ON STONY GROUND

Russländer Mennonites and the Rebuilding of Community in Grunthal

On Stony Ground presents a historical ethnographic account of a generation of Mennonites from the Soviet Union who, following Russia's revolution and civil war, immigrated to Manitoba during the 1920s. James Urry examines how they came to terms with a new land and with their new neighbours, including other Mennonites, Ukrainians, French Canadians, and Indigenous Peoples.

The book discusses the impact of the Great Depression and how the immigrants struggled with their identity in Canada as Hitler and Stalin rose to power in Germany and the USSR. It reveals the immigrants' desire to maintain their faith, language, and culture while encouraging their children to take advantage of an education conducted mainly in English. *On Stony Ground* explores how prosperity following the Second World War helped the immigrants to build a community in conjunction with others, including Mennonites and non-Mennonites, and to accept their new home in Canada.

(Transnational Mennonite Studies)

JAMES URRY is an anthropologist and historian who has published widely on Mennonites and the history of anthropology.

TRANSNATIONAL MENNONITE STUDIES

General Editor: Aileen Friesen

On Stony Ground

*Russländer Mennonites and the
Rebuilding of Community in Grunthal*

JAMES URRY

UNIVERSITY OF TORONTO PRESS
Toronto Buffalo London

© University of Toronto Press 2024
Toronto Buffalo London
utorontopress.com

ISBN 978-1-4875-4737-0 (cloth)   ISBN 978-1-4875-4740-0 (EPUB)
ISBN 978-1-4875-4742-4 (paper)   ISBN 978-1-4875-4741-7 (PDF)

Transnational Mennonite Studies

___

Library and Archives Canada Cataloguing in Publication
Title: On stony ground : Russländer Mennonites and the rebuilding of community in Grunthal / James Urry.
Names: Urry, James, author.
Description: Includes bibliographical references and index.
Identifiers: Canadiana (print) 20230563821 |
  Canadiana (ebook) 20230563848 | ISBN 9781487547424 (paper) |
  ISBN 9781487547370 (cloth) | ISBN 9781487547400 (EPUB) |
  ISBN 9781487547417 (PDF)
Subjects: LCSH: Mennonites – Manitoba – History – 20th century. |
  LCSH: Immigrants – Manitoba – History – 20th century. |
  LCSH: Mennonites – Soviet Union – History – 20th century.
Classification: LCC FC3400.M45 U77 2024 | DDC 289.7/71274 – dc23

___

Cover design: John Beadle
Cover images: (top) The first building for the Russländer meeting house moved from Schönsee to Grunthal in the winter of 1932/33. Courtesy of Johanna Kellett. (bottom) The building of the community auditorium in Grunthal, 1956. The *Carillon* Archives, Steinbach, Manitoba.

We wish to acknowledge the land on which the University of Toronto Press operates. This land is the traditional territory of the Wendat, the Anishnaabeg, the Haudenosaunee, the Métis, and the Mississaugas of the Credit First Nation.

University of Toronto Press acknowledges the financial support of the Government of Canada, the Canada Council for the Arts, and the Ontario Arts Council, an agency of the Government of Ontario, for its publishing activities.

To the Memory of
Harry Loewen and Al Reimer – Colleagues and Friends

Contents

List of Maps, Illustrations, and Tables   ix
Preface   xi
Acknowledgments   xv
A Note on Names and Transliteration   xvii
Abbreviations   xix

Introduction   3
1 Russia and Canada: The Consequences of the First World War   15
2 Russländer Find Homes   31
3 The Bases of Community   55
4 Re-establishing Institutions   78
5 Schools and Education   93
6 Debts, Depression, and a New Grunthal   111
7 Old World and New World Politics   129
8 Conflicted Identities   140
9 The War Years   159
10 Post-War Prosperity   178
11 A United and Divided Community   198
12 Generational Transition and Succession   221

13 Becoming Canadian   242

Conclusion: The Past in the Present   262

Appendix One: Elim Congregation Statistics   269

Appendix Two: Agreement with the Intercontinental Company over Land on East Reserve   271

Notes   275

Bibliography   315

Index   347

Maps, Illustrations, and Tables

Maps

1.1 East Reserve settlements, 1870s 17
1.2 Mennonite settlements in southern Russia, 1914 19
2.1 Landownership in 5–5E, before the Russländer, 1923/1927 41
3.1 Landownership in 5–5E, 1931 62
6.1 Landownership in 5–5E, 1936 127
10.1 Landownership in 5–5E, 1946 182
10.2 Road system, RM of Hanover 189
12.1 Plan of Grunthal township, 1967 231

Illustrations

1.1 Canadian Mennonites leaving for Paraguay, 1926 22
1.2 Russian Mennonites leave Lichtenau, Molochna for Canada, July 1924 29
2.1 Jacob J. Rempel in a non-combatant role during the First World War 48
3.1 Grunthal young women in Winnipeg, c. 1935 60
4.1 The first Russländer meeting house, 1932 86
4.2 Choir festival (*Sängerfest*) held in Grunthal, 1936 89
5.1 Schools in Schoenfeld, Russia, and Grunthal 98
5.2 Heidebrecht's German grammar, c. 1936 106
6.1 Executive of the Canadian Mennonite Board of Colonization, 1935 115
7.1 Jacob J. Rempel and family, c. 1934 132
8.1 Advertisement for a Mennonite Nazi book 147
9.1 Wartime advertisement encouraging farmers to increase production 171

9.2 Chornoboy's tractor dealership in Grunthal   176
10.1 Advertisement promoting electrification   180
10.2 Joseph LaFrance, agricultural advisor   185
11.1 The Grunthal Red Wings Hockey Team, 1950   203
11.2 Opening the Grunthal Auditorium with music, 1956   205
11.3 Later Elim churches that served the Russländer community   217
12.1 Elder J.J. Enns and his wife Anna (Rempel), 1942   232
13.1 Grunthal Centennial Parade float, 1967   245

Tables

2.1 East Reserve land and property sold to Russländer in 1926/1927   43
2.2 East Reserve land original contracts, 1930   54
2.3 East Reserve land adjusted contracts, 1930   54
6.1 Selected travel debts of Grunthal Russländer   113
6.2 Tax receipts and arrears for 5–5E and the RM of Hanover, 1926–46   118
7.1 Voting percentages according to political parties in federal, provincial elections in Provencher and Carillon, 1930–6   138
9.1 Increase in farm values, property, livestock, and income, 1936/1941 in Grunthal   172
10.1 Increases in production following artificial breeding scheme in St. Pierre, 1947–52   186
10.2 Number of taxable landholders in Grunthal town according to Hanover municipal records, 1938–70   196
11.1 Selected referenda results for forming new Secondary School Division No. 15 in 1959   214
11.2 Selected referenda results for forming Unitary School Division No. 15 in 1967   216
12.1 Grunthal Russländer enrolled in the *Mennonitische Verein zur Pflege der deutschen Muttersprache*, 1952   240
C.1 Hanover RM population, 1921–2021   263
C.2 Population of Grunthal district and town, 1951–71   263
C.3 Elim membership, 1946–2020   264
C.4 Bergthaler membership, 1965–2000   265
C.5 Results of the 2021 Canadian Census using categories presented to respondents in three Mennonite population areas of southeastern Manitoba   268
A.1 Elim Congregation, 1927–75 (selected statistics)   269

Preface

Grunthal is situated on stony ground. During the last Ice Age much of the area was covered by soils and rocks left by the retreating ice. The title of this book in part refers to this fact. But some readers might recognize another reference to the New Testament and the parable told by Jesus of the seed sown on stony ground that did not flourish in contrast to seed sown on fertile soil (Matt. 13:3–8, 19–23; Mark 4:3–9, 14–26; Luke 8:4–8, 11–15). The title of this book may suggest that it deals with the failure of community. It is, however, a more complex story: one of both failure and success. Passages citing stones and rocks appear in many places in the Bible. Some are positive, others are negative. A number concern the establishment of foundations, the building of faith communities, and the renewal of belief.

When in the early 1930s Mennonite immigrants from the Soviet Union constructed a meeting house for their Elim congregation in Grunthal, a short passage from Ephesians 2:20 was painted in large letters across the front of its interior: "Jesus Christus der Eckstein" or "Jesus Christ the Cornerstone." The present meeting house prominently displays the same words across its front arch, still in German even though today services are in English. The various historical accounts of the founding of the Elim congregation do not fully explain why this passage was chosen although it is worth considering the text from which it was selected. The words come from Paul's letter to the new Christian congregation at Ephesus:

> ... you are no longer strangers and aliens, but you are citizens with the saints and also members of the household of God,/built upon the foundation of the apostles and prophets, with Christ Jesus himself as the cornerstone./In him the whole structure is joined together and grows into a holy

temple in the Lord;/in whom you also are built together spiritually into a dwelling place for God (Eph. 2:19–22 from the NRSV).

The choice of this passage by the founders of Elim appears appropriate both at the time and with regard to my title. The favourite motto of the leading Anabaptist Menno Simons, from whom the name Mennonite is derived, was "For no one can lay any foundation other than the one that has been laid; that foundation is Jesus Christ" (1 Cor. 3:11). The new settlers in Grunthal hoped to be "no longer strangers and aliens," desired to be good "citizens" (*Bürger* in Luther's translation), and wanted to build a community in a new land, however stony it might appear.

I first visited Grunthal in 1974 when I was taken to the settlement to speak with an elderly Mennonite as part of my research on Mennonite life in Russia before the Russian Revolution. At the time I had no intention of further study in Manitoba but in the 1980s, encouraged by a new generation of Mennonite scholars, I decided to research a Mennonite community in Manitoba. By this time Mennonite archives I had consulted earlier were professionally organized and Mennonite historical societies established. There was also a new chair in Mennonite studies at the University of Winnipeg occupied by Professor Harry Loewen, who was giving Mennonite studies a scholarly foundation. He drew around him a cadre of scholars with expertise in different fields: Al Reimer, professor of English at the University of Winnipeg; Victor Doerksen, professor of German at the University of Manitoba; and Roy Vogt, professor of economics at the same university. They established several publishing ventures. Vogt helped found a popular magazine, the *Mennonite Mirror*, and supported by Reimer, Loewen produced several edited volumes covering diverse subjects such as history, sociology, and literature. Finally, the *Journal of Mennonite Studies* was begun in 1983 and often included papers delivered at annual symposia. A scholarly renaissance clearly had emerged among Mennonites in Manitoba and elsewhere in Canada since my first visit in 1974. During this time of change in Manitoba I moved from Britain to Australia and then to New Zealand. I also moved into new research areas not involving Mennonites. But in 1984 I was invited to a Mennonite conference in Ontario, and I later agreed to turn my thesis into a book, which was published in 1989 by the Mennonite Literary Society. In need of a new research topic, I started to conduct research on Manitoban Mennonites despite the tyranny of distance between New Zealand and Canada. I chose Grunthal, a localized community I had first visited in 1974 that had a mixed population from the two major Russian Mennonite immigrations to Manitoba, those of the 1870s and the 1920s. I therefore returned to Canada in 1989 and although delighted by the new scholarly environment, my research proved more complex than I had initially thought, and I returned to carry out further research over subsequent years.

This study attempts to combine ethnographic approaches based on discussions with Grunthal's inhabitants and Mennonites elsewhere, with primary and secondary historical sources. It might therefore be called interdisciplinary as I am an anthropologist although I also consider myself a historian. The ethnographic methods used are sometimes described as "participant observation," where an anthropologist lives among the people to understand their way of life. The ethnographic research in this account was conducted mainly in English. I stayed with those willing to host me and I was taken to visit worksites, farms, and the homes of relatives and friends. I also attended religious services, funerals, and other congregational events. This does not exactly conform with "participant observation" but my links with Mennonites go back to the early 1970s and my contacts have been extended through correspondence and, in recent years, email. Rather than conducting formal interviews or setting up a recording device, which tends to make people cautious and does not work in group sessions or outdoors, I took notes. However, my notes were always written up soon after discussions occurred.

Historians often record people as "oral history," but ethnographers rarely collect accounts in such a formal manner. Ethnography, however, tends to lack a historical dimension and is based largely on the period the ethnographer was a participant in a community. Anthropologists sometimes claim that their people's past cannot be discovered in the absence of literacy and reliable written sources but in the modern world such claims are difficult to sustain. In the case of most Mennonites, they have been literate since the foundation of their faith and in this account, I have used a wide range of published and unpublished material written by or concerning Mennonites. Some of the material used in this book deals specifically with Grunthal and its local area, other research involves contextual matters.

Research and writing have involved a balancing act incorporating material from a wide range of sources. I have been concerned with how to give voice to people, many of whom have since died, based on discussions at the time of the research. This account has also been restricted by other factors. There were people I could not discuss matters with due to time restrictions and occasionally their unwillingness to talk with me, although thankfully this was very rare. No research can ever be considered comprehensive, and I make no claim to have included everything that might be available. I have, however, scoured newspapers and other published sources produced by Mennonites and non-Mennonites and visited several archives. Finally, the writing of this account has involved making decisions about what to include, what to exclude, and what to avoid, recognizing people's privacy.

All research begins with a question or questions in search of an answer. Unfortunately, some studies appear to begin with an answer in search of a question. If pursued properly, questions change, although oddly a researcher can end up back where they began or circumstances can radically change from their original intent. This is not to deny that research, to use an overworked phrase, is "a journey" that leads the enquirer back to, or at least close to, their initial question. This is what occurred during the process of this research and writing. The writing itself proved difficult and extended over several years from the early 1990s. The ethnographic aspects of the research reached into the "present," but this "present" is spread over a long period of time. After much deliberation, I decided to end with the passing of the first generation who arrived from the Soviet Union in the 1920s. This proved difficult as in the 1920s some immigrants were young, others elderly. Senior members of the initial cohort of immigrants had died before my research began, although in 1974 I had interviewed a few of these people although I was not focused on how they rebuilt their lives in Canada but instead on their experiences in Russia. Even so, some of the material collected assisted in this study.

Acknowledgments

My first debt is to the many people, Mennonite and non-Mennonite, of Grunthal, past and present. The lead minister of the Elim congregation, Dietrich Gerbrandt, and his wife, Agnes, helped establish my first contacts with the community. Others included Peter Block, Werner Braun, Gary Chornoboy, John A. and Lena (Krahn) Driedger, Johnny and Judy (Hildebrand) Driedger, Cornelius Friesen, Agatha (Driedger) Guenther, Eric Guenther, Ernie and Margaret (Warkentin) Guenther, Dietrich and Agathe (Regehr) Heese, Margaret Hildebrand (Peters, Franz), John Janz, Nick Janz, Jake and Helen (Woelke) Janzen, Gertrude Klassen, Helen Klassen, Peter P. Klassen, A.F. Krahn, Udo and Charlotte (Enns) Penner, George Rempel, Peter Rempel, Jack Thiessen, John D. and Margaret (Voth) Warkentin, Werner Warkentin, Jacob Wiebe, Frank and Mary (Sawatzky) Wiens, and Jake and Helen (Fuchs) Woelke. In 1974 I spoke with David J. Fast and Dietrich J. Rempel. Although not resident in Grunthal, Carl Driedger of Winnipeg provided details of life in Schönfeld before the Russian Revolution and Civil War.

Finally, I am grateful to all the private individuals and archivists who have helped to locate illustrations. Mennonite archivists at the Mennonite Heritage Archive past and present include Lawrence Klippenstein and Conrad Stoesz; the Mennonite Brethren Archives: Ken Reddig, Alf Redekop, Jon Isaak, and various volunteers and support staff; the Mennonite Archives of Ontario: Sam Steiner and Laureen Harder-Gissing; the Mennonite Library and Archives, Kansas: John Thiesen; the Mennonite Library and Archives, Fresno, California: Kevin Enns-Rempel. I was helped by the staff at the Archives of Manitoba in Winnipeg and the Glenbow Museum Archive in Calgary, Alberta. The archives of the Rural Municipality of Hanover, now in Mitchell, were in Steinbach at the time of my research. In Steinbach, Delbert Plett assisted me and Rick Derksen provided access to local newspapers since transferred to the Mennonite Heritage Archive. A short visiting fellowship at the University of Calgary's Institute for the Humanities Faculty of Arts provided a base to begin writing up. Vic Doerksen, Abe Friesen, Ruth and Chuck Emerick, and Peter Letkemann helped with accommodation in Winnipeg.

The Mennonite Studies Centre at the University of Winnipeg provided a base for my research and friendly contact with numerous Mennonite scholars over many years has helped me understand Mennonite society and culture. Of particular importance in Winnipeg was my association with Victor and Margaret Doerksen, Harry and Gertrude Loewen, Al and Joan Reimer, Roy and Ruth Vogt, and Irmgard Wiebe. It is impossible for me to name all the other people who have assisted me over the years so I will not try in case I leave someone out. But Ernest N. Braun of Niverville provided important insights into the history of the East Reserve, made numerous suggestions and corrections to earlier drafts, and helped locate illustrations and prepare maps with Brent Wiebe. I am also grateful to the comments and corrections of two anonymous readers, as well as Royden Loewen, and Aileen Friesen for their help in improving the text. The staff of the University of Toronto Press turned my text into a book and Emily Reiner indentified numerous inconsistencies and errors as well as generally improving my sometimes clumsy expressions.

Finally, my wife Rita and son Nicholas accompanied me to Canada and at times helped with my research and independently my daughter Judith, then teaching in England, was made welcome to Grunthal by Jake and Helen Janzen.

A Note on Names and Transliteration

This work is written in English but contains Russian, High German, and Mennonite Low German words and place names. Mennonite Low German is transcribed according to that used in Jack Thiessen's dictionaries. Place names appear in English, German, and Russian; the latter were once part of the Russian and Soviet empires but today many are in Ukraine. Russian place names are used as Mennonites in this study lived in the region before Ukraine became an independent state. Russian place names often given in sources transliterated into German are presented in their Russian forms. Thus Chortitza is Khortitsa and Molotschna as Molochna; German "j" and "w" have therefore been changed to "e" and "v" as in the case of the Russian city and province, Ekaterinoslav (or Yekaterinoslav) instead of Jekaterinoslaw. Where places have entirely different names in German and Russian, I retain the German form as commonly used by Russländer in Grunthal.

Abbreviations

AM	Archives of Manitoba
Bote	*Der Bote*
CM	*Canadian Mennonite*
CMBC	Canadian Mennonite Board of Colonization
CN	*Carillon*
CO	Conscientious Objector
CPR	Canadian Pacific Railway
GAMEO	Global Mennonite Encyclopedia Online
HG	High German
JMS	*Journal of Mennonite Studies*
KfK	Kommission für Kirchenangelegenheiten
LG	Low German
MB	Mennonitische Brüdergemeinde/Mennonite Brethren
MCI	Mennonite Collegiate Institute (Gretna)
ME	*Mennonite Encyclopedia*
MFP	*Manitoba Free Press*
MH	*Mennonite Historian*
MHA	Mennonite Heritage Archives
ML	*Mennonite Life*
MLSB	Mennonite Land Settlement Board
MM	*Mennonite Mirror*
MQR	*Mennonite Quarterly Review*
MR	*Mennonitische Rundschau*
NEP	New Economic Policy (in the Soviet Union, 1921–8)
RCMP	Royal Canadian Mounted Police
RM	Rural Municipality
SP	*Steinbach Post*
UofM Archives	University of Manitoba Archives

WFP *Winnipeg Free Press*
WT *Winnipeg Tribune*
ZMIK *Das Zentrale Mennonitische Immigrantenkomitee*
  (Central Mennonite Immigration Committee)

ON STONY GROUND

Introduction

Between 1923 and about 1926, over twenty thousand Mennonites immigrated to Canada from the Soviet Union, at the time probably the largest single "group" immigration to Canada and occurring within just a few brief years. These immigrants would eventually be known as Russländer (Russians) in contrast to earlier immigrants from Russia called Kanadier (Canadians). The terms Russländer and Kanadier were first used to differentiate between the Mennonite immigrants of the 1870s and those who arrived in Canada from Russia before 1914. After 1923, however, the term Russländer was generally applied to Mennonite immigrants of the 1920s.[1] In more recent years the term Russländer has become widely known through Sandra Birdsell's novel, *The Russländer*.[2] However, most of the novel is set in Russia before and during the Russian Revolution and Civil War where the term Russländer was unknown, even though the novel is concerned with a Mennonite immigrant to Canada who had similar experiences to the people central to this study.

It is remarkable that while there are numerous "insider" Mennonite accounts of Russländer immigration and settlement, the group has received little attention from Canadian historians. This is odd considering their number, the numerous and widespread communities they established, their significance, and especially the importance of their descendants in Canadian society and culture.[3] Especially in Manitoba, however, the distinctions between the peoples of these different immigrations might be described as "invisible" and not widely understood.[4] One problem is that while the first generation of many non-British immigrants can be identified and studied, especially where groups settled in rural areas, second and third generations of such immigrants are more difficult to identify and their impact on Canadian society is more difficult to assess. Jewish groups have tended to settle or resettle in urban areas and have maintained communities better than the descendants of other immigrants who live in urban locations.[5] The descendants of these other immigrants, having received a largely Canadian education in English or French, have often moved away from their home communities, leaving rural locations to pursue careers in metropolitan areas or even abroad. This is true for later generations of Russländer who became physically and socially mobile in Canada. Distinctive ethnic surnames often indicate they have Mennonite ancestry as Mennonites have a limited number of surnames, although it is often difficult to say whether they are either of Kanadier or Russländer origin or even of mixed parentage from the different immigrations. Some descendants are even the result of marriage between Swiss American Mennonites and people of Kanadier and/or Russländer backgrounds. It is also difficult to identify later generations where Mennonites have married non-Mennonites, as in the case of Birdsell, whose mother was Russländer and whose father Métis, hence her non-Mennonite surname. The number of Mennonite-derived surnames in academia is obvious from faculty lists across a wide range of disciplines of North American universities; a number of these people, although not all, are descendants of Russländer. Only a few studies have examined this issue of generational change: while individuals may have an ethnic Mennonite surname, it does not imply they remain Mennonite by faith.[6]

This study is an account of one Mennonite community in southeastern Manitoba: first established in the 1870s, most of its Kanadier descendants emigrated and the earlier Mennonite settlement area was remade by Russländer immigrants. Today it is a community in and around the unincorporated urban district of Grunthal and this study deals with the period between the early 1920s and roughly the late 1970s. The exact dates are not particularly significant as, like many immigrant communities, while relatively clear beginnings can be identified, there is no sudden end as some of the first immigrants lived on into later decades and the community exists into the present.

Before the new Mennonite immigrants from the Soviet Union settled in a place today spelled Grunthal, the original form of the name was Grünthal, meaning "green valley" in English. The original umlaut in the place name has been lost, much to the regret of one of its most learned and colourful sons, Jack Thiessen, who once wrote that the "difference ... between Grunthal and Gruenthal [i.e., Grünthal] is one of a visitor and one who belongs ... like being in love and loving, like plastic flowers and [real] flowers, like the artificial and the artistic."[7] The first village of Grünthal, established in 1876, lay close to the modern town of Grunthal and its founders were settlers from southern Russia, today part of the nation of Ukraine but in the 1870s situated in the Russian

Empire. These first immigrants to western Canada came as a group of roughly seven thousand settlers to what was to be the new province of Manitoba.[8] Later, smaller numbers of Mennonites from Russia followed this initial immigration, some to settle in Manitoba and others further west, mainly in Saskatchewan, where they joined other Mennonites who had moved westwards from Manitoba and northward from the United States in search of farmland.[9]

During the 1870s the Canadian and newly formed Manitoban governments sought out settlers like the Mennonites with little regard for the Indigenous populations. Although the First Nations and Métis had performed essential roles in the development of the local economy through trade and agriculture, state officials viewed Manitoba as a territory to be developed through European settlement.[10] These governments hoped to transform the territory into "a respectable space" through the introduction of European systems of agriculture and ideas of private property, especially after the Red River Resistance led by Louis Riel forced the Canadian government to negotiate with the Métis over land and other rights.[11] The government also entered into negotiations with Indigenous groups represented by the Anishinaabeg (Ojibwe) and Ininew to gain control over the land in preparation for European settlement.

Concerned that an influx of settlers would affect their way of life, Indigenous negotiators sought a treaty with the government to ensure that future generations would have continued access to their lands. Treaty One, signed in 1871, covered most of the area included within the 1870s boundaries of the Province of Manitoba.[12] From the perspective of the Dominion of Canada, the treaty extinguished Aboriginal title to their lands, and paved the way for Canadian and European settlers. From the Indigenous perspective, the treaty created an alliance between the state and the Indigenous population, offering both parties access to land.[13] Although the government quickly surveyed lands for settlers, it only slowly addressed land claims of both the Anishinaabeg and the Métis. The Métis received only a fraction of the land promised to them; the Anishinaabeg experienced similar treatment and were moved to the Roseau River Reserve, sixty kilometres southwest of Grunthal. The move was at considerable cost to their way of life and well-being as it severely reduced their access to land in favour of European settlers.[14]

The government settled the first Mennonites in areas designated as "Reserves."[15] One, the East Reserve, lay to the southeast of Winnipeg to the east of the Red River, and a larger West Reserve lay to the southwest of Winnipeg bordering the United States. To Mennonites on the East Reserve, the West Reserve lay on the other side of the Red River, or *jant-sied* in Mennonite Low German, and the reverse was true for those on the West Reserve.[16] On the East and then West Reserves, Mennonites encountered First Nations and Métis as they established villages and farms.[17] Early diaries and journals of Mennonites refer to these encounters as the settlers often relied on the knowledge of Métis neighbours to understand their new environment, although they also benefited from their experience of steppe regions in Russia.[18] Mennonites, however, were not always considered acceptable immigrants and some officials and settlers of British background considered them inferior because of alleged "Germanic" origin, their Russian background, and their "peculiar" religious ideas. Such negative views, though, initially were of little influence in accommodations made by the state in favour of their settlement and at provincial and federal levels Mennonites generally found officials sympathetic to their settlement.

Both the Métis and Anishinaabeg were impacted severely by the new settlers, especially with regard to their access to land. In the case of the Métis, the Mennonite Reserves included territories they viewed as their own.[19] Without access to land, many Métis families moved west but the threat to their communities intensified into the 1880s, culminating into the North-West Resistance, in which they, and some First Nations allies, fought the Canadian government. In the case of the Anishinaabeg, the surrender under government pressure in 1903 of prime farmland at the Roseau River Reserve further reduced the ability of the community to provide for future generations.[20]

While these events were occurring in Canada, those Mennonites who had remained in Russia after the 1870s were faced once again with the decision as to whether to emigrate, especially following the collapse of Russia's imperial regime in the revolution of 1917 followed by civil war and widespread destruction. Once order returned, many Mennonites had to decide whether to emigrate or remain and rebuild their lives in what was now the Soviet Union. Those who had lost land, factories, and businesses without any hope of regaining them, chose to emigrate and follow the path to Canada taken by earlier Mennonites. Those who immigrated, often as refugees, lacked resources to rebuild their lives immediately on arrival in Canada. The first generation of Russländer, however, were often well educated, especially compared to many existing Canadian Mennonites and other settlers from Eastern Europe and even the United Kingdom. These Russländer would lay the foundation for their successors to participate successfully in Canadian society beyond the narrow confines of the world envisaged by many earlier Mennonite immigrants of the 1870s.

By the time the 1920s Mennonites arrived in Canada, Indigenous populations in southern Manitoba represented just a small proportion of the province's population and their communities had been displaced and severely disrupted. In contrast to the 1870s when Indigenous peoples were acknowledged as part of the Canadian landscape by Mennonite settlers, the Mennonite immigrants of the 1920s had little reason to interact with them. Instead, the Grunthal immigrants interacted with earlier Mennonite and other European settlers to the west and north. There are few signs of sustained relations between Russländer and Indigenous peoples although Mennonites were aware of their presence. The nearest settlement of Indigenous peoples is the Roseau Reserve, located south of Grunthal, but until after the Second World War roads in this area were extremely poor, limiting contacts. Neither Russländer nor the local Indigenous people had much understanding of each other's pasts and given the infrequency of their contacts, this study will not attempt to address settler colonialism as it pertains to Mennonites and other groups in Grunthal.[21]

Unlike the first Mennonite immigrants from Russia to Manitoba who came as congregational communities (HG *Gemeinde*) and settled as such, the 1920s immigrants were rarely organized into single religious groupings. Instead, they were interconnected by a complex of religious and secular organizations closely resembling those established in Russia before 1914. These were intended to develop social and cultural life and respond to changes in official policies that threatened the Mennonites' continued existence. Settlement in Canada added to the need to recreate and build upon these, especially as Russländer did not settle in single locations. Instead Russländer were scattered across several provinces, principally the prairie provinces of Alberta, Saskatchewan, and Manitoba, and to a lesser extent in Ontario. In time several Russländer drifted towards urban areas, a step few Kanadier had taken despite living longer in Canada. In this drift Russländer followed a trend that was increasingly common among Mennonites in late Imperial Russia. In areas of Manitoba and Saskatchewan, some Russländer lived among, or close to, communities of earlier Mennonite settlers from Russia; in Ontario they lived close to Swiss American Mennonites and related groups who had settled from Swiss and German states as well as the United States from the eighteenth century onward.

There are numerous Mennonite accounts of Russländer immigration, settlement, and community-building. Some are of a high calibre and avoid the romantic and triumphalist tone of those written by local historians. Frank Epp wrote a major study of the Russländer and their adjustment to life in Canada and another wave of refugees mostly from the Soviet Union following the Second World War. His study is based primarily on the records of the Canadian Mennonite Board of Colonization (CMBC), the major body concerned with these immigrants, their settlement, and cultural integration. Epp's study is Canada-wide rather than an examination of a single province or community. However, he was willing to deal with some of the difficult issues involved in resettlement and adjustment to a new environment.[22]

Other major Mennonite studies are two theses that focus on Russländer in Ontario written by Henry Paetkau.[23] Paetkau has only published one article based on his research and his theses remain unpublished.[24] Paetkau, along with Stan Dueck, recorded Russländer recollections of Russia and settling in Canada and these are deposited in the Mennonite Archives of Ontario, Conrad Grebel University College, Waterloo. These include interviews with former Grunthal residents. Another project conducted at about the same time by a sociologist, Ellen Baar, included interviews with Russländer and post–Second World War Mennonite immigrants in the Niagara area of Ontario. Again, these appear to have only resulted in a single publication.[25] However, her recordings in the archives and special collections of Brock University have been used by Cynthia Jones in her study of Mennonite identity in the Niagara area.[26] Outside Ontario there are few detailed academic studies of Russländer, although Jenna Klassen recently examined Russländer material culture and identity in Manitoba.[27] Most other academic accounts of Russländer are included in general accounts of Mennonites in Canada.

Despite this dearth of academic publications, there are numerous accounts of varying quality of individual Russländer communities written by members of the community, past or present. Occasionally these have been put together by a committee organized to mark an important date in the history of the community such as its "foundation" and Grunthal had such an account published in the 1970s.[28] Even if local histories are written by a single author with academic training aided by members of the community, these can vary in quality. They often follow a common format, divided into a series of topics: economy, social life, schooling, and, naturally, congregation and faith. Historical aspects may either be sketched in an introduction or scattered through the different topics making an integrated history difficult to discern.

Russländer, or their descendants, have also authored histories of communities even when they involve Kanadier or other ethnicities and in doing so they have appropriated others' pasts. Single community studies are written primarily for local consumption and therefore there is a particular emphasis on biographical details concentrating on worthy citizens and occasionally "colourful" inhabitants. More detailed biographical accounts are usually restricted to specific genealogical studies of families; these studies are often self-published or merely typed and mimeographed for distribution among family members. These occasionally contain details relevant to understanding the communities in which they lived.

Of greater importance, however, are literary autobiographical accounts of growing up in Russländer communities, of which those by Rudy Wiebe and Arthur Kroeger are significant examples.[29] Other community studies focus on a single religious congregation within a community that may contain more than one congregation. The Russländer congregation in Grunthal has produced two such volumes: the first published around 1972 is primarily a list of membership arranged under family names with additional detail on the congregation's history, its ministers, organizations, and snippets of community history.[30] A later volume follows roughly the same format but provides more detail on congregational organizations, links with the wider world, and community involvement.[31] Grunthal's other Kanadier congregations such as the Chortitzer and Spencer Bergthaler Churches have also produced studies.[32] Often their congregations, such as the Kanadier Chortitzer congregation, were more dispersed than Russländer, as their members lived in surrounding rural areas.[33]

Some accounts do not focus on a single community but instead on larger areas of Mennonite settlement. Two important earlier studies of Manitoba Mennonites, one by a non-Mennonite sociologist, E.K. Francis, and the other by a Mennonite geographer, John H. Warkentin, deal with Mennonites mostly in rural Manitoba.[34] More recent studies are often concerned with either the West or East Reserves, which were eventually incorporated into rural municipalities; most of the East Reserve became the Rural Municipality (RM) of Hanover.[35] Occasionally historical accounts focus on sections of a Reserve or founding villages that developed into major population centres, especially within or close to the West Reserve.[36] Others concentrate on areas that are home to religious groups such as the Reinland Church on the West Reserve, and the Bergthal Church in the same Reserve but also extending to the East Reserve.[37] Initially many villages were established on the East Reserve but the major centre in this area was Steinbach, founded first as a village but today a city in its own right.[38] Recent academic studies of the East Reserve and Municipality of Hanover have included accounts of the history of Steinbach, especially its most important religious group, the Kleine Gemeinde and their descendants.[39] Local historical societies have also published accounts of the major villages, their settlers, and "sketches" of life on the Reserve.[40]

Beyond the Mennonite world several Canadian historians have promoted the study of local prairie communities in western Canada. The pioneer scholar of modern prairie studies is Paul Voisey who in 1985 called on professional historians to match the enthusiasm of amateur historians and produce scholarly studies of local communities based on detailed research. This call was followed by his study of Vulcan.[41] Other scholars have followed his lead and written accounts of prairie communities utilizing a variety of approaches based on different research methods.[42] Some of these accounts involve communities in Manitoba, including some close to Grunthal, like John Lehr's historical-geographical study of the Ukrainian community of Stuartburn.[43] A recent study of Chinese communities in Western Canada has examined how ethnic communities have changed.[44] It is beyond the scope of this book to discuss these or other works in detail apart from acknowledging that by combining historical and ethnographic approaches in the study of community, this account is intended to be a contribution to an expanding field of research and scholarship.

The word "community" is central to this study. Since the nineteenth century the concept of community has been the subject of considerable debate and while many academic books and articles have been written on the topic, there is little common agreement on its meaning. At the basic level of intellectual activity, closer to the types of knowledge pursued by anthropologists, sociologists, psychologists, social workers, and others, this has involved a search for an all-encompassing definition of community. By doing this it was hoped it might be possible to finally nail down the elusive concept. Others have attempted to build taxonomies that might provide support for the weight of a "grand theory," if only one could be constructed.[45]

It is not the intention of this study either to construct theory or be involved in a quixotic quest to settle finally what community *is*. However, for the purposes of this study, it is helpful to keep in mind Ferdinand Tönnies's pioneering 1887 German study that contrasted *Gemeinschaft* with *Gesellschaft*, usually glossed in English as *community* and *society*, that created the basis for scholarly debate around the concept of community in sociology and other academic fields.[46] For Tönnies, *Gemeinschaft* involved an older form of social cohesion than *Gesellschaft*, which was the offspring of, and an alternative to, the more organic and cohesive idea of community. As a modern form of organization, *Gesellschaft* threatened the established bases of community and the bonds of social cohesion found in *Gemeinschaft*. Like other nineteenth century writers such as Marx, Durkheim, and others, Tönnies was aware that Europe was undergoing a time of radical change from pre-industrial, agrarian societies into urban, industrial societies. Industrial societies with their increasing populations were supported by commercial agricultural production, often derived from expanding colonial frontiers settled by immigrants. Mennonites were not isolated from these changes, especially the Mennonites who settled in Russia and North America as immigrants.

A useful approach to the question of what community might be in a context such as Grunthal is not to impose external ideas but instead to consider insider ideas, or "native" categories as they are often called in anthropology. The English term "community" was unknown to adult Mennonites who arrived in the Grunthal area in the 1920s. The immigrants spoke three languages: Russian (with some Ukrainian), High German (HG), and most also spoke, or at least could understand, the common Mennonite patois, Low German (LG).[47] The descendants of the 1870s immigrants primarily spoke Mennonite Low German and some English, while High German was largely restricted to worship, sermons, and the language of hymns. As well as the Bible, other books of the Mennonite tradition were owned and consulted, the most important of which details the fate of Mennonite martyrs in the sixteenth century. Originally published in Dutch in the seventeenth century with vivid woodcuts, it was translated into High German during the eighteenth century.[48] People also read Mennonite newspapers in High German though more often to obtain news of kin and friends than to learn about current affairs. Generally, most Kanadier by the 1920s possessed only basic literacy skills but educated Russländer were more literate and read not only the Bible and other religious texts, but also a wide range of German literature. What Kanadier and Russländer shared, however, with minor dialect differences, was Mennonite Low German. This meant they shared an understanding of concepts of society mainly in Low German although Russländer, being multilingual, could access other meanings. Immediately following immigration there were few opportunities for Russländer to speak Russian to non-Mennonites and English was something new to most. Younger adult Russländer soon developed a working knowledge of English and both Kanadier and Russländer children became reasonably competent in English from attending school.

If the shared Mennonite language was Low German, what does this say about the concept of community? In Mennonite Low German one important term, *Jemeenschauft/Jemeenschoft*, can be glossed as "community" and is translated as such in two modern Mennonite dictionaries.[49] The equivalent High German *Gemeinschaft* in common speech was understood as something "mutual" or "jointly shared," between people in association, because *gemein* formerly meant "(in) common." Today, however, it can also be translated as "nasty," "mean," or "base." The Mennonite Low German *jemeen* can also mean "lowly," "menial," or "ordinary." However, Mennonite Low German *Jemeenschauft/Jemeenschoft* is not from the root word *jemeen*, but from the word *Jemeend* which is closer to the High German *Gemeinde* and can refer literally to a congregation and/or denomination in Mennonite High German. As a people of the faith, members of a *Jemeend* stand in opposition to "the world" (LG *de Welt*; HG *die Welt*), a place and situation outside the Mennonite universe with distinct overtones of evil. Association with "the world" leads believers astray and puts in peril their hope of salvation in the final days when God will judge the living and the dead. The inhabitants of this "other" world lack the proper sense of faith that unites Mennonites, a faith made manifest in the fellowship of baptized members who together must assist other members to follow the narrow path of faith in hope of salvation.

Mennonite Low German *Jemeenschauft* also refers to a parish (in terms of a place) as well as a congregation and denomination in terms of a body of believers and worshippers. A related term glossed as "community" in Mennonite Low German dictionaries is *Nohbaschoft* or *Nohbaschauft*. This implies a connectedness in the sense of neighbourhood, a place that establishes social links between neighbours (LG *Nohba*) who act towards each other in a neighbourly fashion (LG *nobalijch*). The related High German terms are *Nachbar* and *Nachbarshaft*.

There are other Low German terms that might be considered despite not being translated as "community" in dictionaries. These are related to the importance of social ties in an organized, closely bound group. Mennonites who speak Low German possess the terms *Ve'waundschoft* (HG *Verwandtschaft*), meaning kin and relations based on ties of descent and marriage. A related term, *Frind'schauft*, also means people connected through ties of kinship by descent and marriage, although speakers of Low German also commonly use the English terms "friends" and "friendship," as there is no equivalent for the term "friendship" in their own language. The Low German *Frind* (friend) certainly exists and there are words for "friendly" (*Frindlich*) and "friendliness" (*Frindlichkeit*) that indicate accepted forms of social interaction. These can involve those persons who are not related through ties of kinship and marriage to the speaker, but they do not carry the same sense of obligation and duty required of those who are so related. The English terms "friend" and "friendship" are not unlike the High German *Freund/Freundschaft* and in these languages can include broader and less focused forms of social interaction than those in Mennonite Low German.

There is another related term, *Jeschwista* (literally siblings), which also means "brothers and sisters" in a larger sense when applied to members of the congregational community. When speaking Low German in less formal settings, such as a special religious service, a minister may for instance say *"leewe Jeschwista,"* meaning "dear brothers and sisters," even though not everyone in the congregation is related through actual relationships of kinship or marriage to the speaker. The term is probably derived from the Biblical phrase "brothers and sisters in Christ" although this, too, was based on kinship terminology.

Important Mennonite social connections are maintained through the practice of visiting and conversing amiably about matters of common interest (LG *spezeare*). Visiting is almost a social ritual among Mennonites with everyone either visiting or being visited, especially on Sunday afternoons. A visitor is considered a guest (LG *Gaust*), and there is also a term for a visit by friends and relatives (LG *gaust'reahre*) and another for a social gathering, usually by invitation, at which a meal is served (LG *Gaust'jebott*). Visiting and sharing a meal create and maintain important social bonds, especially between relatives and close, although unrelated, friends. However, a phrase such as "the community of Grunthal" still defies an exact translation. Instead of "the community of Grunthal," locals might say *daut Darp Jrienthol* ("that village or place of Grunthal") or *de Jrientholla* ("the people of Grunthal"). When the township of Grunthal is referred to, the word "town" (LG *Staudt*) replaces the word for "village" (LG *Darp*). None of these phrases contain a sense of togetherness that might constitute a community. *Dee Nobaschoft vonn Jrienthol* refers literally to the neighbourhood of Grunthal but again this phrase lacks any sense of social togetherness.

If we prioritize native categories as expressed in Mennonite Low German, it is impossible to talk of *a* Mennonite community in Grunthal. However, as anthropologists are aware, there is an observer's point of view as well as that of the natives. Grunthal might possess a variety of Mennonite congregations and Mennonite and non-Mennonite inhabitants with differences in occupations, ideas, and practices, but it also possesses common values founded on a shared history that reaches back into the past. This past for Mennonite people today is in Manitoba and beyond Canada: first in Russia, then further back in time to Prussia, to the Netherlands, and somewhat vaguely to the Reformation. There are other markers in time: events such as persecution, martyrdom, and a succession of emigrations, settlement, and resettlement forming new groupings in different places and times.

Mennonite connections are also based on a knowledge of kinship and marriage ties further traceable through genealogy; these were once enshrined in memory or entries in the family Bible but today are found through the popular pursuit of searching in archives, newspapers, and through the internet. In the past, such connections indicated regular social interaction in particular locations, codependency that centred on the ownership and cultivation of land, and involvement in enterprises and businesses that later in Grunthal assisted in the rebuilding of community. During the 1920s when many Kanadier left Grunthal, those who remained or later returned lost many of the aspects essential for a functioning and continuous way of life. Aspects of this existence certainly survived, but it would take another generation to re-establish a sense of community. Russländer also lacked many of the essential features of connectedness following their experiences in Russia and emigration to Canada. They also needed to rebuild their lives and way of life. In a sense, both Kanadier and Russländer had to rebuild a community among themselves and with others. This study focuses particularly on the dominant group in this process, the first generation of Russländer immigrants and how they came to terms with Canada, Manitoba, and their local area. But it also recognizes that this process involved Kanadier and non-Mennonites who came to live, work, and contribute to the rebuilding of community.

Chapter One

Russia and Canada: The Consequences of the First World War

The outbreak of the First World War in 1914 and its consequences in the years that followed had a profound impact on Mennonites living in both western Canada and Russia. The groups of Mennonites were connected as western Canadian Mennonites had immigrated from Russia, mostly in the 1870s, and were sometimes linked by ties of kinship to their brethren who remained in Russia. Both groups maintained the principle of non-resistance which meant that they refused to serve in military units. The ancestors of Mennonites in western Canada immigrated from Russia when the state threatened them with compulsory military service. Canada already recognized that Mennonites and other non-resistant religious groups such as the Quakers were able to claim exemption from military service on the grounds of religion.[1] In Russia, the state, faced with a mass exodus of economically valuable Mennonites, compromised and negotiated an exemption whereby young Mennonites were conscripted into non-military units to serve the state by planting trees. This system was accepted by most Mennonites but following the outbreak of war in 1914 numerous young Mennonite men volunteered to serve the state in new ways in non-military organizations that helped care for wounded combatants in hospitals and on trains transporting injured soldiers away from the fighting.[2] No such roles were required of or volunteered for by Mennonites in western Canada, although some joined other faiths and served in military roles.

When a minority of Mennonites left Russia in the 1870s to settle in Canada and the United States, they left behind a country in the process of undergoing major reforms in governance, society, and the economy.[3] The reach of the Canadian government in western Canada was limited in the early 1870s and until the building of rail links the established regions of eastern Canada were poorly connected to western Canada. In Russia Mennonite emigrants mostly used newly established railroads to reach the steam ships that brought them to North America. The Mennonites who settled first in Manitoba and later in other provinces of western Canada usually broke in areas of land to establish a commercial agricultural economy and develop markets for their produce. The settlements on the East Reserve were not located close to railroads and therefore took longer to develop than on the West Reserve, where settlements were founded closer to rail links (see map 1.1 for East Reserve village settlements). In contrast, the Mennonites who remained in Russia continued to expand their activities in rural and industrial settings founded in the late eighteenth century and greatly expanded in the nineteenth.[4] Therefore in 1914 Mennonites in western Canada and Russia inhabited very different worlds in terms of economy and social complexity. They also interacted with local, regional, and central administrations in the areas in which they were located.

The map shows the East Reserve first granted to Mennonites from Russia by the Canadian government in the 1870s. The village locations first built by the Mennonite settlers are shown by black rectangles and named Bergfeld, Bergthal, Blumenhof, Blumenort, Blumstein, Burwalde, Chortitz, Ebenfeld, Eigengrund, Eigenhof, Friedrichsthal, Gnadenfeld, Grünfeld (Kleefeld), Grünthal, Hespeler (Niverville), Heuboden, Hochfeld, Hochstadt, Kronsgart, Kronsthal, Landskron, Lichtenau, Neu-Bergfeld, Osterwick, Reichenbach, Reinfeld, Rosenfeld, Rosengart, Rosenthal, Schönfeld, Schönsee, Schönthal, Steinbach, Tannenau, and Vollwerk. Many villages were soon abandoned as their inhabitants moved onto their own sections, building houses on their land. However, the sites of the villages often remained places of importance especially if they were located as shown on the roads that crossed the Reserve. Non-Mennonite French and English settlements (Arnaud, Carey, Clearspring Settlement, Dufrost, Otterburne, and St. Pierre-Jolys) are named in the shaded areas. The English centres are shown, situated on the railroad that ran to the west of the Mennonite Reserve but did not cross it.

By 1914, Mennonites in Russia had established a variety of educational institutions ranging from elementary to secondary schools, while some attended Russian higher educational centres, including universities. Canadian Mennonites in western Canada founded far fewer centres of higher education comparable in scale to those in Russia. From the late nineteenth century, leaders of progressive Mennonite congregations in Canada encouraged members to adopt new ideas and especially to develop institutions of higher education. In Manitoba in 1889 the institution was founded that would become the Mennonite Collegiate Institute and that would eventually be located at Gretna.[5] Under

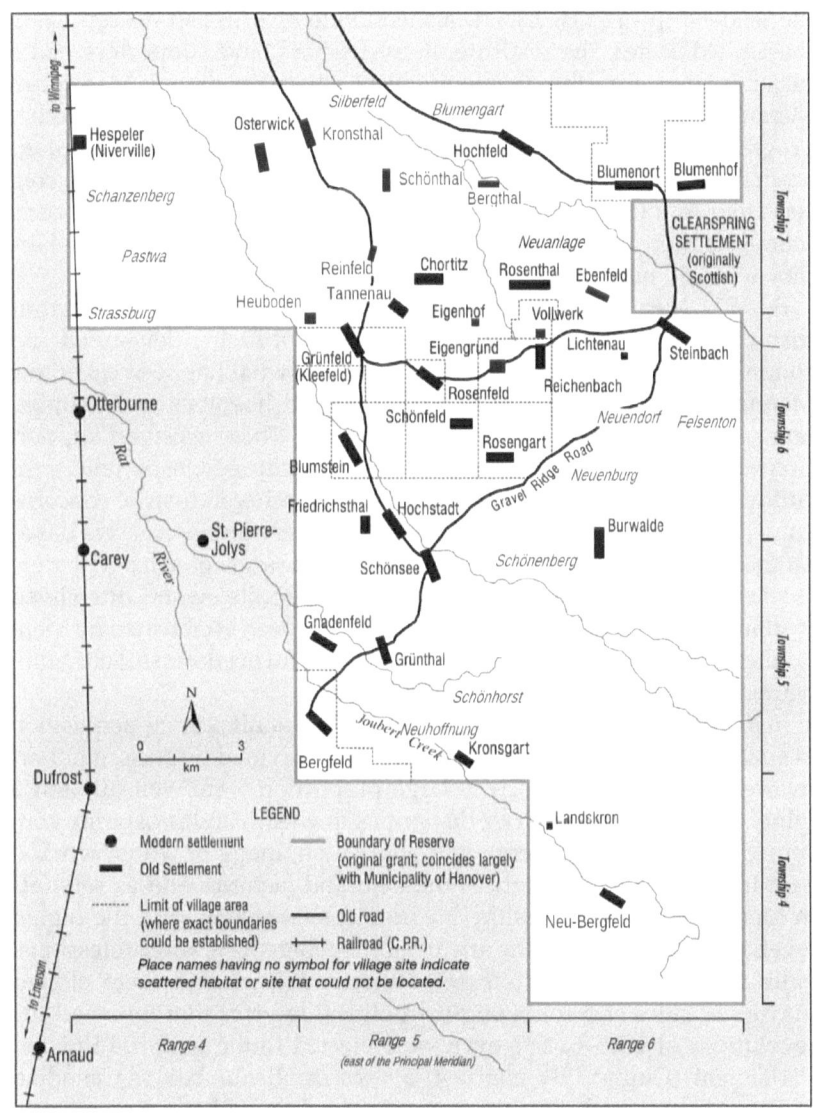

Map 1.1. East Reserve settlements, 1870s.

Sources: Based on map in E.K. Francis, *In Search of Utopia* (Glencoe, IL: Free Press, 1955), redrawn in Urry, *Mennonites, Politics, and Peoplehood* (2006) and amended by Ernest N. Braun (2023).

the leadership of H.H. Ewert, a Mennonite of Prussian descent from the United States, the institute, its instructors, and supporters had a major influence on the development of education among Manitoban Mennonites before the arrival of the Russländer. In Saskatchewan other progressive Mennonite leaders also established a German-language academy at Rosthern in 1905.[6] In areas of western Canada where conservative Mennonites lived, however, most children attended rural schools, either provincial or Mennonite private establishments, where they received only a rudimentary education.

By 1914 Mennonites in Russia were considerably more prosperous than those in western Canada, with a range of highly developed and community-funded institutions. The world of what has been called the Mennonite Commonwealth by 1914 included hospitals, old peoples' homes, sanatoriums, and other institutions.[7] These received support from the owners of numerous large-scale businesses, especially agricultural machine manufacturers, millers, and other industrial concerns valued at millions of rubles. The wealth of other Mennonites was based on the purchase of large estates covering thousands of acres that were worked by peasant labourers while their Mennonite owners often lived in grand houses. Nothing resembling this had been established by Mennonites in Canada although there were a handful of successful entrepreneurs often involved with the grain trade.

In Russia, however, there was a cost for Mennonites in the acquisition of such wealth. Mennonite society itself was divided by class: a minority were fabulously wealthy, a large proportion were well off, and a minority were poor.[8] The real disparities in wealth and prosperity concerned the larger, non-Mennonite population, many of whom worked for Mennonites as labourers in the field and factories and as servants in Mennonite homes. Wealthy Mennonites associated with the higher levels of Russian society, the aristocracy, intelligentsia, and professional elites. Some Mennonites entered Russian politics and were elected mayors of cities and following the political reforms that followed the revolutions of 1905–6, two even were elected to the Imperial Russian Parliament (Duma).[9] By contrast, a very small number of Canadian Mennonites associated with provincial leaders and officials in local towns but most Mennonites living in rural areas avoided contact with Canada's political system and refused to vote in local, provincial, or federal elections. Secure in their mostly rural communities, Mennonites in western Canada continued to be educated in German but spoke Low German at home and the community and despite living in Canada for forty years many had only a basic knowledge of English. Mennonites in Russia were educated in Russian and High German, worshipped in

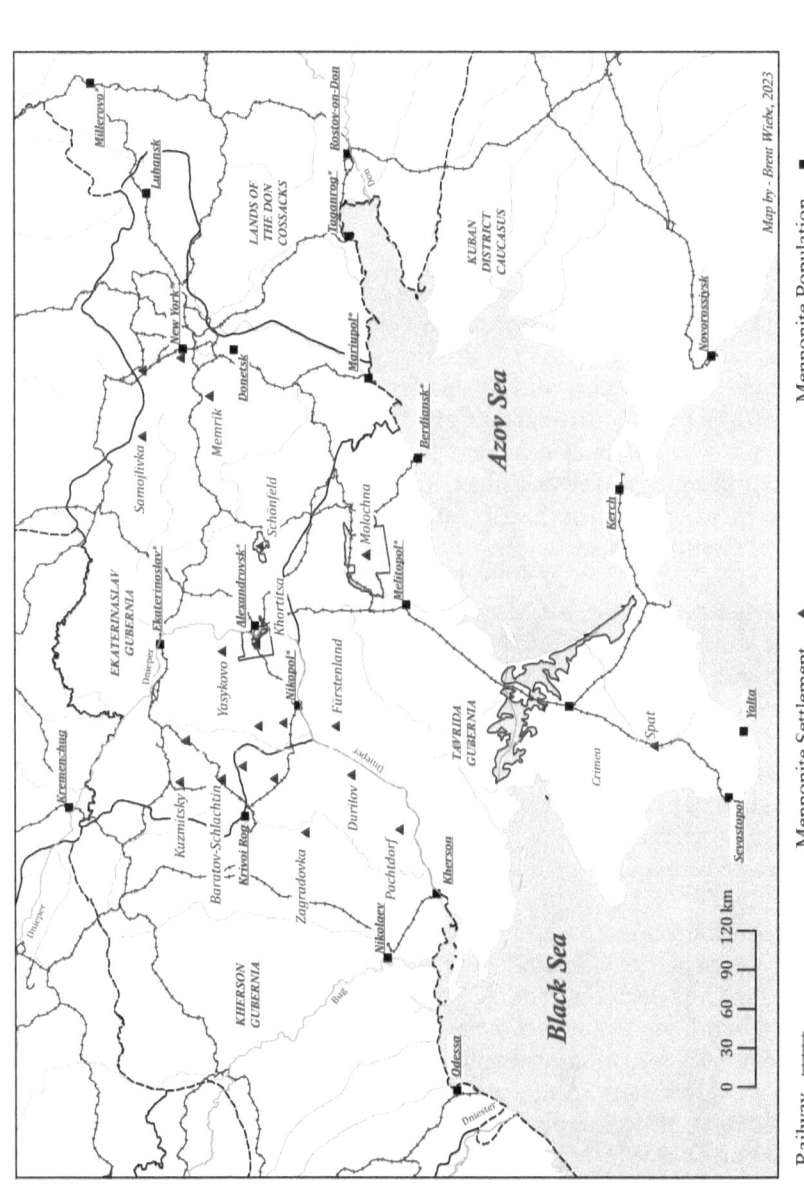

Map 1.2. Mennonite settlements in southern Russia, 1914.

Source: Map by Brent Wiebe.

High German, and could speak not only High and Low German but also Russian and Ukrainian, the latter when communicating with non-Mennonite employees. The generation which had reached adulthood by 1914 could also read and write in Russian if they wished.

The First World War involved several allied powers against the German Empire and its supporter states, principally the Austro-Hungarian Empire. The British Empire, of which Canada was a member, and the Russian Empire became allies and consequently, so were the Mennonites resident in both empires. Problems that had little to do with their non-resistant stance on religious grounds soon emerged in both countries. This was to do with allegations in western Canada and in Russia that Mennonites possessed an allegiance to Germany because they spoke Low German and used High German in publications and religious services. Even before 1914 Russia's geopolitical position with frontiers bordering Germany and Austro-Hungary made nationalism a more sensitive political issue than in Canada. The accusation that Mennonites in Russia supported Germany was entirely false, but such accusations had first emerged towards the end of the 1890s as Great Russian nationalism increased. Also, while Russia and Canada had multi-ethnic populations, Russia was more sensitive than Canada to the political allegiance of its minorities before 1914.

War changed everything for Mennonites in Russia and Canada but in different ways. In Russia, publication in High German was quickly suspended and even speaking German in public forbidden.[10] Despite Mennonite contributions in the form of the service of its men along with considerable financial gifts, the state began a process that would have resulted in the expropriation of Mennonite land and property because they were considered of "enemy descent."[11] In response, Mennonites attempted to prove they were of Dutch, not German, descent, a suggestion that created the basis for later disagreements in Canada on Mennonite identity.[12]

Nothing on the scale of what occurred in Russia during the First World War happened in Canada, but restrictions steadily increased for Mennonites in Ontario and western Canada.[13] Although during the war Mennonites had been exempted from military conscription based on their non-resistant religious principles, there was widespread public opposition towards them. As patriotism during the First World War increased, so did political opposition to the presence of many non-British ethnic minorities.[14] In Manitoba, as elsewhere in the prairie provinces, the war and its aftermath had a marked impact on Mennonites.

The major issue that soured relations among Mennonites, provincial governments, and the public concerned schooling. Mennonite immigrants who came in the 1870s requested the right to organize their own schools with their own teachers and provide instruction in German. The original Kanadier settlers believed this right was part of a special "charter of privileges" negotiated between themselves and the Canadian government.[15] In Russia, and elsewhere in Europe, Mennonites had been granted such charters at least since the seventeenth century. But in Canada there was no charter and Mennonites merely had been granted the right to organize their own schools within the provisions of existing laws. Under Section 93 of the British North America Act (1867) schooling was a provincial matter where a legislature "may exclusively make laws in relation to education" subject to the provision that no law enacted should "prejudicially affect any right or privilege with respect to denominational schools."[16] The Act did not apply to persons recognized as subject to the Indian Act (1876) where schools and education were recognized as a federal matter.[17]

Between 1874 and 1916 Mennonites were permitted to opt out of the provincial school system, establish private schools, employ their own teachers, and teach in German. During the First World War, however, the Manitoba authorities made teaching in English and school attendance for children between the ages of five and fourteen compulsory. If a local community refused to abide by these new regulations, the authorities either closed the schools or appointed an official trustee to manage education, employ teachers, and ensure provincial regulations were followed. Prior to the outbreak of the First World War the Manitoba public school system permitted bilingual education and some progressive Mennonites established public schools and encouraged young Mennonites to train as qualified teachers. Conservative Mennonite communities, however, maintained their private German-language schools that often provided only a very rudimentary level of education with unqualified teachers. These conservative groups took great exception to wartime changes in official policy, but their appeals to provincial and federal governments, and even resorting to the courts, failed to produce a result in their favour. Consequently, once the First World War ended several conservative groups in Manitoba and Saskatchewan investigated the possibility of emigration from Canada.[18]

Between 1922 and 1930 almost eight thousand Kanadier Mennonites left Canada for Mexico and Paraguay, vacating large areas of farmland in Manitoba and Saskatchewan. For some on the East Reserve, emigration to Paraguay started later than emigration to Mexico as the investigation of lands in Paraguay and subsequent negotiations took longer and the emigration "fever," as it became known, did not begin in earnest until 1926. The Mennonite descendants of the 1870s immigrants

Fig. 1.1. Canadian Mennonites leaving for Paraguay, 1926. Kanadier Mennonites at Carey rail station close to Grunthal leaving for Paraguay, November 1926.

Source: Courtesy of Ernest N. Braun, Niverville.

who emigrated to Paraguay from the East Reserve were all members of the Chortitzer congregation and their Elder and ministers actively promoted the move. Not all members of the congregation, however, wished to move thousands of miles and pioneer the Paraguayan Chaco. Congregational meetings in 1921, though, indicated that 65 per cent of Chortitzer were willing to emigrate, a much higher percentage than members of other congregations on either the West Reserve or in Saskatchewan.[19] Such was the authority of congregational leaders that by 1930 over 1,200 Chortitzer Mennonites, just over 40 per cent of its East Reserve population, moved to Paraguay and 90 per cent from the Grunthal township area (see fig. 1.1).[20]

The problems faced by Mennonites in Canada during the war and following its end, however, pale into insignificance when compared with the tribulations Mennonites faced in Russia between 1917 and the early 1920s.[21] When the imperial regime collapsed in 1917 and Russia began to withdraw from the First World War, many Mennonites welcomed a change in government. Young men serving in the medical services were easily radicalized and as the revolution began some participated in political debates, especially in urban areas. Soon, however, order started to collapse in many cities and the countryside. Whereas the First World

War for Canada ended in 1918, in Russia war continued into the 1920s.[22] Between 1918 and 1921 Mennonites, especially in the most densely settled areas of southern Russia, were caught between warring forces trying to control the region and establish new regimes. Many Mennonites lost their lives through fighting, murder, disease, and famine; their lands were devastated and, in some cases, seized by land-hungry peasants. Farm stock, especially horses, were either stolen or destroyed. Factories and mills were seized or left in ruins. Only in 1921, following the victory of Bolshevik forces over the White Army and the suppression of local anarchist bands, was order restored. Soviet control, however, did not result in the restoration of the privileged world so many Mennonites had previously known as within a few years the Soviet authorities embarked on major reforms all of which, in one way or another, many Mennonites viewed as a threat to their faith and identity.

Adult Russländer who later settled in Grunthal experienced these years in very different ways depending on gender, age, former life, and exactly when they emigrated from the Soviet Union. Those who came from an area called Schönfeld and who later settled in Grunthal can help illuminate these troubled times. Schönfeld, located in Ekaterinoslav Province, consisted of a central village and scattered estates settled between the 1840s and the 1870s. The area was inhabited predominantly by Mennonites from the colony of Molochna who sought land, prosperity, and independence away from the constraints of colony life.[23] All its settlements consisted of private land, purchased mainly from the estates of impoverished Russian nobles, acquired by Mennonites who were often related and who pooled their resources to buy land following the prosperous years of the Crimean War (1854–6). Although the incomes of the Schönfeld inhabitants were far higher than those of an average colonist, most Schönfelders were careful with money and lived frugally. They grew accustomed, however, to think of themselves as different from most colonists, whom they considered their social inferiors. Despite this, Schönfelders remained closer to other colonists in terms of their world view than they were willing to admit. In Schönfeld they had their own schools and meeting house, and while some had been educated to high school level, the real centre of intellectual and spiritual life still lay in the Molochna Colony. Before 1914 they still considered Molochna their mother settlement even though Schönfeld lay closer to the Khortitsa Colony than Molochna, from where their ancestors had come and where their congregation was associated. Nearly all Schönfeld's inhabitants maintained close contact with the colony, principally through family ties, congregational affiliation, and business connections.

At the outbreak of the First World War Schönfeld was a microcosm of a wealthy section of the Mennonite Commonwealth, as their prosperity was derived from commercial wheat growing, livestock raising, and from shops, flour mills, and industry. Schönfelders lived in large houses, mostly built in the same style as those in Molochna but much grander and better furnished. The average size of landholdings in Schönfeld was greater than the largest Molochna farm. In Schönfeld and its surrounding districts just 202 families owned almost 135,000 acres of land, an average of 659 acres per family. By comparison, the average size of a full-farmer's landholding in Molochna was 175 acres, although many only owned half or quarter farms (88 and 43 acres, respectively). Although there was considerable variation in the size of individual Schönfeld holdings, as most farms ranged from between 810 acres and 2,700 acres, a number were much larger, including an estate of 14,400 acres named Silberfeld.[24] In farming they utilized large machinery for ploughing and threshing that before 1914 included steam-powered tractors. Unlike colony farmers, the Schönfelders were not restricted to cultivating small strips of land in different village allotments but instead farmed large fields.

The prosperity of the area, however, was not based solely on technology but also on the availability of cheap Ukrainian labour. Referred to as Little Russians these largely peasant workers were employed as farm labourers and as servants in households. They were drawn from an extensive pool of cheap local labour from large neighbouring peasant villages and often employed as seasonal workers, especially at harvest time. Their ancestors had previously helped cultivate the land owned by Russian nobles but to which peasants believed they possessed an inalienable right. Following the 1861 emancipation decrees that freed peasants from serfdom the peasants had hoped they would be given titles to land.[25] But instead what they considered rightfully theirs was sold to others, including Mennonites, and the new Mennonite owners often proved stern and demanding masters and mistresses. The peasants, reduced to poorly paid labourers and servants, increasingly resented their condition as a landless, impoverished underclass.[26] In the 1870s, during the reorganization of local government in Russia, Mennonites managed to locate most of their settlements around Schönfeld into a separate administrative canton centred on the village of Schönfeld but in places including non-Mennonite peasant communities. These were now dominated by Mennonites and their inhabitants exploited as cheap labour.

During the First World War many men were away in service so older men and women had to maintain farms and businesses. The fall of the tsar and the promise of peace raised hopes of better times, as the correspondence between a man from Schönfeld in service and his family reveal.[27] As Schönfeld was situated beyond its more established and populated mother colony it was more exposed to the anarchy that followed the end of imperial rule. During the earlier 1905 Revolution confrontations had occurred between Schönfeld Mennonites and local peasants and similar problems happened elsewhere.[28] Following these events some Mennonites felt vulnerable on their estates and employed Cossacks and other armed guards to defend their lives and property.[29]

In 1917/18, radical groups promised peasants land and freedom, and local peasants renewed their efforts to reclaim land from Mennonites. The situation was further exacerbated during the brief period when German and Austrian troops occupied southern Russia and supported Mennonite landowners in retrieving seized land; their efforts turned violent so that when the occupying troops withdrew, the attacks on Mennonites only intensified. Unfortunately, Schönfeld was located close to areas where warlords competed to gain peasant recruits to fight the various forces operating in southern Russia. In Mennonite opinion the most infamous warlord was Nestor Makhno, who during the Civil War raised a large peasant army and sought to establish an anarchist society.[30] In the chaos of the time Schönfeld Mennonites suffered robbery, assault, and a number were brutally murdered.[31] A confused attempt was made to form a self-defence force, like those organized in Khortitsa and on a larger scale in Molochna.[32] These actions, contrary to Mennonite principles of non-resistance, merely worsened the situation. In the autumn of 1919 Schönfeld Mennonites packed a few belongings and fled to the relative safety of neighbouring colonies. The Schönfeld district was seized by peasants and according to one account its orchards and other trees cut down, some buildings dismantled, and the land subdivided among local peasants. Within a short time Schönfeld as the Mennonites had known it ceased to exist. Most of its inhabitants now lived with relatives in Molochna, joining other Mennonites refugees from isolated estates and farms of southern Russia, and from the Terek Colony in the Caucasus region whose settlements were overrun by the local population.[33]

In other areas where Mennonites formed self-defence units, severe countermeasures occurred, such as in the village of Eichenfeld where eighty Mennonites were massacred.[34] Similar mass killings occurred in another Molochna-connected colony called Zagradovka.[35] In Alexandrovsk, bordering the Khortitsa Colony, factory workers attempted to seize power and Makhno's forces briefly held the city. Wealthy urban and estate-owning Mennonites became easy targets for robbery: some were held for ransom and others murdered. Vulnerable settlers who fled to Khortitsa found little comfort as the colony, situated as it was at a strategic crossing of the Dnieper River, quickly became a centre of military activity. Villages on the borders of the colony of Molochna experienced thefts and intimidation from local peasants and later attacks by bandits aligned with Makhno.[36]

Even though the Bolsheviks eventually brought peace, much of pre-war Mennonite life was ruined. Not a Mennonite family was left untouched by the events of 1917–21. Practically every Mennonite lost family members or knew of someone who had experienced terror, threats of violence, robbery, and for women, rape. Death from disease and famine followed the coming of peace as grain reserves had been requisitioned or destroyed.[37] Many fields remained uncultivated; seed was difficult to obtain; horses had been stolen and farm equipment often proved inoperable. A period of drought further added to the misery. The situation was particularly dire for the refugees living in the colonies who had no hope of regaining their former lands or properties. Instead, they had to depend on relatives and friends, themselves often short of food and resources.[38] The Mennonites were rescued by relief aid sent by North American and Dutch Mennonites and between 1922 and 1923 thousands received food, clothing, and medical supplies, assistance which continued into 1924 in southern Russia and 1926 in Siberia.[39]

For those who survived these years and immigrated to Canada, tales of suffering were woven into their shared sense of being in which Mennonites were victims and others were blamed, including the Bolsheviks. The atheistic ideology of communism and the later persecution of Mennonites who remained in the Soviet Union were attributed to the false claim of a worldwide conspiracy led principally by Jews who it was claimed were prominent in Russian revolutionary movements. If the suffering of these troubled years had thrown all Mennonites together, the experience of being refugees added a special meaning to the sense of identity for people such as the Schönfelder and others who had lost their land and hopes for a future. By 1920 most Schönfelder were scattered in various Molochna villages while a few had fled to Memrik, another Molochna-connected settlement.[40] Once wealthy and proud, the Schönfeld refugees were now forced to live in crowded, temporary quarters, subsisting on the charity of others.

As the Soviet government established its control and as economic reconstruction began, the refugees were increasingly seen as a burden. But there was nothing for them to return to as their former lands were redistributed among local peasants and their businesses nationalized by the state. Social and economic pressures steadily increased and for many young people any thought of pursuing a career was overwhelmed by the family's struggle to survive. Opportunities were few, there was no money to pay teachers, and village schools hardly functioned, least of all the pre-war high schools, and so a generation failed to complete their education. During the First World War while men were in state service, many couples delayed marriage or starting a family, but following demobilization men returned home and as children were born there were more mouths to feed and new responsibilities to bear. Despite these seemingly hopeless conditions, peace led some Mennonites to welcome the early years of Soviet rule as an opportunity to establish a better Mennonite society. But others, probably a majority, hoped the regime would not survive and there would be a return to a free market economy.[41] The refugees, however, could not await any change that might or might not happen and emigration seemed the only option.

Emigration had been part of Mennonite life almost since their formation as persecution and economic demands forced people to seek new lands and opportunities. This meant that almost every generation had some experience of migration whether within the Russian Empire or abroad. Before the First World War the possibility of emigration to South America, and even the distant Antipodes, had been discussed in the Mennonite press, but the best possibility remained North America where Mennonite communities from Russia and Prussia had been established before 1914. By the early 1920s, given the scale of destruction in the Soviet Union, interest in emigration increased, and many had little choice but to contemplate leaving their homeland. The post-war world, however, was not an easy place to find a new home. Nationalist sentiments increased during the war and afterwards as millions of displaced people sought new homes as victims of conflicts and as new nation states were created.[42] The situation in Soviet Russia and Soviet Ukraine was particularly serious as there had been large-scale urban depopulation and a massive dislocation of populations of which Mennonites were just part.[43]

Canada and the United States presented a possibility of new homelands for Mennonites and other peoples but government regulations either prohibited or severely restricted further immigration. During the First World War most Mennonites in the United States and Canada had maintained their non-resistant stance and in 1919 this resulted in a ban on the further immigration of pacifist religious groups, including Mennonites and Hutterites. This was part of a broader range of policies that also identified "preferred" immigrants. [44] Only after considerable intervention by Canadian Mennonites were the restrictions on Mennonite immigration lifted in 1922.[45] Of major significance was a special agreement negotiated between Canadian Mennonites and the Canadian Pacific Railway (CPR) that would aid Mennonite immigrants from the Soviet Union to receive a loan to cover the costs of their transportation to Canada. The loan was to be guaranteed by the Canadian Mennonite community. To impoverished Mennonites in Soviet Russia and Ukraine the opportunity to seek a new life in Canada seemed like a blessing from God.

To support the move, North American Mennonites organized their scattered and religiously diverse communities and established a Canadian Mennonite Board of Colonization (CMBC) to handle immigration. Emigration from Khortitsa began in 1923 and in 1924 a larger number left from Molochna. These immigrants included many refugees despite considerable economic reconstruction in the USSR during the period known as the New Economic Policy (1921–8). Other Mennonites began to be concerned about freedom of worship and the future of their children under communist rule and in succeeding years this added to the desire to emigrate. Between 1923 and 1929 over twenty-one thousand Mennonites left the Soviet Union, the vast majority to settle in Canada, a small number in Germany, and in the final years of emigration, in South America.[46] Most emigrants after 1923 secured group passes that permitted trainloads of Mennonites, often related or from the same settlement, to legally leave the Soviet Union. At first the Soviet authorities recognized that permitting refugees to emigrate would assist in economic reconstruction. In April 1924 ministers from Schönfeld stated that their members' "need is great" as they "no longer have a homeland on this earth."[47] Unlike some later emigrants there was little to leave behind as their belongings were few and most of their close relatives and friends were also emigrating. Most took with them only a few essential belongings along with memories of a way of life now vanished (see fig. 1.2).

As a degree of prosperity returned to rural areas in the Soviet Union following the implementation of new policies of reconstruction, fewer Mennonites left but individuals and groups continued to emigrate, some paying their own way, others taking a CPR loan. Emigration often involved chain migration as people joined relatives who had already moved abroad. These later emigrants had more experience of life under the Soviets than the earlier groups, and this sometimes made them suspect to those who confused Bolshevism with anarchism. However, many later settlers were motivated to leave not just to join family, but also by changing conditions in Soviet Ukraine and reports of the opportunities in Canada. Most emigrants who arrived in Canada departed the Soviet Union by 1926/27 as further emigration officially ended

Fig. 1.2. Russian Mennonites leave Lichtenau, Molochna for Canada, July 1924.
Source: Centre for Mennonite Brethren Studies, Winnipeg (NP012-01-40).

in 1926.[48] Immigration into Canada was also increasingly restricted because of opposition from various groups, particularly by some prairie provincial governments as after 1929 economic conditions worsened in Canada. In Saskatchewan a Royal Commission on Immigration and Settlement, established in 1930, recommended significant changes to the province's immigration policies.[49]

In the USSR the New Economic Policy ended in 1928 and the collectivization of agriculture started as forced industrialization began, intended to build a truly socialist state. Social disruption followed along with political repression, famine, and arrests that eventually led to the Great Terror. In the new situation Mennonites and other groups attempted to emigrate. In 1929, Mennonites from all over the Soviet Union, especially from Siberia, rushed to Moscow hoping to obtain exit passes.[50] In Moscow passports proved difficult to obtain as further emigration was not permitted and further immigration to Canada drastically curtailed. In 1932 the Canadian government permitted the entry of only twenty thousand immigrants, down 82 per cent from 110,000 in 1929/30 and a dramatic fall from a high of four hundred thousand in 1913/14.[51] A few Mennonites waiting in Moscow, however, discovered the German Weimar

Republic would help to obtain German passports and a lucky few entered Germany until they could find alternative homelands.[52] Some eventually reached Canada, but the majority moved to Latin America, settling in Brazil and Paraguay. Those unable to obtain passports in Moscow were forced to return home and face the same terrible fate of other Soviet citizens in the years that followed.[53] Few Mennonites were able to leave the Soviet Union until after the Second World War, when a number retreated from Ukraine with German troops to Germany; many were forcibly repatriated to the USSR after 1945 but others eventually managed to join other Mennonites in Canada and Paraguay.[54]

Chapter Two

Russländer Find Homes

When Russländer arrived in Canada in the early 1920s the country was recovering from the First World War. It was a period of social, economic, and political turmoil, as the war had distorted the way of life for all Canadians. The absence of so many men in the armed forces changed the face of the labour force and raised wages in industries that flourished from wartime demand. Others, however, had not prospered and during the war the cost of food rose due to limited supplies while uneven harvests further increased prices.[1] Generally, if the war years had seen increased production and price rises, the immediate post-war period saw the economy falter and social unrest increase, especially in the larger cities. By 1922, though, there were signs of economic recovery.

The war also brought changes to society and politics especially when urban electorates challenged long established agrarian parties and new political groups emerged. In western Canada these new political groups included radical forces on both the left and the right.[2] During the war, mainly right-wing groups opposed settlers of non-British descent and encouraged restrictions be placed on Mennonites and any further immigration of their kind. The imposition of public schooling on Mennonites in Manitoba and Saskatchewan fuelled the Mennonites' decision to emigrate. The Russländer immigrants shared few concerns with conservative Kanadier over public education and were generally unsympathetic to their recent difficulties with government. In Imperial Russia, once Mennonites had immigrated to Canada in the 1870s, those who remained largely accommodated themselves to the demands of the state. Whereas before 1870 some Mennonites had felt threatened by the policies envisaged by the Great Reforms, future generations largely accepted the changes concerning education and alternative service and gradually some Mennonites even became active in local and regional administration.[3]

The new immigrants were therefore willing and eager to adapt to their new land. A number accustomed to the political institutions of pre- and post-revolutionary Russia acquainted themselves with the system of central, provincial, and local government of Canada, obviously with an aim of wherever possible contributing and even participating in civic life.[4] It is unsurprising therefore that from the outset of Russländer immigration to Canada leading Mennonites were keen to take advantage of the educational opportunities offered by the provinces who were responsible for education. As several immigrants had been teachers in Russia, a number quickly set about learning English and requalifying as provincial teachers. It seemed as if the new immigrants would soon re-establish their old ways of life and develop strong Mennonite communities in Canada but on their own terms.

These were adjustments required of many adult immigrants to new lands, especially those who considered themselves refugees, in order to establish a new sense of place and identity. Some Russländer achieved this transition with greater ease than others. While the first immigrants often extolled the virtues of Canada, a land of freedom protected by a democratic political system and the rule of law, a number soon realized that Canada's social and political system was very different from that of Imperial Russia. They understood this might work to their disadvantage, especially because of their poverty and lack of English. In Russia, despite increasing official restrictions, Mennonites had maintained several privileges granted at the time of initial settlement or acquired later through negotiation with the state. In Canada they found themselves identified as foreign immigrants who were expected not just to conform, but also to assimilate to the dominant English culture. Mennonites could only influence matters at the local level and then in limited ways. To many this lack of power seemed to threaten their separate identity and one early immigrant equated becoming Canadian with Americanization and complained of the aggressiveness of assimilation and its dangers.[5] But another, no doubt reflecting the chorus of complaints heard among Russländer in private and the insidious way some would constantly compare pre-revolutionary Russia and its ways with their new homes in Canada, warned Russländer to stop complaining about their losses and adapt to their new land, in spite it being no paradise.[6]

The natural allies of Russländer among existing prairie Mennonite settlers were not conservative congregational ministers but the educated leaders of progressive congregations and communities. Since the late nineteenth century such leaders encouraged their members to adopt new ideas and become involved in municipal and provincial politics. In Manitoba the more progressive groups were centred in certain southern areas of the province and there were others in Saskatchewan. In Manitoba the major progressive congregation was the Bergthaler whose members were involved in commercial agriculture and other entrepreneurial activities. The Bergthaler consisted largely of settlers who had moved from the East to the West Reserve where their leaders also encouraged the development of higher education.

A related development was the formation in 1903 of a regional conference, the Conference of Mennonites of Central Canada (*Konferenz der Mennoniten im mittleren Kanada*), later to become the Conference of Mennonites in Canada.[7] This connected progressive Mennonite congregations and their communities across western Canada, including the Bergthalers of Manitoba, progressive Mennonite immigrants from the United States, late immigrants from Russia, and a few from Prussia settled in Saskatchewan.[8] As the immigrants came from such diverse backgrounds they often formed new congregational communities rather than joining established, kinship-based congregations that had moved to Saskatchewan from Manitoba. One such new congregation was Rosenort, which established several affiliates in areas to the north of Saskatoon. This group possessed outstanding leaders, especially its first Elder originally from Prussia, Peter Regier, and later Elder David Toews, a Russian Mennonite from the United States.[9] The Canadian Mennonite Board of Colonization (CMBC), which negotiated the contract with the CPR and guaranteed the debt permitting Mennonites to immigrate from the USSR, was only made possible because of the existence of such progressive Mennonites and their organizations. The CMBC was based in Rosthern and later Saskatoon and was managed by both Kanadier and Russländer. It was here that leading Russländer first started to re-establish the social and cultural institutions they had known in Russia, and which seemed so essential to their sense of being Mennonite.

While willing to join with some Kanadier community structures such as local and regional religious conferences, Russländer also believed they needed to establish their own institutions. These would cater to the needs of the new immigrants and assist in maintaining communication with their homeland and the immigrants scattered across Canada. To assist in this a newspaper was established in 1924, *Der Immigranten Bote*, later just *Der Bote*, under the editorship of Dietrich H. Epp. Independent of the church conference it did publish its reports, only much later becoming an organ of the conference. Before 1914 Dietrich's brother David had edited a Mennonite newspaper in Russia, *Der Botschafter*.[10] Before 1914 another Mennonite newspaper, *Die Friedensstimme*, had been published in Russia by the evangelical Mennonite Brethren (MB), formed in Russia after the 1860s. Its followers were already established in North America before the Russländer immigration but Russländer Mennonite Brethren took over an established newspaper, *Die Mennonitische Rundschau*, and relocated its headquarters to Winnipeg. Here it would eventually become the official organ of the Mennonite Brethren Conference. In this manner the major religious divide that existed among Mennonites in pre-revolutionary Russia was transferred from Russia to Canada and was reflected in the publication of separate newspapers that deeply influenced how Mennonite readers, especially Russländer, viewed the world.[11]

Other specifically Russländer social and cultural institutions developed in Canada during the 1920s and 1930s. Some came from initiatives stemming from Rosthern, but others were responses to local needs in the various provinces where Russländer settled. In this way the political geography of the Canadian provincial system quickly asserted itself on the structure of Russländer organizations. Upon their arrival in Canada, however, most Russländer were concerned with meeting their immediate needs and less with building cultural institutions. These needs included finding somewhere to live and a means of support for themselves and their families. In 1923 the first immigrants from the Soviet Union mostly came to Rosthern and were given temporary housing and work by Saskatchewan Mennonites in both progressive and conservative communities. In Ontario and in Manitoba other Mennonites provided similar early support and aid to later immigrants.

The Russländer, however, neither intended to live off charity for long nor did they relish working for others, whether Mennonite or non-Mennonite. Their aim was to achieve a degree of independence, rebuild their lives, re-establish communities, and thereby regain their lost dignity. This involved finding the means to control their destiny as individuals, families, and communities and to start to repay the travel debt. The immigration debt hung like the sword of Damocles over many families for years to come. The most immediate problem, however, was that most had arrived with little but a few cherished items that had survived the Civil War and had not been discarded when they emigrated.[12] Some brought with them small items of china, most possessed photographs and other documents that proved their educational qualifications. A few carried maps and legal documents that might prove their right to land and property if ever the Bolsheviks lost power and they could return to Russia. In a sense, therefore, settlement in Canada remained problematic. Should they commit themselves totally to the new land? Or should they wait for an opportunity to return? After their experiences in Russia, however, most realized they had to make do with what they had and begin life anew. The best way to achieve this was through farming and once they had become established, built up some capital and seen to their children's needs, they might be able to pursue another career.

Most immigrants had families, often with children on the way, or expected to marry and start a family. There were also aged parents to support as well as sick relatives, and physically or mentally impaired family who might have passed the medical examination before leaving the Soviet Union but who later needed assistance. Immigrants were held responsible for members of their families and in the first instance care fell on immediate kin. Ultimately, however, if deemed a burden on Canadian society, they risked deportation. In serious cases the CMBC would come to the aid of any person threatened with deportation, and CMBC levied an additional sum on all immigrants to assist with the increased costs involved in such cases.[13] Anyone convicted of criminal activity might face deportation as in one infamous case when a person was deported to the Soviet Union.[14]

Immigrants preferred to settle close to other Mennonites, preferably fellow Russländer, and specifically those from similar backgrounds. This included people related in various ways, through kinship and marriage, having roots in the same village, community, or colony, people with similar religious allegiances, and finally people who were similar in their previous social and educational status. For instance, Mennonites from Khortitsa preferred fellow immigrants from the Old Colony as they shared many things including speaking Low German with the "correct" pronunciation in comparison with say Molochna or Molochna-connected people. Despite attempts to forget old religious divisions and to worship together, Mennonite Brethren chose to live and worship with Mennonite Brethren while non-Mennonite Brethren preferred the reverse. Where possible, educated people and former owners of estates tended to associate with each other. But all these desires were extremely difficult for most Russländer to achieve.

At first the quest for a secure future was sought in the countryside but for other reasons than just need. Russländer were initially permitted to immigrate to Canada on the well-deserved reputation of Kanadier as an agricultural people, renowned for hard work and honesty. As such the new Russländer immigrants were expected to settle in rural areas and devote themselves to farming as this was where their "skills" were most needed.[15] It was for this reason the government and CPR had thrown their support behind Russländer immigration. Among the immigrants there was a widespread belief that they had little choice in the matter, and it was their duty to become farmers and remain on the land. A CMBC source from 1926 suggested that in 1923 Mennonites had agreed with the Canadian government that they would "be placed on the land as farmers."[16] While government immigration policy in fact strongly favoured agricultural settlers, it could not control immigrants once they entered the country.[17] The initial agreement was in fact between the CMBC and the CPR not the federal government and was intended to assist new immigrants to settle on land owned by the CPR, develop it, and thus further the company's freight business involving mainly agricultural produce.[18] For many Russländer the move onto the land was unproblematic as they had been successful farmers in Russia. For others, however, farming presented a challenge as while some had been raised in farming families, before 1914 a generation of men and women emerged who looked to a life beyond farming and instead contemplated careers in the professions.

Before 1914 some young Mennonites in Russia were increasingly better educated privately or with community assistance than their parents had been and were expected to pursue such careers especially when they were considered essential to their community. But following the revolution and the destruction of the Civil War, most young people were unable to finish their qualifications or pursue careers in their chosen fields. Under the Bolsheviks formerly wealthy land, mill, and factory owners and their offspring were redefined as members of a despised class of the bourgeoisie and excluded from participation in the new Soviet society.[19] These people, who had largely lost their land and businesses, had little option but to emigrate and were consequently over-represented among early Russländer immigrants to Canada. The Soviets also dismissed teachers if they were congregational ministers. For many the loss of social status and respect was sometimes difficult to bear. Writing in the 1940s and 50s, no doubt after discussions with Russländer, E.K. Francis described the adjustments many faced in Canada: women were forced into "unaided household work" when once they had employed servants; for men it meant "working out and dirt farming," when in Russia they had employed peasant labourers; "college professors," unaccustomed to manual labour were forced to spread "manure," and finally, former "millionaire mill owners" now had to earn "a living from small raspberry plots."[20] Some Russländer simply lacked the necessary knowledge, skill, and even the will to become farmers. Some turned to farming out of necessity and even succeeded. Others took up farming and continued with it even if they never felt at ease with it as a way of life. Farming ensured a basic level of subsistence for those with families, at least at first. Some thought that they could later take up careers, but language barriers and poverty often prevented them from pursuing this dream, so the hopes of parents were thrust upon their children who were pushed to succeed where their parents had failed. Some Russländer simply abandoned any pretence of farming and drifted to towns and cities, a move that was often criticized by those who remained on the land.

Access to farmland varied from place to place. Early in 1924 a Russländer, Peter Rempel, noted in a publication of the Conference of Mennonites of Central Canada that the immigrants were faced with five options when they considered where to obtain land. First, there was land owned by the CPR, which possessed extensive areas of the prairie granted to them in return for developing the rail network. It was available at $15 an acre on credit at 6 per cent a year, but Rempel also noted that much of the land was unbroken and consisted of bush and stone. Secondly, there was homesteading land, offered by government to anyone who would pioneer it, but such land was often located in marginal or remote areas and was even poorer than much CPR land. There was also the land that had become available, or which would become available, once conservative Kanadier Mennonites emigrated from Saskatchewan and Manitoba to Central and South America. Lastly, they heard that there was land to be vacated by some Doukhobors who, following the Russian Revolution, decided to return to Russia.[21] The obvious advantage of areas to be vacated by conservative Kanadier and Doukhobors was that large Russländer settlements could be established where families and friends could live in proximity. But at first these were unavailable.

In 1924 a second, even larger wave of over five thousand immigrants arrived from the Soviet Union. A statistical survey of this 1924 cohort reveals the structure of the immigrant group by age, gender, and number of children in a family.[22] In terms of the latter, the average was just over four but at least two had 11 children, five had 10 children; and fourteen had 9 children. There was also an imbalance between men and women in the age group twenty-one to thirty with fewer men than women (41 per cent to 59 per cent), undoubtedly a reflection of war and revolution. In terms of ages, 70 per cent were aged one to forty.

To deal with this large number the CPR assisted Mennonites to form a Mennonite Land Settlement Board (MLSB) in conjunction with its own Colonization Association. The Association was to assist immigrants, Mennonite and non-Mennonite, to find and settle prairie land.[23] Offices of the MLSB were opened in major centres of CPR activity on the prairies. A highly skilled and competent Russländer, Gerhard W. Sawatzky, whose brother Wilhelm would later settle in Gnadenfeld, close to Grunthal, ran the Winnipeg office. The MLSB soon identified possible areas of settlement, including some in the categories identified by Rempel as well as new possibilities. One such option was for groups of families to settle on large farms established during the late nineteenth and early twentieth centuries in Saskatchewan and Manitoba by British and American entrepreneurs, often speculators. By the 1920s many of these farms had proved unprofitable and their owners wished either to sell or lease them. If groups of Russländer moved onto such lands and farmed cooperatively, they might eventually raise sufficient capital to purchase the farm and subdivide it among themselves and so reproduce a localized Mennonite community as in Russia. Special agreements were drawn up for Mennonites to settle the large farms, with Russländer groups often taking over their extensive buildings, machinery, and livestock. While some ventures proved highly successful, others quickly foundered.[24]

Future Grunthalers who emigrated before 1925 experienced all the early hardships associated with the search for suitable land. Some proceeded straight to Saskatchewan where they worked for Mennonite farmers, others stopped over in Ontario, living and working alongside Swiss Mennonites or in non-Mennonite factories. All wanted to find farms of their own and by 1925 many had moved to Manitoba and settled on farms they hoped to purchase or at least rent long enough to accumulate capital and repay some of the travel debt. The Schönfelder who emigrated in 1924 exhibited a strong sense of solidarity and a desire to remain in close contact in the hope of settling in the same neighbourhood. An indication of this is illustrated by an appeal issued in 1925 to former members of the Schönfeld community to provide financial support for an elderly and sick former minister of their congregation, Johann Abraham Driedger, still living in Molochna where his poor eyesight had prevented him and his family from emigrating.[25] Those who moved to Manitoba joined together in the Westbourne area, 115 kilometres west of Winnipeg, where there were a number of large farms with buildings and equipment. The often-absentee owners were in financial difficulties so by April 1925, 112 Russländer had settled in the area. Johann J. Enns, later a minister and the first Elder of the Grunthal Russländer congregation, reported in a Mennonite newspaper that a group of thirty-four "refugees" from Schönfeld and Terek had moved to Westbourne from Ontario and established a new "household."[26]

A letter from one Schönfelder written to a non-Mennonite German-language Winnipeg newspaper, also noted that their preference had been to settle in a "closed" village in an area to be vacated by Kanadier.

The preference for establishing "closed" settlements was widespread among the first Russländer and their failure to do so was later seen as one of the major reasons for their social problems, loss of identity, and economic poverty.[27] However, until Kanadier land became available, living together in a "commune" on the Westbourne farm was the next best thing. The article sought to strike a comic note, saying that while the settlement lay in the "north" they had yet to see an "Eskimo" [Inuk].[28] Living and working on the Westbourne farm, though, was no laughing matter. The idea of living in a commune, which ironically recalled peasant farming households in Russia, was an indication of the cramped and unhappy situation in which they found themselves.[29] Unmarried men were forced to sleep in the outside bunkhouses built for labourers, while married couples, including those with children, shared the single, albeit large, houses. The women took turns to cook and bake bread for the entire group. These living arrangements proved most unsatisfactory and were a cause of considerable conflict and ill-feeling, even though many of the families were related and had suffered together in Russia. Although the farms were well stocked and equipped, cultivating the land was not always easy. Even Russländer with experience of farming had difficulty using Canadian farm machinery and controlling horses with harnesses so different from those they had used in Russia. This led to several misadventures. Horses tended to bolt, damaging machinery, leaving inexperienced farmers ignominiously dumped in fields or ditches. Similar difficulties were experienced by Russländer in Ontario.[30] Working together proved as difficult as living apart. Accustomed to employing Ukrainian and Russian peasant labourers, every man wanted to be boss, and few were willing to take orders from others. To make matters worse the weather turned wet and the harvest, although reasonable, proved below expectations.[31]

The settlers hoped to earn enough to purchase the Westbourne land, but it soon became clear that the price was beyond their slender means. Half the crop had to be turned over to the owner, but when this proved insufficient to cover the owner's debts his creditors seized the stock and farm implements. Unable to spend another year at Westbourne, the Russländer moved on. Some went to Grosse Isle in northern Manitoba, clearing land so it could later be sold as farms. Others moved to the Aitkins Farm at Pigeon Lake, named after the British entrepreneur who had established it. Another large farm close to Portage la Prairie was sharecropped by Russländer. A few families joined Schönfelder relatives near Marquette or close to Glenlea where prospects for agriculture and the purchase of land looked more promising.[32] This uncertain, peripatetic existence was the common lot of many Russländer during their first years in Canada. Some indeed were to spend years uprooting their families in search of land and a secure life. By 1926 the situation of many Russländer immigrants remained precarious. Families still had not secured a satisfactory home or means of sustenance. Indeed, many groups had been divided by the need to gain a regular income. Self-sustaining communities remained unformed, at least unlike those in their former homelands. What the immigrants needed were large areas of land, where family groups could establish viable economic foundations, rebuild communities, and look forward to a better future.

Parting from their old homelands had been both a joy and a sorrow. Relatives and friends had been left behind along with memories of established landscapes, settlements, and ways life. In time these tended to be idealized. Within a short period, the immigrants discovered that Canada was quite unlike their Russian homelands. While the prairie landscape reminded many of the Russian steppe, the climate, especially in Manitoba and Saskatchewan, could be considerably harsher and more unpredictable than in Russia, with colder winters that lasted longer than in southern Russia. The onset of spring seemed particularly unpredictable in comparison with the southern steppe, making it difficult to decide when to start seeding. Then there were many little, everyday things that were absent: the steppe's turn of the seasons, familiar wildflowers, birds, and especially the rich harvest of summer fruits such as the wild pear (LG *kruschtje*). In time people around Grunthal came to appreciate the taste of wild saskatoon berries but older Russländer yearned for the taste of the fruits of their homeland.[33] When life proved hard and the winter season especially long and cold, such things were recalled at family gatherings and community events where adults would reminisce about the "good old days" in Russia. The sound of spoken Ukrainian and Russian and Slavic songs was also missed although in some areas of immigrants from Slav lands were encountered and even sought out by Russländer to ease their loss. Russländer in Saskatchewan visited neighbouring Doukhobors and around Grunthal there were opportunities to encounter Ukrainians.

Some of the land vacated by emigrating Kanadier in Manitoba and Saskatchewan was settled by Russländer once their former owners emigrated.[34] In Manitoba the areas available for settlement included villages and land on the West Reserve where some Russländer settled as early as 1924 to replace Old Colony Reinländer and Sommerfelder Mennonites moving to Mexico.[35] On the East Reserve, however, the emigration mostly started later, beginning only in earnest after 1926 (see map 2.1 for changes in land ownership during the 1920s). Early vacated houses in Alt-Bergfeld, southwest of Grunthal, were settled briefly by a

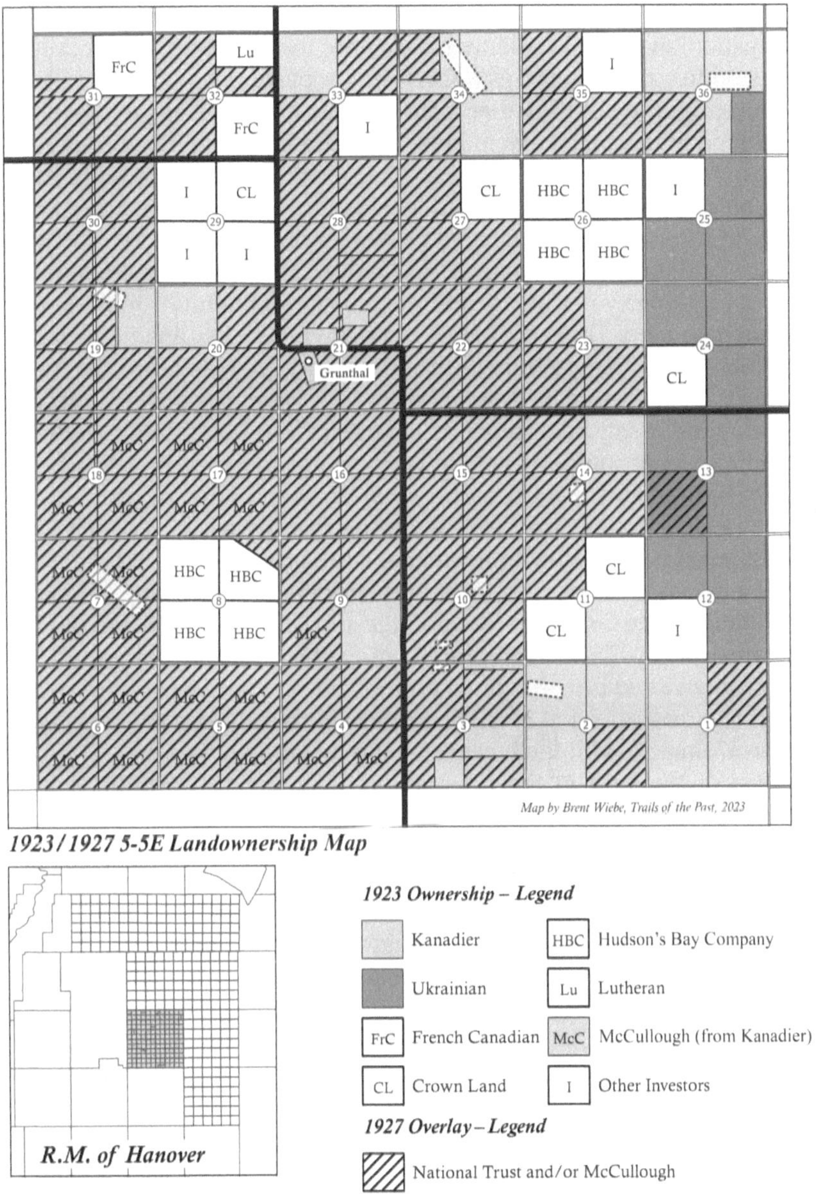

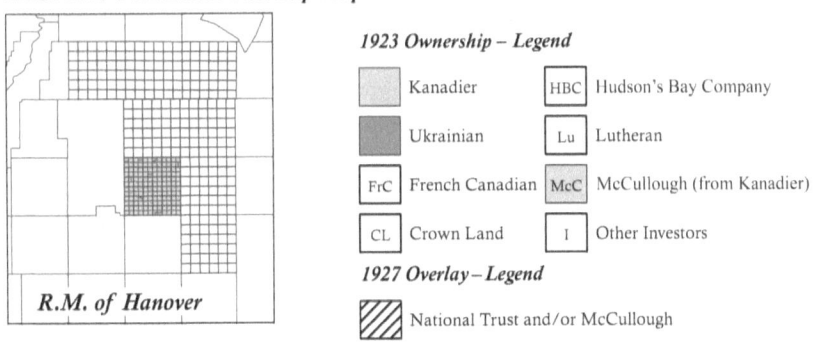

Map 2.1. Landownership in 5–5E, before the Russländer, 1923/1927. Map shows land sold by Kanadier leaving for Paraguay in c. 1926.

Sources: Map by Brent Wiebe, *Trails of the Past* (2023). Government of Manitoba, licenced under the OpenMB Information and Data Use Licence (Manitoba.ca/OpenMB).

few Russländer families, but the land proved too rocky and sandy for cultivation, even by Russländer desperate for farmland. Eventually it was sold to a rancher, James Robertson, for pasture.[36]

The emigration of Kanadier from the East Reserve was greatly aided by United States financiers in New York and Philadelphia with investment interests in South America. One provided contacts with Paraguayan government officials and local landowners purchasing land in 1921 on the Paraguayan Chaco. Once Mennonites agreed to settle in Paraguay their finance companies arranged for the sale of Mennonite land and property in Canada and the transfer of the funds to Paraguay to purchase land. Three companies were involved. In Canada the Intercontinental Company Limited (the "Company" to later Grunthal Russländer), incorporated in Manitoba in 1925, purchased the Canadian Mennonites' assets held in bonds to be repaid in March 1941. In Philadelphia another company helped raise capital and to meet Paraguayan legal requirements a local corporation arranged land purchases and assisted Mennonites to settle once they reached Paraguay. However, the Paraguayan corporation so mismanaged their part in the scheme that the American investors lost most of their money.[37] Following extensive negotiations, the Canadian Mennonites sold 49,998 acres of land (20,234 hectares) for $902,900 to the Intercontinental Company, although the land value varied between $6.50 and $42 an acre with a few areas close to urban areas priced at $50. The price paid to the emigrants averaged out to $7 an acre with the balance paid with land on the Chaco.[38]

Most of the land in the International Company's portfolio, which included buildings, some livestock, and farm machinery, came from the East Reserve.[39] In the Chaco the Company purchased by far the largest area for Mennonite settlers.[40] In total, 1,201 Mennonites emigrated from the East Reserve between 1925 and 1930. Of these 41 per cent belonged to the Chortitzer congregation, numbering 2,930 as of 1927.[41] The Intercontinental Company was backed by large private financiers, American institutions, and by small individual investors that included some American Mennonites and Amish wishing to help their Mennonite brethren in Canada.[42] American and Canadian investment banks and trusts also participated, the most important of which was the National Trust Company of Canada, which acted as trustee for all property and funds involved with East Reserve and Saskatchewan lands. One Grunthal Russländer later suggested that as a Canadian-registered company the National Trust handle Intercontinental Company's affairs because the latter, as an American-based company, could not operate in Canada.[43] While the investments of the banks and trusts were secured by 7 per cent mortgages held in "A" Gold Bonds due for

Table 2.1. East Reserve land and property sold to Russländer in 1926/1927

Location	Acreage	Value of land and chattels, $	Cost per acre, $
North end	8,935	554,596	62
South end	25,179	624,677	25

repayment in 1941, the investments made by private individuals were held in "B" Bonds and unsecured. This situation was later to have dire consequences for those involved. In 1926, however, the position of the Company looked secure.

The arrival of the Russländer provided the Intercontinental Company with an ideal opportunity to capitalize on the lands it held in Canada. It calculated there would be sufficient land to settle 154 families, of which land 36,800 acres (14,892 hectares) was situated in Manitoba and sufficient to settle 132 families.[44] The East Reserve land consisted of approximately 30,000 acres (12,140 hectares) the Company valued at over $1.46 million (see table 2.1).[45] This was spread across townships four through eight but the largest area, about 14,000 acres (5,666 hectares), was situated in Township 5, Range 5, an area centred on Grunthal. The other large concentrations of land were located to the north of Grunthal around Chortitz, towards Dufrost and the town of Niverville. In later documents a distinction was drawn between lands situated in the northern areas of the Reserve and those towards the south (see table 2.1) and the latter were considered poorer and commanded lower prices than those in the north. The value of the land as calculated by the Company was reported to vary from as low as $10 an acre to as high as $65, with an average of about $32 an acre.[46] This valuation included not only land, but also houses, buildings, and other chattels including livestock that had not previously been disposed of at auction by departing Kanadier. In 1926 the German consul in Winnipeg reported to Berlin that he considered the Company had overvalued the land in comparison to what was paid to Kanadier to sell to the Colonization Board and settle Russländer.[47] The board, however, was not able to turn down such an offer since land had to be found for Russländer.

The contracts offered by the Company to prospective purchasers were complex, but not unreasonable. Prospective purchasers did not have to put down a deposit but instead had to pay interest at 7 per cent annually on the principal and to repay part of the principal according to a prearranged agreement. Payments could be made either as a proportion of the crop or in cash. As part of the agreement, any settlers were obliged to work the land, preparing and planting areas in ways carefully detailed in the agreement, and were also responsible for all taxes and assessments on the land as well as any insurance. Special conditions were written into the contracts concerning existing crops and livestock for the period 1926/27, and the Company agreed to assist with the maintenance of properties and improvements to livestock. Ownership of the land and property remained with the Company until a farmer had paid 42 per cent of the purchase price. Upon signing the agreement, the prospective owner, or initially family groups, gained almost immediate possession of the land, buildings, and chattels and could begin farming as soon as the Kanadier left, and the new farming season began.

Once they learned Kanadier land would become available, the Mennonite Board of Colonization began negotiations with the Intercontinental Company to settle Russländer on vacated farms. The board had its own conditions and was willing to act as an agent of the Company to facilitate Russländer settlement. When the Canadian Colonization Association of the CPR learned of these negotiations it intervened through the newly organized MLSB and insisted on amendments to the Company's contracts to ensure that they conformed to the Association's standard contracts. Their agents also inspected the lands and arranged for prospective buyers to deal only with the Company through the MLSB in Winnipeg.[48] The Company appears to have agreed to these conditions and the Mennonite Board of Colonization drew up a statement outlining the conditions for the purchase of the land with chattels and an obligation on the part of the Company to supply the basics needs for farming if these were not included. The land and chattels were to be purchased under a "crop sales contract." The average price of the land with chattels was to be $32.50 an acre and the statement went on to outline how payments were to be made in later years and other details of settlement.[49] With terms agreed, the availability of land and the cooperation of the Mennonite Board of Colonization were publicly announced in the immigrant press.[50] The Company, however, would not allow the deal with the MLSB to proceed to finalization unless 90 per cent of the land was sold. In November the Winnipeg Board announced that after a concerted six week "campaign" they had managed to finalize agreements on almost 34,000 acres of land, enough to settle 136 families and thereby fulfil the Company's conditions.[51]

Mennonites interested in the land offered by the Company through the Mennonite Board of Colonization travelled to Winnipeg and, after being checked as to their suitability, they could then view the land. In the East Reserve the board employed the services of a local Kanadier to show prospective settlers around the area.[52] This was Peter A. Braun, a farmer-entrepreneur, also known by his nickname Red Beard (LG *Root'boat*) Braun, well known as a shrewd businessman who had been involved in several commercial ventures around Grunthal and later developed extensive business contacts with Russländer in the Grunthal area. Some farms offered for sale were quite isolated and scattered across areas of trees and bush; others were still grouped close to original village sites such as Schönsee. A few Russländer were already living in the area, including Tobias Janz who had settled in early 1925 on an Alt-Bergfeld farm vacated by Kanadier.[53]

Around Grunthal the farms offered for sale were situated mostly on accessible adjacent quarter sections but further south they were often scattered through areas of partially cleared bush. The land prospective buyers viewed with Braun varied considerably in quality.[54] There were gravel ridges, the remains of old beach lines of the vast, ancient Lake Agassiz that once covered much of southern Manitoba after the last great ice sheet began to melt and retreat northward. The original village of Grunthal was situated on an ancient beach ridge that extended to Steinbach. A surveyor in 1872 described the soils in the area to later include Grunthal as "generally of a sandy, gravely, stony nature" and a "considerable proportion of this township [5–5E] is covered with drift, consisting of large granitic limestone and other boulders."[55] He suggested this "must render its successful cultivation a matter of some difficulty" and indeed many areas would remain uncultivated, covered with trees and low-lying scrub, including poplar, tamarack, willow, and oak. Today this cover has been roughly cleared for pasture or cultivation but in the 1920s much remained uncultivated. The entire region is known to Mennonites as the land of "brush and stone" (LG *Struck enn Steen*). According to the Russländer author Arnold Dyck's comic characters Koop and Buhr (*Koop enn Bua*), written in the 1930s, in the southern areas of the East Reserve, brush and stones grew naturally with little help.[56] Elsewhere, the soils were better, especially where rotting vegetation had formed in ancient swamps and lakes. Such pockets of soil could be found towards the north and west of Grunthal where there were patches of richer, heavier loam that, once they were cleared of timber and brush, could be cultivated intensively.[57] Nowhere, however, was the land on the East Reserve as rich or fertile as much of the West Reserve.

Many established and developed sections of land contained a house, usually in the form of the classic Mennonite house-barn construction in which the main house was connected to a barn for wintering livestock (HG *Stall*; LG *Staul*) leading to a larger annex for storing produce and machinery (HG *Scheune*; LG *Schien*).⁵⁸ There were also outbuildings and a range of equipment as well as livestock depending on the land's productivity, the wealth of the previous owner, and what had not been sold by emigrating Kanadier. Good water was available if wells had been properly maintained but this varied from place to place like the buildings, livestock, and machinery. Houses might be in good repair, but others, including barns, were in a state of collapse; houses had only earthen floors, timber frames were rotting, and the buildings and yard were liable to flood in the spring. The landscape often reflected earlier Kanadier attempts at cultivation. In Gnadenfeld and Alt-Bergfeld, for instance, there were old field ridges in the form of strips to be divided among the village community still visible at the time of Russländer settlement.⁵⁹ Kanadier in most of the Grunthal area had not farmed this way for many years. The villages, often only half formed before they were broken up and farm households relocated on their own quarter sections, were barely visible.

Each farmer had utilized land in their own way although in the Grunthal area most cultivated land was still in quarter sections of between 158 to 160 acres. Some Russländer secured whole sections, sometimes two in poorer areas. By 1928 there were about 130 Russländer families living in the southern areas of the East Reserve including the area in and around Grunthal.⁶⁰ In Township 5–5E there were about seventy farms available for settlement and by the early 1930s these had been occupied by about fifty Russländer families. The land value of a quarter section in 5–5E prior to the Kanadier emigration, as reported in municipal tax records for 1927, averaged around $600, ranging from a low of around $400 to a high of almost $1,600.⁶¹ The more highly valued land lay to the west of the old village of Grunthal in an area known as Gnadenfeld, so named after a village once located there but which by the 1920s had disappeared except for a few remaining houses and barns.⁶² The poorer land lay to the south and the east of the central area of Township 5–5E. Here adjacent sections tended to be combined into single holdings or linked to neighbouring areas to maximize cultivatable land and avoid areas of poor soils and brush cover. Timbered areas, at first seen as useless, later proved a source of cordwood some farmers could utilize to supplement their income.

While there are records detailing where individual Russländer settled on vacated East Reserve lands, there is no clear indication as to how decisions were arrived at concerning the choice and distribution of land. Later memoirs sometimes discuss the choice of farms but do not detail the importance of the quality of land chosen.⁶³ The first settlers, dealing with the Company through the Winnipeg Board, undoubtedly first personally viewed the farms and then came to their own decision based on need, their knowledge of the area's potential, and a calculation of their ability to repay the costs involved. Their skill at making a wise decision depended on their ability to assess the potential of a farm and the more experienced farmers were better able to do this than others. There was also the appeal of being near centres of communication, to stores, and services as they clearly wanted to be at the centre of things once a community developed and hopefully prospered. A store in what remained of the old village of Grunthal indicated an important location despite it being situated on the gravel ridge and on marginal soils. Additional factors besides economic considerations may also have been involved in the selection as social factors were also important. These included the desire of families with previous social connections in Russia, often reinforced by shared experiences as refugees, to settle close to each other. Once initial Russländer settlement took place, there was occasionally a readjustment of holdings and a movement of people in search of advantages that became apparent only after they had lived in the area.

It soon became obvious to the Company that a local Russländer agent was needed to act as an intermediary between the Company and the settlers as well as to assist in the distribution of land still to be sold or which was vacated by Russländer moving out of the district. In 1927 the new settlers met in the local Grunthal schoolhouse and elected Jacob J. Rempel as their spokesman and representative in all matters concerning land and settlement. Rempel, a former Schönfelder, had been born in 1886 into a wealthy family whose estate, Tiegenhof, consisted of over 1,350 acres (546 hectares) of land. As the eldest son, he had been forced to assume responsibility for the estate after his father's death in 1901 and his management skills were developed further during service in the First World War, first in a Red Cross unit and after he transferred to naval ships operating on the Black Sea (fig 2.1).[64]

In Grunthal Rempel's role in civic affairs increased rapidly proving that he was a born leader, in recognition of which he would acquire the nickname Kaiser (LG *Tjeisa*) Rempel. In Mennonite Low German *Tjeisa* can refer to both the German emperor and the Russian tsar and, like many Mennonite nicknames, is suggestive of both positive and negative opinions of Rempel.[65] Initially the settlers agreed to contribute towards Rempel's expenses, providing him with a small salary; this arrangement permitted him to devote time to their interests and compensated for the time he was away from his farm. Later reports suggest the promised contributions were either only partially paid or not at all as everyone was extremely short of money. Rempel's services were

48   On Stony Ground

Fig. 2.1. Jacob J. Rempel in a non-combatant role during the First World War.
Source: Courtesy of Eleanore (Rempel) Woollard, Edmonton.

eventually recognized by the Company who provided him with a salary and supplied a vehicle. Rempel later wrote that his salary was $600 a year but some Russländer believed it was $1,500, a figure unlikely at the time. Naturally, the salary and vehicle immediately raised Russländer suspicions, and some claimed he was working either in the Company's interests, or in his own, but certainly not theirs.

The MLSB may also have backed Rempel's nomination as in 1928, Gerhard W. Sawatzky, head of the board, referred to him as the Grunthal Group Leader (HG *Gruppenführer*). Another Russländer, Franz (Frank) Steingart was also referred to as *Gruppenführer* for the Chortitz area north of Grunthal, but he never became such a dominant leader as Rempel.[66] In 1937 Steingart moved to St. Catharines in Ontario and in old age merely spoke of himself as a "field man" for the Intercontinental Company and collector of debts owed to CMBC.[67] In 1931 an agent of the Board of Colonization referred to Rempel as *Oberschulze*, a term used in pre-revolutionary Russia for elected district mayors of areas that included several villages. An additional factor in Rempel's selection may have been that the Russländer wanted one of their own to speak on their behalf and not the Kanadier businessman Braun who, however, continued to represent the Company and give advice to new settlers on farming and local government regulations. Later Rempel was referred to as the "Representative of the National Trust Co. for the entire settlement" indicating how, by the early 1930s, the Russländer's influence extended beyond the immediate Grunthal area.[68]

The change in Rempel's title occurred once the Intercontinental Company's liabilities were transferred to the mortgage-holding National Trust now referred to by the Russländer as "The Company." Both companies had a considerable interest in the new settlers' welfare as it was in their long-term interest that the settlers succeeded so they could continue to pay interest on their land and eventually purchase it. The CPR's Colonization Association also attempted to involve the companies in assisting the settlers. On the East Reserve, well into the 1930s the National Trust Company employed a graduate of the Manitoba Agricultural College, Andrew Robertson, to help the farmers and through him, Russländer received specialist advice on seed, livestock, and how to farm successfully. Robertson arranged for professors from the Agricultural College to address local meetings based on their expertise: the raising of cows, chickens, pigs, vegetables, and grain cultivation, and on the different qualities and uses of soils. Starting in 1928 the new settlers organized an annual agricultural fair where farmers could exhibit products that then were judged by invited experts and cash prizes awarded.[69]

Initially Russländer were bound within a human landscape moulded by Kanadier to meet their economic needs and distinctive sense of community. Remnants of the original villages established in the 1870s survived, not as large settlements but usually as sites of stores, post offices, an occasional blacksmith and dairy, and in certain places, a meeting house. Other meeting houses were isolated at crossroads where members in the district gathered to worship. In the early 1920s, today's road system that mostly follows section boundaries did not exist.[70] Instead roads and paths meandered across sections at angles, linking key centres by the shortest and most convenient routes. Some roads associated with Métis cart tracks predated Mennonite settlement. But while many farms were quite isolated from the outside world, Kanadier and later Russländer still needed access to markets to sell farm produce. The Ridge Road linked Grunthal to Steinbach and Peter A. Braun owned a trucking business, known locally as a transfer service, and in 1928 he purchased a new truck to carry goods and people between local settlements and Winnipeg and even the West Reserve.[71] Russländer settlers used his services to ship and collect goods and to visit Winnipeg. The other way to contact the outside world was to drive a horse and buggy to the railway station at Carey, situated west of St. Pierre, from where produce such as cream could be sent to Winnipeg. In 1928, however, the City Dairy in Winnipeg opened a plant to process milk and cream into butter and cheese in a disused feed mill located a short distance from the old village of Grunthal.[72] Also, in 1928 lambs were sold by the Russländer farmers to the Hudson's Bay Company and the Ideal Meat Market Company in Winnipeg for more than $9 a head.[73]

From the outset most Russländer accepted the challenge of making a living from the land, clearing debts, and hopefully purchasing their farm. But so much was new and while some learned quickly on the job, others struggled. A great deal depended on external circumstances: the fertility of the land, the weather, and the returns received for produce. The unpredictable climate was a major factor as the area's long, cold winters were succeeded by unpredictable springs where winter would suddenly return, freezing newly planted seed, destroying early pasture growth under snow and ice just as winter feed started to run out. The short growing season limited the range of vegetables and fruits available. A few new Russländer settlers attempted to break in new land only to discover why certain areas had been left fallow or uncultivated by Kanadier. As bush was removed and the soil exposed, immense rocks appeared which had to be dragged clear with teams of horses. Smaller stones broke ploughs and damaged other farm machinery as the fields were prepared. Even today when farmers employ specialized teams and machinery to clear land considered suitable for cultivation, stones continue to surface for years, even quite large ones. In the past farmers just abandoned efforts to clear or maintain certain fields, turning them over to pasture or leaving them to return to brush. Later, particularly stony areas would be sold for gravel to dredging companies for road paving and today close to Grunthal is a large water-filled hole that locals joke might be turned into a water-sport venue in the future.

The variable soils of south central parts of the East Reserve are more suited to mixed farming than single crop, commercial cultivation. This mixed farming had been the practice of the better Kanadier farmers, many of whom made a reasonable living from the land before they emigrated.[74] In southern Russia, however, Russländer had been more accustomed to grain production, overwhelmingly wheat, for commercial markets. The mixed farming of the Kanadier, often combined with the gathering of wild products from the area's mixed ecology, appeared to many Russländer as a return to a subsistence economy. The Russländer author Arnold Dyck described the way of life of local Kanadier through his comic characters, Koop and Buhr:[75]

> When these folks do sow something, wherever they can among brush and stones, then it's wheat and barley, oats and rye. They also plant potatoes and raise cucumbers and other vegetables. The women and small kids dig seneca [*Polygala senega*] roots, hunt for wild strawberries, blueberries, cherries and whatever else grows among the *struck* [LG: brush] and stones that can be eaten or even sold. In winter the men cut firewood to sell, take care of the stock and catch bush rabbits by the ton. Na, and in season they shoot deer, prairie chickens, grouse and wild ducks ... Wolves and bears they shoot the year round, or hack at them with a hatchet when there's nothing handy to shoot them with ... All this shows that these folks live quite close to nature.[76]

From the outset Russländer settlers were advised to establish a broad-based mixed farming system, combining some grain cultivation with pasture improvement for dairying and stock rearing. They were also encouraged to raise vegetables.[77] In the first planting season of 1927 the settlers were instructed to sow sweet clover, alfalfa, and other grasses. The Company also supplied them with breeding stock, including Yorkshire boars and a bull to improve dairy herds. Up to this time most cattle in the area were Ayrshires with a few Holsteins and an occasional Jersey cow. Peter A. Braun was sent to Alberta to purchase farm horses.[78] In 1929, Jacob J. Rempel reported that an agent of the Company, a Mr. Bowman, had travelled to Ontario and Saskatchewan to purchase improved livestock for the settlers.[79]

In southern Russia Mennonite farmers had mainly cultivated crops on land with deep loam and very few or no stones. In southern areas of the East Reserve grain crops could be grown, but only in limited areas and in small quantities. Many Russländer yearned for the ease of cultivating a single crop and especially for the sight of fields of ripening wheat. One Grunthal farmer recalled how his Russländer father would plant a small field of wheat and as it matured, visit it every day, just to stand and recall his lost homeland. But the reality for most Russländer was mixed farming, producing fodder for livestock, but little commercial grain. Dairy produce, however, could be sold at a profit. In Russia Mennonites kept dairy cows to produce milk, butter, and cheese mainly for home consumption. In colonies a herdsman was hired by villagers and every morning he would collect the individual farmer's cows and drive them all out to a common pasture, returning at evening in time for milking. Milking was done by women as it was deemed women's work. Most adult Russländer men would only milk a cow at times of dire emergency when a suitable female was unavailable. There is a local story of a man whose wife fell ill so he brought the cow to her sickbed to be milked. On the other hand, women preferred men not to touch their cows, as men were inexperienced and handled a cow's teats roughly. Dairying was fine if a man had a skilful wife or, even better, several daughters, but not if he had only sons or lived alone. W.W. Sawatzky in Gnadenfeld, close to Grunthal, was a highly successful dairy farmer blessed with daughters and in 1930/31 his cows produced ten thousand pounds of milk and four hundred pounds of butter.[80]

Russländer in Russia were accustomed to raising livestock for household needs – mainly pigs and milk cows – but now they were encouraged to keep sheep both for their meat and wool, no doubt because Kanadier once raised sheep on the East Reserve.[81] By 1931 there were almost 1,500 sheep in the area but they proved a challenge as although in early nineteenth century Russia the Russländer's ancestors built much of their wealth rearing sheep, this had long been replaced by grain farming. In Grunthal Russländer found sheep extremely difficult to manage as most fences in the area were in poor repair and sheep, not the cleverest of God's creatures, were always getting lost in the brush or trapped in snowdrifts. Wolves killed some, or so it was reported.[82] A surprising number died "accidentally," ending up in the immigrants' cooking pots where, as one Mennonite put it, they proved much easier to handle than when they were alive. Finally, chickens provided meat and eggs for domestic needs while eggs also could be sold. For any real profit, however, eggs needed to be supplied in large quantities and transported to major market centres rather than sold to local storeowners who usually sold them on. Some immigrants resorted to selling eggs themselves as a means of raising extra money although others considered such practices as an indication of a lowering of social status: "chickens scratch backwards," as a saying expressed it.

Within a few years of their arrival in the East Reserve, Russländer, particularly those settled around Grunthal, appeared to be prospering and 1928 proved to be a good year for the sale of produce. The Grunthal Russländer held a harvest festival in the schoolhouse, with their choir and a sermon from a guest minister. They even raised $150 for Christian missions.[83] The community was heralded as a great success with excellent prospects for further development. Gerhard W. Sawatzky, head of the MLSB in Winnipeg, published a glowing account of the settlement, reproduced in all the leading Mennonite newspapers.[84] Jacob J. Rempel was justly proud of his fellow Russländer's achievements. In 1929 he attended the provincial meeting of the Mennonite cultural organization the Central Mennonite Immigration Committee (*ZMIK*) and delivered a paper on livestock improvement based on his experience of farming in Grunthal.[85] The following year he offered a paper to the provincial meeting of Russländer immigrants on farming, but it is unclear whether it was delivered as although he is listed in the proceedings, no paper is included in the minutes.[86] However, the agricultural correspondent of the *Manitoba Free Press* visited the Grunthal area and wrote a favourable account of the success of the new settlers.[87]

The real situation, however, was that in spite of all the assistance the Russländer received and access to markets for their produce, the returns were insufficient to cover their costs, debts to the Company, debt repayments, or even local taxes. The CMBC also imposed additional levies on all Russländer to support other activities and aid for sickly and needy immigrants. The local congregation also required financial support. Adults and children needed clothes, footwear, and essentials as no household was totally self-sufficient in terms of foodstuffs such as coffee and sugar. Often a decision had to be made as to where best to spend the limited cash available. Some chose to pay the travel debt before paying the Company. But the Intercontinental Company was itself in financial difficulties.

In 1929 the Company's receipts from its mostly Russländer tenants in Manitoba were insufficient to meet the Company's tax and interest liabilities. Despite it having lowered the interest rates charged to tenants from 7 per cent to 6 per cent so that the Company could receive more in repayments, this proved insufficient to cover its debts.[88] The Company then attempted to provide its tenants with new contracts that wiped out the interest payments due in 1929 while also reducing the value of the land (see table 2.2).

These readjustments, however, failed to save the Company from collapse. In 1933 the holders of first mortgage bonds began foreclosure proceedings but the Company could not meet the required payments, and the Company's charter in Manitoba was cancelled in November 1935.[89] The holders of "A" Gold Bonds secured by liens over the land had already taken control of the Company's assets, mainly its mortgages. This was reported in a letter from the Intercontinental Company Ltd to holders of farm lien bonds at the end of March 1933.[90] The largest creditor was the National Trust Company. These events meant little for Grunthal's Russländer as for a long time the National Trust had been the agency they had dealt with. But the American holders of second, unsecured "B" Bonds included several Mennonite and Amish farmers who discovered they had lost their entire investment. David Toews reported to the Mennonite Conference in Canada that these losses amounted to

Table 2.2. East Reserve land, 1930: Original contracts and accumulated charges/interest (in $)

Area	Original principal	Accumulated charges	Accumulated interest	Totals	Per acre
North end	554,596	41,996	50,730	647,323	72
South end	625,677	56,696	50,329	732,703	29

Source: Figures from a letter dated 13 May 1930 from the Intercontinental Company Ltd. to David Toews, CMBC Records, MHA, Vol. 1171, No. 58.

Table 2.3. East Reserve land: Adjusted contracts 1930 (in $)

Area	New contract	Per acre	Loss on adjustment	Adjustment per acre	Adjustment, %
North end	400,557	45	246,766	27.62	38
South end	517,124	21	215,579	8.56	29

Source: Figures from a letter dated 13 May 1930 from the Intercontinental Company Ltd. to David Toews, CMBC Records, MHA, Vol. 1171, No. 58.

over $250,000.[91] American Mennonites had believed that in taking out the "B" bonds they were supporting fellow Mennonites and that the CMBC had guaranteed their investments. Now they discovered that this was not so. The losses, occurring at the time of the Great Depression, generated a great deal of bad feeling between American Mennonite and Amish investors and the CMBC that would last for years.[92]

Chapter Three

The Bases of Community

While the first Kanadier had mostly immigrated as members of existing congregations ready to settle in corporate village communities, Russländer did not immigrate as cohesive groups ready to re-establish the united communities they had known in Russia. The way of life Kanadier sought to recreate was like that they had known in Russia, focused on membership in a congregation, and interconnected by ties of kinship. In the early 1870s Kanadier discovered a land inhabited by a variety of peoples with their own ways of life. During the 1920s Russländer came as nuclear families or as members of small, non-corporate groups, loosely affiliated by ties of kinship and friendship but not as congregational communities. Some came as individuals, with some later immigrants trying to locate family, relations, and friends already resident in Canada. Where there were pre-existing connections, these were based on those established in Russia and reinforced by identification with a common place of origin, previous place of residence, schooling, and occupation. Another factor involved shared experiences, even if these were often painful. For some, pre-immigration connections formed the basis on which a new community could be built, but such previous associations also contained the potential for discord, social division, and eventually separation.

Ties could be relatively easily broken and new ones established, as in their homeland Russländer as individuals and groups had been more physically and socially mobile than Kanadier ever were before they emigrated in the 1870s. The greater mobility of Russländer was not just a consequence of recent events, for in 1914 economic opportunities made Mennonites in Russia a more mobile people willing to seek new opportunities even if this meant moving away from their home and community. In Canada many Russländer were only connected because they once had lived in Imperial Russia, experienced terrible events, and been forced to emigrate. At one level they appeared to share similar ideas, values, and hopes for the future, but this was not always so. While to Kanadier who had not joined the emigration southward and still inhabited areas of the southern East Reserve, Russländer at first presented themselves as a unified group, there were differences between them that often took time to resolve. At least one early settler, Nikolai Thiessen, left Grunthal for Coaldale in Alberta during the 1930s as he lacked kinship links with others in Grunthal, and his move to Coaldale may indicate a wish to join the Mennonite Brethren who were dominant in the Coaldale community.[1] In Canada Russländer had to come to terms not only with a new land, a new political system, and new neighbours, but also with each other. It is important to examine the structure of the Grunthal community more closely, starting with their different places of origin in Russia, previous connections, social status, and past occupations.

From the outset of Russländer settlement in Grunthal it was people from Schönfeld or who had connections to Schönfeld who at first dominated the attempts to form a community. Their unity was reinforced by their shared experiences in Russia: loss of family and friends, the seizure of land, destruction of property, life as refugees in Molochna, and by the fact that almost all had immigrated to Canada in 1924. These factors combined to bind them together in a special way when compared with many other Russländer. Close ties of kinship and marriage among Schönfelder established either in Russia or later in Canada provided another source of connectedness, sometimes extending back through several generations and further sustained by a sense of distinctiveness associated with their self-perception as members of a privileged class, real or imagined. Between Schönfelder families, however, there were also distinctions based on social status already present in Russia related to the size of landholdings and additional ties of kinship and marriage. These are difficult to reconstruct as in some ways the terrible events in Russia made everyone "equal."

The Schönfelder in Grunthal also maintained links with other Schönfelder in Manitoba, especially in Glenlea, and as far away as Leamington and Vineland in Ontario.[2] There was movement between these groups and later some Schönfelder left Grunthal to join relatives and friends elsewhere. Other Schönfelder from these places were attracted to settle in Grunthal, encouraged by the presence of relatives. This included those with special skills in need of a farm or those wanting to start a business.

While living as refugees in Molochna, some Schönfelder married into local Molochna families and some of these relatives immigrated to

Canada and settled in Grunthal. In Schönfeld in 1912 Jacob J. Rempel married Maria Thiessen, a member of a neighbouring estate-owning family. In 1918 he was forced to flee from Schönfeld to relatives in the Molochna Colony with his family, widowed mother, and siblings, but soon his wife died. With four children to support, Rempel was soon remarried to Lena Woelke, youngest daughter of a Molochna villager, and together they had six more children, two of whom died young. When Rempel immigrated to Canada from Molochna in 1924 he was the leader of the third departing group that included many related members, including Rempel's sisters and brothers and his wife's Woelke family.[3] After early years of struggle in Canada they eventually all reunited in Grunthal, including a pair of Woelke bachelors. In Grunthal the Schönfelder initially identified with other Mennonites from Molochna or from other Molochna-related daughter colonies. However, none of these other settlers formed a cohesive group although a number came to identify with the core Schönfelder settlers. These included the Enns brothers, Johann and David, and members of the Driedger, Peters, and Rempel families as well as Wiens and Warkentins.

Surprisingly, few families of Russländer in Grunthal came directly from the established colonies of Khortitsa and Molochna although the Woelkes came from northern Molochna and a family of Kasdorfs from the village of Burwalde in Khortitsa. But a number proudly identified themselves as coming from one of Khortitsa's daughter settlements. One included people from the settlement of Grigorievka, some of whom were related through kinship and marriage, including members of the Bartel, Froese, Krahn and Loewen families. They could also trace connections to other Khortitsa-related Russländer settled in the Grunthal area. The predominant Khortitsa-connected Mennonites were those from the colony of Baratov Shlachtin, also often related through kinship and marriage ties. They predominantly came from the villages of Grünfeld and Steinfeld.

Former Grünfeld inhabitants included Dietrich and Franz Warkentin, later joined by their brother-in-law, Julius Klassen. W.W. Sawatzky, who would settle in Gnadenfeld close to Grunthal, although born in Yasykova was also raised in Steinfeld. He married Maria Klassen, also from Baratov Shlachtin, and they immigrated in 1925, settling on the East Reserve in 1926. In 1929 Maria's brother Peter, a recent immigrant, joined them. Heinrich Olfert, also from Steinfeld, settled in Grunthal before moving to McCreary in 1930. Other Steinfelders living close to Grunthal were the Nikkels and the Kaspers. Another family was centred on the patriarch Abram P. Martens, who was born in Steinfeld in 1875 and immigrated in 1926, and who with his large family eventually settled close to the former settlement of Schönsee on the East Reserve. Later he purchased land closer to Grunthal. As well as his own large family, relatives of Martens through marriage, such as the Bestvaters and Schapanskys, arrived in the Grunthal area during the late 1920s and early 1930s. Members of the Thiessen family, also late immigrants from Khortitsa-connected settlements, settled close to Grunthal. Members of other families who had been born either in Khortitsa or Molochna later immigrated from later-established daughter colonies; one such immigrant is Franz Guenther who, although born close to Molochna, came from Orenburg, a daughter colony close to the Urals.[4]

The end of emigration from the USSR and restrictions on immigration to Canada affected the relatives of Tobias Janz, who had settled in the Grunthal area before most other Russländer. The Janz family came from Molochna and after 1906 moved to Pavlador in Siberia. Tobias had joined them but soon felt ill-suited to life in Siberia and returned to Molochna where he established a photographic studio.[5] His brother Abram remained in Siberia but shortly before the implementation of Soviet collectivization policies he and his family fled to Moscow and managed to reach Germany. Because the family included healthy, adult sons capable of agricultural work, it was permitted to enter Canada in 1930 and at first stayed with Tobias in the Neu-Bergfeld area.[6] Two brothers, John and Nicholas, found work in Glenlea whose mainly Schönfelder inhabitants had close connections with relatives in Grunthal. The brothers had little choice but to work here as the Depression now gripped the country and they knew no English. John married in Glenlea, but the couple was forced to live in the summer house of John's employer. In search of better conditions in 1939 they moved to the Alt-Bergfeld area, just south of Spencer. Nicholas also worked in Glenlea and married Sara Peters, who was closely connected with Schönfeld people, so when he moved to the Grunthal area in the 1940s he found it easy to join the community. Both brothers' parents had belonged to the Mennonite Brethren, and this probably meant that at first, they were suspect in Grunthal.[7] Even when they and other immigrants from Siberia, such as the Spensts, settled near Grunthal, they were forced to live on marginal lands south of Grunthal.

A family that was interesting but very different from other Grunthal settlers was the Heeses, descendants of a noted nineteenth-century teacher, administrator, and entrepreneur, Heinrich Heese.[8] They lived in the provincial capital of Ekaterinoslav and as they were intermarried with wealthy milling, factory, and estate-owning families they maintained connections with the Khortitsa Colony.[9] The family was the most Russianized of all Grunthal settlers. Dietrich Heese's first language was Russian, and he used the Russian form of his name, Dmitry, before eventually adopting the German, Dietrich. Members of the family reached Canada by several different routes. In 1923, fourteen-year-old Dietrich Heese travelled alone from Germany to Saskatchewan where he worked for a Mennonite farmer.[10] Earlier, in 1922, he had fled Russia with his widowed mother, a younger brother, and a sister after his father died of typhus. The family lived in a German refugee camp before they came to Canada although his mother and the family were delayed when trachoma, a common eye condition that frustrated the hopes of many emigrants, was diagnosed.

Dietrich's elder brother Nikolai served in the White Army, but in 1920 after their defeat he was evacuated with other troops on a French warship to Tunisia. Here he married a Russian nurse, Antonia Pridovorova, who immigrated with him to Canada. In North Africa Nikolai spelled his surname Guezé, obviously a French transliteration of his Russian surname. Reunited in Canada, the family share-farmed 1,300 acres close to Dominion City with a former miller, Heinrich Janzen, from Yasykova. The group had an option to purchase the land at $42 an acre, but rain ruined the crop so, unable to make the required payments, they sought work elsewhere. Dietrich meanwhile married Janzen's daughter, Elizabeth, before both families settled close to each other south of Grunthal. Heinrich Janzen died soon after but his son Peter, denied conscientious objector status and conscripted into the Soviet Navy, was only able to immigrate in 1925 to join his relatives near Grunthal.

To earn money for the family, Margarethe Heese, Dietrich's sister, joined other young Mennonite women in working as a maid for a wealthy Jewish family in Winnipeg. This was a common practice for many Russländer girls who found employment in wealthy English and Jewish urban households, sending home most of their earnings to assist families to pay bills and establish themselves on farms or in business. Although many of the girls enjoyed and profited from the experience, gaining a knowledge of English and often receiving gifts and support from their employers, for their parents it was a humiliating but necessary evil and revealed how low the immigrants had fallen. In Russia prosperous Mennonites had employed servants rather than providing them, least of all to members of other ethnic groups. Young women were also seen as at risk in the city and to ensure their moral safety and provide them with social and religious support, several girls' homes were established in the major cities where they were employed, including two in Winnipeg: one for General Conference Mennonites, the *Ebenezer Mädchenheim*, and the Mary Martha Home for Mennonite Brethren young women (fig. 3.1).[11]

Fig. 3.1. Young women from Grunthal meeting at the Ebenezer Young Women's Home (*Mädchenheim*) in Winnipeg while working as maids in Winnipeg, c. 1935.

Source: Mennonite Heritage Archives, Winnipeg (629-M-20.0).

Like members of the Heese and Janzen families, later immigrants to Grunthal came to join relatives. This kind of chain-migration steadily swelled the ranks of Khortitsa-connected Mennonites in and around Grunthal but as most arrived in Canada after 1924, they encountered Schönfelder whose men had already taken advantage of the new country and even acquired a working knowledge of English. Despite their common backgrounds and sometimes connections through kinship and marriage, Khortitsa groups were never as united as the Schönfelder and were unable to control the community even if some individuals eventually held important offices and contributed to specific projects. The reasons for this are not entirely clear, although a lack of forcefulness of Khortitsa-connected immigrants may also reflect a natural Khortitsa reticence to promote themselves, perhaps because they were less concerned with status and power than Schönfelder. Several Khortitsa-connected people came from close-knit villages in Russia and were unaccustomed to living on separate, individual farms like the Schönfelder.[12] Khortitsa-linked Russländer did, however, manage to achieve a degree of solidarity in the area around the old Gnadenfeld village where they associated with the Kanadier who had remained or returned. Some of the land in this area had been rejected by Schönfelder as it appeared stony and sandy, whereas in Russia the Schönfelder had known mostly heavier loam. But there was sandy soil in areas of the Khortitsa Colony that was excellent for growing watermelons and other crops and the land around Gnadenfeld proved equally suited for cultivation and pasture. In 1931 the distribution of land in the Grunthal area did not always reveal these subtle differences as they gradually would became more significant with time (see map 3.1).

Divisions between Khortitsa and Molochna Colony Mennonites that were established in Russia were often enhanced in immigration. An attempt in Russia in 1897 to establish a daughter colony at Orenburg with settlers from both colonies proved less than successful due mainly to social and cultural disagreements among the settlers.[13] But although differences between Russländer settlers to Canada might be marked by problems of different origins, other issues complicated relationships such as distinctions based on education, perceived social status, and religious affiliation. Disparaging remarks were whispered in Grunthal. "Just another Steinfelder," one Schönfelder was reported to have remarked about an impoverished neighbour. Insults, however, could go worth ways. Some Schönfelder were referred to by Khortitsa immigrants as *Zarakofelda*, a term coined from the vulgar Mennonite Low German word *Zarako*, one of several words for the "posterior."[14]

This name-calling reflected the complex practice of inventing colourful names for villages and their inhabitants, as well as personal nicknames. Some were spoken in jest, attributed, adopted, rejected, and openly exchanged. Others were circulated more discreetly. The practice was common not only among Grunthal Mennonites but wherever Mennonite settlements were established.[15] In Canada the divide between Mennonite settlers of Molochna and Khortitsa backgrounds could further be reinforced by different cultural aspirations. Mennonites from or with connections to Khortitsa were considered more "down to earth" than many from Molochna. As one Old Colony Russländer put it, when the time came to butcher a hog, Khortitsa people just "stuck" it with the knife, but in order not to upset the hog's feelings, Molochna people "tickled the beast to death with a feather." Khortitsa people liked to give the impression that they did not aspire to the "high culture" (HG *Hochkultur*) promoted by their Molochna neighbours. Khortitsa people knew they were just as knowledgeable as Molochna folk, but the difference lay in how they presented themselves. To openly claim superior learning and interest in culture would make them little better than their Molochna neighbours, who seemed eager to parade their superiority, not to mention their piety. Pride, after all, is a sin.

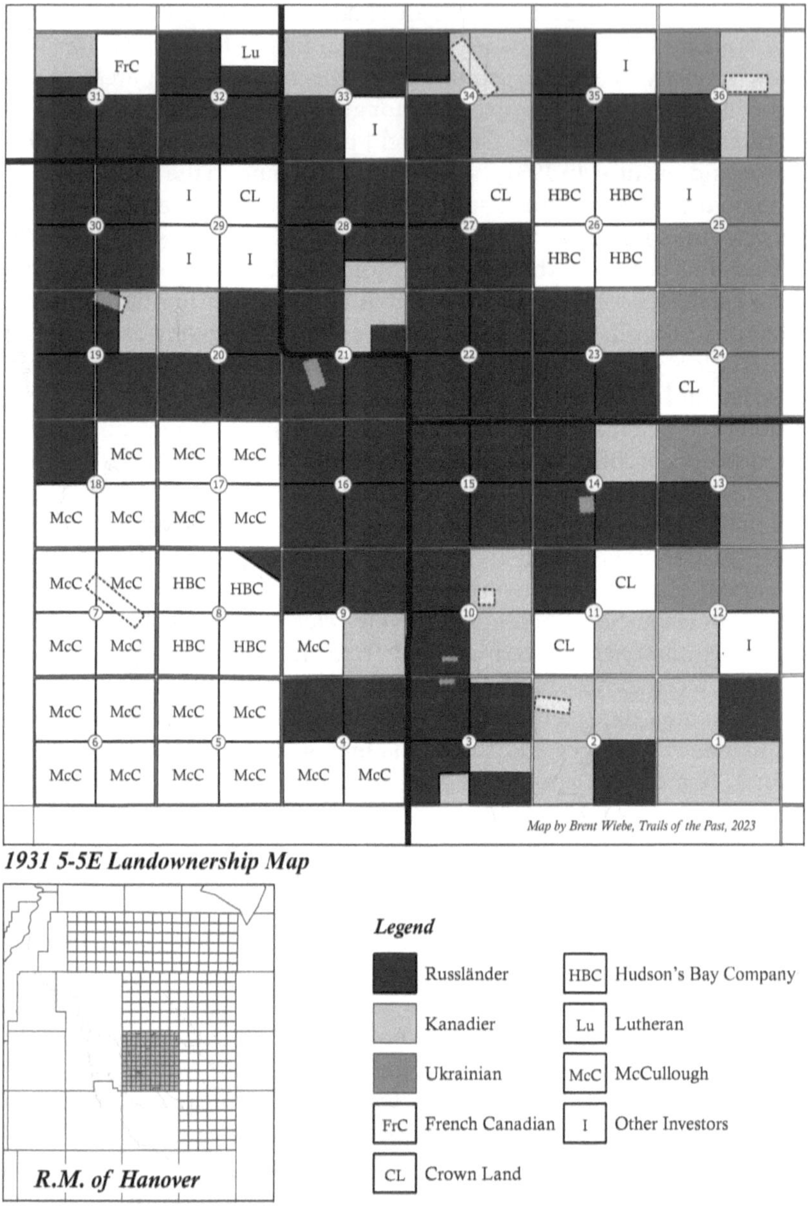

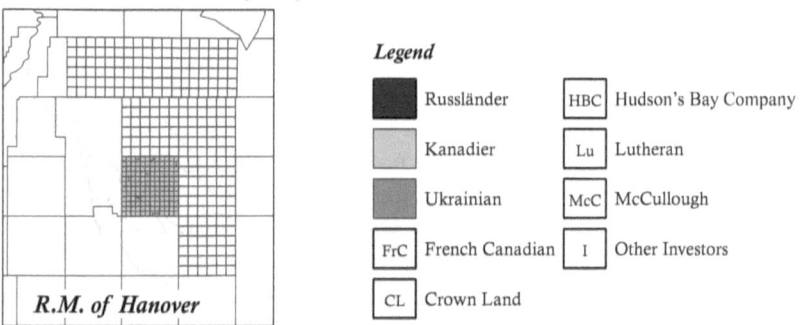

1931 5-5E Landownership Map

Map 3.1. Landownership in 5–5E, 1931. From tax records of the RM of Hanover.

Sources: Map by Brent Wiebe, *Trails of the Past* (2023). Government of Manitoba, licenced under the OpenMB Information and Data Use Licence (Manitoba.ca/OpenMB).

In terms of claims to religious piety there was a divide between Kirchliche Mennonites and Mennonite Brethren. This was also manifested in different attitudes to High German and Mennonite Low German. This too went back to pre-revolutionary Russia where some community leaders attempted to suppress Low German in favour of High German and parents were encouraged to speak only High German and not Low German to children at home, a situation that could result in the odd situation where parents spoke Low German to each other and community members of the same generation, but not to their own children. Low German was also suppressed in schools, even during break time. The reasons given for the emphasis on High German and suppression of Low German varied. Apart from the obvious connection between High German and religion there were also concerns with the growing influence of Russian, like those later expressed in Canada about English. But there were also social and cultural factors involved. High German was seen as a real language linked to German culture and literature. With increased education and wealth some Mennonites acquired bourgeois tastes, so knowledge of High German was essential for the maintenance of social status. By contrast, Low German was basically an unwritten language lacking an extensive, distinguished literature. Instead, it was considered a form of peasant speech inappropriate for transfer to a younger generation as it possessed expressions that could not be spoken of openly either in High German or English without losing something in translation.

In Russia support for High German over Low German was particularly marked in areas of the Molochna colony and its affiliated settlements. In Khortitsa opposition to Low German was not as marked, as members of the elite before 1914 saw less conflict between High and Low German and considered them as distinct languages, not in competition, and either was available without prejudice for use in a range of social contexts. In Molochna Mennonite Brethren leaders were strong supporters of High German mainly on religious grounds and it followed that they held negative views of Mennonite Low German. This was unlike many Kirchliche, including some of its educated religious leaders who, while keen to see High German promoted, did not view Low German as inappropriate.

Another related issue before 1914 involved the increasing use of Russian among educated elites who tended to see High German and Russian as both being important languages connected with literature. Low German was sometimes seen as equivalent to Ukrainian, spoken by peasants. Such different attitudes towards languages and their place in Mennonite life continued after immigration to Canada where

English quickly replaced Russian as an important language and literature to be mastered. However, lacking a local peasantry, Low German had no equivalent. Most members of Khortitsa and Khortitsa-related groups treasured Low German, although their spoken dialect was easily distinguishable from Molochna Low German. This difference was an important feature of a shared identity between Russländer and local Kanadier as around Grunthal most Kanadier had immigrated from Khortitsa-associated communities. Also, although Kanadier supported the teaching of High German in schools, their understanding of the language was often less sophisticated and more archaic in form than it was for educated Russländer. For Kanadier and Russländer Low German, essentially an oral language used in everyday discourse, was the language of the home, of sociability between friends and neighbours, as well as the community at large. Moreover, Low German could be colourful and amusing although it was fortunate that most non-Mennonites could neither understand it nor its nuances. To Kanadier Low German was part their sense of being and although some Russländer shared this view, others did not.

Opinion over language was just one aspect that influenced Kanadier and Russländer opinions of each other, opinions that already began to form before large-scale Russländer settlement in Grunthal. On arrival in Canada Russländer often encountered conservative Kanadier who appeared extremely backward in their knowledge of the world. In 1938, J.J. Hildebrand recounted his experience of arriving in Saskatchewan in 1924 from the Soviet Union to the Swiss American Mennonite J. Winfield Fretz, then researching Mennonite Mutual Aid at the University of Chicago. Hildebrand claimed that he had innocently remarked to his Kanadier hosts how he had journeyed "halfway around the globe" from Siberia to reach Saskatchewan. The following morning, he discovered his comment had spread widely through the community and he had been condemned because his views contradicted the Bible as understood by his hosts. To them the world created by God was flat, not something a person could go "around."[16]

However, while some conservative Kanadier might have held such views, others undoubtedly did not. In the Grunthal area Kanadier initially provided work and shelter for individual Russländer when they arrived in 1923/24, but by 1927 most had left, some for Steinbach and others further away. But after large scale Russländer settlement to the area began Kanadier and Russländer opinion of each other tended to concentrate more on differences rather than similarities. These were still apparent in the 1940s when E.K. Francis carried out his sociological research.[17] He noted how to Kanadier the Russländer appeared arrogant (LG *hüach'näsijch*), proud, haughty, and vain (LG *prautzijch*), and to walk with a swagger (LG *stolzeare*).[18] This was reflected in their bearing and dress, their emphasis on social etiquette, and their use of language, especially High German. In a 1924 fictional account of a discussion between Kanadier concerning Russländer, one speaker suggests that although "as poor as church mice," the new immigrants "should have left their pride" behind in Russia because they still considered themselves "lords because they were once wealthy in Russia."[19] Russländer were also too "worldly" for many Kanadier, too interested in higher education and reading newspapers to follow world affairs. Some were also interested in reading fiction, listening to classical instead of just religious music, and even visiting movie theatres. Finally, to make matters worse, while a Kanadier's word could always be trusted in business dealings, a Russländer's word could not. As one elderly Russländer in Grunthal remarked, "Russländer might be more religious, but Kanadier are more honest."

Russländer found their Kanadier "benefactors, on whose good will they depended, uncouth, backward, miserly, and, above all, ignorant and uneducated."[20] To Russländer, Kanadier appeared to know little High German and spoke a vulgar (LG *prost*) form of Low German. Moreover, they muddled High German and Low German with English words and phrases, even while, unknowingly or not, Russländer had incorporated Ukrainian and Russian words and phrases into their Low German since the Kanadier had emigrated from Russia in the 1870s. To Russländer, Kanadier appeared to lack any interest in "culture" or acquiring polite manners. Their dress was seen as backward, even primitive, and their eating habits more concerned with gaining sustenance than maintaining social convention. Whereas Russländer hosts plied guests with food, Kanadier just placed meals on the table and left visitors to help themselves. At first this caused confusion to Russländer who waited for an invitation to take food and start eating. Russländer guests also discovered that if out of politeness they feigned unwillingness to appear hungry by at first declining food or by rejecting a second helping, this might result in getting nothing more to eat, as uneaten dishes were simply removed from the table by their Kanadier hosts. The truth was Kanadier had merely remained close to the way of life of their peasant ancestors whereas in Russia, Russländer had adopted the trappings of middle-class culture and respectability. However, this is not necessarily how some Russländer viewed the situation. Instead, they believed it was they who had remained close to the traditions of their ancestors whereas Kanadier had somehow degenerated to a lower state in the primitive backwaters of Manitoba. Here was a warning for all

Russländer of the dangers of settling in Canada, dangers that seemed all too real as they failed to re-establish what they considered the civilized ways they had known in Russia. Moreover, the later Depression merely increased the impression that they too would soon be reduced to the same condition as many Kanadier.

Despite these apparent differences, Kanadier and Russländer also found they had much in common although neither would admit it openly. A few were even distantly related or had family connections dating back to Prussia and Russia. They also shared various customs, including preferences for certain dishes and a sense of humour, when the occasion presented itself, usually expressed in Low German. Many stereotypes both groups held of each other proved unfounded on closer acquaintance. Finally, even if they belonged to different congregations, there were enough common features such as adult baptism to assure each other that they were Mennonites. In time Russländer also discovered there were considerable variations among different Kanadier. Some who had not moved to Paraguay were progressive Kanadier who, while they may have lacked as high an education as many Russländer, were knowledgeable about the world and were skilled entrepreneurs. Such people proved essential to the first Russländer settlers as they adjusted to a new society and these Kanadier gave important advice on how to deal with the non-Mennonite world. However, other Kanadier had stayed behind in Canada because they were not entirely welcome to join the voyage to Paraguay. Documentary evidence of such selection is lacking, but it was common knowledge, and similar processes were at work when immigrants were chosen to leave the Soviet Union.

Family reputation rather than wealth, education, and status played an important role in the differentiation of Kanadier society; it also influenced the choice of marriage partners. On some outlying farms Russländer encountered Kanadier with very backward farming practices, dress, and other habits that reinforced negative opinions. Some Kanadier houses still has earthen floors from the time they were constructed in the 1870s. Children ran around "half-naked," and one grandmother cursed fluently in Low German. A Russländer who had been a schoolteacher in Russia where he and his wife were accustomed to being treated with respect and addressed by their patronymics (Jacob Jakobavich/Maria Jakobova) and with the formal use of "you" (HG *Sie*), were shocked to discover their Kanadier neighbours cared little for such niceties. They addressed Russländer visitors with the more familiar form of "you" (HG *du*). Similar differences in usage between Kanadier and Mennonites of Prussian and Russländer origin in Saskatchewan have been noted by linguists; formal terms were commonly used between older and younger kin and more familiar terms spoken where age differences were less than ten years. This has been described as establishing "an asymmetrical pattern" with deference paid to older people.²¹

In time some Russländer developed close social relationships with their Kanadier neighbours who were considered fine, upstanding figures with whom they could associate freely. One such relationship developed between W.W. Sawatzky's family and his Kanadier neighbour, Peter K. Toews. This was in the area around Gnadenfeld where relations between Kanadier and Russländer were closer than in Grunthal and where other Kanadier who had left the area for Paraguay had returned to Canada when faced with the realities of a pioneering life in South America. This meant most families were unable to reoccupy their former family farms and were forced to take up marginal lands that the Russländer had rejected. Most of this land lay to the south of Grunthal in areas with brush, stones, and gravel that, because of its poor farming potential, acquired the dubious name of the "Chaco." The name reflected the recent misadventures of the region's inhabitants and only coincidentally the harsh landscape and poverty of its people as an ironic counterpoint to the real Paraguayan Chaco. But it was also ironic in another sense as it pointed to negative opinions held by Kanadier who remained in Canada and by those left behind in Paraguay concerning these "returnees" (HG *Rückkehrer*).²²

Some of the land reoccupied lay outside the RM of Hanover in which Grunthal was situated, and instead was located to the RM of De Salaberry. This included Weidenfeld, an area that overlapped with Neu-Bergfeld (Barkfield); another area was Spencer, which encompassed the Kronsgart area where Mennonites had farmed successfully for fifty years. Here a few Russländer, such as the Heese family, first farmed, and their children attended the Spencer school. During the 1930s as the Depression deepened, these areas received an influx of Kanadier from the West Reserve and Saskatchewan who cut cordwood to keep them warm over winter as they attempted to scratch out a living. Many of these new arrivals were connected through ties of kinship and marriage as well as religion to East Reserve Mennonites.

Steadily Russländer and Kanadier were drawn into each other's social networks. These included networks created through neighbourly contacts and meeting in stores and workplaces. The fact that Russländer and Kanadier could communicate through Low German helped but some social situations remained limited and restricted. All Russländer, despite their differences, attended the weddings and funerals of their own group and Kanadier did likewise. Close Kanadier and Russländer neighbours might attend each other's events on a personal basis, but not as representatives of their respective communities. For members of both groups, however, there was no need for a formal invitation as people just turned up once an event was announced.

Weddings and funerals were life cycle rituals usually held in the homes and barns of a relative although both rituals involved sacred and secular aspects.[23] A couple wishing to be married first had to have been baptized, a process that involved memorizing the 199 articles of faith and an examination by the minister and deacons. Baptism took place before the entire congregation where the candidate had to promise to follow the narrow path of life in hope of salvation. Marriage was based on Biblical precepts and involved a man leaving the sphere of his father and mother to "cleave unto his wife" so they might "be one flesh" (King James Bible, Gen. 2:24; see also Matt. 19:5). Therefore, marriages concerned matters of religious significance and also worldly aspects, as the couples' offspring were legitimized in the eyes of the community. Only baptism was marked by ritual in the meeting house but for a long time marriages and funerals were considered worldly events and marked with little ritual ceremony. An indication of this was that both were held not in the meeting house but in the yards of one of the families concerned. Usually, the part of the barn used for storage was cleared and set out with the food and drink prepared for the marriage or the wake. However, religious ritual marking the right of passage of marriage or death was not completely absent, as a minister was present to bless the happy couple or eulogize the deceased. The Low German terms used for both are closely related: for weddings, the term in Low German is *Trüräd*, "wedding sermon," and for funerals, *Trüaräd*, literally "the sorrow oration."[24] The latter was often delivered in the form of a sermon announcing the ending of another life.

Once the minister and any unrelated deacons present had departed, the "celebrations" could begin with eating, drinking, and general socializing. Sometimes, particularly at weddings, alcohol might be served to adults. Marriage celebrations (LG *Nohtjast*) usually occurred in the evenings when the couple were crowned with wreaths that were subsequently distributed among any other young people considering marriage. Young people also played games such as circle games, a practice that went back at least to Russia and continued in Canada and could be mistaken by an outsider for dancing.[25] The bride's veil and wreath were distributed among women of marriageable age (LG *Kraunz enn Schleia uetspaele*).

Death also had both religious and social significance as any death is more a concern of the living than the dead because it ruptures longstanding social bonds. Funerals were sombre events expressed through the singing of hymns of sorrow and hope. This was followed by the long trek to the cemetery, on foot if not too far away, where the interment occurred with another hymn. This was then followed by a funeral meal (HG *Trauermahl*; LG *Traumohl*) in many cases at the expense of the entire community. It was not acceptable to laugh during the meal, although gossip was often exchanged between relatives and friends who had often come from distant places.

Everyday secular life in Grunthal, however, was similar in one important aspect for both Russländer and Kanadier: it was male dominated. This was particularly so in the home and beyond. Women largely were tied to the domestic sphere where they cared for young children not attending school, baked and prepared meals, did the washing and cleaning, and during certain seasons preserved fruits and vegetables.[26] Men handled most of a family's money and conducted financial transactions as they were free to move beyond home and their fields to interact with neighbours and go into town to shop, visit the post office, or go to machine shops. These visits also gave men an opportunity to purchase non-essentials such as their tobacco and newspapers and to converse with other men in the community. The stores became hubs of social contact, particularly in the winter months when there were only a few chores to do on the farm. The building often filled with tobacco smoke as men lingered, some even playing chess.

At first there were few ways Russländer women could congregate, although they could meet when visiting kin or neighbours after religious services on Sunday. On designated occasions they helped prepare food for weddings and funerals as well as cleaning up afterwards. Kanadier women were accustomed to this restricted way of life but for Russländer women the change in status and role was profound. In Russia before 1914 the social position of young women, especially for those from more prosperous families, changed radically as they entered a higher level of education than their mothers, advancing beyond village elementary schools to high schools or even further. But after immigration to Canada, they often found themselves with few opportunities for advancement. While some young, unmarried women managed to escape from the limited Grunthal world to work as maids in Winnipeg, their mothers remained behind.

Marriages between Kanadier and Russländer at first were resisted by both groups as both Russländer and Kanadier were concerned about maintaining a degree of continuity across generations. This involved a degree of endogamy in both groups. Intermarriage between Kanadier and Russländer established new social exchanges between them with duties and obligations that involved crossing the networks of both groups. Before the Russländer arrived Kanadier established marriage alliances between families, which in some circumstances extended across generations; these alliances were occasionally connected with a family's reputation. In Russia Russländer had also considered similar matters and in Canada attempts were made to recreate them based on education, occupation, and class, often seen as existing prior to immigration. Formerly wealthy parents sought marriage partners for their children from among those of a similar background even if they no longer possessed either land or wealth. Schönfelders preferred their children to marry other Schönfelders or people from Molochna; marrying into a Khortitsa family was frowned upon, especially if they were from a "poor" family. Siberians, even if they or their parents may have come from Khortitsa or Molochna, were often looked down upon as it was thought only poor people had moved to such a remote area.

Love, sex, and human fecundity, however, care little for social boundaries and conventions. Marriages did occur between Kanadier and Russländer, either through a process of men and women marrying or remarrying neighbours, or even by an unexpected pregnancy. Russländer seemed to view such unions with greater misgivings than Kanadier. However, one senior Kanadier Mennonite Brethren minister on the West Reserve, when hearing of such a marriage, is reported to have remarked: "See how a Russian louse has now entered our fur coat!" Offspring of such marriages reminded some Mennonites of non-Mennonites of mixed Indigenous and French descent (LG, *Haulf'britt*), especially Métis who developed as a new nation in northwest North America before the first Mennonite migration in the 1870s. Métis were seen as wild and rebellious and for Russländer were representative of the kind of cultural degeneracy that stemmed from a mixing of "races." Such views were not restricted to Mennonites.[27] Certainly in Imperial Russia Roma were disliked and distrusted as were Central Asian peoples when Mennonites settled in their regions. In Low German offspring from marriage with the "wrong" type of Mennonite or a non-Mennonite might be referred to as *Mischeehe*, related to *mische*, "to mix."[28] It was clear that some Mennonites thought that nothing good could come of mixed marriages, whether between unconnected Mennonites and especially Mennonites and non-Mennonites. Being Mennonite was still a matter of history, descent, and at its heart, religion.

Most Russländer relations with Kanadier in and around Grunthal involving religion were with members of the Chortitzer and later Bergthal congregations. But the religious affiliations of East Reserve Kanadier were almost as varied as for Russländer. Due to the emigration of the Chortitzer elder in 1927, those Kanadier who remained were served during the 1920s and 1930s by the Sommerfelder elder from the West Reserve. Since the Chortitzer clearly identified with them, they were called Sommerfelder (LG *Sommafelder*) both among themselves and by others around Grunthal although they were not actually members of the Sommerfelder congregations on the West Reserve.

Located to the north of Grunthal around Kleefeld and beyond were descendants of the Kleine Gemeinde who had also emigrated from Russia in the 1870s. The largest concentration of these people lay further to the northeast in the Steinbach area. The Kleine Gemeinde had immigrated from Molochna-based settlements in Borosenko and Crimea and elsewhere, unlike most Kanadier around Grunthal and to the north around the village of Chortitz who in the 1870s had arrived from Khortitsa or the related Bergthal colony. The Kleine Gemeinde was formed in Molochna in the early nineteenth century by a small group committed to the re-establishment of a pure congregation.[29] In the 1920s most remained faithful to their interpretation of established Mennonite principles, but others had not escaped the influence of North American Protestantism and evangelical influences had penetrated their communities. One was known as Holdemans, so named after an American Mennonite who had introduced his own form of conservative evangelical witness to some Kleine Gemeide during the late 1880s. Their males were clearly distinguishable by their dress and beards.[30] Another group based in the United States were the Bruderthaler, later renamed the Evangelical Mennonite Brethren, who had been present in Steinbach since the 1890s. Whatever their affiliation, descendants of the Kleine Gemeinde were well established in economic affairs before the arrival of Russländer and had developed commercial farming as well as a range of entrepreneurial businesses based mainly in and around Steinbach. By the 1920s Steinbach was already a town, not a village, and it showed clear signs of further expansion.[31]

A few individual Russländer settled in Steinbach and their numbers increased through the 1930s. But although they established successful ventures, including a general store, a local printer's shop that published a newspaper founded by Kleine Gemeinde, Russländer never became a dominant force in the town or its businesses. Russländer, especially those in Grunthal, viewed Steinbach and its Kanadier with suspicion and envy. Steinbach's Kanadier failed to correspond to many Russländer stereotypes of the 1870s immigrants as they easily matched Russländer in their approach to business. To Grunthal Russländer, Steinbach presented a challenge if not a threat to their hopes of building a prosperous community. Social relations with Steinbach Kanadier were kept to a minimum although some Russländer maintained contacts with Kleefeld. At first, however, apart from occasional visits to service motors or obtain medical help, Grunthal Russländer avoided Steinbach's Kanadier.

If marriage between Russländer and Kanadier was problematic, marriage with non-Mennonites was almost unthinkable for the first generation of Russländer immigrants. Russländer, however, did develop contacts with some who had non-Mennonite backgrounds living in the Grunthal area when they first settled. These included Bruno Hamm, who had come to Grunthal from Germany in 1911 and worked in a Kanadier-owned grain mill, been baptised Mennonite, and married one of his employer's daughters. When Russländer first arrived he contacted them, emphasizing his knowledge of High German and German culture in contrast to most Kanadier. But this did not impress Russländer, and Hamm was put firmly in his place. In pre-revolutionary Russia Mennonites looked down on other Russian German "colonists," and German nationals known as *Reichsdeutsche*, who came to work in their factories and mills, were treated as outsiders and considered as unsuitable marriage partners for Mennonite women.

Mennonites in Grunthal had limited interactions with Indigenous people. In the spring some Indigenous people from the Roseau River Reserve would pass through Grunthal to hunt coyote, camp on road reserves, pick saskatoon berries, or harvest hazelnuts. They exchanged produce with local farmers or at the Grunthal store and Mennonites recall being asked for food and other goods by Indigenous people passing through. A farmer might provide them with casual employment, especially at harvest time, but anecdotally, the labour relations that developed between Mennonites in the West Reserve and Indigenous people from Roseau River Reserve were not replicated in the East Reserve. Although scholarship on this topic remains underdeveloped, some Mennonite farmers living in the West Reserve remembered the importance of Indigenous labour during the summer. In contrast, the inhabitants of Grunthal could only recall that Indigenous workers often left the farm after a day or two.[32] The opinion of some Russländer was that Indigenous people lacked the Mennonite devotion to hard work and negative comparisons were drawn with Russian peasant workers they once had employed in Russia at harvest time.

Also living in Grunthal when the Russländer arrived was a Jewish general goods dealer and postmaster, Baruch (or Benjamin) Gerstein, who had good relations with local Kanadier who preferred not to own or run trading businesses but instead to deal with non-Mennonite traders. Jewish storekeepers were a common feature of several Mennonite settlements on the East and West Reserves and a succession of Jewish stores existed in Grunthal before the arrival of the Russländer.[33] The Jewish merchants could often speak Mennonite Low German, a language not unlike their Yiddish as many had immigrated from western Russia.[34] After working through the week their owners returned home to Winnipeg, where their families lived, for the Sabbath. While Gerstein had a wife in Winnipeg, he also maintained a relationship with a woman in Grunthal which resulted in offspring.

Many Russländer viewed most Jews with suspicion. They were considered sharp operators but as one Mennonite Low German saying puts it: "If a Mennonite wants to cheat a Jew, he has to get up before breakfast; if he wants to cheat another Mennonite, he should not go to bed at all."[35] In southern Russia Jewish traders, especially grain dealers, purchased Mennonite wheat in competition with Mennonite businessmen. Ordinary Mennonites interacted mostly with Jewish peddlers and shopkeepers in neighbouring towns, while a few Jewish tailors lived in Mennonite colonies. However, antisemitism was endemic to Late Imperial Russia and violent pogroms common in urban and rural areas. Mennonite prejudice against Jews, acquired before the revolution, was reinforced during the Civil War. During this period the White forces were led by members of the nobility who blamed Jews for their defeat, claiming the Bolsheviks were dominated by Jews, and such antisemitic views later influenced Nazi ideology.[36] In Canada during the interwar period antisemitic views, often promoted by right-wing groups, openly opposed Jews although in Manitoba such views were mostly held by people of British descent and in Quebec by French Canadians.[37] Russländer antisemitism argued that Jews had been behind the Russian Revolution, controlled key positions in the Soviet government, and were part of a worldwide conspiracy.[38] Such views grew stronger during the 1930s and influenced Russländer relations with Gerstein and other non-Mennonites.

Russländer relations with their other non-Mennonite neighbours varied. During the 1890s Ukrainian settlers, mostly from eastern areas of the Austro-Hungarian Empire, settled to the east and south of Grunthal.[39] They moved onto their sections and built houses in the style of their old homeland often living surrounded by uncleared bush. Their faith was either Orthodox or Uniate and like Mennonites they re-established many of their traditional institutions, recreating religious and social customs from the old world. To the east of Grunthal, in Sarto and Pansy, they built Ukrainian-style churches, with onion-shaped domes that, set among trees, still look like a scene from Galicia.

When Ukrainians first settled a few older Kanadier could understand what they said as often the Kanadier possessed a limited knowledge of Russian and Ukrainian, even if the dialect of the Ukrainian settlers was often different from that of southern Russia. In 1902, a principal of the bilingual English-German Winkler District School, which had many Mennonite students, noted that older Mennonites could still write Russian.[40] The Galician Ukrainian spoken in the Grunthal area also possessed German loan words, so the differences in the languages were less significant. Kanadier and their Ukrainian neighbours developed contacts based on trade and mutual aid before the arrival of Russländer. The Kanadier Johann Braun was fluent in local Ukrainian through his extensive business dealings with their communities. At first Russländer thought they could exclude Kanadier within earshot by speaking in Russian or Ukrainian but discovered that some Kanadier could understand what was being said. Some Russländer adopted a similar tactic with greater success when discussing private matters in front of their children.

Russländer attitudes before the revolution towards Ukrainians and Russians were more extensive and complex than those of the ancestors of Kanadier who emigrated in the 1870s. Russia's rapid economic development after 1880 created numerous opportunities for interaction between Mennonites and Russians and Ukrainians. Wealthy Mennonites often associated with the upper echelons of Russian society while Russians and Ukrainians were widely employed as servants, agricultural labourers, or seasonal workers during the harvest season. They were considered underlings, and Mennonites, masters. A common opinion was that peasants were simpletons, summed up by the phrase "the foolish/stupid Russian" (LG *dee domma Russ*). The Mennonite sense of social and cultural superiority, however, was combined with a paternalistic attitude as peasants were considered children, not full adults. They therefore needed to be carefully watched and occasionally disciplined with beatings, despite Mennonite religious principles of non-resistance. Wayward peasant adults could be ill-treated like some Mennonite children.

On the other hand, educated Mennonites possessed an appreciation of Russian history and literature, although the average colonist knew little of such things and cared less. But all adult Russländer possessed some knowledge of the Russian language and music was included in the repertoire of school and choral groups so that the haunting melodies of peasant folk songs and religious chants were recalled by Russländer with poignancy.[41] In Canada some Russländer and Ukrainians developed close economic and social contacts. Dietrich Heese often cut cordwood with Ukrainians and relished the opportunity to speak Ukrainian with neighbours. Ukrainians also distilled illegal alcohol (LG *selwstje-moakta Schnaups, Gnuj*; Ukr/LG *Samogon*) of variable quality in bush stills (LG *Schnaups'brennarie*).⁴² In Ukrainian territory outside Mennonite areas of settlement, some younger Mennonites participated in a range of intercultural activities with a greater freedom than at home, where they were subject to the oversight of neighbours and religious leaders. But at this period no marriages occurred between members of the communities.

To the west of Grunthal were the "French" (LG *Fraunzoose*), separated from Mennonites by language, religion, and history. This included people of Métis descent. Most were Catholic, a religion Mennonites knew little about apart from the stories of earlier Catholic persecution in the *Martyrs Mirror*. Catholic churches looked entirely different from humbler Mennonite meeting houses and their cemeteries, visible from the road, contained crucifixes, angel statues, and other symbols alien to Mennonites as at the time the Grunthal cemetery only had simple markers. On the roadside leading to Grunthal, however, close to the boundary between the RM of Hanover and the RM of De Salaberry, a large wrought-iron crucifix has been erected, probably by a French-Manitoban farmer.⁴³ Crucifixes were seen as an indication of Catholic misunderstanding of the true nature of Christianity and a morbid emphasis on Christ's crucifixion whereas Mennonites knew that the resurrection was what was important. In this Mennonites were closer to their Orthodox neighbours, an indication of which was a custom Russländer brought with them from Russia involving the baking and sharing of a sweet bread at Easter (LG *Pastje*; Russ. *Paska*). Boundaries between the French and the Mennonites, both Kanadier and Russländer, therefore were clearly marked. Mennonites would go to St. Pierre-Jolys to shop and do banking, but social relations with its inhabitants were kept to a minimum although some Kanadier exchanged letters with French neighbours after emigration to Paraguay.

Beyond St. Pierre lay Carey, with the closest Canadian Pacific Railroad (CPR) railroad station to Grunthal. In the 1920s and 1930s this was a predominantly British settlement area centred on the town of Niverville although Russländer, often Mennonite Brethren, settled there. For Mennonites the term "English" (LG *Enjle(ä)nda*) was used to identify a person from a multitude of other ethnic groups. It included not just people of British descent, but also anyone who was not clearly French, German, or Ukrainian. Thus, the manager of the City Dairy until the mid-1930s, John Helgi Bjarnason, was considered "English" because he spoke English but in fact he was of Canadian-Icelandic descent and came from Mary Hill in the Interlake area. Later, a Danish worker by the name of Christiansen employed in the Grunthal cheese factory in the 1940s and was also referred to as "English." Later, Joseph LaFrance, an important figure in the development of dairy farming in Grunthal and obviously of French background, was classified as "English" because he represented the Manitoba Department of Agriculture. Others in positions of authority including government officials, employees of the Intercontinental Company and later the National Trust, were "English," along with those from the Agricultural College, bankers, policemen, and wealthy city residents who employed young Mennonite girls as maids.

The English were both admired and feared by Russländer. They were admired because they were the dominant force in Manitoba and most of Canada, controlling its economy and political culture. But they were also feared because their culture and language appeared powerful and pervasive, quite unlike the Russländer's experience of Russia. Prior to the revolution Mennonites believed they could participate in Russian life on their own terms as Russian culture and language could be assimilated to Mennonite ways, following careful negotiation. It was clear to Russländer that their young people might quickly be submerged into English ways and the German language, the Mennonite faith, and their way of life might be lost. This threat was contained in the phrase "to become English" or as it was expressed in Mennonite Low German, "*den Gloowe aun daut Mennonitentum veschmiete*," and in High German, to become *verenglischt*, literally "Englished."[44] One definition for English (*enjelsch*) in Mennonite Low German is "worldly," to "become unfaithful to one's own," and "no longer identifying with the Mennonite faith."[45] No such negativism applied to the French, presumably because no Mennonite could conceive of anyone becoming French. Russländer probably adopted such ideas about the consequences of being "Englished" from Kanadier but provided them with their own meanings. Whereas for Kanadier concern about the English primarily focused on the dangers of a loss of religious faith, for Russländer it indicated something more: not just a loss of faith, but also of Mennonite culture, tradition, language, and identity. For some, it seemed a betrayal of a religious and cultural sense of being Mennonite, so strongly developed in Russia, but increasingly connected with their "racial" destiny, the purity of their blood, and links to German culture. The reality was, however, that in the early days few Mennonites had direct dealings with English people on a day-to-day basis. The English remained an elusive presence beyond the Mennonite community, inhabiting the city of Winnipeg or large farming settlements far to the west. During the 1920s and 1930s English voices were present on the radio or in newspaper reports but in everyday activities Russländer mostly associated with other Mennonites or with their immediate, non-Mennonite neighbours. Together the groups formed the bases of the Grunthal community. But the Russländer community needed a focus and soon after their arrival they began to establish their own institutions, religious and secular.

Chapter Four

Re-establishing Institutions

Kanadier in the southern regions of the East Reserve had not been major institution builders and instead were primarily focused on their families, social connections between kin and friends, and religious links with other members of their congregations. The record books of the congregation, some transferred from Prussia to Russia and on to Canada, were not located in one place but instead were held by the congregation's secretary and usually handed on from one holder to another. The other and most important set of records was associated with the Orphans Office (HG *Waisenamt*), which valued the property of a deceased person and ensured that any surviving dependents were cared for, especially underage children whose inheritance rights were secured. Male guardians were appointed to oversee a widow's rights and any children until they reached the age of majority. The funds were held in trust, and these funds also acted as a source of community credit to be lent at a rate of interest with the profits credited to the beneficiaries. The only other institutions local Kanadier re-established in Canada were German-language schools which by the time Russländer arrived had been closed. In contrast by 1914 the Russian Mennonite Commonwealth was almost a state within a state with a wide range of institutions.[1]

Immigrant Russländer moving to the East Reserve had the choice of several places to re-establish institutions and link up with other Russländer. Towards the centre of the Reserve was Chortitz, a settlement originally founded by Kanadier and named after the Russian colony of Khortitsa; the Chortitzer Congregation was also named after Khortitsa, possibly because its first Elder lived in the village.[2] By the 1920s, however, the village no longer existed and like Grunthal was merely a collection of houses. To the south of Chortitz, Russländer were scattered on farms close to old settlements around Kleefeld, Schönsee, Rosengart,

Burwalde, Gnadenfeld, Alt-Bergfeld, and Grunthal itself.[3] A number of these places could have become the focus of a Russländer community, but Grunthal eventually emerged as the major centre. An important factor in this was the establishment close to the old Grunthal village of a Russländer congregation and meeting house.

Although Russländer did not come to Canada as congregational communities, their immigrant groups included ordained Elders and ministers. The nominal leader of the first group from Khortitsa was the Elder of the Frisian congregation from Schönwiese, Johann P. Klassen. Most Khortitsa Mennonites were members of Flemish congregations and Frisians were a minority religious grouping, but at the time of immigration such distinctions were less important than differences between Church and Mennonite Brethren Russländer.[4] Both Frisians and Flemish were Church Mennonites although Frisians were considered more pious than many Flemish. During the First World War the Khortitsa Colony village of Schönwiese was incorporated into the city of Alexandrovsk and when a congregation was established by Russländer in Winnipeg, it was named Schönwiese.

Elder Klassen was noted for his liberal outlook and on occasion was willing to accept non-Mennonites into communion. He also wrote poems and prose in an elegant High German.[5] But he could also express more negative views, condemning dancing, women's use of make-up, drinking coffee and tea, and the use of tobacco.[6] But his authority was recognized by other teacher-preachers and members of the educated Mennonite elite, and he immediately began to establish institutions for new immigrants to Manitoba scattered across different areas often in small, isolated groups. Eventually he and others re-established a network of travelling preachers (HG *Reiseprediger*) like that used in Russia to unite scattered Mennonite groups. Where immigrants had no minister and especially when they needed an Elder to ordain new ministers and deacons, baptize, and preach supportive sermons, an Elder could be found to serve them. The Board of Colonization helped with money from the Conference of Mennonites in North America that defrayed an Elder's costs while the CPR supplied free or subsidized travel passes. As Russländer in western Canada were willing to associate with established conferences in Canada and the United States, they joined the Manitoba and Saskatchewan conference founded by less conservative congregations whose members had arrived in Canada before 1914.[7] The Russländer were to play an important role in the development of the main western conference and helped establish provincial conferences and eventually a more central, Canada-wide conference. In the early days of settlement, however, Russländer also created their own organizations and held meetings to develop a sense of religious and communal solidarity.

Gradually, as immigrant groups formed local congregations for worship and companionship across Manitoba, they chose ministers to manage local religious affairs on a regular basis while remaining affiliated with a central congregation and particularly its Elder. As new immigrants arrived after 1924, particularly from Molochna, the number of groups needing to be served increased and eventually while Klassen served some groups, another Elder, Franz F. Enns, served others. Enns had been born in Molochna but later moved to the Terek Colony in Central Asia; when Terek was attacked by locals in 1918, he fled to Molochna, and the Colony was abandoned. Like the Schönfelder he lived as a refugee in Molochna before immigrating to Canada in 1926, eventually settling in Lena, close to Whitewater, one of the largest Russländer settlements in western Manitoba with an active congregation. Enns served several immigrant groups including for many years Grunthal Russländer.[8]

Regular worship services and the sociability associated with local congregations were central features of Mennonite life. The Christian calendar provided a regular order to life as significant as changes of season and agricultural work, which meant that the re-establishment of congregations in Canada was a matter of concern for all Russländer. Scattered on prairie farms, they would meet to worship in homes, schoolhouses, and even English churches, if they were available. In cases where an ordained minister could be found, he would be asked to lead the service; if not, an unordained member had to suffice. Russländer might also attend Kanadier services and sometimes these proved to be like those they had known in Russia. For instance, Mennonite Brethren from Russia often joined congregations of North American Mennonite Brethren for worship. But many Kanadier services on the East Reserve, particularly those of conservative congregations, appeared strange to Russländer, with sermons often read from old handwritten texts rather than freely delivered and containing Low German phrases that occasionally amused Russländer even if some of their own preachers were not immune from doing something similar.[9] Quite soon the new immigrants withdrew from Kanadier services to worship among their own kind.

When settled in Westbourne before moving to Grunthal, the mostly Schönfelder group held services together and decided to choose men to serve the community "with the word."[10] Those selected were Johann J. Enns, Jakob J. Rempel, and Heinrich J. Wiens, the latter an elderly man from Fischau in Molochna who eventually moved to Grunthal but died shortly after. The provisional group was included as an affiliate of the Schönwiese church in Winnipeg and its chosen leaders attended meetings with other immigrants to discuss the organization of the religious life of Russländer in Manitoba.[11] Out of these only Johann J. Enns became a minister once the Westbourne people settled in Grunthal. At first the Grunthal Russländer investigated the possibility of joining local Kanadier for worship.[12] Some attended the Chortitzer church in Grunthal and despite obvious differences they opened discussions on further cooperation. Some accounts claim the Chortitzer rejected the Russländer, but others insist that just as an agreement to unite had been reached, a senior Russländer who had led religious services in Russia refused to accept any compromise on the form of worship and consequently the negotiations collapsed. Red Beard Braun, who had shown Russländer around the Grunthal area, invited them to hear preachers from his Holdeman Church in Kleefeld. The Holdeman Church's free preaching appeared familiar to Russländer as did their singing in four-part harmony. But Russländer did not like aspects of their religious requirements if they joined the congregation, including that men should grow full beards.

The only alternative for the immigrants was to form a new congregation. Until this could happen groups met for worship without ordained ministers in their immediate localities: schools in Grunthal and Rosengart and a house in Neu-Bergfeld (Barkfield). Some travelled to Steinbach to attend services with Mennonite Brethren. At this time there was hope among Russländer that Mennonite Brethren and Church Mennonites could unite in Canada as such a union had been attempted in Russia before 1914 and during the early years of Bolshevik rule. But the existence of a well-established Mennonite Brethren Church in the United States and parts of Canada, along with the desire of some immigrants to form separate groups, saw the re-emergence of the division between groups in many parts of Canada, including Grunthal. To further complicate the issue of leadership, Russländer settlers in Grunthal also discovered that one of their number had been ordained as a minister in Russia but now refused to lead a new congregation. The responsibility of leadership therefore fell to a former Schönfelder, Johann J. Enns, and he collected the names of seventy-five families in the area who might be members of a new congregation. In February 1927, G.A. Peters, the minister from Winnipeg, was invited to the Chortitzer meeting house in Grunthal where forty-five people agreed to form a new congregation. At the same meeting the group also agreed to join the Conference of Mennonites of Central Canada and the General Conference of the Mennonite Church of North America.[13] Enns was chosen as the lead minister.[14] The members then decided to name their congregation "Elim" after Exodus 15:27, even though the Bible passage speaks of an oasis of palm trees, unknown in the land of brush, poplar, and willow surrounding Grunthal. It was, however, a name entirely appropriate for a group who saw themselves as a people saved from a condition of slavery.

The new congregation stated its desire to be affiliated with the Winnipeg Schönwiese congregation and so in 1927 Elder Klassen was invited to baptize the first group of young people.[15] Klassen baptized a second group in 1928 and a meeting of the Schönwiese Church in July indicated that Elim was considered an affiliate congregation although it is not listed in later histories of the Winnipeg church. Overworked, Klassen told the Grunthal congregation to use Elder Enns of Lena not only to perform baptisms but also to oversee the election and ordination of ministers, a deacon, and leaders of congregational hymn singing (HG *Vorsänger*, or precentor). As Johann J. Enns was already chosen as a minister, the members elected two more from a field of six candidates. By a show of hands, Dietrich D. Mirau of Grunthal received the most votes (thirty-seven) with Abraham A. Peters from Gnadenfeld not far behind (thirty). None of the other candidates achieved double figures, with Jacob J. Rempel receiving only six.[16] Peters accepted the ministerial position and Abram Driedger, who received only six votes for the role of minister, was chosen as the deacon and four song leaders were appointed, Dietrich J. Rempel, Jakob J. Rempel, H.J. Enns, and P.P. Hübert (or Hiebert). Mirau refused to accept his election and later left Grunthal for Alberta.[17]

A.A. Peters, the new minister, was born in 1878 in Ladekopp, Molochna and attended the Halbstadt Zentralschule and a Realschule, a higher level educational institution, in Melitopol. After starting a business in Molochna he moved to Terek in 1908 and later managed an estate near Ufa, close to the Urals. Following the revolution, he had been a religious leader of a Moscow-based group organized to serve Mennonites in Russia's eastern regions. Finally, he moved back to Ukraine and immigrated to Canada in 1926.[18] His brother, Gerhard A. Peters, was the minister in Winnipeg who helped in the formation of Elim. Apart from the election of Peters, Schönfelders were strongly represented in the selection of congregational leaders and all of the first office holders were immigrants with Molochna connections. Although the new congregation was based in Grunthal, its exact territory was unclear as it served members in surrounding areas still identified by their separate names. In March 1928 the congregational books indicate that the Congregational Governance Board (HG *Gemeinderat*) was divided into different *Rayon*, an administrative term meaning district in the Soviet Union but which soon fell out of use in Canada. Each district sent an elected member to sit on the board. A.J. Kasdorf was elected by the Neu-Bergfeld (Barkfield) *Rayon*, with another member for Rosengart and one for Gnadenfeld, closest to Grunthal.[19]

At the same March meeting additional ministers were chosen, all from Russian Khortitsa-connected settlements, to serve Russländer living beyond Grunthal. One, Heinrich H. Janzen, originally from Khortitsa, later left Grunthal in 1930 for Crystal City and the second, Heinrich Olfert of Rosengart left in 1930 for McCreary, a settlement northwest of Winnipeg at first considered a potential major area for Russländer settlement.[20] The third, Jacob K. Penner, also originally from Khortitsa, lived in Neu-Bergfeld (Barkfield) but moved to Ontario in 1935. Elder Klassen ordained all the new ministers but made it clear that the Grunthal congregation fell within Elder Franz Enns's jurisdiction. The leadership of the new congregation therefore reflected the mixed origin of Grunthal Russländer and its surrounding area, but members soon discovered that even if they all came from Church Mennonite backgrounds, their understanding of religious matters and patterns of worship frequently varied.[21] Elder Enns insisted on foot washing to accompany communion, a practice that symbolized humility. Most in Grunthal had never practised this in Russia as it reflected Enns's Frisian background rather than the Flemish traditions of a majority of Elim's congregation.

Other tensions between ministers and members soon emerged. Minister Peters by all accounts was a difficult person, inflexible in his attitudes and sharp of tongue. After he settled in Gnadenfeld he quarrelled with his neighbours over land issues as he wanted a farm for his son, but this proved difficult. Several other issues appear to have caused discord between Peters and members of the congregation. A report of a congregational meeting held in December 1930 referred obliquely to these difficulties but not in detail. After discussion the matter appeared resolved and was sealed "with a kiss and song."[22] In 1933, however, problems re-emerged, and Peters and his wife resigned their membership of the congregation and his position as minister. Peters's disagreements were both with the congregation and with Minister J.J Enns, but exact details remain unclear from Enns's surviving papers. However, it must have been a serious matter as indicated by a letter from the Elder of the Blumenort congregation on the West Reserve, Johann P. Bückert, to Elder David Toews in Saskatchewan.[23] In 1934 after Peters had resettled in McCreary, he wrote a letter to Minister Enns in which he appeared to place all the blame for the difficulties on Enns. Instead of trying to make peace and ask for forgiveness, which would have been a normal way to resolve disputes, he merely asked for Enns's forgiveness "where your conscience says you have done something wrong to me and my family in word, deed or thought."[24] Enns's response was brief and correct: he forgave Peters for everything.

In McCreary Peters again became embroiled in controversy with his local congregation and with a fellow minister, Heinrich Olfert, who had moved there from Grunthal. Olfert wrote to Minister Enns asking for details of the Grunthal community's difficulties with Peters, but Enns refused to supply them. The disagreement with Peters, whatever its cause, also involved Elder Enns, who was placed in a difficult position as he was related through marriage to Peters.[25] The Elder felt he no longer enjoyed the full support of the congregation and in particular Minister Enns so he offered to resign, but the congregation voted overwhelmingly for him to remain.[26] In 1934, however, Elder Enns performed his final baptisms and from 1935 until 1942 Elder P.H. Enns from St. Elizabeth, some thirty kilometres west across the Red River, served the Grunthal congregation. Religion, supposedly the centre of communal solidarity, in practice proved a source of as much discord as any secular activity.

The crises of the early 1930s, however, involved more than just Peters. Within a few years of the original congregational leaders' selection only Minister Enns and deacon Abram Driedger remained in office; all the others had resigned and moved away from Grunthal. In 1933 it was necessary to hold elections for two new ministers. Eventually five candidates put themselves forward and three were chosen, Isaak Penner of Rosengart, Abraham A. Fröse of Neu-Bergfeld, and David Fast of Chortitz. As Fast and Penner received the same number of votes in the second round, both were declared as elected.[27] Two of the new ministers were obviously intended to serve members of the congregation around Rosengart and Neu-Bergfeld. In the end only Fast was ordained in 1934, although Fröse eventually joined him in 1943. While Fast lived beyond the immediate area of the Elim congregation, Chortitz contained a few Russländer, some of whom were attracted to congregations in Steinbach rather than Grunthal. Fast, however, had connections with Grunthal people as he had been born in Schönfeld, although he had not immigrated with most Schönfelder in 1924. During the time of troubles in Russia he fled not to Molochna but to its daughter colony, Memrik, where he married into a former estate-owning family and left the Soviet Union in the final rush to Moscow in 1929.[28] Fröse came from Grigorievka, a Khortitsa-linked settlement. In 1934 another minister who had been ordained in 1920 into the Khortitsa Flemish Church in Russia,

Wilhelm J. Peters, moved to Chortitz and served as a minister of Elim until 1943.[29] Although neighbours, Peters and Fast fell out in 1939, and Fast offered to resign but as the most senior minister, Enns refused to accept his resignation.[30]

In one sense, the Elim congregation was reconstituted in 1933/34 with an almost new ministry. At the same time the church books appear to have been restarted and the first membership book abandoned. All members were asked to re-register but at least one refused and continued to attend services although his name, and that of his family, were only added some years later once his stubbornness and that of the congregational secretary were resolved. The secretary in the early years was Jacob Block and his successor was Dietrich J. Rempel, brother of Jacob J. Rempel. Both brothers had stood for election as ministers in 1933 but were not chosen. With Rempel as secretary, Abram Driedger as deacon, and J.J. Enns as leading minister, the Schönfelder in Grunthal basically controlled the reorganized congregation. For almost ten years, however, members of the Elim congregation remained scattered, worshipping and holding meetings in their own localities. The congregation, like the Russländer in the area, still lacked a central focus. But with Minister Enns leading the congregation and Jacob Rempel as representative of the Intercontinental Company and later of the National Trust, both residing close to the old village of Grunthal, the settlement became the logical centre for the Russländer congregation. The position of Grunthal as the central place was further strengthened in 1932 when the Company offered the immigrants a surplus dwelling around the old village of Schönsee to use as a meeting house. During the winter when the ground was frozen, members of the congregation with teams of horses pulled the building to a site in Grunthal on land purchased from A.B. Krahn. Here it was converted into a meeting house and dedicated by Elder F.F. Enns in July 1933 (see fig. 4.1).

The congregation followed patterns of worship established in Russia. Minister Enns was very interested in religious matters and closely studied religious texts, often neglecting farm work. As he and his wife were childless there was less pressure on them to establish a farm for any descendants although the couple helped raise several of their relative's children. Enns's religious outlook was probably in line with the views of most of his fellow ministers except for those of David Fast. Fast had studied at the Bible College founded by A.H. Unruh in the Crimea after the assumption of Soviet control and later Unruh helped found Mennonite Brethren Bible colleges in Canada.[31] A pious man, Fast's sympathies lay more towards the Mennonite Brethren than most Church Mennonites, who were strongly represented in Grunthal. Many in the

Fig. 4.1. The first Russländer meeting house, 1932. The first Russländer meeting house being converted into a place of worship for the Elim Congregation in 1933.

Source: Picture courtesy of Johanna Kellett, Winnipeg.

congregation found his sermons difficult to follow as they appeared abstract or dealt with unfamiliar themes. He had an interest in discerning God's future for the world, which he illustrated with detailed time charts that he claimed revealed the imminence of the Day of Judgment. The impact of the charts was somewhat reduced when the chronology was revealed to be pasted onto the backs of old calendars and breakfast cereal packs. Other visiting preachers shared Fast's concerns with the end times, including Jacob W. Reimer known as "Revelation Reimer" (*Offenbarung Reimer*) after the final book of the New Testament.[32] Such ideas, however, were also more common among some Mennonite Brethren than Church Mennonites.

A minister's responsibilities, however, went well beyond delivering sermons as servants of God and their congregation; they were expected to visit all their members, especially the poor and the sick. But as laypeople they were the unpaid servants of the Lord, family men who needed to support families, mostly through farming. Their religious duties had to be fit around the other demands and occasionally members of their flock could be both demanding and unforgiving. In 1938 Minister J.J. Enns complained to Elder P.H. Enns on the attitude of one individual in his congregation who was ill, but when visited by Minister Enns had been rude. This individual also demanded that only an Elder could serve him communion. Elder Enns replied, "We preachers are servants of God in the church but definitely not servants for men ... we proclaim Christ's death, and this should not be belittled without reason." He recommended that Minister Enns remind the member of this, preferably in the presence of a witness.[33]

Being a member of a congregation was more than an excuse to meet for worship on Sundays: they were expected to be involved in a wide range of activities directly or indirectly connected with the congregation. Under the auspices of the congregation other community institutions were established and fostered. Sunday Schools for children were started and a Young People's Group (HG *Jugendverein*) organized, first headed by Abraham Peters, which by early 1927 had twenty-five members.[34] Through the long winter nights study groups met to read the Bible and discuss religious ideas in the light of current events. These activities reflected practices established in Russia and continued by other Russländer in Canada.[35]

One of the most active members involved in such work was Jacob Block, first secretary to the congregation. In the early 1930s Block assumed responsibility for the choir from Abraham Peters and Dietrich Mirau and Block also took over the Young People's Group after Mirau and Peters left. Block was a popular leader and an experienced school-teacher skilled at preparing programs for choirs and young people. Participation in choirs was important in establishing bonds between young and old, especially as members came from different backgrounds in Russia. During breaks from choir practice Block would read excerpts from the comic writings of the Low German writer Fritz Reuter whose books were popular among Mennonites in Russia and following immigration to Canada.[36] Block's enthusiasm for Low German reflected his Khortitsa background. As well as singing and Bible study, the Young People's Group also read secular prose and poetry, a practice that reflected the broad cultural interests of Russländer and the influence of non-Mennonite knowledge and culture among educated Mennonites in late Imperial Russia. In summer Block also organized excursions into the surrounding bush leading to a better appreciation of the new land. This mirrored Mennonite interest in nature and nature preservation in Russia, particularly as it was promoted by teachers in Khortitsa.[37] It was also a good way for young people to get to know each other away from the oversight of parents and laid the foundations for relationships of friendship and marriage that would bring sections of the community together.

Russländer brought with them well-established hymn collections such as the *Gesangbuch*.[38] But the resources available to them in Canada were only part of a much larger musical repertoire that reflected major developments in pre-revolutionary Russia. Choir singing had a special place in Russländer communities as a love of music united their sense of faith with a broader interest in non-religious culture.[39] In Russia Mennonites often used a numerical notation system introduced by the Prussian schoolteacher Heinrich Franz before 1840. Towards the end of the nineteenth century organized choirs using four-part harmony were formed and these gradually became commonplace, often led by schoolteachers. The enthusiasm of young people for singing quickly secured a central role for such music in congregations. Although the position of Lead Singer (*Vorsänger*) to guide congregational singing was retained, choir singing in meeting houses and elsewhere grew in importance.[40]

In Russia the use of musical instruments in services was rare although guitars, pianos, and other musical instruments were used in schools and in the homes of more prosperous Mennonites. The voice, however, remained the most important musical instrument. Some hymns and melodies were adapted from old Mennonite sources and others borrowed from German evangelical groups while a few choirs were ambitious enough to select music by eighteenth- and nineteenth-century classical composers. Teachers and music directors also selected items from collections of German folk songs and even from Russian sources. Various songbooks published in German and Russian between 1900 and 1914 reflect a rapidly changing situation and an increasing Mennonite adaptation to the Russian cultural environment.[41] Music from the Russian Orthodox Church was even included in at least one published collection. The music in these collections was adapted to the numerical note system as song collections were published for wider use by Mennonite choirs. In Canada Russländer re-established and developed this musical tradition and in time it became an important unifying factor at the local, provincial, and national levels. As choirs developed choir leaders held special courses for conductors and choir festivals (HG *Sängerfest*) were held in different locations. One, hosted in Grunthal in 1936, lasted three days and included choirs from seven other settlements as well as instrumental performances including a musical quartet (see fig. 4.2).[42] But such festivals took time and money to arrange and at first the immigrants lacked resources and so at first these events were restricted.

Fig. 4.2. Choir festival (*Sängerfest*) held in Grunthal, 1936.
Source: Centre for Mennonite Brethren Studies, Winnipeg (NP035-01-012).

Once Jacob Block assumed control of the Young People's Choir, he followed the system of musical instruction used in Russia. It was in schools that children first learned the rudiments of singing and music-making and eventually this improved congregational singing. Under Block not only did congregational choir singing flourish, but also the singing of secular songs. Religious hymns were sung at funerals and secular songs at marriages and other celebrations, such as family anniversaries and reunions. Young people also produced special programs presented in the meeting house during services or at social events in the summer. Sources of music were limited because only a few songbooks had been brought out of the Soviet Union, so the few existing copies were often laboriously reproduced by hand although eventually the use of carbons eased the task. Block himself transposed and rearranged other hymns and songs with musical notation into the numerical note system more familiar to Mennonites. Block remained in charge of music until 1939 when a younger man, John A. Driedger, the son of deacon Abram Driedger, took over. As a child in Russia, Driedger developed a deep love of music and later was involved with musical events in Grunthal. He taught himself to read musical notation in addition to the numerical system learned at school.

Block's repertoire consisted mainly of songs brought from Russia, mostly in German. In Canada Russian items were gradually dropped and new German songs, religious and secular, added using musical scores obtained from Germany. This shift reflected the emergence of a new generation of Mennonites willing to accept innovations although there was some opposition to change, not only concerning Block's views and the attraction of new music for younger singers, but also to an increase in use of choirs in services. To some, choirs appeared to restrict the role of Lead Singers in congregational worship. One change, however, took much longer to implement and it was not until the late 1940s and early 1950s that a few English hymns were introduced and English songs presented at social gatherings.

In Russia several welfare institutions were associated directly or indirectly with congregational matters and could concern the rights of widows and orphans, burial societies to cover funeral costs, and mutual fire insurance coverage. The Mennonite Orphans Offices were incorporated within the Russian legal system but in Canada re-establishing such offices proved difficult due to the different legal systems concerned with inheritance rights in different provinces. Russländer in Grunthal did not establish an Orphan's Office but other forms of mutual aid were attempted. In 1934 Jacob Block published an account in the immigrants' newspaper *Der Bote* on how Grunthal's Russländer in 1932 had established a mutual fire insurance scheme providing cover for buildings, equipment, and crops.[43] How well and for how long the scheme operated is uncertain.[44] Block also founded a burial society in 1933 where members paid a set sum into the scheme so on the death of a subscriber any accumulated funds would help to cover funeral costs.[45] The funds could also be drawn upon to contribute towards health care costs which were high.

Control of congregational affairs and the administration of various welfare institutions were basically the domain of senior males in the community. The Congregational Council (HG *Bruderschaft*) by its very name was run by men even though women were nominally full members of the congregation. In Russia, in the brief period between the fall of the tsar and the collapse of civil order, a Mennonite conference had discussed the right of women to vote in congregational affairs but without reaching an agreement.[46] The issue was raised again in Canada by members of the Schönwiese Church who in 1928 agreed that women had a right to vote in congregational matters concerning the selection of ministers. They also could teach in Sunday School and be deaconesses, but not ministers.[47] Various Russländer congregations took different positions on the role of women in congregational and community affairs. In practice it mattered little as even where women were granted rights, men still dominated affairs and they chose congregational candidates in advance of voting.

Women, however, did have important roles in other areas of community life. In 1928 Lena Rempel, the wife of Jacob J. Rempel, organized a sewing course for young girls and other interested women.[48] Under the leadership of Eva Enns the group produced items to raise money in support of the congregation. A 1932 report by Lena Rempel on the sewing group indicates how the work had expanded with the assistance of a Liberal member of the Canadian House of Commons, Howard Winkler. This may have been motivated by the Canadian National Railway's Community Progress competitions for ethnic groups held between 1930 and 1932 which the RM of Hanover entered every year, gaining two placings before winning the final one. The competitions encouraged farm improvements and a range of educational and community projects including craft and sewing.[49] Winkler arranged for the Extension Department of the Manitoba Education Department to provide support from English female instructors to advise unmarried women on sewing and acquiring other domestic skills such as cooking and the preserving of fruit.[50] While obviously having a practical advantage, the Grunthal sewing group developed into a congregational activity where female members could meet in small groups (HG *Kränzchen*) in members' homes. While useful for acquiring new skills, the meetings were also important social gatherings and women's activities expanded to include money raising to support missions and other good causes. The organization became known as the *Tabea Verein* after Tabitha in Acts 9, and for many years it was led by Margarethe Enns, wife of David D. Enns.[51] Another women's group was organized in the Rosengart area and continued to meet until the late 1930s.

Russländer settlers therefore quickly reconstituted the core institutional organizations associated with religious life, centred on the Elim congregation in Grunthal. In this way they played an important role in bringing together Russländer from different backgrounds and places in their old homeland. These organizations, however, were specifically Russländer not only in terms of membership, but also in their form and operations. While congregation and community ideally had always been coterminous among Mennonites, in Russia more diverse patterns of religious and community life had developed with members belonging to different congregations and where not all institutions were based solely on just one congregational group. In Grunthal almost all Russländer were members of the Elim congregation and therefore when involved in the other more secular institutions they did so with fellow members. While a few settlers may have come from other religious backgrounds, for instance the Mennonite Brethren, they either joined Elim or moved away to places where they could join a Mennonite Brethren congregation, either in Steinbach or elsewhere. A few late immigrants from Russia were not always made welcome in either the congregation or community and felt alienated by the treatment they received from established Russländer. Such people sometimes opted to join a local Kanadier congregation, but they were few and later joined Elim. In other ways, however, even they soon became members of a wider community that in everyday life included Russländer, Kanadier, and non-Mennonites involved in a network of economic interdependency and secular institutions such as schools that went beyond separate congregations.

Chapter Five

Schools and Education

Most Russländer held education and teachers in high regard. Throughout the nineteenth century Mennonite interest in education increased and was crucial in their economic success and cultural advancement. A commitment to basic instruction in order that children acquired the rudiments of literacy and numeracy had existed from the formation of Mennonite communities in the sixteenth century. All members had to be able to read the Bible, learn the catechism, and in the case of men, prepare themselves for possible election to the ministry. But the aim of instruction was the acquisition of basic skills, not greater knowledge; children were to learn to read and write, not to investigate the ways of the world.[1]

Although Mennonite schools existed in Prussia before immigration to Russia, more formal education was encouraged in Russia by the authorities.[2] Initially the government's concern was that Mennonites acquire knowledge and skills in High German to administer the civil system it had imposed. To meet the demand for trained teachers and administrators some Mennonites advanced beyond the elementary school level and with Russian support secondary schools were founded.[3] By the 1860s most school children were instructed by Mennonite teachers either trained in Russia or Prussia. Teaching emerged as a distinct profession in a Mennonite world consisting largely of farmers and gradually teachers gained status and respect. By the turn of the twentieth century several teachers had been chosen as ministers producing a clerisy which did much to advance both religious and cultural life.[4]

From early 1880 onward all school instruction was in Russian, and German was taught as a "foreign" language, including German literature. Religious instruction given in German was also permitted. Gradually the standard of elementary education improved but most pupils still left school without progressing to higher education. Schooling, however, was liberated from conservative religious leaders and secular school boards were elected, a process that began in Molochna and following Russia's Great Reforms a unified school system was established in Khortitsa. Later Mennonite attempts to expand their educational institutions were impeded by reactionary forces but with the granting of greater political freedom to Russian subjects after 1905, some new establishments were founded.[5] Before the revolution small numbers of Mennonite men and women who attended Russian higher education institutions gained qualifications to pursue careers in professions such as teaching, law, medicine, architecture, and engineering. The generation educated in Russia before 1914, many of whom immigrated to Canada, viewed education as essential for individual and community development. Although their own hopes to pursue their dreams were frustrated by subsequent events Russländer retained a respect for education and were determined that their children would have access to education and serve the community for the benefit of future generations.

Mennonites who immigrated to Canada in the 1870s were mostly unaffected by the educational reforms in Russia although one of the reasons they immigrated was because they opposed Russian plans for changes in education. All accepted that their children needed to acquire basic skills but proposals to expand education and teach in Russian were rejected as they might lead young Mennonites astray. They were also suspicious of progressive Mennonite leaders, backed by Russian officials, who wanted to remove control of the schools from the hands of the congregation and its leaders. In one case a government proposal to grant scholarships to intelligent young Mennonites so they could attend Russian universities was a factor in the decision of one Mennonite to emigrate, as it reminded him of the Prussian government's attempts to integrate Mennonites into that country's society so that they would accept military conscription.[6] As a precondition for settlement in Canada the Mennonites included a desire to control their own schools.

In Canada education was a provincial not a federal matter, but as separate French Catholic schools already existed in Manitoba, Mennonites were permitted to establish German schools under their control. Mennonites mistakenly believed this right had been granted by the Canadian authorities in a Charter of Privileges (*Privilegium*), similar to those granted by the Russian government in 1800 and earlier by Polish and Prussian rulers.[7] In Manitoba local congregations and religious leaders chose the teachers and basically decided what could be taught and as a consequence teachers were often unqualified, the curriculum limited, and with instruction as much in Low as High German along with little or no English.[8] A teacher's pay was low, often supplemented with firewood and food so during the holidays some were forced to take up manual work.[9] The existence of Mennonite schools, separate from the English-language schools and essentially a Protestant provincial public school system, continued until challenged along with the French Catholic school system.[10] Issues concerning schools increasingly became a subject of dispute between Mennonites and provincial governments in Manitoba and Saskatchewan.[11] Some individual progressive Mennonites, and in places entire communities, however, joined the public school system, accepted government funding, and taught English as well as German. This move entailed a degree of official oversight of the schools, the curriculum, and the qualifications of teachers. The increased demand for better-trained Mennonite teachers was a factor in the establishment of Mennonite higher education institutions in Manitoba and eventually, in the late 1880s, the creation of the Mennonite Collegiate Institute at Gretna.[12]

However, two congregations, the Chortitzer of the East Reserve and the Reinlander or Old Colony Mennonites of the West Reserve and their communities remained strongly committed to the private German school system.[13] Most Mennonite children left school at the mandatory age which gradually increased from twelve to thirteen reflecting the basic education Kanadier considered sufficient for a child and the needs of the community. For male children an ability to farm successfully, and for females to establish a home and raise a family, could not be taught at school. Before 1919 the Grunthal area had several private Mennonite schools, mostly under the control of religious leaders of the Chortitzer congregation. For instance, there was a school in Grunthal and another in Gnadenfeld. In Grunthal a timber-framed building replaced the first log structure that had originally served as the school after classes moved out of the home of the first teacher in the 1880s.[14] Mennonite schools in this area of the East Reserve were not particularly well managed; the single classroom buildings were often crowded and pupil attendance poor. Local congregational leaders opposed the teaching of English and when in 1908 one teacher, Peter A. Braun, attempted to do so and to organize a choir in Grunthal, he was dismissed.

But the days of the private German schools were numbered as during the First World War there was considerable opposition to the existence of German schooling.[15] In 1916 the Manitoba provincial government made school attendance compulsory, the last Canadian province to do so, and in 1919 gave itself the power to establish public school districts in all areas of the province. These changes were not just concerned with improving education, but were also a consequence of anti-foreigner sentiments that intensified during the war.[16] In Grunthal in 1919 the new public school district was first named "Aldershot" (#1967) after a military training base in southern England although this was later changed, perhaps in a spirit of reconciliation, to "Goodwill."[17] To the south of Grunthal the "Spencer" (#1969) school district was founded at the same time and to the southwest, "Woolwich" (#1968), named after English military barracks near London. The Chortitzer religious leaders, unlike some Mennonites of the West Reserve, first attempted to compromise over the new school districts and did not ban members who sent their children to public schools. In the meantime, to find common ground they petitioned the provincial government.[18] But as the public schoolteacher reported to the official trustee in 1922, many locals remained unreconciled "with our system and an unsettled attitude is the result."[19] A parallel private German school system continued to function until the early 1920s when one after another schools started to close. As late as 1925 parents in the district were fined for not sending their children to public schools.[20] But by this time Chortitzer Mennonites had begun their search for an alternative homeland where they could continue to control their own schools.

When the Russländer first settled in the Grunthal area they had the choice of several public schools. Many schools had Kanadier teachers although some, like Woolwich, had English teachers until 1929. The Kanadier teachers were often of Kleine Gemeinde background as sections of this congregation had been more willing than most Chortitzer to accept the advantages of a bilingual education in English and German. Indeed, from the early 1920s a new generation of male and female schoolteachers from Steinbach and surrounding areas, trained in Winnipeg, began teaching across the RM of Hanover.[21] The number of pupils in the Chortitzer area attending public schools was low as sometimes parents failed to enrol their children despite the threat of being fined and even when enrolled, attendance was often irregular. In 1925 the teacher in Grunthal, George M. Neufeld, reported that out of forty-two children enrolled the average monthly attendance was thirty and in September, with children kept home to help with the harvest, it dropped to almost twenty. In tests, half the pupils scored below average for their age.[22] Only rarely would a parent permit their child to attend school beyond Grade 6, and some left even earlier. In 1922 the Grade 1 pupils ranged in age from six to fifteen and several pupils in Grade 3 were aged twelve to thirteen.[23] The grouping of children of different ages is a reflection of the fact that students coming from private Mennonite German schools were all enrolled in Grade 1 in their first year, regardless of age, because most were only just starting to learn English as required by the school curriculum. It was simply unrealistic to have a new school year begin with students spread across grades according to age. The arrival of Russländer dramatically altered this situation. Just a year after the new immigrants settled in the area the school inspector reported that Russländer children "seem anxious to advance."[24] The children had already attended Canadian schools elsewhere and the older ones could build on schooling interrupted in the Soviet Union. Soon they not only began to fill classrooms, but also to progress to the higher grades offered by rural schools.

The Grunthal School was in a disused general store, a two-storey building with a basement markedly different from the type of building the Russländer had constructed in Russia to further education that before 1914 were rather grand constructs. The Schoenfeld *Zentralschule* for instance was custom built as a school complete with a grand entrace and separate classrooms to teach different grades (see fig. 5.1a). At a cost of over $1,000 the ground floor of the Grunthal schoolhouse had been converted into a one-room classroom with a teacherage upstairs (see fig. 5.1b).[25] The classroom was entered through a cloakroom "where the children got spanked."[26] There were large windows on one side and high windows on the other. Children were arranged in rows according to grade with the lowest grades at the front, and the higher grades at the rear. Pupils sat two to a desk, the teacher's desk was at the front, and he dealt with each grade in turn, setting them work. Sometimes older children would assist beginners, taking them into the cloakroom for reading. English was the only language of instruction, and no German was taught in the early years when the teacher was not a Russländer. Kanadier teachers in Grunthal before the Russländer arrived rarely stayed more than two or three years.

The first teacher in the new school, Frank Isaak, did not possess a teaching certificate but this did not stop some Kanadier parents from suggesting that he was too committed to education.[27] When the first Russländer arrived in 1927 the Kanadier teacher was David Heinrichs, with whom the new immigrants appeared to get on well, in part perhaps because he was very strict with children. He later taught at the Spencer School until 1931 and maintained contact with the community once he left. Some Russländer adults took advantage of Heinrichs' offer to teach them English after school. But when Heinrichs left in 1928/29, he was succeeded by another Kanadier, Cornelius L. Toews. He was followed soon after by Jacob B. Warkentin, a bachelor who stayed two years until 1931. Warkentin was the brother of the school inspector in the Beausejour area, Benjamin Warkentin, and according to one account cared little for either Mennonite religion or community traditions.[28] He lived the classic life of a bachelor, eating fried eggs for dinner every day and leaving the dirty plates for a week before senior pupils were

(a)

(b)

Fig. 5.1. Schools in Schoenfeld, Russia, and Grunthal. (a) The Schoenfeld Central School (*Zentralschule*) in Russia before 1914 and (b) Grunthal schoolhouse around 1927 shortly before the arrival of Russländer immigrants.

Sources: (a) Mennonite Heritage Archive, Winnipeg (44-224); (b) Archives of Manitoba, Department of Education, District School Inspector's photograph album, GP 1-3-1-3-3, p. 69, A 0233, GR 8461.

charged with cleaning them. The dirty state of the school and teacherage was noted by the school inspector. Warkentin, however, was popular with the children as he adopted a rather unorthodox approach to the teaching timetable. He loved sports and if the weather looked suitable, he would suspend class and take the children out for an impromptu physical education lesson. Apparently he was unable to cope with brighter students in the higher grades and this, along with his sports activities and lack of commitment to the local community, drew muted criticism from Russländer parents.[29]

By the early 1930s the Russländer decided that the time had come for them to take charge of education. But they had already faced difficulties in assuming control. In 1927 Minister A.A. Peters of Gnadenfeld and other Russländer parents requested that a new school district be formed for children around Gnadenfeld as there were fifteen children of school age and it was difficult in winter to travel the three to four miles to the Goodwill School. Local Kanadier, however, were opposed to the move, as was the local Hanover Municipal Council, who pointed out that Kanadier paid school taxes, while the Russländer did not as their lands were still under control of the Intercontinental Company. The request was therefore turned down, although the following year the Gnadenfeld residents requested a closed vehicle as winter transport for children to Goodwill.[30] In 1927 a separate request was made to the Hanover Council, most likely by Russländer, to alter the Grunthal School District boundaries but the council decided this was unwarranted.[31]

These rejections were probably due to opposition from the larger non-Russländer community in Hanover. They started to complain that as landowners they paid the bulk of school taxes, but the benefits had begun to flow to Russländer whose children stayed on into the higher grades which most Kanadier considered unnecessary. In 1929, a request by Russländer to the Deputy Minister of Education to elect a district school board was also rejected.[32] Before the Russländer arrived the Goodwill School District, like others around it, was imposed on Kanadier by the government without consultation. At that time the government did not expect local people to be capable of electing a representative school board, so an external official trustee was appointed. Until 1930 this was J.F. Greenway, and between 1930 and 1942, Albert A. Tomlinson.[33] In 1931 Jacob Woelke organized a meeting to make a further request to the official trustee for local representation, but again the request apparently was denied.[34] While Grunthal was not to have its own elected local school board until 1949, over twenty years after their initial settlement of the district, in 1931 schooling was transformed through the appointment of a Russländer teacher.

The community already possessed a highly experienced teacher, Jakob H. Block, who was born in 1892 in the village of Grünfeld in Baratov Shlachtin. Educated at the Nikolaipol High School, Block was a graduate of the prestigious Khortitsa teachers' college.[35] He immigrated late to Canada in 1928 and like his brother Julius, also a teacher, was unable to retrain and resume a teaching career. By the early 1930s there was little support available to retrain older men instead of younger immigrants. Totally unsuited for farming, Block acquired land to the south of Grunthal where he and his family lived in poverty, his main income coming from beekeeping.[36] As he came from a Khortitsa-connected colony in Russia, Block lacked pre-existing links with the dominant Schönfelder residents in Grunthal.

However, another teacher, David P. Heidebrecht, did possess the right credentials. Born in 1893 in the Molochna village of Rosenort, he secured financial assistance to attend the Ohrloff High School in Molochna, the oldest Mennonite secondary school in Russia.[37] Desiring to continue his education and qualify as a teacher, but unable to afford the expenses involved, he became the tutor to children of wealthy Mennonites on an estate in Schönfeld. Here he learned the rudiments of teaching at first hand and established contact with Schönfelders including the landowner, Jakob J. Heidebrecht, who was murdered in 1919.[38] As Heidebrecht's forebears emigrated at a late date from Prussia to Russia and had never taken out Russian citizenship, David was interned as a German citizen during the First World War. Later he escaped from exile and returned to southern Russia at the end of the war, shortly before Russia's Civil War began. During this troubled period, he held teaching positions in various Mennonite villages and immigrated to Canada in 1924. After attending the Mennonite Collegiate Institute at Gretna in 1926 he accepted a teaching position in a Russländer pioneer settlement at Reesor in northern Ontario. Here during the 1920s and 30s a group of immigrants attempted to establish a Russländer settlement away from outside influences.[39] In 1930 Heidebrecht left Reesor and returned to Manitoba to finish his training as an English teacher in Winnipeg and in 1931 accepted a teaching position in Grunthal.

Heidebrecht was to remain in Grunthal for the next twelve years and during his tenure the school grew. The number of pupils increased, and the range of grades offered was extended. New teachers were employed, and new buildings were added to cope with the growing enrolments. The teaching of German returned as Heidebrecht's teaching was influenced by his Russian experiences and this included an emphasis on instruction in High German. In time Goodwill School became known locally as "The German School" in contrast to Spencer, the nearest school to the south which, despite also containing Russländer pupils and even Russländer teachers, was known as "The English School."

The Great Depression was not an auspicious time to take up a new post, but any form of regular employment was better than none. In September 1931 the regional school inspector, Archibald A. Herriot, told the Hanover Municipal Council that the Department of Education would pay only half the salaries of teachers if they decided to open for ten months and any more had to be paid by the municipality. The offer was rejected so schools opened for only nine months and teachers were paid a lower salary.[40] Herriot was a sympathetic inspector who had served in the Boer War and would regale students with stories of his role in the conflict, apparently unaware that in Russia Mennonites had supported the Boer cause. Al Reimer described him as "a very epitome of the Anglo-Saxon ruling class," a large figure with a "military bearing" who when he spoke, made children tremble.[41]

In Heidebrecht, Grunthal Russländer had a teacher qualified in the Manitoba school system but experienced in old-world methods and values. Although at first an outsider, Heidebrecht's Schönfelder connections were enhanced by his wife, Anna Fast, who had been born on an estate in the same area. She had attended the prestigious Halbstadt Girls' School and a Russian girls' *Gymnasium* in Berdiansk and thus was as highly educated, if not more, than her husband.[42] With Heidebrecht's appointment therefore the Russländer community gained the skills of not one, but two teachers as his wife once taught school in Russia and in Grunthal she assisted her husband despite her poor health. Heidebrecht had amassed numerous debts associated with the expense of immigration and retraining in Canada. In his autobiography Heidebrecht gives his starting salary as $60 a month and his debts at the time as $3,000.[43] In part the debts were because he had been forced to pay medical expenses for his wife who had fallen ill during their immigration and after delays in Europe she miscarried once they arrived in Canada. Later she underwent a series of major and, at the time, expensive operations but she could not bear children.

Because of his status as a teacher in Russia and the couple's earlier connection with Schönfeld, they initially had little difficulty in being accepted by most in the Grunthal community. Transfer of membership from the Reesor congregation to Elim, however, was complicated by religious divisions in Reesor and subsequently Anna found aspects of the Elim congregation "conservative."[44] She may have held Mennonite Brethren sympathies, and this might explain why her obituary later appeared only in their newspaper, *Mennonitische Rundschau*, while his appeared in the more General Conference paper, *Der Bote*. Other factors may also have been involved, particularly Heidebrecht's attempts to play a more dominant role in the congregation. His efforts were rebuffed, perhaps because he also lacked direct kinship ties with leading Russländer families, and because he and his wife had no children, they were unlikely to establish affinal connections. In his later memoirs Heidebrecht wrote that while he was considered "a good teacher" people thought "he interfered too much in congregational and community affairs."[45]

Heidebrecht faced a daunting task following his appointment as the number of pupils in the one-room schoolhouse rose rapidly. In 1931 there were around sixty pupils, by 1933 there were almost seventy, and the numbers continued to rise as Russländer children born after immigration reached school age.[46] Improvements in attendance also meant that unlike in the past, most children attended every day, so the single classroom was soon overcrowded. The increased expectations of Russländer parents meant that older children stayed on to take higher grades, so Heidebrecht had to deal with children ranging from Grades 1 to 8. Some parents wanted the children to continue to take even higher grades, but this could only be done through correspondence. Preparing pupils for correspondence courses, however, involved further work for an already overextended teacher. In 1935, although the school did not possess the status of a secondary school and Heidebrecht only held a second-class teaching certificate, he was given permission to teach to Grade 10.[47] Heidebrecht was an organized, methodical teacher and carefully structured classroom activities, arranging the children into groups with each receiving an allotted portion of his time according to their ability and grade. He described his method in a school journal article in 1935 where he suggested that in teaching it was not the number of pupils that was crucial issue, but the "correction of seatwork, individual help, and discipline." He admitted, however, that he was concerned about time commitments.[48]

The problem, however, really was a question of numbers. In October 1934 the school inspector noted the "overcrowding" caused by the number of pupils was "too heavy for one teacher," as classes had now reached almost eighty.[49] In January of the same year J.J. Rempel, supported by other "ratepayers," successfully petitioned the Minister of Education for a second teacher, and in 1935 a female teacher was appointed, Susanna Nettie Reimer, a Kanadier from the Steinbach area.[50] The school's classes were now divided so that Reimer took Grades 1 to 4, and Heidebrecht 5 to 9/10. To accommodate the increasing numbers, a new, separate teacherage was built and the old upstairs teacherage was converted into a second classroom. This proved rather unsatisfactory as the upstairs room was small, dark, and cold in winter.[51] In January 1936, on a bitterly cold morning before school Heidebrecht's wife stoked the fire in the school's basement and later the building caught fire and burned to the ground.

Teaching continued in alternative places while a new, modern building was erected on the site, containing two large classrooms and a smaller room near the entrance.[52] The new school was the pride of the local community, but it had been desperately needed long before the fire. The British-Canadian school inspector noted in 1936 that the "people are stirred up to new interest with the prospect of a new two-roomed school."[53] By the late 1930s the number of pupils often exceeded one hundred. In 1938 a third teacher was employed to assist with the first four grades and in 1939 three classes were formally established with Dora Sudermann caring for the first two grades, Peter Jacob Rempel, a Russländer also originally from Schönfeld, in charge of 3 to 5, and Heidebrecht responsible for only the senior grades. Sudermann taught at the school for ten years (1938–48) and Rempel later succeeded Heidebrecht as principal (1943–8).[54] Another building was added to the school complex in 1940 to accommodate these new classes. In 1942–3 the school enrolment reached a high of 125 with 29 pupils in Grades 7 to 10.[55] In just over a decade the school had been transformed from a rural one-room school teaching only to Grade 6, into a newly constructed complex with three staff teaching almost to secondary school level.

When Heidebrecht began work in 1931–2 his salary was less than his predecessor Warkentin and in total he was paid $772 in his first year of teaching. During the Depression all provincial public service salaries, including those of teachers, were cut.[56] In 1931 the annual report of the Education Department reported that salaries "are likely to be perceptibly lower than for some years past" and indeed they remained low until the 1940s. In the years that followed Heidebrecht's monthly income dropped to $60, the teaching year was reduced to nine months to save the government money, and for the 1933–4 teaching year his total income was reduced further to $557 a year. Only in 1935, when the school teaching year was increased, did his salary return to the 1931–2 level and it was not until 1941–2 that it increased in real terms.[57] In spite of little financial reward, Heidebrecht impressed both the school inspector and community by his commitment to teaching. In 1932 school inspector Herriot reported that Heidebrecht was "giving good service" and in 1933 strongly recommended that the department keep "this teacher and give him what help you can afford." It was also apparent that Heidebrecht went out of his way to improve the school, often purchasing teaching material himself. Herriot noted this and reported that the school library was "well-used and tidy ... things are in splendid order here" as well as that Heidebrecht "is very interested" in teaching.[58] In later years, however, the inspector graded him as "fairly adequate" and only "adequate" as a teacher, but improvements to the school and the community's support for education were noted with approval.

There are no contemporary records of the parents' opinions of Heidebrecht, but obviously most Russländer found him more than satisfactory: he ran an ordered, strict school which achieved results. He also taught German and German literature within the provincial curriculum and continued instruction outside school hours. Most Russländer parents would not criticize a teacher, at least in front of children, and always backed them in matters concerning the discipline of their children. However, many Kanadier parents whose children attended the school had misgivings concerning Heidebrecht and his methods. At school Kanadier were often clearly distinguishable from Russländer children, most obviously in their clothing, footwear, and haircuts. But the food Kanadier children brought to eat, their use of Low German in the playground, and difficulty in grasping High German also set them apart. In his autobiography Heidebrecht notes that he was careful not to distinguish between his pupils, especially between Russländer and Kanadier.[59]

Whatever his recollection, this is not how many Kanadier pupils remember him and how they were treated differently from Russländer children as well as how their parents complained about their exclusion and neglect. Russländer pupils also recall differential treatment towards some Kanadier children who received less attention than themselves, especially when Kanadier children were left to work on their own while Heidebrecht concentrated on those, mostly Russländer, children he believed would move on to higher grades. One Russländer suggested this was only sensible as most Kanadier children left school early. Given the number of pupils, his limited resources and time, Heidebrecht probably had little option but to budget his efforts despite his claims of careful "time management." It was certainly true that some Kanadier parents did not expect much from school and would not permit their children to move on to higher grades. But there were Kanadier children, such as those of Peter A. Braun and the Krahns, who were eager to learn and received parental encouragement although even for progressive Kanadier, gender remained an issue. Intelligent girls received less support than boys. However, Russländer pupils and parents were not as united about the benefits of education as might at first appear, nor were they so certain about Heidebrecht and his methods.

A short, stocky man, Heidebrecht was a Mennonite schoolmaster with a proud Prussian sense of discipline, always tidily dressed, his hair cropped, and moustache clipped. Many of his ideas on education remained unchanged from Russia. This included the view that teaching High German in school was essential for the preservation of Mennonite religion and culture. During his first year in Grunthal, Heidebrecht received official permission from the Department of Education to teach German in school from 8:15 to 8:45 in summer, although it was also taught in winter and sometimes after school.[60] Past pupils recall leaving home early on cold, dark mornings to take German lessons, clustered around the dim light of a kerosene lamp before "English school" began. Heidebrecht did not teach German from the Bible like Kanadier private school teachers. His emphasis was on "correct" German grammar taught through German poetry, songs, and classical literary texts. By 1935 Heidebrecht was teaching German to select pupils intending to take the language at Grades 9 and 10 by correspondence.[61] For Heidebrecht teaching German was a duty and he went to considerable lengths to achieve his end, even writing and publishing his own textbook on the subject in 1935 (see fig. 5.2).[62]

During the late 1920s and early 1930s the teaching of High German to a new generation was a particular concern of many Russländer in Canada. In newspaper articles, at meetings and conferences, community leaders stressed the importance of learning German. Their message was not just directed at teachers and ministers, but also parents. A clear connection was drawn between the need to preserve German for the sake of religion and the maintenance of a distinctive identity in Canada, and so this became a central focus of activity in many Russländer communities. Consequently, considerable pressure was placed on congregations, schools, and homes for young people to learn and appreciate the language and for it to be a "good, pure and correct" High German.[63] Implicitly this contained a criticism of the persistence of Low German in certain immigrant families as continued interaction with Low German–speaking Kanadier was seen as a hinderance to a child's ability to learn "proper" High German.[64] Increasingly, however, English and not Low German was seen as the major threat to continued use of High German, especially because children appeared to acquire English with ease. Worse, those receiving instruction in higher grades in schools, particularly when attending schools with English-speaking pupils, often appeared to prefer English to High German. Russländer leaders therefore argued that it was crucial for Mennonite teachers to correct these tendencies through intensive High German instruction.[65]

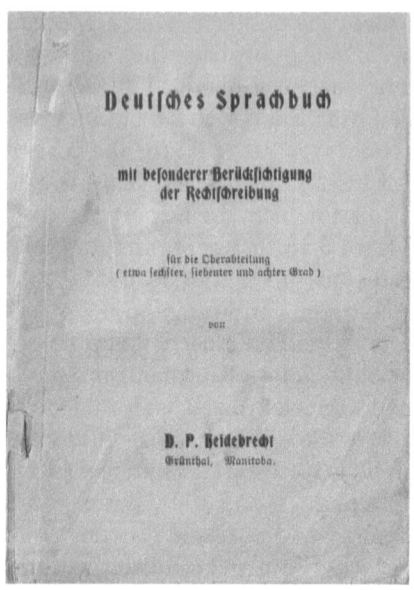

Fig. 5.2. Heidebrecht's German grammar, c. 1936. Front page of Heidebrecht's c. 1936 *German Language Book with Special Consideration of Correct Spelling for Senior Classes (For Example the Sixth, Seventh, and Eighth Grades)*. Heidebrecht wrote and published textbooks probably at his own expense. They were most likely printed by Arnold Dyck, the Russländer author and publisher in Steinbach.

Source: Heidebrecht, *Deutsches Sprachbuch*.

However, the response of both Russländer parents and children to High German varied. The strongest response in Grunthal came from those parents who came originally from Schönfeld, Molochna, or other Molochna-based colonies. It was primarily in their households that High German was spoken in the hope of reinforcing what was taught in school. Among many parents from Khortitsa or Khortitsa-related backgrounds, the response to the emphasis on High German varied. Low German usually continued to be spoken at home and support for High German was influenced by the attitudes of one or more of the parents. In some households reading and writing in High German was encouraged even when it was not spoken in everyday life. In others it received little reinforcement. Where Low German was spoken at home parents were often not very concerned about their children's use of English. Indeed, some even encouraged it, realizing that access to

English improved a child's chance of success in the new world. Heidebrecht strictly observed what he perceived to be the Education Department's rules so the language of school, including the playground, was English except at those times when High German was taught. Use of Low German within the precincts of the school was expressly forbidden and subject to punishment, a ruling that impacted heavily on Kanadier children who often started school without a word of English.

Heidebrecht was eager to exhibit his pupils' command of High German. The visiting school inspector would often request that the children sing a song in German and Heidebrecht would arrange for children to perform in the Elim meeting house, singing songs and reciting items in German. The high point was the Christmas program delivered almost entirely in High German. However, Heidebrecht experienced opposition from some members of the congregation who objected to the non-religious tone of the children's presentation.[66] To most immigrants though, such presentations by school children followed accepted patterns established in Russia where festive occasions, including the erection of a Christmas tree, had become commonplace by the end of the nineteenth century. To many Kanadier such Christmas programs were "worldly" activities and in schools where Kanadier were in the majority and the teacher was a Russländer, Christmas trees and celebrations were either frowned upon or strictly forbidden.

Another important event for Russländer transferred from Russia was the public testing (HG *Prüfungen*) of senior pupils before an assembly of parents, ministers, the deacon, and other community leaders. Each pupil was required to make a presentation and be tested on their knowledge and skill, including their knowledge of Biblical texts, fluency, and ability to recite and sing in High German. This was a formal event and for some an ordeal. Older Russländer both from within and outside Grunthal acknowledged the community's continuation of this practice including B.J. Schellenberg, the archivist of the immigrants, who praised Heidebrecht for continuing tradition.[67] But public testing also became the source of controversy. Once more Kanadier pupils felt largely excluded from school programs that prepared pupils for the test, a practice not followed in neighbouring "English" schools where the end of the year was a time of celebration with enjoyable activities such as comic skits and community sports. In the early 1940s, with the arrival of young female Kanadier teachers in Grunthal, similar "field days" were introduced in a more relaxed atmosphere that involved the entire community. These younger teachers had been raised in a more relaxed Mennonite environment than Heidebrecht and attended teachers' college where new forms of training had developed since he qualified.

Gradually formal testing at the time of graduation declined although Heidebrecht disapproved of the new ways.[68]

For Heidebrecht and older Russländer parents the teaching of High German and established customs had a larger purpose than just the continuity of the faith for a new generation in Canada. Even in Russia by 1914 many children still left school with only a basic elementary education, although an increasing number attended secondary school. Talented students were selected to train abroad with the expectation that they would return home and serve their communities. Russländer attempted similar strategies and soon after the first immigrants arrived in 1923 a few young men were selected to retrain in colleges in Canada and the United States, later to return and serve as educators or administrators. To support them and other leaders, money was raised often through interest-free loans or gifts from wealthy Mennonite benefactors in North America. Some individuals in Grunthal received such loans, including J.J. Rempel and J.J. Enns, from wealthy Mennonite benefactors in Buhler, Kansas.[69] In Canada the major retraining centres for teachers were the Mennonite Collegiate Institute at Gretna and the Rosthern German Academy in Saskatchewan, founded by Kanadier and immigrant Prussian Mennonites before the Russländer arrived. These institutions received a considerable boost once the new immigrants from the Soviet Union took advantage of their facilities, including employing their most talented instructors and administrators.[70] Russländer leaders viewed these institutions as a substitute for the teachers' seminaries (HG *Lehrerseminaren*) located in Halbstadt and Khortitsa before 1914.

In Canada Russländer parents eager for their children to progress in education often were faced with the prospect of sending them away from rural communities to such institutions so they could complete their education, especially in Grades 11 to 12. Completing such grades was essential for anyone hoping to teach, especially to gain a full teacher's certificate. Young people with Grade 12 secondary education could teach in rural schools with a temporary teaching certificate but were required to obtain a full certificate by attending the normal school in Winnipeg. Schoolteaching was seen as a particularly suitable career for clever Russländer and if they returned to their home community, they could replace Kanadier and non-Mennonite teachers. It sometimes proved difficult for teachers with a Russländer background to secure such positions, so some taught in other schools including in Kanadier districts where they were often viewed with suspicion. In the 1930s a Russländer teacher, Victor Peters, taught mostly Kanadier and Ukrainian pupils at Lister, close to Grunthal, and discovered it very different from a Russländer school.[71] The ideal, however, was for a Russländer teacher to return to their own community and this is what eventually happened in Grunthal. The major problem facing most parents whose children hoped to train as teachers was the cost. There were fees to pay for each higher grade taken, but there were also accommodation and boarding costs once young people were sent away to other institutions. The family also lost the productive labour of their young people from farms and households. To advance children into higher education, undoubtedly the ideal for many Russländer parents, therefore involved considerable sacrifice. In 1931 for instance the cost of taking Grade 9 was calculated at $70, Grade 10 at $100, 11 at $150, and 12 at $200.[72] In 1930 the purchasing power of $200 in today's terms would be over $3,000. While it is impossible to calculate the average income of a Grunthal Mennonite during the 1930s, it was undoubtedly low and in 1931 overall farm incomes in Manitoba were negative.[73]

Demand for higher education increased when Heidebrecht started to teach to Grade 10. After 1936 to reduce costs a few pupils who had completed Grade 10 with Heidebrecht were sent to the Kornelsen School, a public elementary school in Steinbach which taught Grades 11 and 12.[74] Two Russländer children from Grunthal who attended the school boarded with local Mennonite families. The place proved very different from the Grunthal school as pupils of the same level worked in separate classrooms. Some only attended for one year such as Erich Guenther, who was forced to return to Grunthal to help in his father's store and failed to complete Grade 9. The Steinbach school was considerably more "English" in orientation than the Grunthal school and in 1936 it included no special Bible classes or German language instruction.

Margaret Peters from Grunthal continued her education to Grade 12 at the Mennonite Collegiate Institute in Gretna where religious instruction was strongly emphasized, so it is unsurprising that Russländer favoured it. Indeed, it was viewed as *the* educational institution in Manitoba for Russländer and its graduates, especially those who became teachers, were highly respected. However, it was very expensive to attend, as was the provincial Department of Education's normal school in Winnipeg. Margaret Peters's parents received additional support from Heidebrecht and in his memoir, he recalled her as one of his most successful pupils.[75] She began her career in 1942 at Gravel Ridge, a one-room school located north of Grunthal.[76] The majority of her pupils were Kanadier, but she initiated a new teaching program, including early morning German lessons, based on her Grunthal experience. She returned to teach in Grunthal in 1945, initially for another nine years. She was a good example of a new generation of Russländer born or raised in Canada, educated, and trained as a teacher in Manitoba who returned to their communities to help recreate a sense of communal continuity. Other Grunthal graduates followed Peters in the later 1940s and 50s, until Grunthal's school was dominated by Russländer teachers, as were many other Mennonite settlements.

In this way, and despite financial hardship and inexperience in English, Russländer were largely successful at integrating themselves into the provincial education system. By retraining immigrant teachers, investing time and effort into rural schools, and by gaining access to and eventually controlling established Mennonite colleges, they succeeded in training a next generation of Mennonite teachers. As Heidebrecht proudly reported, some of his pupils had gone on to become teachers, others had entered important professions, and two even gained doctorates from German universities.[77] What he did not mention, however, is that most of his pupils never moved on to higher education or advanced beyond Grade 10. Due to their parents' poverty, younger people never had an opportunity to complete their schooling, especially his Kanadier pupils. But this was also true of those Russländer who left school to work on local farms, in workshops, or at best, as clerks. Some remained entirely satisfied with their lives, but others felt a degree of sadness at having been unable to fulfil their hopes of advancement. If many of their parents' lives had been frustrated by revolution and Civil War in Russia and consequently had to abandon hopes for their own futures by immigrating to Canada, so some of their children would never achieve their full potential. A major cause of this was the impact of the Great Depression.

Chapter Six

Debts, Depression, and a New Grunthal

The Great Depression had a worldwide impact but proved particularly devastating in Canada.[1] Between 1929 and 1931 the Canadian prairie provinces were severely affected, and real incomes dramatically declined; in Saskatchewan they fell a staggering 72 per cent, in Alberta by 61 per cent, and by 49 per cent in Manitoba.[2] The worsening situation gave rise to several radical political movements.[3] Russländer, who since immigration had attempted to rebuild their lives through farming, were particularly hard hit. In Manitoba farm values decreased from $637,388 in 1921 to $301,543 in 1936 with similar decreases in land value from $380,855 to $153,219, buildings from $112,955 to $71,628, and farm machinery from $67,047 to $35,792.[4] Cash incomes from farming in Manitoba that in 1926 were recorded at $89,879 had fallen to just $31,785 by 1931, and only began to show signs of recovery in 1936, when they reached $47,856.[5] The index of farm purchasing power taking 1926 as 100, fell to 38 in 1932, to recover to 49 in 1935, and to 62 in 1936 with Hanover's economic rating described as only "average."[6] In Manitoba in 1926/27, $9,640 was paid out in unemployment benefits by the provincial government but in 1929/30, this had grown to $64,283. In 1930/31 to the end of the financial year in April, the sum expended on benefits by Dominion, province, and local municipalities combined was $1,543,000, but reached the staggering figure of $8,475,000 in 1931/32 before starting to decline. Between 1930 and 1932 the contribution of municipalities to the total rose from $427,254 to $2,276,574; by 1936 the figure was $3,000,423. Between 1931 and 1937 Manitoban municipalities spent $15,125,506 on benefits and relief works, almost $11.6 million on direct benefit payments, and $3 million on relief works.[7] In Hanover many unemployed and poor Mennonites worked on relief work schemes, including those forced to pay off tax arrears. The municipal debt in

Manitoba rose 63.6 per cent between 1919 and 1934, the highest of all the prairie provinces.[8]

Many Russländer entered the Depression heavily in debt and as the economic situation worsened their indebtedness increased. Although in the Grunthal area sufficient food could be produced to survive from day to day, money was still required to pay taxes, service debts, and purchase essential household items. Beyond survival and subsistence, the pursuit of money during the 1930s became an abiding feature of life for many Russländer across Canada and the worries and hardships they endured at this time left a legacy of stress, parsimony, and ill-feeling long after prosperity returned. The immediate debts were varied for Russländer in Grunthal, but the most immediate concern involved payments for land and livestock owed to the Intercontinental Company's successor, the National Trust, and meeting local taxes payable to the municipality. There were also an assortment of personal debts associated with their education and that of their children, as well as medical expenses if anyone was unfortunate enough to require treatment. The most significant debt for a majority of Russländer, however, involved the CPR's travel loans payable through the CMBC although repaying this was less pressing than meeting immediate needs. Even so most Russländer during the 1930s tried to make the occasional repayment.

Not all Russländer immigrants came to Canada on credit or on full credit, but a majority did so. Even those without a travel debt were still considered to have a collective responsibility for their co-religionists and the CMBC periodically levied additional charges to support its work. The amount of individual debt varied considerably but from the moment people arrived, interest on the debt accumulated, usually at about 6 per cent per annum. If levies remained unpaid, they were added to the principal owing. The levies were five cents a month per immigrant to support patients committed to mental health institutions and fifty cents a year to cover CMBC's administrative costs.[9] After marriage the debts of wives were usually added to the husbands' responsibilities and occasionally other people's debts were transferred to close kin and in-laws. Additional loans were sometimes advanced to settlers to cover education and other costs, but CMBC had little money for such purposes and during the 1930s even less. The board was ultimately responsible for any debts incurred by immigrants, such as medical expenses, whether for physical or mental health. The board guaranteed to pay these to prevent an immigrant from being deported from Canada as in official eyes, they had become a burden on the Canadian community. Once again, matters became increasingly

Table 6.1. Selected travel debts of Grunthal Russländer

Name	Dofe	#inf	idebt	fdebt	dfp
Diet. Heese	1923	1	$138	$196	1928
Abr. A. Driedger	1924	8	$730	$1,138	1933
Jac. Neufeld	1924	2	$372	$813	1929
J.J. Rempel	1924	4	$373	$722	1926
J.G. Woelke	1924	0	$124	$177	1940
D.J. Rempel	1924	3	$456	$1,022	1944
P.H. Janzen	1925	1	$146	$349	1944
J.J. Friesen	1927	4	$882	$2,530	1944
Jac. H. Block	1928	3	$496	$1,377	1946*
Peter D. Klassen	1929	5	$493	$1,474	1946*
A.P. Janz	1930	6	$841	$1,732	1944
A.J. Bestvater	1930	4	$414	$919	1946*

Notes: Dofe = date of emigration; #inf = number in family; idebt = initial debt; fdebt = final debt; dfp = date of final payment.
* Paid off other than by debtor and no promissory note issued.

Source: CMBC Records.

difficult during the 1930s when the number of people who genuinely could not pay such costs increased. In 1932 Canada deported 7,131 immigrants, 4,916 because they had become a charge on the public purse.[10] Only one Mennonite was deported to the USSR because of a criminal conviction and another with psychological issues about whom the CMBC learned too late to prevent his removal back to the Soviet Union.[11]

In Grunthal almost all Russländer had travel debts. A few like W.W. Sawatzky and Franz Guenther paid their own way to Canada, but most had not. A comparison of some of the individual debts reveals how much the debts varied (table 6.1). The size of the initial debt was related to family size but any increase in the debt could be managed if regular repayments were made. Immigrants who arrived early in the 1920s and secured good, cash-paying jobs could choose to devote some money to reducing or even clearing the debt and therefore were in a much better position than others once the Depression began. The most unfortunate were those who immigrated late in the 1920s or even in 1930. They were almost immediately swept into the Depression and had fewer opportunities to make repayments. However, this general rule varied in practice from individual to individual.

Details contained in CMBC account books and in reports by board representatives sent to collect debts indicate that Russländer looked upon their responsibility for their travel debt in different ways. Those who considered the debt as something to be cleared as soon as possible and regarded repayments a first responsibility went out of their way to make regular payments often at considerable sacrifice to themselves and their families. There were those who believed that they had little or no responsibility for the debt. Some claimed that CMBC and the CPR were involved in a business for profit and that repaying the debt was not a prime responsibility compared to other demands placed on their scant resources. So, the immigration board "could wait." Others just flatly refused to pay and a few even denied that they had a debt. These differences of opinion and attitude were found in many Russländer communities, so it is unsurprising they were also present in Grunthal.[12] One local told of a meeting in Grunthal held to discuss the problem of those who refused to repay the travel debt where a Kanadier offered a solution: "Shoot the lot of them," he advised in Low German, amid general laughter. Ministers might also intervene and emphasize the moral responsibility of debtors, but as one farm wife reportedly told a minister after he gave a sermon on the duty of members with debts, "you feed the sheep in the tender, green, pastures [on Sunday], and on Monday already you come to shear them."[13]

After an initial rather haphazard policy concerned with collecting outstanding debts, CMBC became serious about chasing debtors (fig. 6.1). By 1930 the total debt had risen to over a million dollars, interest payments alone were accumulating at $60,000 a year, while in 1931 the immigrants repaid less than $46,000.[14] The appointment of C.F. Klassen, a new immigrant who had managed the Mennonite Agricultural Association in Moscow during the early Soviet period, brought new vigour to the task.[15] Klassen criss-crossed the country visiting Russländer communities, often personally calling on individual debtors. It was a godforsaken task and Klassen frequently was met with hostility and abuse.[16] But he was a strong-willed person who could be blunt and to the point with troublesome Russländer. His reports on districts and individuals, often written in clear, colourful language, present a striking picture of those he encountered.[17]

To assist his work Klassen enlisted the support of local Russländer representatives or "district-men" appointed to liaise with CMBC and other immigrant organizations established during the 1920s. As many of these organizations had declined in importance by the 1930s and CMBC basically controlled all immigrant affairs, the principal role of district-men was to support the board and in particular its debt collectors. Often local

Fig. 6.1. Executive of the Canadian Mennonite Board of Colonization, 1935. Standing, left to right, J.A. Harder, C.A. DeFehr, G.J. Derksen, J.J. Gerbrandt; seated, B.B. Janz, David Toews, C.F. Klassen, J.J. Thiessen.

Source: Centre for Mennonite Brethren Studies, Winnipeg (NP108-04-01).

Russländer schoolmasters were enlisted to calculate sums owing and reckon up any repayments that Klassen had squeezed out of debtors. In 1931 Klassen spent two weeks in the East Reserve area where ninety Russländer debtor families were scattered in and around Grunthal, Spencer, Gnadenfeld, Neu-Bergfeld, Burwalde, Chortitz, and Rosengart. Each location had its own district-man although Klassen noted that Jacob J. Rempel seemed to have some overarching control.[18]

Klassen reported that there was considerable misunderstanding and opposition to the additional taxes being added to the initial travel debt to support other activities. In Grunthal one individual claimed he had no debt even when confronted with the evidence that he had just taken out "the contract" to cover his travel expenses, not other activities.[19] In the area there was also a general unwillingness to view the debt as something to be repaid as soon as possible. Klassen also reported that some district-men were competent, maintained good records, and attempted to keep track of any debtors who had left the district so the board could maintain its records. Other district men, however, he found less satisfactory. One close to Grunthal Klassen described as "a wretched figure," "absolutely good for nothing." This individual had attempted to unload responsibility for his own debts onto some one else.[20] Others claimed poverty which Klassen was willing to accept if it was confirmed. But in other cases, it was a matter of how immigrants viewed their priorities. One person who claimed he had other debts and illness in the family Klassen described as "a miserable person" and found his excuses to be unacceptable. Another was described as having "no initiative and no will to [re]pay."[21] A leading community and congregational figure with a large family argued he farmed insufficient land to repay the debt but the collector noted he owned a large holding and "could pay more."[22] In 1939 a farmer with seventy acres under plough who owned a radio and other "luxury" items claimed poverty in order to justify having not cleared his debt, a claim the collector rejected.[23] While the debt remained unpaid "luxuries" such as radios, cars, and fine clothing were considered "unnecessary."

The reality for Russländer was that they had numerous and competing claims on their limited resources and these mounted during the Depression. Many were also trying to support kin in the Soviet Union as Stalin's first Five Year Plan was initiated, and collectivization extended into most rural areas. Russländer started to receive horrifying reports of famine, arrests, and banishment. Individuals, congregations, and other institutions struggled to find ways to help those "trapped" in the "Red Paradise." Appeals to the Soviets to alleviate suffering were largely ineffective and further emigration was impossible.[24] The CMBC tried to coordinate whatever aid might still reach Soviet Mennonites by arranging for Canadian Mennonites to send money to the board who transferred it through various agencies to the USSR. Between 1929 and 1943 over $212,000 was sent in relief to Soviet Mennonites, of which 84 per cent was sent between 1929 and 1933, years that corresponded with the worst period of North America's Depression. Over $62,000 was sent to the USSR in 1933 as reports of famine, especially in Ukraine, were received.[25] Funds were forwarded through a German agency to *Torgsin*, the Soviet hard currency shop in Moscow so Soviet Mennonites could receive credit and purchase food, clothing, and other essential items.[26]

Not all Russländer in the Grunthal area still had many relatives in the USSR. The Schönfelders had few, but those with Khortitsa connections did, including Russländer from Baratov Shlachtin. Contributions from communities and not individuals can only be identified from reports periodically published in Mennonite newspapers. Grunthal's contributions were smaller than those from some other communities: in 1929, for instance, $70.50 was contributed from Grunthal, and $218 by the Whitewater community to the west.[27] Meanwhile, reports from the old homeland grew increasingly worrisome and communications infrequent. The Soviet security system closely watched anyone with links outside the USSR and Mennonites living in Stalin's paradise feared sending or receiving letters from abroad. The *Torgsin* offices closed in early 1936 and soon the Great Terror began in which Mennonite men were arrested in large numbers, sentenced to the Gulag, or executed.

As well as the travel debt and the board's levies and moral obligations to donate money to Mennonites in the Soviet Union, Russländer also had to pay for their land under the sharecropping agreements they had signed with the Company. Often half a farmer's income was owed to the Company. In 1931 the travel debt collector reported that one farmer paid half his weekly cream cheque of $2.10 to the Company, and his total income was only $225 in 1930.[28] How the Company kept an eye on an immigrant's sources of income from a farm is unclear. Cheques received from the creamery were easily traceable, but goods exchanged, sold to local shops, or sold in Winnipeg for cash could only be accounted for if the farmer declared them. It was unlikely that a farmer would be forced off their land as during the early 1930s it was almost valueless and the owners, the National Trust, were unlikely to find new tenants. On the other hand, the Trust did not abandon the settlers. In 1933 their adviser, Mr. Robertson, in conjunction with J.J. Rempel, once again brought experts from the Ministry of Agriculture and the University of Manitoba to advise farmers. This time they concentrated on how farmers might better produce goods suitable for changing markets during the Depression.[29]

Taxes owed to the local municipality also had to be paid. These paid for local services including roads and the control of pests, but at least a third went to schools. Taxes were calculated on the value of land and properties which for a period even included livestock, although by the early 1930s this apparently had been dropped. The taxes were not high but in a world of competing demands and falling resources, especially cash, the ability to pay taxes became increasingly problematic. During the 1930s, the number of people in arrears steadily increased especially in the Grunthal area (table 6.2). To reclaim outstanding debts the municipality could seize land and property and auction them. As people slipped into arrears, they received reminders, then warnings, and eventually public notices were placed in local newspapers signalling the intention of the municipality to sell the debtor's land and property. Many debtors developed a strategy of delaying payment for as long as possible and clearing all or a sufficient part of the arrears to prevent their land and property from being sold.

An examination of arrears owed by Russländer in the Grunthal area during the 1930s reveals that while many could be considered

Table 6.2. Tax receipts and arrears for 5–5E and the RM of Hanover, 1926–46

	5–5E		Hanover totals	
Year	Taxes	Arrears (a%t)	Taxes	Arrears (a%t)
1926	4,048	993 (24%)	67,511	7,189 (11%)
1931	4,479	3,600 (80%)	66,321	27,230 (41%)
1933	3,115	2,287 (73%)	42,294	21,839 (52%)
1936*	4,068	3,579 (88%)	52,286	32,479 (62%)
1938*	4,668	2,069 (44%)	74,404	22,185 (30%)
1940*	5,562	3,550 (64%)	85,178	41,281 (49%)
1942*	6,872	4,196 (61%)	98,931	14,903 (15%)
1944*	6,992	4,906 (70%)	109,743	17,467 (16%)
1946*	8,495	5,434 (64%)	139,772	20,389 (15%)

Note: a%t = arrears as percentage of taxes.
* Each year arrears include carry-overs from two previous years.
Source: Collectors Rolls, RM of Hanover Office.

poor, others were obviously employing the strategy of delayed payments. Paying taxes usually meant finding sufficient cash but some arrears could also be paid off through contributing labour, horses, and machinery to municipal works, the most important of which during the 1930s involved building roads. A farmer would supply an agreed number of days' labour, supplying his own horses and equipment to help remove large stones, build banks, and grade roads. The St. Pierre highway received considerable attention from Grunthal farmers who would often spend days away from their farms, sleeping out in the countryside. In many ways this work benefited everyone in the community. Farmers cleared some of their debts, the municipality got essential work done at minimal cost, and improved highways assisted communications, bringing trade and the hope of prosperity to previously isolated communities.

An additional problem for some Grunthal residents involved costs incurred through illness, especially serious illnesses that required specialist treatment and even admission to hospital, either in Steinbach or Winnipeg. It brought some Russländer in Grunthal close to bankruptcy. As the CMBC was ultimately responsible for debts incurred by Russländer, in October 1930 the secretary to the Hanover Municipality, J.D. Goossen, sent a bill to the board detailing outstanding debts for hospital treatment accumulated since 1926 by Russländer in the municipality. Four individuals from Grunthal are listed owing sums ranging from $8.75 to $56. In November the board replied saying they had forwarded

Goossen's letter to J.J. Rempel as "Supervisor for the Intercontinental Company." In December, Goossen replied that the municipality had agreed that only half the sum owed needed be paid now and more could wait until later but also stated that the municipal council had resolved that ultimately all the money owed had to be repaid and that it still held CMBC liable.[30]

Problems relating to hospital care were alleviated to an extent when Russländer Abram A. Vogt and his sister Marie, who had trained as a nurse in Germany and Russia, opened a medical centre in Steinbach.[31] From 1928 onward it operated as a maternity home but in 1931 added an operating theatre and two additional wards. In 1937 a new Bethesda Hospital was opened in Steinbach and a hospital aid organization was established to help cover costs of treatment.[32] As the hospital was a private venture anyone admitted still had to pay towards their treatment even though it was founded to serve the local community rather than be run at a profit. A number of other Russländer communities established mutual aid organizations to help cover health care costs during the Depression.[33] The main Russländer medical centre in Winnipeg was the Concordia Hospital, which opened on a small scale in 1928.[34] Provincial support was minimal and dependent on the number of patients a hospital could handle.

In order to pay for all these costs and secure their futures, the farmers were involved in a pursuit of money. This involved finding markets for produce from farms or the establishment of businesses that could meet local needs and connect with the wider economy. The main farm produce was milk and cream sold in a variety of markets. In summer cream was often suspended in a churn at the end of a rope in a farm's well until it was ready to take to market. It could be sold in Winnipeg directly or more often by taking it to the railroad station at Carey and from there forwarded to an agent in the city. In the early period this might involve two trips a day to the station with a team of horses.[35] After 1927 cream could also be sold directly to the Grunthal creamery or at one of the other plants such as that in the Kanadier hamlet of Kleefeld, ten kilometres to the north, where it was mostly turned into butter and later cheese.[36] Grunthal once possessed a cheese factory owned since the 1890s by the Kanadier Braun family but by the time Russländer arrived it was no longer in operation. In the late 1930s a cheese factory was established in Grunthal with important consequences for the town and farmers in the district. Creameries, shops, and agencies paid different prices for produce, and these changed from season to season. The best thing a farmer could do was to maximize returns while not expending too much time and effort to secure a better price. Payments were usually by monthly cheque that required access to a bank, usually for Grunthal farmers in the nearby French-Canadian parish of St. Pierre.

While milk was the major farm product sold to raise money, there were other ways money could be raised: through the sale of grain, fodder, vegetables, fruit (including watermelon), eggs, and meats such as chickens, pork, sausages, and hams. Seneca roots collected in the brush could be sold to the local store by enterprising youths. Farm produce was also sold in neighbouring English and French towns. The best returns were obtained by taking produce to Winnipeg and selling directly to shops or hawking produce from door to door through the wealthier suburbs. Only a few Russländer favoured the latter course as most considered it demeaning. Others, however, enjoyed the cut and thrust of bargaining with shopkeepers, maids, and housewives. Some even dressed in old clothes and would plead abject poverty in hope of gaining the sympathy of potential customers: a not easy strategy during the Depression, as the city was overrun with the unemployed on relief, themselves in search of money and employment.[37] Local transfer operators would also carry produce to markets and return with merchandise from Winnipeg.

Another major source of obtaining either credit or cash was through supplying firewood sold by the cord, a measure of 128 cubic feet or 3.6 metres "stacked." Cordwood was an essential source of fuel to keep houses warm through Manitoba's long winter months, especially in rural prairie regions devoid of timber. The brush around Grunthal, especially to the south, was ideal for obtaining cordwood although people had to travel much further away to the tamarack for supplies for building lumber and fence posts.[38] Cordwood was usually cut in summer or fall and then transported in winter by sleigh as the snow and hard ground made its movement easier. All through winter horse teams, and even an occasional bullock team, their owners wreathed in steam and frost, could be seen hauling large loads of cordwood towards centres to be exchanged for cash or credit. At first the creamery purchased fuel, but later shopkeepers in Grunthal and neighbouring towns took cordwood in exchange for supplies. The collection and transportation of cordwood was often dangerous if loads were not properly secured or stacked, as they could roll and crush people. In 1939 Johann Wiens, a Kanadier, was killed in Grunthal when he fell under a sleigh carrying cordwood.[39] Not only was cordwood a source of income but certain Russländer and Kanadier also purchased machinery and hired themselves out to cut and prepare it. Such "custom" work was also employed for other tasks, especially in late summer when threshing teams would move from place to place threshing farmers' grain for a fee or a share of the grain.

As the Depression continued, prices paid for produce plunged dramatically. Cream that in 1929 was sold for forty cents a pound sold for only thirty cents in 1930, and fell as low as nine cents by 1932, although the average price was about eighteen cents.[40] Cordwood, which in 1929 sold for $3.00 a cord in St. Pierre and $2.75 in Grunthal, brought only $1.00 to $1.50 in 1934; even in 1936 it had only recovered to $2.00 a cord.[41] Eggs varied in price according to quality, season, and market demand but through the 1930s they maintained their price better than other produce.[42] During the early 1930s when the Depression was at its worst, people who had money were not Grunthal farmers but those with other sources of income, such as J.J. Rempel, agent of the Company, and teacher Heidebrecht. The search for money naturally led away from the land towards a range of entrepreneurial activities. While these could include direct selling of produce in Winnipeg, the desire to stay close to the community encouraged people, Russländer and Kanadier, to develop a local market and service centre in Grunthal itself. In this way New Grunthal, as opposed to the remains of the original village of Old Grunthal, began to be built from the early 1930s onward.

The establishment of business enterprises within or close to Old Grunthal began long before the Russländer arrived, and was led by the Braun and Krahn families.[43] Johann Funk Braun first farmed in Gnadenfeld and in the 1880s became a local dealer in farm machinery. In 1892 he moved to Grunthal and with his brother-in-law, Johann Krahn, established a store. Soon they were involved in other ventures including the farm machinery dealership, a cheese factory purchased from a local Frenchman, and a Midget Flour Mill that ground flour and prepared animal feed.[44] The mill was powered by a large mobile steam engine that was also used for threshing and lumber cutting. With the settlement of Ukrainians in the district the ventures flourished. Additional custom came from further away, as Mennonites and non-Mennonites travelled to Grunthal to consult the famous "Dr." Peters (LG *Dokta Petasch*), who would later emigrate to Paraguay but die shortly after.[45] Peters was renowned for his healing arts particularly through massage and the manipulation of bones (LG *trajchtmoaka*).[46] After 1900 a succession of Jewish shopkeepers operated in the old village area although their stores seemed to burn down rather often.[47] In 1911 Braun and Krahn built a new store away from the old village site and close to the Grunthal Milling Company's enlarged mill. A bachelor, Jacob H. Hiebert, acted as clerk to the Milling Company and later became postmaster, a farm machinery dealer, and owner of a second-hand store; hence he was known as Second-hand or Store Hiebert (LG *Stua Hiebert*). As businesses flourished, especially through the prosperous years of the First World War, reports from Grunthal detail the expansion of the mill and its facilities.[48]

The downturn of the post-war economy, and uncertainty over the future of local Mennonite settlements following opposition to school reform, resulted in the Milling Company being closed. Around 1920 the store building was sold to the provincial authorities and converted into the Goodwill public school, while the mill's machinery was sold to an enterprise outside the district. By the time the Russländer arrived, Grunthal's thriving trade and service centre was no more. Soon, however, the situation changed as the City Dairy purchased the Milling Company's empty buildings in 1927. The company converted them into a creamery to process mostly skimmed milk and butter. The opening of the dairy, close to the school, further refocused the business centre along a new axis away from the old village. Farmers coming to the creamery sometimes had to queue to deliver their cream, so the area became an ideal location to establish other businesses and soon a farmers' cooperative was constructed to supply the new immigrants with essential items.

In Russia the cooperative movement had grown in importance in many Mennonite settlements from the late 1890s and in the early Soviet period Mennonite cooperatives received official approval. In Canada Mennonites were also attracted to the cooperative movement but more strongly in some areas than others. On the East Reserve there were few cooperatives, but the movement prospered on the West Reserve, under the energetic leadership of a Kanadier, J.J. Siemens.[49] Siemens was eager to involve Russländer and often spoke at their meetings but while some supported the movement, others considered it to resemble "communism," which they despised. It is unclear what motivated Grunthal Russländer to start their own cooperative venture but undoubtedly a shortage of money and credit hastened a desire to establish and control a trading system to their own advantage. A correspondent in 1929 noted the store, ideally located next to the creamery, was small and lacked a proper basement to store goods.[50] To manage it the cooperative members sought out the services of the Russländer Franz Guenther, who had been a shopkeeper in Russia. Guenther came from Sergievka in the Orenburg Colony founded in the 1890s by settlers from Molochna and Khortitsa. His father owned a retail business although on his mother's side his relatives were farmers. In Orenburg Franz Guenther took over his father's store in 1922 but problems with the local Soviet confirmed his view there was little future for private enterprise in the USSR. In 1925 he immigrated to Canada with his wife, Anna Penner, and three sons. He worked first in the West Reserve before taking on a Company farm in the Neu-Bergfeld area.

Guenther was no farmer, but the cooperative needed a manager, and in 1929, he started work. In 1930 was joined by Johann G. Peters as the cooperative's bookkeeper. Peters was directly related to Grunthal's leading group as he had been born and educated in Schönfeld where he had managed a large general goods store. He too was forced to flee to Molochna with his wife, Margarethe Warkentin, and they immigrated to Canada in 1925 and farmed with relatives in Glenlea. Neither a farmer by inclination nor by physique, and even though extremely skilled with accounts, he later proved to be a poor businessman, lacking drive and ambition.

As the Grunthal cooperative was established for the benefit of farmers, particularly leading Russländer settlers, differences soon emerged between a manager like Guenther, accustomed to running a private enterprise for profit, and the shareholders. In Russia competition between Mennonite farmer cooperatives and privately owned stores increased before the revolution and similar issues emerged in Canada. Peters' connections with leading Russländer further complicated relations as Guenther had no relatives in Grunthal or anywhere else in Canada. In 1932 therefore, with a $400 loan from a Steinbach lumber merchant, he built a store in the vicinity of the creamery and set himself up in direct competition with the cooperative located close by. His business was met with fierce opposition from Russländer who supported the cooperative where Peters now was appointed as manager. An attempt was made to boycott Guenther's new venture, but he soon developed good contacts with a wide range of customers: Russländer, Kanadier, and particularly Ukrainians, people from the French community, and even Indigenous people from the Roseau Reserve.

Guenther also contacted Winnipeg suppliers and distributors and sometime around 1935 his store become part of the Red and White Store network.[51] His store was stocked from floor to roof with a variety of goods, and soon it became a central place for shopping or just visiting, although some Russländer continued to avoid his store for many years. Guenther excelled at business and had a willingness to work all hours, so the store flourished despite the bad economic times. He accepted goods in exchange instead of cash and extended credit to customers when money was in short supply. The latter problem was widespread as people hoarded cash. To alleviate this a Russländer storekeeper in Steinbach, Peter Vogt, issued his own metal tokens or barter coins, but these were deemed illegal in 1938.[52] In 1936 Guenther managed to move his family out of his living quarters located at the back of the store into a new house across the street and in 1941 the store was relocated into an expanded building close by.[53]

In 1932 the cooperative and Guenther's store were located away from the old established village area. Both areas were controlled by Russländer as three had positioned themselves in the old area of town during the first period of Russländer settlement. These were Jacob J. Rempel in the old home of "Dr." Peters and his father-in-law Jacob Woelke in an old house and barn at the southern end of the street. Jacob's brother Dietrich took over the house and farm long in the possession of its previous owners, the Kanadier Kauenhoven family. These people were not just related through kinship and marriage but also would hold important roles in the Russländer congregation and wider community. Close by was Gerstein's store and post office, supported by the former clerk of the Grunthal Milling Company, Jacob Hiebert, who collected the mail from Steinbach.

The post office was established in the old village in 1894 and Johann Braun was its first postmaster. Mail was very important to Russländer as it brought letters from friends and relatives in Canada as well as the Soviet Union before connections with the latter became almost impossible. The mail delivery also included newspapers and magazines which relieved the boredom and sense of isolation for many in Grunthal. The post office was visited regularly, but the late arrival of mail annoyed many. In 1931 Russländer succeeded in getting the post redirected through St. Pierre rather than Steinbach so it could arrive by 8:00 a.m. Some complained about the change at a Hanover Council meeting in Steinbach.[54] Jacob Woelke now became responsible for mail collection instead of Hiebert.[55] The post office itself moved out of Gerstein's store after his death in 1933 and was relocated in a separate room in Jacob J. Rempel's house.[56]

Rempel claimed his right to the position of official postmaster under provisions of the *Civil Service Act*. This gave preference in government employment to men who had served as soldiers overseas during the First World War. Rempel's entitlement was questionable as he served as a non-combatant with the Russian Black Sea fleet and earlier, on the eastern front in a non-military role. Many years later Russländer who served in similar roles were denied ex-servicemen pensions.[57] In 1935 the post office was relocated to the house of John F. Warkentin on what would be called "Main Street" although Rempel remained postmaster until 1942 when he left for Ontario. Warkentin had been born in the Khortitsa-related settlement of Steinfeld in Russia and immigrated in 1924.[58] The new mail location was now situated closer to the creamery, the cooperative, and Guenther's store than it had been at Rempel's place and farmers could collect mail while taking milk to the creamery and shopping. In 1942 Warkentin, now known by his Low German nickname, Post Warkentin (*Post Woatjentien*), became postmaster, a position he held until 1966.

These developments produced two business areas. The older one became known as Old Grunthal, the other New Grunthal or the Company's Place (HG *Kompanies Platz*), thereby identifying the new location with Russländer.⁵⁹ This identification was enhanced by the location of the Elim Church building constructed in 1933 and later by the rebuilt school. Other businesses run by Russländer and Kanadier followed, and people also began to build houses parallel to the street. In 1935 Julius Klassen, a Russländer who had tried to farm close to Grunthal, purchased some old millstones and opened a small business grinding feed for cattle. This replaced small, inefficient mobile motorized milling machines that operated on a "custom" basis. As his business expanded, he produced more diverse feeds to meet different customers' needs, especially Mennonites and Ukrainians.⁶⁰

During the Depression former Schönfelders from Glenlea moved to the Spencer and Grunthal areas but struggled to farm successfully.⁶¹ In 1937 John D. Warkentin, a young man from Glenlea of Schönfelder background with relatives living in Grunthal, established a motor garage in New Grunthal. A qualified mechanic from the Dominion Trade School in Winnipeg, he first worked in a French-owned garage in nearby St. Pierre and met his wife, Margarethe Voth, in Niverville. They lived in humble circumstances as he built a garage with a wind powered electric generator on the roof on Grunthal's emerging new main street. Warkentin repaired and serviced local vehicles and sold oil and petrol, bringing new skills to the district such as welding which was previously only done crudely by blacksmiths. In 1939, after a brief period selling International Harvester farm equipment, Warkentin became an agent for Allis-Chalmers.⁶²

Russländer who failed as farmers started commercial ventures around town, some more successfully than others. They attempted to operate as blacksmiths, but never as successfully as Kanadier who also took advantage of the developing town. These Kanadier included Peter P. Friesen and especially David F. Toews, who skilfully mended damaged farm machinery. The Kanadier Peter Braun relocated his auto repair shop and transfer service closer to the new service area.⁶³ Other Kanadier such as local carpenters and builders also flourished as Grunthal developed. As the Depression eased, a "restaurant" was opened by David F. Hiebert in 1938. Grunthal started to serve non-Mennonites in the district that reached as far as the French settlements around St. Pierre and St. Malo, towns that previously dealt mainly with their own people. The most important non-Mennonites in the growth of the town, however, were Ukrainians from around Sarto and Pansy whose entrepreneurs chose to settle in Grunthal and compete with Mennonite businesses. Ted Chornoboy from Sarto started by hauling supplies for Ukrainian farmers from his district to neighbouring centres. In 1937 he purchased a transfer service from Henry Unger and named it "Grunthal Transfer," moving supplies in trucks from Sarto and Grunthal to Winnipeg. The centre of his operation gradually became based in Grunthal rather than Sarto and in 1940 he sold the transfer business to establish a dealership in International Harvester farm machinery in Grunthal.[64] Another Ukrainian, Steve Block, had already built a garage in Grunthal in the late 1930s.

Most of these new ventures established themselves or relocated on what was increasingly considered Grunthal's main street and a new road was constructed connecting it to the old, "downtown" Grunthal.[65] The town begun at the height of the Depression grew rapidly through to the late 1930s from a few scattered businesses to a supply and service centre whose residents often lived close by for ease of access to their businesses. One correspondent reported in 1935 that people in the district no longer had to travel to Winnipeg or Steinbach to do business when money could remain in the town, although he added, "if your money is burning a hole in your pocket, New Grunthal is as good a place to spend it as anywhere."[66] As most people had little money, spending what little they did have in Grunthal was not as cynical a matter as this comment might suggest. The town played an important role in lifting the community out of its economic woes. In June 1936 a correspondent noted proudly that the town had a new school, fine houses, four stores, two blacksmiths, one cobbler and a creamery, as well as transfer services that ran to Sarto, St. Pierre, and St. Malo, and on to Winnipeg on improved roads.[67]

Recognition that Grunthal had indeed changed occurred in 1935 when J.J. Rempel requested the municipality to carry out a new survey of Section 21–5–5 East to identify the new town site, prepare funding for new roads, and revise property taxes in the area (see map 6.1).[68] From 1936 the "village" of Grunthal appears separately in district tax records and it becomes easier to trace the growth of its enterprises. In 1931 Section 21, which covered most of what would become the town of Grunthal, had fourteen lots, six of which belonged to individual businesses, the cooperative, or outside concerns like the City Dairy. By 1936 there were thirty lots and eight identifiable businesses, and by 1941 the businesses had increased to over a dozen.[69]

The growth of New Grunthal was also reflected in the increased density of settlement in the surrounding area, especially to the south. The settlers here included a few Russländer, but the majority were Kanadier: either Chortitzer people, some of whom had returned from Paraguay,

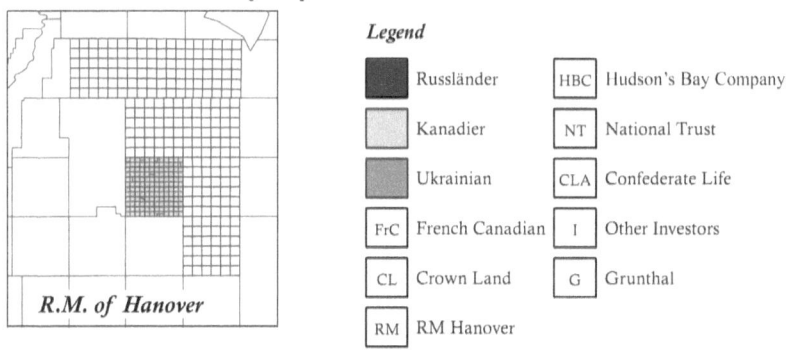

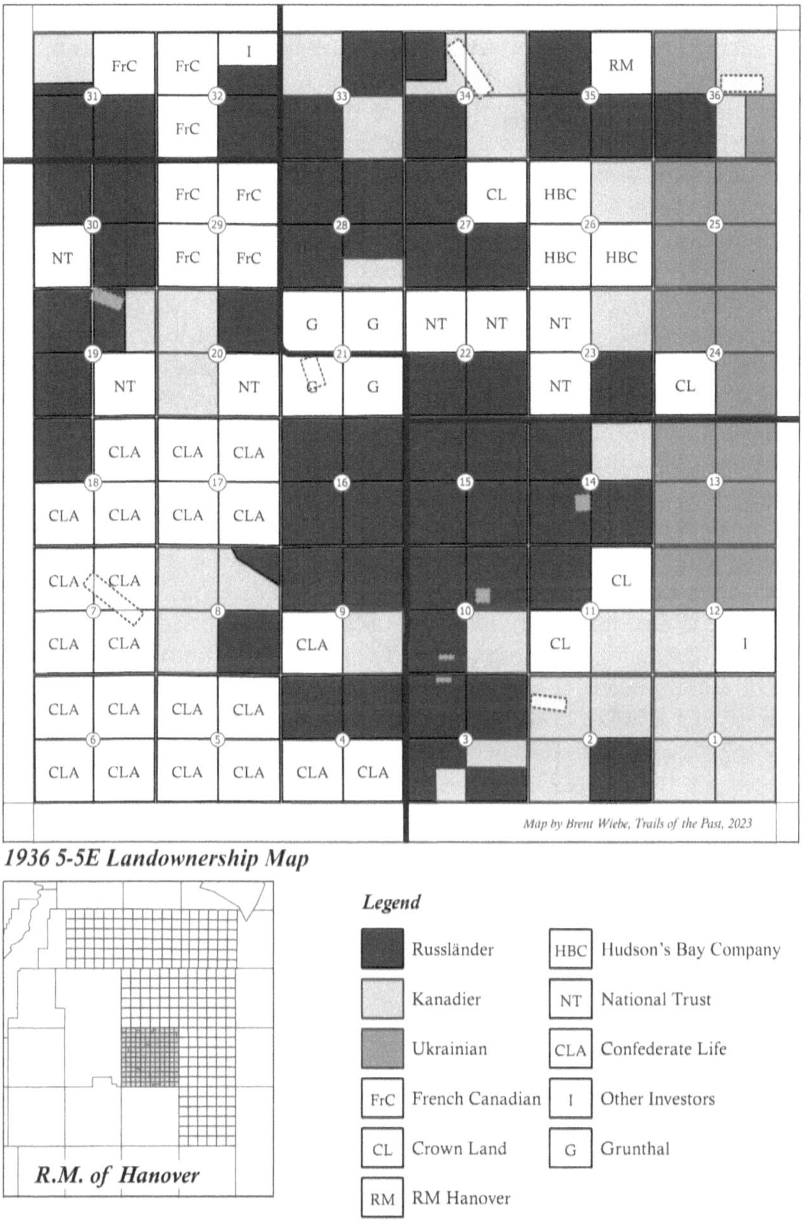

Map 6.1. Landownership in 5–5E, 1936. From tax records of the RM of Hanover.

Sources: Map by Brent Wiebe, *Trails of the Past* (2023). Government of Manitoba, licenced under the OpenMB Information and Data Use Licence (Manitoba.ca/OpenMB).

or members of the Bergthaler congregation from the West Reserve who arrived in the 1930s. The effects of the Depression combined with appalling weather conditions in the mid-1930s left many Mennonites on the West Reserve in a more parlous state than their brethren on the East Reserve. Many depended for a living on a limited range of grain crops and prices for grain almost collapsed in the Depression while drought, locusts, and soil erosion often devastated what could be produced. Suddenly the marginal soils of the East Reserve's bushland looked like a promising way to make a living as at least here people could grow enough for subsistence, cut cordwood, and keep warm. Cordwood could also be sold to relatives on the West Reserve, an area with little firewood. The Bergthalers often had distant relatives among local Chortitzer, so it was easy to establish social relations. In other matters, such as their attitude to education and religious practices, Bergthalers were more progressive than most Chortitzer. In 1936 a Bergthaler minister, William Heinrichs, moved to the village of Neu-Bergfeld southwest of Grunthal and served Bergthalers living in the area close to Neu-Bergfeld and nearby Spencer. In 1939 a new congregation was formally organized with a blessing of the Elder David Schulz from Altona on the West Reserve.[70] Although living outside Grunthal, the settlement of Bergthalers added an additional impetus to the development of the district and eventually to the town.

The experience of the Depression helped reshape the Grunthal community in a number of ways. While Russländer experienced difficulties due to a lack of capital they all had experienced previous hardships in Russia. By the mid-1930s, however, Russländer in Grunthal had succeeded in relocating the town and establishing new businesses. While the rebuilding of the town may have been advanced by Russländer, it was built around a pre-existing business area where Kanadier entrepreneurs had once prospered. The building of New Grunthal involved developing relations with more than just other Mennonites as gradually the economic hardships of the Depression pulled all people of the district together: Mennonites, Ukrainians, and French. The Depression affected everyone, as all had to find the money to pay taxes and meet the demands of everyday life. All peoples experienced poverty, shared similar concerns, and were forced to adapt to changing economic conditions. In poverty there are few distinctions of class, background, or even religion. Old attitudes and prejudices may have persisted, but they were not an immediate concern of everyday life.

Chapter Seven

Old World and New World Politics

The Mennonites' Anabaptist ancestors eschewed "worldly politics," separated themselves from state-supported churches, formed new Christian communities based on their understanding of the New Testament, and abandoned earthly concerns along with power backed by force. But separation from the "world" and the denial of force and the ultimate authority of earthly rulers were political acts that challenged the existing political order that viewed them as subjects. To gain political recognition Mennonites often obtained special protective charters that also gave them special privileges. Those who had immigrated to Russia from the eighteenth century onward secured such a Charter of Privileges, as they had earlier from Polish and Prussian rulers. By immigrating, Mennonites turned their backs on a rapidly changing world where bureaucratic nation states were being formed and once subservient subjects were mobilized into useful, productive citizens ruled not by royal decree, but instead governed by legal statutes approved by elected assemblies within constitutional frameworks. The reform of old political systems often met with opposition from conservative forces which in turn fomented rebellion and revolution. In autocratic Russia modern political systems were delayed despite attempts at reform that affected Mennonites in both negative and positive ways. Following Russia's Great Reforms, roughly between 1860 and 1880, the bodies created to administer Mennonites were abolished and thereafter Mennonites dealt directly with Russian ministries.

The establishment of Mennonite communities after the sixteenth century necessitated the formation of internal authority structures that created opportunities for internal political action, as individuals and families attempted to gain and maintain power in a community. By attempting to escape the worldly web of external politics, Mennonites spun internal political webs of their own.[1] This is what happened following Mennonite settlement in Russia and conflicts occurred between religious leaders and the new secular leaders established by the Russian government, mostly concerned with spheres of authority. Compromises were sometimes reached but when conflicts reoccurred, Mennonite civil leaders were nearly always backed by Russian officials. The new political environment provided opportunities for progressive Mennonite leaders to force through economic, social, and cultural reforms generally opposed by conservative congregational leaders.[2] Mennonite-led reforms occurred prior to Russia's larger Great Reforms that fundamentally changed political relationships between Mennonites and the state and that contributed to the emigration of some Mennonites to North America in the 1870s.

Those Mennonites who remained in Russia were integrated into Russia's new administrative systems that mostly ignored Mennonite religious authority. In the wake of the Great Reforms Mennonites founded a range of institutions and administrative bodies until their world resembled a "state-within-a-state," a Mennonite Commonwealth.[3] The urge to organize, establish boards, elect officials, control finances, hold meetings, write up and distribute minutes, became an established feature of Mennonite life before 1914. Interest in political matters led to closer Mennonite involvement in politics within and beyond their communities. With the establishment of constitutional government in Russia in 1905/06, Mennonites faced new challenges while the First World War threatened the Mennonite Commonwealth's foundations. Long before the collapse of the commonwealth after 1917, Mennonites were a highly politicized people but also politically polarized with conservatives, liberals, and a small minority of radicals. The 1917 revolution initially resulted in calls for the reform of Mennonite society by young alternative servicemen, young men who had served in alternative services (*Sanitätsdienst*) during the war. All adult Russländer immigrants to Canada in the 1920s had grown up during this time of political change, witnessing the collapse of the imperial state and the Mennonite Commonwealth and the rise of the early Bolsheviks.

Following immigration to Canada the Russländer leadership attempted to re-establish the religious and secular institutions of the Mennonite Commonwealth but were also faced with a need to create new institutions. The CMBC became the dominant secular Mennonite organization in Canada, initially concerned with immigration and settlement, but after immigration from the USSR ended it focused on managing the travel debt and caring for the welfare of immigrants.[4] The board's membership was soon dominated by Russländer although Mennonites from earlier immigrations remained members. Closely associated with leading ministers, it also contained professionals:

Mennonites trained in Russia as teachers, accountants, and businessmen. During the 1920s other organizations developed, directly or indirectly connected with the CMBC, to aid, direct, and inform Russländer.

One indication of CMBC's shift from immigration to rebuilding a sense of political and cultural unity among Russländer was the creation of the Central Mennonite Immigration Committee (*ZMIK*). Founded in 1923 as an advisory body, it adopted a more formal constitution in 1927. This secular organization, separate yet still connected with conferences of different religious bodies, resembled Mennonite organizations developed in Russia before 1914 and after 1921 to unite Mennonites.[5] At that time a clear differentiation was drawn between the religious conference (HG *Kirchenkonvent*) and the central Mennonite civil organization (HG *Mennozentrum*). The latter was to negotiate political, social, and other cultural issues with whatever government came to power.[6] While leading Russländer in *ZMIK* attempted to establish a similar distinction of roles in Canada, the more immediate needs of the immigrants such as a shortage of money and the worsening economic conditions limited their activities and in 1934 *ZMIK* was merged with a reorganized CMBC.

Russländer by this time had abandoned any hope of re-establishing a single united body for immigrants because of religious divisions and the scattered Russländer settlements. However, other religious and secular conferences provided ways of maintaining and developing contacts between Russländer at a provincial level. Participants usually met annually to receive reports on the work of the CMBC Board and to hear presentations covering a range of social and economic issues. These were followed by discussions where ideas were shared, resolutions put forward, and agreed to or rejected. Some conferences lasted for several days. Local communities elected or delegated people to attend, reports of meetings were published in Mennonite newspapers, and in some provinces, separate, extended reports were also printed. In time, however, provincial secular assemblies declined in importance and eventually were subordinated to religious conferences although this did not occur until the late 1940s and early 1950s.

In Manitoba the first Russländer provincial assembly was organized in Winnipeg in 1928, a year after *ZMIK* was constituted, although a less formal meeting was held in 1926.[7] Grunthal Russländer were involved with provincial assemblies from their foundation and sent representatives, some of whom delivered papers. The key person was once again J.J. Rempel, who on more than one occasion represented Grunthal as a delegate and delivered addresses on farm improvement.[8] In 1930 Rempel was elected to the organizing committee for the next assembly.[9] The provincial assembly continued to meet in Winnipeg but in 1933 it gathered in Grunthal's new meeting house when several members

Fig. 7.1. Jacob J. Rempel and family, c. 1934.

Source: Courtesy of Eleanore (Rempel) Woollard, Edmonton.

of the community delivered papers. Rempel provided an overview of the settlement's history and their experiences, his brother Dietrich discussed the value of mixed farming, Peter H. Janzen spoke on dairying, J.G. Peters reported on the cooperative, and G.A. Peters discussed the need to train young people in agriculture. Finally, Jacob Block spoke on how the fire insurance scheme operated in the community.[10] The holding of the event in Grunthal was a major coup for Russländer in the area, and Rempel was elected as president of the assembly for the following year.[11]

If Russländer settled on more productive farms in western Manitoba had once sneered at their poorer brethren living on the stony ground of eastern Manitoba, calling them "bush-bunnies" and other derogatory names, by 1933 the devastating impact of the Depression on the once prosperous western prairie farms gave Grunthalers something to crow about. The Grunthalers might have been poor, but in their own newly renovated meeting house they could "preach" to other Russländer on their own achievements. However internally divided Grunthal Russländer might have been, to outsiders, whether other Russländer or non-Mennonites, they presented a united front. By the early 1930s J.J. Rempel was the undisputed civil leader of Grunthal Russländer and he was also active in the affairs of the RM of Hanover (see fig. 7.1).

The Mennonites who settled in Canada in the 1870s first attempted to re-establish the congregational system and the secular offices of civil authority they had known in Russia. By the early 1880s a municipal system replaced Mennonite local government previously based on assemblies headed by village and regional mayors. In Canada the civil system was centred on villages and the Reserve but as villages were abandoned and individuals relocated onto quarter sections, the position of village mayors became redundant. The move also created changes to the system of land tenure.[12] Unlike in Russia, however, except in the very early years in Canada, the authority of Mennonite civil officers was not fully backed by Manitoban authorities. Instead, those holding civil positions were subordinated to religious leaders, especially the Elders, considerably more than in Russia before immigration.[13]

On the East Reserve Chortitzer people and their religious leaders seemed more willing to recreate Russian forms of civil administration than Kleine Gemeinde, and a previous regional mayor of the Bergthal Colony in Russia, Jakob Peters, managed many of the affairs of the Reserve.[14] In stark contrast to episodes of conflict and confrontation between religious and civil leaders in Russia and on the West Reserve, the adoption of the Manitoban municipal system on the East Reserve between the early 1880s and 1910 went smoothly.[15] For a brief period the East Reserve was divided into two municipalities, Hespeler and Hanover, but they tended to operate together.[16] Annual elections were held for the positions of reeve and representatives of local wards who with the reeve formed a municipal council. Some wards included Mennonites, but the council included non-Mennonites, some from the German Lutheran community and for Ward 6, which largely covered of the area of 5–5E in which Grunthal was located, Ukrainians. The election of Ukrainians to Ward 6 was aided by the fact that many Chortitzer, like some Kleine Gemeinde, refused to stand candidates, to vote, or otherwise be involved in local government.

Mennonites who remained in Russia after the Great Reforms mostly continued to control their own local affairs even as Russian replaced German as the language of administration. As Mennonite officials were integrated into the imperial system of local government it is not surprising that after immigrating to Canada Russländer had few qualms about being involved in local government and indeed many were keen to participate. The fact that the official language of administration in Canada was not German, but English and French, matched their experience in Russia of conducting official business in another language. The real difficulty at first lay in their lack of proficiency in English although in Hanover discussions were probably in Low German and other languages. A more important concern involved sharing local government with non-Mennonites. This had little to do with religious principles and more with the well-established view that Mennonites should control their own affairs. Other Mennonite immigrants from Russia, however, had experienced sharing local affairs with non-Mennonites and therefore some Grunthal Russländer saw no problem with neighbouring Ukrainians and other non-Mennonites holding office in the municipality. Grunthal, however, was dominated by Schönfelders who in Russia had controlled local affairs. Although it was obvious Schönfelders would never be able to dominate the entire municipality or even Ward 6 it was essential that they were represented in municipal affairs, hopefully by getting one of their own elected to the ward in which Grunthal was located.

Before the Russländer arrived and before the majority of Chortitzer emigrated to Paraguay, Ward 6 was represented by members of the entrepreneurial Braun and Krahn families. Between 1908 and 1916 Johann Braun had been a councillor and reeve.[17] It is unclear, however, whether the positions of councillor or reeve were ever contested before the 1920s and candidates may have been appointed unopposed as so few Mennonites voted.[18] By the time the Russländer arrived, the Hanover Municipal Office had shifted from the village of Chortitz to the town of Steinbach. Minutes of meetings were now recorded in English as were local by-laws enacted to manage farming practices, maintain roads, and other matters under the municipality's purview. The council possessed the power to levy taxes and appoint local people in their ward to collect fines from any who contravened the by-laws. After 1922 the reeve was Adolf F. Müller, postmaster in the Lutheran settlement of Hochstadt. It is unclear how Müller interacted with Russländer when they first arrived, but it may be significant that in 1928 he married a Mennonite, Elisabeth Schellenberg, and later joined the Russländer Elim Congregation.

He was still in office when, early in 1927, J.J. Rempel was appointed "pathmaster" (roadmaster) for Ward 6. Rempel's duties mainly concerned the upkeep of roads in the local area, and he was also the assistant weed inspector.[19] In March 1930 Rempel submitted the names of property owners in his district so that they could be entered into the Court of Revision and be entitled to vote. Another Russländer, Franz Steingart, submitted the names for his area. Steingart competed with Rempel for control of the district until he moved away.[20] Late in 1932, following the resignation of the Kanadier Jacob T. Wiebe of Neu-Bergfeld (or perhaps Pansy), with the support of Russländer Rempel was elected as councillor for Ward 6.[21] He stood against two Ukrainian candidates and his election was described in a letter from Chortitz to a German-language newspaper, probably written by a Russländer, as a "defeat" of "two Slavs."[22]

Rempel joined the council at a time of change as local government in the municipality become increasingly politicized. Since 1928 Müller had been challenged as reeve, including by a Steinbach businessman who was supported by members of the town's Kleine Gemeinde, the dominant congregational group in Steinbach and surrounding areas. His first challenger was an English lawyer, N.S. Campbell, then businessman J.J. Reimer, and finally Jacob H. Peters, son of a former reeve and grandson of the founding district mayor.[23] In 1930 Müller lost the election by just twenty-one votes and lost again in 1931 but in 1932 he retook the position by just fifty-three votes.[24] His victory, however, was short-lived. Early in 1933, just as Rempel joined the council, Müller resigned after a dispute with other councillors although he did run unsuccessfully for re-election in 1935.[25] For Rempel these events were a rude introduction to municipal politics. In time, however, Grunthal's Russländer would come to consider Ward 6 as their political territory by right and Rempel remained its representative until he left Grunthal in 1943.

However, Rempel came to understand that he was a member of a council that represented the interests not only of his fellow Russländer, but also all people of Ward 6 and the good of the entire municipality. He now acted for a larger constituency of Kanadier Mennonites, Ukrainians, and others in the district who sought his assistance with tax issues, roads, livestock, and building permits. His promotion of Ward 6's interests is apparent in council resolutions that included road improvements and the resurveying of Grunthal town, central not just to Russländer but also to the economic development of the entire area. But as Russländer gained full ownership of their land, his work for the Company decreased and as Russländer assemblies became less important, Rempel's influence waned. Mennonite respect for persons in power was always tenuous; "Kaiser" Rempel, like Germany's last imperial ruler, looked increasingly as if he had lost his crown. The increased politicization of municipal affairs apparent from the late 1920s onward, however, cannot be attributed solely to the presence of Russländer. The emigration of conservative Mennonites resulted in changes to the social fabric of the East Reserve and altered the outlook of remaining Mennonites which, when combined with improved education and the rapid development of Steinbach as an economic hub, were probably as important as the presence of Russländer.[26]

During the late nineteenth and early twentieth centuries Mennonites in Russia were informed of political events occurring within and outside their country although they had limited experience of national elections or democratic processes as long as Russia remained an autocratic state. This was until 1905/06 when publishing in Russia became more open. It is often claimed that the Mennonites' congregational system was "democratic," but this was not so. Those who held congregational office were often chosen from a limited set of candidates drawn mainly from leading members of the community. Women also had no direct say in congregational elections. In Mennonite local government elections before 1914 the franchise was restricted to landowning males so the poor and landless were excluded as well as most females. As Russia moved towards democracy a small number of Mennonites became involved in local and eventually national politics. Some were chosen as mayors of major cities, and after 1906 others joined newly formed political parties and were elected to the Russian Parliament.

Although a small number of Russländer immigrants to Canada were politicized their direct experience of politics beyond their communities was extremely limited. In Russia Mennonites had been concerned more with asserting and protecting their privileges as a religious and cultural group, than becoming politically active. Direct involvement in politics was restricted to a small, educated elite as before 1914 most older Mennonites remained deeply suspicious of any parliamentary system and instead supported the autocratic rule of the tsar, God's ordained ruler. Similar attitudes prevailed in Canada among older Russländer, not just regarding the Romanov dynasty, but also the British monarchy. British politicians, however, were widely disliked, especially Winston Churchill who was thought to have failed to aid the White forces fighting the Bolsheviks. It followed that many Russländer in Canada also remained suspicious of popular democracy. Their distrust increased as it was clear an English and French-Canadian ruling elite dominated political affairs.

In Canada Russländer encountered a more established democratic system than in Russia at the municipal level and beyond in provincial and federal elections. The East Reserve and later the municipality lay within the federal riding of Provencher and the provincial constituency of Carillon, the latter divided in 1969 into the constituencies of La Vérendrye and Emerson. Although Kanadier Mennonite names appear on voters' rolls, on religious grounds they rarely turned out to vote. In Provencher federal elections held between 1887 and 1911, only 12 per cent of registered voters, most of them non-Mennonites, voted and it is estimated that only 3 per cent of Chortitzer congregational members voted.[27] Although this situation had begun to change by the time Russländer arrived, once the immigrants obtained citizenship, usually five years after their arrival, most entered their names on electoral rolls and voted in provincial and federal elections. To many Russländer Canadian politics appeared complex and confusing because its populist nature was so different from their experience in Russia. Canadian politics was often chaotic during the 1920s and 1930s, especially in western prairie provinces. This occurred in both provincial and federal elections. Power shifted between conservative and liberal political parties while new alliances and new political parties materialized, some of which represented regional interests, and others social and interest groups. But around Grunthal there was a degree of stability and continuity in elections until the 1940s, dominated not by most Mennonite voters but by Manitoban French and English interests. The provincial district of Carillon was represented almost continually by Albert Prefontaine, at first a member of the Conservative Party, then a member of the United Farmers of Manitoba, and finally as a member of the Liberal Progressive Party. In 1935 he was succeeded by his son, Edmond Prefontaine, who held the post as a Liberal Progressive, then as an Independent Liberal, and finally as a Liberal until 1962.[28] Federal politics followed a similar pattern with Arthur Lucien Beaubien, a farmer, holding the seat from 1925 to 1940 as a Liberal or Liberal Progressive, and then by René Jutras, a teacher and Liberal, who succeeded him until 1957.[29]

As in other regions where Russländer settled in established Kanadier Mennonite districts, such as the West Reserve, their presence dramatically increased local voter turnout and in regions without Kanadier, they were also keen to exercise their franchise.[30] In the Grunthal area where some Kanadier were registered as well as most French Manitobans and numerous Ukrainians, full participation by Mennonites would not arrive until the late 1940s. However, Russländer who were eligible to vote undoubtedly did so from the early 1930s on.[31] Federal voting rolls for 1935 and 1940 clearly indicate that most Mennonites listed in the Grunthal district were Russländer. In 1935 Grunthal people voted in Sarto along with Ukrainians, but from 1940 onward they voted in Grunthal. The overall voting patterns of Russländer in provincial or federal elections can be identified for the 1930s with reasonable accuracy. Most Russländer in Manitoba voted overwhelmingly for Liberal Progressive candidates (see table 7.1).

The voting pattern appears to confirm anecdotal evidence that the first generation of Russländer tended to vote Liberal because in the 1920s the Liberal prime minister Mackenzie King and his party had permitted them to enter Canada. Apocryphal stories also abound of leaders exhorting members during congregational services to vote Liberal. The stories are retold by later generations to emphasize the political naivety of their

Table 7.1. Voting percentages according to political parties in federal, provincial elections in Provencher and Carillon, 1930–6

Year	1930 (F)			1932 (Prov)		1935 (F)		1936 (Prov)	
Party	L	Con	O	LP	Con	L	Con	LP	Con
P/C v%	58	29	13	80	20	63	37	65	35
eMv%	Nk	Nk	Nk	91	9	61	39	53	47
Gv%	Nk	Nk	Nk	Nk	Nk	81	19	84	16

Notes: Voting percentages according to political parties in federal (F) and provincial elections (Prov) in Provencher (P) and Carillon I, 1930–6. (L = Liberal, LP = Liberal Progressive, Con = Conservative, O = Other; v = votes, eMv = estimated Mennonite votes, Gv = Grunthal votes [in 1935 Grunthaler voted in Sarto with Ukrainians], Nk = not known.)

Sources: Scarrow, *Canada Votes*, 85, 99; *History of the Federal Electoral Ridings*; Gordon Driedger, "South-East Reserve Voting Trends 1920–1986, Provincial Elections Manitoba" (unpublished paper, Canadian Mennonite Bible College, 1987) in MHA, Vertical Files; AM Legislative Assembly, Voting Patterns, GR 430 G 2880 gives slightly different figures for Carillon for the period 1922–45 than Driedger, who used contemporary newspaper reports.

parents, although these have been challenged in a study of changing Mennonite voting patterns for the West Reserve.[32] The strong support for Liberals during the 1930s around Grunthal, however, may reflect other factors than a continued sense of loyalty to the Liberal Party. The presence of long-established figures in office such as the Prefontaines, the succession of father and son, probably appealed to Russländer who valued kinship connections and generational succession.

In Russia a proverb known to most adult Russländer claimed "God is on high and the tsar is far away." The concerns of political parties in Winnipeg or Ottawa were also "far away." Political matters within their local community and those concerned with municipal affairs were of primary interest to Kanadier, Russländer, and others on the East Reserve. The local German-language newspaper published in Steinbach carried little on politics and where it did its focus was on municipal affairs, the building of major roads, and the installation of electrical power by the province. In terms of the latter the local member of the legislature favoured his core French constituency who would receive such benefits long before Mennonites because it appeared Mennonites were unlikely to influence his re-election as he assumed they did not vote. Also, at this period Ottawa's reach into local affairs was still extremely limited. During the 1920s and 30s most Russländer did not understand federal politics and for a long time Russländer viewed it as a system that operated mainly for the benefit of English Canadians, not for new immigrants like themselves.

Before the outbreak of the First World War Mennonites in Russia had read newspaper reports on international affairs. The outbreak of the First World War, the revolution, and Civil War thrust Mennonites from the role of distant observers of such matters into participants in world events. After immigration Russländer continued to receive regular communications from relatives in the Soviet Union including the occasional Soviet newspaper. But as communications became irregular, Russländer continued to submit letters received from relatives in the USSR to Mennonite newspapers in Canada so others could learn about friends and relatives. During the 1930s, however, people were forced to be more circumspect as they understood that the publication of anything from the USSR might compromise those still living under Soviet rule. Mennonite newspapers controlled by Russländer editors provided insight and opinion on foreign affairs especially on events in the Soviet Union and increasingly in Germany. Other German non-Mennonite newspapers subscribed to by Russländer and published in Canada, such as the *Nordwesten*, founded in Winnipeg in 1889, and the *Courier*, founded in 1907 in Saskatchewan, also carried extensive reports on European politics especially on Germany.[33] Russländer interest in events in the USSR and Germany, however, was increasingly combined with other issues concerned with their identity.

Chapter Eight

Conflicted Identities

Social identity involves ideas of being and belonging acquired through membership of groups. Identities are defined by gender, age, and relationships of kinship, inherited status, or status acquired through education often closely related to occupation.[1] All human groups, including Mennonites, have possessed these basic forms of identity although life in a community of believers intensified connections when members remained separated from the "world." Religion for Mennonites therefore played a crucial role in identity formation and although in principle a person chose their religious affiliation as a young adult by accepting baptism, for most the choice was a result of socialization in a family and community of believers. While religion had been crucial to the Mennonite sense of being and belonging, it was not the only source of Russländer identity as before immigration they had been exposed to other forms.

Most Mennonites in Russia before 1914 lived in villages situated in colonies that provided an additional identity beyond kinship and congregation. When Mennonites were born and raised in locations such as a private estate or an urban centre indirectly connected with either their parents' or grandparents' colony or village, they and their descendants usually continued to identify with a particular colony where relatives resided. This was also required because as Russian subjects they had to hold passports even for internal travel, and after the 1880s Mennonite males liable for alternative service frequently were registered in their ancestral settlements.

By the end of the nineteenth century Mennonite religious identities in Russia involved not just association with a single congregation, but also larger parish-like groupings linked with larger conferences of affiliated congregations. The conferences took on a denominational appearance where members recognized a common confession. A network of regional and general religious conferences brought Mennonites together but differences between Church Mennonites and Mennonite Brethren remained. Before 1914 the leaders of different Mennonite religious groups established a Commission for Church Affairs (HG *Kommission für kirchliche Angelegenheiten* or *KfK*) to overcome long-standing religious differences among Mennonite groups and move towards a common confession of faith. It was hoped this would ultimately bring all Mennonites into a united alliance under a single system with equal representation, but it failed to gain total support.[2]

The attempt at unity, although made in a spirit of reconciliation by liberal-minded leaders, was primarily motivated by external events rather than by popular support from lay members of congregations. In 1905 the Russian government signalled its intention to reclassify Mennonites as a sect rather than as a confession because they lacked a central religious organization or a common confession of faith, a move that threatened the privileges Mennonites had hitherto enjoyed.[3] The religious divisions among Mennonites proved difficult to resolve even after the Bolsheviks gained power and the *KfK* attempted to continue its work. Jacob H. Janzen, later leader of Russländer in Ontario, revealed in a highly critical unpublished account of the *KfK* how this unity largely failed.[4]

By the late nineteenth century, the Mennonite sense of being and belonging in Russia extended to a larger Mennonite community beyond the country's boundaries as improved means of communication brought Mennonites across the world into closer contact. This was achieved mainly through Mennonite newspapers and journals published in Germany and North America subscribed to by Mennonites in Russia. Similar publications printed in Russia appeared only after the 1905 revolution once official censorship eased.[5] External political pressure from the Russian government and critical articles in influential Russian journals forced Mennonites to conceive of themselves as a persecuted people. Earlier, during the first half of the nineteenth century, matters had been very different. Mennonites were recognized as just another enclave within the multi-ethnic empire belonging to the category of "foreign colonists," specifically those from German-speaking lands who were deemed "German colonists." As the nineteenth century advanced a new category of "Russian Germans" emerged that included German-speakers from Russia's Baltic states.[6]

Towards the end of the nineteenth century, however, a single national identity was promoted in popular and official circles that called for a greater integration of subjects into a distinct Russian, Slav, national identity with an emphasis on the Orthodox faith. Mennonites reacted to this situation in several ways.⁷ At one level many aspects of official Russianization were rejected, a move that further reinforced a sense that Mennonites needed a separate united identity. However, as Mennonites increasingly became involved in the economic and social life of the rapidly industrializing Russia, they also became more patriotic. Therefore, the powerful forces of nationalism created a new sense of being and belonging in addition to Mennonite identification with religion, denomination, and colony.⁸

The First World War and the chaos that followed the Russian Revolution made many Mennonites question their identity, especially as they were accused of disloyalty and being pro-German. When German and Austrian troops occupied their settlements in 1918, Mennonites were deeply impressed by their discipline and the restoration of order. Given the situation in Russia some Mennonite leaders believed they might acquire German citizenship and emigrate to Germany, even if this would entail a change in identity.⁹ Representatives were sent to Germany to investigate the possibility of resettlement and at the time a Mennonite wrote in his diary that "we are Ukrainian since we live or were born here" but Mennonites could "still be able to become German citizens." However, as nothing was certain, Mennonites should "place [their] confidence in the Lord, 'who doeth all things well,' instead of on Germany and the Germans."¹⁰

The writer was correct to doubt German intentions as when they withdrew, Mennonites were exposed to renewed attacks. The triumph of the Bolsheviks and the establishment of a new order added an additional dimension to questions of Mennonite identity as they discovered they were now Soviet citizens living in different republics of the USSR. Those in southern Russia became members of the Ukrainian Soviet Socialist Republic governed from Kharkov/Kharkiv; others, living in the Crimea and outside Ukraine in areas like Siberia, were now members of the Russian Soviet Socialist Republic. No Mennonite was explicitly "Russian" in the sense they had been before the revolution. Although many hoped the Bolshevik regime would not last long, few wished a return to the imperial regime or the chaos they had endured following its collapse.

In papers prepared for discussions over the possibility of emigration once peace was restored, the issue of identity was raised in relation to possible places where Mennonites might settle outside Russia. Peter Braun, an influential schoolteacher, suggested "Mennonites no longer had a fatherland in Russia" and that even before the First World War several countries for possible resettlement had been discussed in the Mennonite press.¹¹ Braun reminded Mennonites that subsequent events had rudely confirmed they were "no more than tolerated strangers" in Russia, even while they had "conscientiously fulfilled ... [their] civic responsibilities."[12] A.A. Friesen, who had been selected as one of those sent abroad to seek new lands for resettlement, also reflected on questions of Mennonite identity. Writing from Herbert in Saskatchewan in June 1921 he suggested that the "basis of our national identity is Dutch," not German, and indeed the "rather widespread assumption among us that we are German is a false one." He argued it was impossible for Russian Mennonites to settle in Germany but instead suggested that either the USA or Canada might be better places to consider. However, Mennonite immigrants from Russia would need to recognize these were English-speaking countries and in the long term they would have to accept an accommodation "in the good sense of the word."[13] During the 1920s most Mennonites on their way to Canada did not stop over in Germany as many departed from Baltic ports, so most Russländer had little direct experience of Germany, a country where hyperinflation followed the end of the war. In Canada, however, Russländer faced new, often conflicting, demands on their identify.

The Mennonite rush to Moscow in 1929 coincided with the onset of the Depression and few were permitted to enter Canada.[14] The German government issued around six thousand mostly temporary visas, many to Mennonites, to enter Germany before seeking new homes, particularly in Brazil or Paraguay.[15] This became known as the German "rescue" of Mennonites, and in Canada had a profound effect on Russländer opinion of Germany especially as it coincided with reports from the Soviet Union of collectivization and the arrest of many Mennonites. The help Mennonites received was reinforced by what increasingly was claimed to be the underlying "Germanness" of being Mennonite. This was summed up in the sentiments of an ode of thanks to the Mennonites' "German brothers" for the rescue of their brethren from Bolshevism. It was written by J.P. Klassen, Elder of the Schönwiese congregation in Winnipeg, where he contrasted Germany to the Soviet Union, a land where now:

Satan commands and governs
And Beelzebub stokes the fire.[16]

Reports from Germany in the early 1930s also spoke of a struggle between communist and conservative forces, the former backed by the Soviet Union and the latter represented by the National Socialist Party and its fellow travellers. Confrontations between these opposing forces often involved violent street battles as the Weimer Republic collapsed. These events did not go unnoticed by Russländer.[17] Even before he assumed power in 1933, Russländer were aware of Hitler and the editor of one newspaper editorialized on Hitler in response to numerous enquiries received from readers. While he warned against direct involvement in worldly politics, he suggested people should remain informed on developments in Germany.[18] Hitler's accession to power and the apparent achievements of the New Germany were now regularly reported in Mennonite and other Canadian German-language newspapers. The renewal of Germany under Hitler after Germany's defeat in the First World War and its humiliation under the provisions of the Treaty of Versailles increased support for the Nazi regime and its conservative values. The latter appeared to include Christian ideals and opposition to Communist atheism reflected in the Nazis' anti-Soviet policies. Writing from Germany, the Russian Mennonite leader B.H. Unruh even claimed Hitler was a peace-loving Christian.[19] Nazi ideas and policies greatly appealed to many Russländer and German Mennonites with whom some Russländer communicated.[20] German and Russländer Mennonites in Canada viewed themselves as victims of the First World War and were eager to reclaim their lost sense of pride, regain a place of importance in the world, and fulfil their destiny.

Russländer identification with the New Germany often involved an implicit criticism of Canada, its English traditions, and above all its democratic institutions. The spirit of anti-liberalism which emerged in Europe following the First World War was aimed at the inheritance of the nineteenth century, its promotion of social reform, and its modernism in art and music.[21] Such anti-liberalism struck a chord with conservative Russländer who viewed ideas of the equality of the sexes, evolutionary ideas, and jazz as a threat to Christian faith and family values. Mennonite reports on jazz, for instance, closely resembled Nazi views.[22] A newspaper report of a choir festival held in Grunthal in 1939 described jazz as "Niggermusik," the music of African "savages" and contrasted it with the fine singing of "our [Mennonite] people (*Volk*)."[23] To avoid assimilation to such vulgar North American culture, Russländer, like Germany, needed strong leaders. One Winnipeg Russländer, J.J. Hildebrand, went even further and suggested that as all Mennonites were "racially" German, they needed to separate themselves entirely from foreign influences, not by forming a closed group founded on faith, but by creating an exclusive state for the "Mennovolk." His views were strongly influenced by an idealized vision of the lost Russian Mennonite Commonwealth now informed by Nazi ideology.[24]

Another aspect of Germanness and Mennonite ideas of identity involved antisemitism. While antisemitism had been a feature of late tsarist society, as it indeed was for many Europeans, it is difficult to clearly identify antisemitism among Mennonites before 1914 apart from passing negative comments on Jews in their publications. Following the revolution and subsequent events, Bolshevik leaders were widely identified as Jews, part of a wider Jewish "conspiracy" to foment worldwide revolution.[25] Some Russländer easily adopted such ideas as explanations of what happened to them in Russia and Nazi antisemitism merely provided an addition to their sense of conspiracy.[26] Nazi thinking on race, however, extended beyond Jews to include Roma, people worthy of extermination, and others classified to be of Slavic descent, and physically and intellectually impaired. All threatened the purity of the Aryan "master race" ideas that during the Second World War would have lethal consequences for entire populations. Some Mennonites who left the USSR in 1929 were subjected to "scientific" racial study and identified as Aryan.[27] Some Russländer changed their names to remove any association with Jews or Slavs. Many Mennonite forenames were derived from those in the Bible and were changed. In Canada an Isaak who considered his surname too Jewish changed it to Janzen and in another case a Sawatzky who thought his surname sounded Slavic, changed it to Siemens.[28] An educated Russian Mennonite in Germany changed his forename from Jacob to Walter Quiring before Hitler came to power.[29]

The rise of the Nazis coincided with a marked increase in Russländer concerns over their future, fuelled by the Depression. Their concerns centred on the continuance of the Mennonites' "German" culture, its connection with Russländer identity, and the future of their Mennonite faith.[30] The increasing Russländer passion for things German and interest in Hitler's regime was further encouraged by the Nazi state in its drive towards developing contacts with "Germans living abroad" (*Auslanddeutsche*) and the Mennonites received special attention from Nazi organizations.[31] In Nazi thinking, anyone of German descent was linked to their German Fatherland (*Vaterland*), its people (*Volk*), and its culture (*Kultur*), and was therefore German, a member of a single community, even if they lived abroad. All Germans living outside Germany (*Volkstumsgruppen im Ausland*) ultimately were to return to the German homeland in the new empire (*Heim ins Reich*). German embassies and consulates abroad were charged with spreading Nazi propaganda and supporting German cultural activities.

A separate organization, the *Deutsche Ausland-Institut*, now devoted itself to collecting information on and maintaining links to German communities outside the German Fatherland, including Canada.[32] The work included supplying books of classical German literature, popular novels approved by the Nazis, men's and women's magazines, and a range of other material. Between 1934 and 1938 there was a *Verband der Deutschen aus Russland* (Union of Germans from Russia) that communicated directly with some Mennonites in Canada.[33] The literature included pamphlets of speeches of Nazi leaders, opinions on racial and political issues, and details of the wonderful new society the Nazis were building. As in Germany, particular attention was paid to the young, with prizes of books and pens awarded to any who showed excellence in the German language. Most Russländer welcomed these new sources of material as many were free and eased the sense of isolation, boredom, and despair of the Depression.

CMBC encouraged immigrants to establish libraries and between 1923 and 1944, when it ceased operations, ZMIK distributed over 121,000 books, mostly in German.[34] Whether the books provided included Nazi texts is unclear, but Grunthal's Russländer library included Nazi material including a copy of Hitler's *Mein Kampf*.[35] Events such as "German Days" held in provincial centres allowed Mennonites to meet German Canadians and to enjoy themselves away from the farm and businesses. These gradually became dominated by Nazi supporters and in Winnipeg they were addressed by the German consul, Dr. Heinrich Seelheim, on the wonders of the "New Germany."[36] A fascist action group, the German Union of Canada (*Deutsche Bund Kanada*), was established.[37] In Winnipeg some young Mennonites were involved in clashes between pro-fascist and anti-fascist supporters, including Jewish activist groups. Out in the countryside there were few opportunities to be directly involved and little reason for Russländer to join political groups. However, they were increasingly exposed to Nazi propaganda. The *Bund* published a newspaper (*Deutsche Zeitung für Canada*) financed by the German government to promote Nazi views. A few urban Russländer became shareholders in the newspaper which was printed on the presses of the *Mennonitische Rundschau* in Winnipeg. A small and ineffective English fascist group also made contacts with the *Bund* and Russländer in Winkler and some of the group's antisemitic material was printed by the editor of the *Rundschau*, Hermann H. Neufeld, who was subsequently prosecuted for his involvement. He claimed he knew little English, so was unaware of its contents.[38] It is a pity his prosecutors could not read German and what he published in the *Rundschau* and printed in the *Deutsche Zeitung Kanada*.

The most obvious public sign of Mennonite interest in Nazi ideas, however, was found in the Russländer's own newspapers, journals, and books. A very popular and widely circulated book was Heinrich H. Schröder's *Russlanddeutsche Friesen*, which contained a brief history of

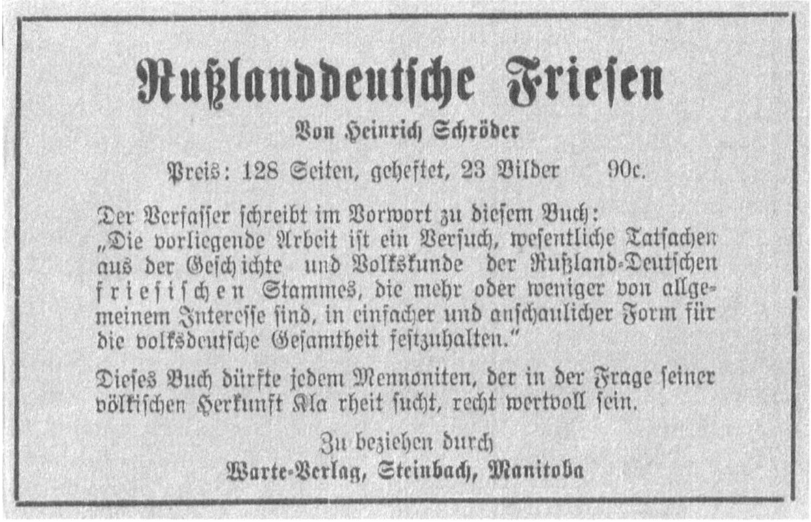

Rußlanddeutsche Friesen
Von Heinrich Schröder

Preis: 128 Seiten, geheftet, 23 Bilder   90c.

Der Verfasser schreibt im Vorwort zu diesem Buch:
„Die vorliegende Arbeit ist ein Versuch, wesentliche Tatsachen aus der Geschichte und Volkskunde der Rußland-Deutschen friesischen Stammes, die mehr oder weniger von allgemeinem Interesse sind, in einfacher und anschaulicher Form für die volksdeutsche Gesamtheit festzuhalten."

Dieses Buch dürfte jedem Mennoniten, der in der Frage seiner völkischen Herkunft Kla rheit sucht, recht wertvoll sein.

Zu beziehen durch
Warte-Verlag, Steinbach, Manitoba

Fig. 8.1. Advertisement for a Mennonite Nazi book. Advertisement for Heinrich H. Schröder's *Russlanddeutsche Friesen*, which promoted Nazi views on the purity of race, that appeared in a number of issues of the *Mennonitische Volkswarte* published by Arnold Dyck in Steinbach.

Source: *Mennonitische Volkswarte* 2, no. 23 (November 1936), back cover.

the Russian Mennonites within a framework of Nazi racial thought and claimed Mennonites were of "pure" Frisian descent (fig. 8.1).[39] Schröder was a teacher of Mennonite Russian descent in Germany, and the book has a photograph of him in a Nazi uniform wearing a swastika armband.[40] Arnold Dyck sold Schröder's book from his bookshop in Steinbach along with other books from Nazi Germany, and published articles by Schröder in his cultural journal, the *Mennonitische Volkswarte*. He also reviewed Schröder's book positively and suggested everyone should read it, irrespective of how they felt about their own identity: German, Frisian, Dutch, Canadian, or American.[41] Throughout the 1930s Russländer newspapers carried numerous articles and reports that argued because Mennonites were of German descent they should be aligned with Hitler's regime.[42] Most were written by a small number of Russländer sympathizers of Hitler and his regime. The articles identified dangers posed by the Jews and "Bolshevism" and some praised alleged Nazi support of German churches. The dangers of German militarism and rearmament was barely mentioned and when negative reports on

Nazi Germany appeared in English-language Canadian newspapers, one Russländer wrote letters openly defending Hitler's regime and condemning communism.[43]

Support for the Nazis, however, did not go unanswered. From the outset several Russländer leaders protested the antisemitic, militaristic, and anti-Christian tone of Nazi ideology. They warned Mennonites against reports published from sources taken directly from Nazi propaganda agencies or submitted to Russländer newspapers by a small clique of Nazi supporters. The counter-reaction mostly came from congregational leaders. On the West Reserve members of the Blumenort congregation were warned explicitly not to join Nazi groups. In Grunthal, however, while there was interest in these issues, no explicit warnings were issued although the Elder responsible for the Elim congregation, Peter H. Enns of St. Elizabeth, grew increasingly concerned about the nature of German-language material circulating among members of the congregations he served. The most important figure to oppose support of the Nazi regime and the idea that the ancestors of Mennonites were German rather than Dutch, was B.B. Janz, leader of the Ukrainian Mennonite organization before he immigrated to Canada that had dealt with the early Bolshevik government. A highly respected member of the Mennonite Brethren, Janz voiced his concerns about Mennonite identification with the Nazi regime as early as 1934 and shortly before the start of the Second World War he issued another strong warning.[44] The opposition of Russländer Mennonite leaders was focused on political issues rather than on the cultural aspects of Germanness, but the issue of Germanness and its links to the Nazi regime polarized Russländer communities. Very few Kanadier, however, were interested in or supported such ideas as they considered them as another manifestation of Russländer fantasies concerned with identity beyond just being a people true to the faith of their ancestors.

The politics of Germanness that played out in Russländer newspaper debates from the late 1920s onward and the increasing influence of Nazi ideas as the 1930s advanced had several implications for Russländer identities in Canada and elsewhere. It encouraged individual supporters of the Nazis in Canada to align themselves with a country, a political system, and an ideology of which very few had direct experience. What they knew about Nazi Germany, its leaders, its ideas, and actions was gained mainly from newspaper reports, propaganda pamphlets, or by listening to an occasional radio broadcast. A few who emigrated from Russia and settled in Germany, like Schröder, strongly identified with the Nazi regime based on their direct experience.[45] Living in Germany, people like B.H. Unruh wrote numerous articles on Nazi

Germany for Russländer newspapers. In Paraguay and Brazil those who left the Soviet Union in the late 1920s strongly identified with the Nazi regime and its views on race and identity.[46] They placed secular, cultural, and political interests over religious concerns, even when the Nazis claimed to support all Christian churches while at the same time attempting to establish a German Evangelical Church aligned with its own ideologies.[47]

Direct support of the New Germany in Grunthal, as opposed to general support in certain quarters, is difficult to trace from surviving records. Some groups of Russländer from Grunthal attended German Days in Winnipeg, sharing rides in cars or using the transfer service. Among them was Peter Klassen, who was such a keen supporter that he was nicknamed "Hitler Klassen" (LG *Hitler Klause*). In 1936 one Grunthal correspondent to the *Mennonitische Rundschau* claimed grandly that local "Hitler Youth" (HG *Hitler Jugend*) in Grunthal had driven a local Jewish storekeeper from town.[48] There was no Jewish storekeeper in Grunthal in 1936 although Jewish peddlers still visited the area. Alternatively, the incident, if it occurred, may have involved local children baiting the offspring of the previous Jewish shopkeeper Gerstein and a local woman. The reliability of the report might also be judged by the correspondent's local nickname, "Cottage-Cheese-Head Neufeld" (LG *Glomm'skopp Niefeld*) or "Idiot Neufeld."

Of greater significance is the reliable report that one late immigrant to Grunthal refused to take out Canadian citizenship and instead registered himself and his family with the German consul in Winnipeg as Germans in the 1930s. After the Second World War this created problems for his family when they applied for Canadian passports. Before the outbreak of the Second World War Russländer in the area either returned or sent their young "home" to Germany. This included Arnold Dyck, previously in Steinbach, who sent his family to Germany just before the outbreak of war. He was delayed in Canada and was unable to join them but in Germany his son Otto was subsequently conscripted into the German army and ironically sent to fight on the eastern front close to where his father had been born.[49] Bruno Hamm, who immigrated to Canada in 1911 from Germany, returned to the country in 1939 to visit his ill father but was unable to return before war was declared. He later claimed he was held in the Sachsenhausen concentration camp but later released and only after the war returned to Grunthal.[50]

The differences between Kanadier and Russländer regarding identity beyond the immediate social level were marked. Mennonites who immigrated to North America in the 1870s took with them aspects of the village and colony system: although for most the village system soon collapsed in the imagination, it was remembered as an ideal form of community. Villages and colonies were often recreated when Mennonites emigrated from Canada to Latin America. What did survive the break-up of most villages in Manitoba, however, were the two Reserves largely inhabited by Mennonites that appeared to resemble Russian Mennonite colonies. Even when the Reserves ceased to exist as official legal entities, they continued as important foci of Mennonite identity and Russländer also recognized their existence in name as historical survivals. In Canada Mennonites of earlier immigrations than the Russländer largely rejected close relations with the state and association with non-Mennonites. Conservative Kanadier avoided the development of national identities although this was more apparent in Canada than in the United States where, by the early years of the twentieth century, several descendants of 1870s immigrants were active in local, state, and even national politics. Mennonites in Canada before the First World War continued to see themselves as a separate people connected primarily to a local congregation, a particular settlement, and place but little else. Conservative Kanadier hardly identified as Canadians, citizens of a dominion linked to a British Empire.[51]

In terms of religious identity, among the Kanadier congregational groupings took a long time to form larger conferences and a number remained opposed to conferences when the Russländer first arrived. Cooperation between Mennonite Brethren and Church Mennonites among Russländer proved as difficult in Canada as it had been in Russia as differences between them re-emerged in many areas, including Manitoba, and religious affiliation became an issue of Russländer identity.[52] Divisions between conferences of Church Mennonites and Mennonite Brethren at the provincial and national levels fragmented allegiances among and between Russländer. In Alberta an effort was made to unite Russländer from Allianz, the new Mennonite religious grouping that had formed in pre-revolutionary Russia, and Mennonite Brethren backgrounds, but this was soon abandoned.[53] Differences between Church and Brethren were eventually reinforced in other areas, for instance in education when separate high schools, including separate Bible colleges, were eventually established. Russländer members of Grunthal's Elim congregation before immigration were overwhelmingly Church Mennonite and practically all Mennonite Brethren who settled in the Grunthal area soon left the district to join Brethren communities elsewhere. Any who remained were isolated and forced either to attend congregational services outside the district or attend Elim and accept its practices, for instance about baptism. Some acquired nicknames that ridiculed their faith: for instance, one member of the Mennonite Brethren acquired the name "Pious Friesen" (LG *Fromma Friese*).

The lack of religious solidarity and a single identity among Russländer was not just a result of a failure to achieve religious unity in Russia but also involved other factors. These included the mixing of Russian Mennonites from different areas of settlement and congregations in the Soviet Union. But the division was also a consequence of Mennonite stubbornness and the conservative and illiberal tendencies of some religious leaders and many older lay Russländer. Finally, the existence of major religious divisions among Kanadier, some formed in Russia before the 1870s and others in North America, further complicated the issue. In Ontario Mennonites and Amish from entirely different backgrounds shared little with Russländer but often proved more welcoming to them than conservative Kanadier on the prairies.[54] Russländer found it almost impossible to join local conservative Kanadier congregations especially in Manitoba and Saskatchewan. But the presence of a strong, well-organized Conference of Mennonite Brethren in North America, founded by late Mennonite immigrants from Russia, quickly eroded any attempt to maintain religious unity between Brethren and Church Russländer.

Academic discussion of Mennonite identity is often based on debates of the "learned" in newspapers and literary studies. But folk aspects also need to be considered. An example of folk views can be seen in a short story by Jack Thiessen, an expert on Mennonite Low German. He starts with a question: "What is a Mennonite, you ask?" and continues to answer it from the stony ground close to Grunthal where he was born and where he grew up. Thiessen writes that a "Mennonite is ... a person of human persuasion who speaks Low German and who patronizes a bonesetter" (LG *trajchtmoaka*). Thiessen also produced another definition: "At pay-up time, a Mennonite is a person of human persuasion whose billfold usually contracts a bad case of constipation."[55] The importance of such ideas is that most, if not all, first-generation Russländer in Grunthal remained closer to the folk traditions of their Low German ancestors than perhaps many were willing to admit.

Another important aspect of identity in Canada concerned language. By the time of Russländer settlement, some Kanadier were competent in English and possessed a knowledge of English-speaking society. In the Grunthal area, however, this varied and many Kanadier still preferred to remain apart from the English world and its language, one indication of which involved their effort to maintain control of their German-language schools. The Russländer believed they could control the situation of schooling in English and indeed even benefit from it through establishing contacts with the English Canadian world. In Russia their strategy had been to control the influence of Russian while developing extensive contacts with Russian society. Older Mennonites in Russia living in established colonies with mostly Mennonite neighbours had fewer contacts with Russian society than those living outside and engaged in industry. Compared with the younger generation they spoke Russian with a German accent, but many Russländer were competent in spoken and written Russian at the time of immigration to Canada. However, the Russian language was not passed on to the next generation in Canada as most Russländer considered the most important thing was to maintain High German while learning English.

They soon realized, however, that the influence of English, more closely related to German and Low German than either Russian or Ukrainian had been in their old homeland, was difficult to control among young people. One Mennonite suggested that the importance of educating children in High German was to counter the influence of English because English, unlike German, was not a "pure language." The writer insisted German was essential for Mennonite "peoplehood" (HG *Volkstum*), as it was connected to the very "essence" (HG *Deutsches Wesen*) of what it meant to be "German."[56] Another complained that children picked up English so easily that the need to maintain a good German in Mennonite homes, schools, and churches was imperative.[57] Similar opinions were expressed in the Mennonite press dating back to the 1920s.[58] The matter was also discussed in Rosthern, Saskatchewan, centre of Russländer immigrant organizations.[59] English was, however, the language of public life as the largest English-speaking group in Manitoba were Canadians of British descent and they constituted the political and economic elite of society both in Manitoba and in all the provinces settled by Russländer. As long as it was to their advantage and on their own terms, most Russländer were eager to learn English and to adapt to the ways of the dominant English society. But there were problems with too much assimilation. The most obvious problem lay with gaining competence in the English language at the expense of German. Those who favoured the English language and English ways potentially betrayed not just the Mennonite faith, but also, especially for the Russländer, their German roots founded in language and culture.

The maintenance of High German and the future of the Mennonite faith were closely related to the preservation of a distinct Mennonite identity. Although the sense of being "German" might have varied among Russländer they were more united on the need to preserve the High German language. This took on a special urgency in terms of the continued competence in the language among younger generations. Here the Mennonites faced several problems, some of which were clearly recognized by Russländer leaders. These included not just competition from English, but also from the continued use by many Russländer of Mennonite Low German. These concerns over language, language usage, and Mennonite identity had been present in pre-revolutionary Russia, and involved the attempts by some leaders to suppress Low German in favour of High German. Parents were encouraged to speak only High German to children at home and this often resulted in an odd situation where parents spoke Low German to each other, relatives, and neighbours of the same generation, but not to their own and other young children.

Reasons given for the emphasis on High German and suppression of Low German varied. Apart from the obvious connection between High German and religion there were also concerns with the growing influence of Russian like those later expressed in Canada with regard to English. But social and cultural factors were also involved. High German was seen as a real language linked to German culture and literature and with increased education and wealth some Mennonites acquired bourgeois attitudes and opinions, so High German, unlike Low German, was essential to the maintenance of social status. For Kanadier Low German was just part of their everyday world and although some Russländer shared this practical view, others did not, as Low German was a source of embarrassment and stood in the way of social advancement.

When he was a teacher in a prestigious girls' school in Russia before 1914, the minister Jacob H. Janzen wrote several comic plays on Mennonite life in Low German to be performed by his female pupils. In part this was a response to the language issue in Russia and to arguments suggesting that drama in Mennonite schools should not be permitted.[60] Janzen immigrated to Canada where he became an important Elder in Ontario and his literary writings, including his dramas, were republished along with new works which occasionally contained subtle shifts to reflect the Canadian worlds of Russländer. His works were well known to Russländer in Grunthal, and he continued to support Low German, lamenting that few "know Low German anymore and aren't even ashamed of it" but instead took pride "in their prodigious learning" by speaking "High German, English, [and] Russian." Such people he condemned as not "worth the rind of a ham."[61]

Therefore, Russländer transferred positive and negative attitudes towards their languages from Russia to Canada but extended them as the relationship between English and Mennonite identity became more critical. Some argued that High German should replace Low German while others continued to promote Low German, even if they were supporters of or sympathetic to the Nazi regime. An example of this was the former Khortitsa teacher Arnold Dyck who during the 1930s encouraged the development of Low German as a literary language, often in the form of comic stories. But Dyck's attitude towards the Nazis remained ambiguous. As editor of the Steinbach Mennonite newspaper and publisher of major Mennonite literary journals, he included articles written by supporters of the Nazis. Dyck also had strong links with some Russländer in Grunthal and recognized that their Low German was closely allied with Kanadier speech as their ancestors had similar Old Colony roots.

Differences in speech and attitudes to Low German thus were yet another source of division among Grunthal Russländer who came from different settlements in Russia. They also lived in a Low German world of Kanadier, who were often neighbours and close associates in certain situations. Low German in its expressions and meanings varied among Russländer and between Russländer and Kanadier. In the Grunthal area for instance, there were distinct dialectical differences recognizable to speakers and these acted as identifiers of different origins before and after immigration. Some claimed that Steinbach Mennonites pronounced Low German differently from Grunthal people. Most Steinbach Mennonites were members of the 1870s immigration of Kleine Gemeinde origin with connections to Molochna, whereas in other areas of the East Reserve, Chortitzer Mennonites, as their name suggests, were linked with Khortitsa. Initially within Grunthal there were also recognizable variations that went back to Russia and even to Prussia and that marked differences in origin, subsequent settlement, histories, religious affiliations, and social prejudices. The most marked divides between Molochna and Khortitsa dialects were in pronunciation, in word use, and even in degrees of bawdiness. Schönfelder spoke with a distinctly Molochna dialect and their attitude to Low German in relation to High German was often as ambiguous as it had been for many Molochna people in Late Imperial Russia.

The divide between High and Low German for Grunthal Russländer, while not unique, possessed its own significance. Russländer from Khortitsa or Khortitsa-based daughter settlements in Grunthal and surrounding areas were in closer social contact with their Kanadier neighbours than Molochna-linked Russländer. The situation varied from individual to individual and from family to family. Because many Chortitzer Kanadier lived on the margins, having either been left behind in the move to Paraguay or having returned, they were often poor, economically and socially, and this affected their relations with Russländer. Russländer who closely associated with Kanadier were not just from a similar Khortitsa background, but themselves were often living on the margins of a world dominated by Russländer with Molochna origins.

These social and economic factors also influenced relationships and nowhere more so than between young people. While parents may have wished their children not to associate with Kanadier, especially those of a poorer background, this could not easily be prevented, especially in marginal areas of settlement or at school. Russländer children growing up in circumstances of poverty could become rapidly declassed in relation to their parents' former status and consequently their sense of identity underwent a transformation. Nowhere was this clearer than among those growing up in the so-called "Chaco," the bushy, stony areas to the south of Grunthal, although not restricted to this area. A good example involved Peter Block, son of Jacob Block, the well-educated schoolteacher in Russia who, unable to retrain in Canada, lived in poverty. Life for the family became increasingly difficult during the Depression so Peter grew up with little parental control, and by the late 1930s was associating with other young Kanadier who lived without the authority of their parents. Together the youths pulled pranks on sections of the community, stealing alcohol from local bachelors as they attempted to "run" it into Grunthal. Peter left school early with little formal education and sought work not with other Mennonites, least of all other Russländer, who he claimed did not treat hired people well. Instead, he chose to work for English farmers and one day simply left home on a bicycle with just an extra clean shirt and joined a threshing team, one of many that every year moved across the prairie as grain crops ripened.[62]

The issue of the discipline of children other than one's own was difficult. To mention concerns with neighbours might point to their failure as parents and their inability to exercise proper authority. Deacons might raise concerns with parents and ministers preach on the issue in general terms, but in public no one was named even if most adults were aware of what was going on and who was involved. Schoolteachers might discipline children in school, as this was their domain, but never outside. As Jack Thiessen noted in one story: "You can cheat a Mennonite, you can insult him [,] and you can glance askance at his wife, and all that might be forgiven and often is, but if you propose to question his divine authority in the raising of his children, you are taking your life into your hands."[63]

Faced with the difficulties of adapting to a new country, a new language and coping with poverty, Russländer parents had to seek a solution for the social problems of wayward children who could not identify with their parents' concerns. It was difficult for children of Russländer, born just before or after immigration, to identify with the feelings their parents had for Russia and their sudden newfound interest in Germany and the Nazis. Unlike their parents they had no direct knowledge of the Mennonite Russian world before the First World War or the terrible events that followed the revolutions of 1917. But like their parents they also had no direct knowledge or experience of the Soviet Union under Stalin's rule, or of Germany and Hitler's Nazi regime. For children all the things that appeared to dominate their parents' discussions and constant search for an identity seemed at odds with their own experiences growing up in Canada and their developing sense of identity. In 1935 the newly appointed principal of the Mennonite Collegiate Institute, Gerhard Peters, addressed the issue of the alienation of Russländer youth from the Mennonite faith. Peters was a strong supporter of the continued use of High German and a strict disciplinarian at the institute, but he kept his political opinions to himself.[64] His comments, however, drew a fierce response from two right-wing Mennonites, Walter Quiring and Gerhard Töws. Quiring suggested all Mennonite youth needed an "active Christianity" linked to Germanness, no doubt associated with the Nazi attempts to forge a fascist "church." Töws called for a strengthening of High German among young people for much the same reason.[65]

There was, however, an aspect of every adult Russländer's personal identity that remained largely unspoken. It involved a sense of belonging absent from the mundane realities of everyday life in Canada but remained in the background, haunting and powerful. This was the Russian side of their identity, contained in memories of the Russian and Ukrainian languages, recalled in poetry and songs they once learned at school. All this was mixed with memories of places and peoples that faded as the years passed. These aspects of identity could also be mixed with sadness and feelings of loss that for some involved recalled memories of terror that at night woke them from nightmares, hot, sweaty, and confused. In Grunthal women who may have been raped relived such experiences as they grew older. In the 1970s one thought Makhno's men were hiding the Grunthal bush waiting to fall on her house and commit unspeakable atrocities. During the 1930s the building of identities among Russländer in Canada was conflicted by the continued pull of older identities from Russia and by efforts to align themselves with Germany. Identity therefore became something both renewed and reshaped in the Canadian environment. The continued significance of Russia can be clearly seen at the end of the 1930s in a sudden interest in holding reunions of the scattered Russländer across Canada based on previous colony and regional affiliations in Russia. These reunions were not in themselves new but had often involved the past pupils of prestigious high schools or men who had served in the alternative forestry camps. Reunions based on their former homes in Russia were more exclusive than such gatherings and were usually held in late summer, once the harvest was brought in.

Although few Grunthal Russländer came from Grigorievka those that did attended its reunion in 1938.[66] A larger number attended the 1938 reunion of former Terek residents held the same year in Whitewater along with Russländer from Steinbach.[67] Other Grunthal Russländer from the Baratov Shlachtin area, well represented in the Grunthal district, met in Grunthal in 1937, a reunion organized by Jacob Block. In 1939 he appealed to them to mark their connection with their former home in a more concrete way by publishing an account of the colony.[68] His appeal, never fulfilled, may well have been influenced by the more ambitious plans for a reunion by Schönfelder, the most significant gathering of Russländer from Grunthal and one that reflected their dominant role in establishing a distinctive community in Canada.

Their reunion in July 1938 was held in Glenlea, just across the Red River, and lasted over two days. People came from all over the prairies and further afield.[69] It was agreed at the reunion that a book be written on the Schönfeld settlement that combined all the information in official documents and those which had survived the settlement's destruction that were held by former members.[70] Three hundred copies of the book were printed in 1939 by the Rundschau Publishing House in Winnipeg. It was written by Gerhard Töws, a former Schönfelder who reputedly had served in the Imperial and White armies as well as in a Mennonite "self-defence unit." Töws was the author of two semi-fictional accounts of events in revolutionary and post-revolutionary Russia under the pseudonym Georg de Brecht.[71] He held strong Nazi sympathies and in 1939 moved to Germany, served with the German forces on the eastern front, and did not return to Canada until 1951. Although Töws's account of Schönfeld begins and ends with references to the reunion, this is more a literary device than a way of providing detailed information on the event. However, Töws does note how the reunion revealed to him the marked contrast between memories of their old homeland and their present life in Canada: "I let my thoughts wander through my memory and the Canadian way of life around me disappears."[72] The text that follows this statement is devoted almost exclusively to the lost Russian settlement, its rise and fall. No information is provided on the subsequent history or present condition of its former inhabitants in

Canada. Russia remained the focus of attention and primary source of identity, as it was for many first-generation Russländer.

In 1938, as these reunions occurred, another extraordinary event occurred in Grunthal when some Russländer became excited by news of the forthcoming confrontation between the German boxer Max Schmeling and the African American boxer, Joe Louis. Nazi propaganda singled out the United States as a degenerate land with a mixed-race population of descendants of African slaves and Jewish immigrants who the Nazis claimed controlled the financial system. The match between Schmeling and Louis was promoted in the Nazi press as a fight between a pure Aryan and a "degenerate" Black American.[73] The Nazis' persecution of German Jews mobilized America's influential Jewish community in support of Louis.[74] In an earlier match in 1936 Schmeling had beaten Louis by a knockout so it was confidently expected that he would also win the rematch. The fight took place in Yankee Stadium, New York, on 22 June 1938, and was broadcast by radio across America and Europe to an estimated audience of seventy million. In remote Grunthal a number of Russländer, oblivious of their faith's non-resistant principles, eagerly huddled around a radio at Franz Guenther's place as he had the best apparatus for wireless reception. The NBC's announcer delivered a blow-by-blow account of the fight as long as it lasted, because Louis took just two minutes and four seconds to end the Nazis' hopes of another Aryan triumph. Across Germany the news of Schmeling's defeat was met with disbelief, and in Grunthal with a sense of disappointment. But worse was yet to come for many of Canada's Russländer and their conflicted sense of identity.

Chapter Nine

The War Years

Since the mid-1930s political events in Europe had pointed towards a military confrontation between an increasingly aggressive Nazi regime and its neighbours. European alliances indicated that, as in 1914, any European war would have global implications while imperial links meant Canada would inevitably be drawn into any war that involved Britain. In 1935 a highly educated but radical Mennonite with socialist views living in California, Dietrich Neufeld (Navall), who had escaped Russia during the revolution, wrote to Elder David Toews in Canada decrying the fascination of Russländer with Hitler and the Nazis. He condemned the regime and issued a warning:

> The Second World War is coming, not because some crazy prairie man discovered it in the book of Revelation ... but because ... politics that are leading to it. It is not likely that we can keep out of it. The Fascists and Nazis will force it on the world, but they ought to be swept away by this new purgatory.[1]

While there is no evidence that Toews replied, Neufeld's views were undoubtedly not shared by most Russländer. In February 1939 a Russländer wrote to the *Winnipeg Free Press* warning readers that "at the present time" communists were "a greater menace to Canada than the Nazis ever will be."[2] Another letter written by the ardent Nazi supporter J.J. Hildebrand somewhat disingenuously defended Mennonites against accusations of disloyalty towards Canada especially when his earlier letters to the newspaper suggested otherwise.[3] These letters followed reports of a meeting held in Winnipeg in support of Germany and its government that was attended by Mennonites and where the Mennonite Young People's Choir entertained an audience giving Nazi salutes.[4] At the same time in a series of articles *The Winnipeg Tribune* exposed the local German consulate's role in funding *Deutsche Zeitung für Canada*, which promoted Nazi propaganda, and Mennonite connections with the paper.[5] Just under seven months later, on 10 September 1939, Canada declared war on Germany, following its invasion of Poland and Britain's declaration of war a week earlier.

War was not unexpected as on 30 January 1939, Hitler delivered a major address to the German Reichstag with the ominous prophesy that if "international financial Jewry in and outside Europe should succeed in plunging the peoples once again into a world war, then the result will not be the Bolshevization of the world and a Jewish victory, but annihilation the Jewish race in Europe." Hitler's entire speech was reprinted in the *Mennonitische Rundschau*.[6] But the outbreak of war seven months later still came as a shock to many Canadians, particularly Mennonites. It is difficult to reconstruct the impact of the outbreak of war on Russländer either in Grunthal or among other Russländer in Canada over the next five years, until peace was restored. Unfortunately, few Russländer appear to have recorded their thoughts or feelings on this subject in any letters or journals that may have survived, and their newspapers are silent on the issue. To appease any English who might encounter their German-language newspapers, some sections were printed in English, usually the front page. While the Russländer press had published numerous comments on politics, race, and identity during the 1930s, with the coming of war all this ceased, and articles concentrated on safer topics. Mennonite newspapers might carry summaries of current events with an emphasis on subjects of interest to readers but reports of the conflict were published in matter-of-fact terms.

In private, however, individuals discussed, debated, and disagreed about the war, its origins, and possible outcome. Some more radical individuals who had expressed support for the Nazis or strong pro-German views during the 1930s now found themselves in a difficult position. A few Mennonite schoolteachers lost their jobs, but none in Grunthal.[7] Russländer on the West Reserve seemed more vulnerable to accusations of disloyalty than those on the East Reserve, perhaps because they were in closer contact with English Canadians and surrounded by more diverse ethnic populations. In Altona in late 1940 a shoemaker, Jacob Kroeger, was arrested and interned in a camp in Kananaskis, Alberta, for possessing a short-wave radio, owning a copy of Hitler's *Mein Kampf*, and for talking openly about the war. A local Mennonite leader wrote to his Liberal Member of Parliament suggesting Kroeger was not really a Nazi but by early 1941 he stated that if Kroeger were released from internment, his "lips be sewn up by his own shoemaker's thread" to prevent his telling of stories, as even his wife agreed he was too "darn dumb" to know better.⁸ Another complaint that Mennonites were listening to German broadcasts on shortwave radios received the reply from the local member that Mennonites were motivated by anti-Bolshevik sentiments rather than support for the Nazis.⁹ Certainly some in Grunthal had access to short-wave radios and it was claimed that Franz Guenther listened in secret to German broadcasts during the war.

It is probably safe to speculate that for many Russländer the Second World War created a roller coaster of emotions. They were new citizens of a country now at war with a nation, people, and for some a regime with which they had increasingly identified. For some there was probably also a sense that Germany might finally set right the humiliation of defeat in the First World War and confront the "Jewish-Bolshevik" menace. Such hopes undoubtedly were almost immediately dashed by the seemingly incomprehensible news of an agreement made between Hitler and Stalin to divide a defeated Poland, with the Soviets also seizing the independent Baltic states. How Russländer reconciled themselves to this realpolitik is also not revealed in the Mennonite press. Poland was soon defeated and then the German army swept into Western Europe, invading other lands, and defeating armies, including the British who were forced to retreat from continental Europe. In Grunthal a small band of mainly bachelors and youths, encouraged by Nick Heese, who had served with the White armies, celebrated the German victories. Liquor and "Mennonite caviar" (tins of sardines) were served much to the regret of the youngsters the following day.

In view of the dire situation in Western Europe and with Britain facing invasion, in June 1940 the Canadian government abandoned its earlier policy of limiting the country's involvement in a war so far away and Parliament enacted the National Resources Mobilization Act. One official later described this legislation as "the most sweeping Act passed by Parliament since the outbreak of war."¹⁰ The Act, modelled on British legislation enacted under emergency provisions for the defence of the country, authorized the Canadian government to order compulsory military service, although anyone conscripted was limited to home defence duties. In part this was in response to the French, particularly in Quebec, who during the First World War had objected to conscription and overseas service and now indicated they would again.¹¹ The Act required every adult citizen to register and "place themselves, their services and their property at the disposal of His Majesty in the right of Canada."¹² Forms were distributed to local registrars and were to be completed over a three-day period between 19–21 August. All adult citizens had to complete the forms without exception. The requirements were summarized in German in Mennonite newspapers that included a government advertisement and a copy of the form that needed to be completed.[13]

The Act, the compulsory nature of registration, and the specific language of the forms immediately caused concern in the Mennonite community. Leaders of the varied and scattered Mennonite organizations had already met in Winkler before war was declared to discuss a common response in the event of a conflict. Most Kanadier and Swiss "Old" Mennonites from Ontario drew upon their experiences with the Canadian government during the First World War. As they understood the law, they were exempt on religious grounds from military service. But the Russländer, who had arrived after the First World War, had very different experiences in Imperial Russia of service during a war and viewed it as a duty as citizens.[14] Many had served during the First World War in the sanitary service, including a number in Grunthal.[15] Many Russländer believed their experiences during the war had positive aspects such as comradeship, and that helping others in need was considered a Christian duty. As war again threatened, leading Russländer saw little reason why their people should not once again contribute their services in similar roles and, given the dubious allegiances of some during the 1930s, it might provide proof of their loyalty to Canada.

In practice, however, Russländer were divided on the issue with some more enthusiastic than others. The important Mennonite Brethren leader B.B. Janz was strongly in favour of them providing some form of service.[16] The problem, as they later learned, was that unlike in Russia, serving in similar roles in Canada entailed joining military units. Such an idea was totally anathema to Kanadier and other Mennonites in Ontario who demanded total exemption from all forms of military service. Differences between Mennonites that had existed prior to the outbreak of war soon re-emerged during negotiations with officials following the passage of the 1940 Mobilization Act. Some Russländer representatives suggested they would serve their country even if this entailed duties in military hospital units. But a compromise was also negotiated with officials in Ottawa whereby young Mennonite men unwilling to accept military roles would instead be classified as "conscientious objectors" (COs) to work in logging camps, on farms, in hospitals (including mental health hospitals), and in a range of other occupations.[17]

The registration forms, however, soon revealed other problems as the instructions asked registrars to collect information on country of birth, nationality, racial origin, and language.[18] The major problem was question number eight which required everyone to state their "Racial

Origin."[19] Just putting "Mennonite" was at first unacceptable to the authorities and the advice some Kanadier received was that as citizens they just write "Canadian" in place of racial origin, as Mennonites lacked a "pure" racial identity. But official instructions to registrars excluded "Canadian" as a racial category along with other ethnic group labels, while racial origin could only be traced through the male line.[20] As a number of Mennonites considered they were ultimately Dutch in origin they could write "Dutch Descendant."[21] The Dutch option was strongly favoured by B.B. Janz, who wrote an article on the subject for an English-language newspaper in Alberta, reprinted in English in the *Rundschau* with a clarification in German.[22]

The question, however, proved a greater challenge for many Russländer than for other Mennonites and soon reopened debates in the Russländer press on identity involving an issue that went back to Imperial Russia.[23] A number of Russländer were unwilling to abandon the idea that by race they were "pure" Germans or at least "Frisians."[24] Many who during the 1930s had been involved in radical discussions and assertions of a German racial identity decided to remain silent or any letters they may have sent to editors of the Mennonite press may not have been published. The idea that Mennonites were racially German also threw into question their status as members of an enemy "race" when they were supposedly loyal Canadians. The issue also caused confusion and debate outside the Mennonite world with one editor suggesting the question be dropped in all future official documents.[25] Elder David Toews, head of the CMBC, following discussions with J.G. Gardiner, the minister in charge of war services in Ottawa, suggested combining the term "Mennonite" with a secondary identity, such as "Dutch Mennonite," "German Mennonite," or "Russian Mennonite."[26]

In the national census of 1941 Mennonite responses under the headings on race, language, and origin showed a marked change from the earlier 1931 census, with an increase in Dutch entries and a decrease in German and Russian. This is undoubtedly another indication of the politics of Mennonite identity, especially for Russländer.[27] At the local level, however, confusion abounded. In Grunthal Dietrich Heese, thinking that he was "German" attempted to surrender the gun he used for shooting wildlife to the local RCMP officer. When asked where he had been born, Heese replied "Russia" and the officer handed back the gun. Heese obviously was confused by the difference between race and nationality.[28]

The confusion over identity and registration was compounded once Russländer of military age, along with Kanadier, began to receive call-up papers for military service at home. It was recognized by better-educated

Russländer leaders that young men were ill-equipped to face Canadian registrars and judges and to make their case for exemption on religious grounds. In response Johann G. Rempel wrote a small pamphlet providing a "catechism" on non-resistance to help young men better prepare when called before registration boards.[29] In Grunthal Peter Block, son of Jacob H. Block, attempted to discuss what stance he should take with the lead minister of the congregation, J.J. Enns, but Enns merely referred him to the senior Elder of the Schönwiese congregation in Winnipeg. Block took this as not a sign of Enns's ignorance as much as his incompetence.

In the end, along with his Kanadier friend Peter Braun, Block decided that instead of risking the complicated and uncertain process of claiming exemption on grounds of faith, they would "volunteer" for military service. Among the risks they might face was appearing before Judge John E. Adamson, infamous for being unsympathetic to Mennonite claims for exemption on conscience grounds and whose decisions often resulted in prison sentences being imposed.[30] Block and Braun also believed they would fail any military medical examination and would be rejected as Block had flat feet and Braun had lost his right index finger and therefore could claim he was unable to pull a gun's trigger. To their surprise both passed their medicals. Block's feet proved to be not as flat as his Low German and the medical officer is reported to have told Braun to use his next finger. Block appears to have been later released from service but Braun at first enjoyed being in uniform. Attached to a unit transporting German prisoners of war from eastern Canada to camps in the west, he found his ability to speak a variety of German extremely useful.

Other Russländer had rather different experiences. Art Guenther, son of the storekeeper, received his papers and managed to gain conscientious objector status but when his younger brother Eric was ordered to report, the family thought he would also be exempted as he was needed to run the store. When he failed to report to the authorities as ordered he was arrested by the RCMP and sentenced to a year in prison with hard labour, a sentence later reduced to six months. Eric's imprisonment caused consternation in Grunthal and Elim's lead minister, J.J. Enns, raised the matter at an assembly of congregational leaders of Western Canada in Saskatoon.[31] Later in the war when the youngest Guenther boys received orders to report for service, they successfully obtained conscientious status but by then the war was nearly over. In fact, few Russländer in Grunthal were of an age where they might be called into service, so the war's impact was less significant in the area than in other Russländer communities. But in the Grunthal area Chortitzer and

Bergthaler young men, often identified as being linked to the Grunthal district by their postal address rather than as active members of the region's community, are among those listed as having served as COs.[32] Any Mennonite who enlisted in the military often found themselves in ambiguous positions in Mennonite society once the war ended and they returned home.[33]

In schools the outbreak of war had an immediate impact as the tone of official directives grew increasingly nationalistic. After the fall of France in June 1940 a questionnaire was sent to all teachers by the Department of Education asking them for information on the range of subjects taught, including how they encouraged pupils to carry out "patriotic exercises" on Empire Day, whether any pupils refused to be involved, and the names and addresses of the parents of such children. Teachers were also asked whether classes had contributed to the Red Cross or other relief agencies, how they, as teachers, presented the "cause of the Allies," and how through their teaching methods they could "serve our war effort."[34] In August 1940 new regulations for "patriotic exercises" were issued to all teachers by the department. These entailed singing "O Canada" at the start of each day and "God Save the King" at the end of the day, "with pupils standing at attention erect." Empire Day, the King's Birthday, Dominion Day, and Armistice Day required additional special exercises such as "suitable readings, recitations, saluting the flag, and pageants of a patriotic character" in order "to impress upon pupils love for and devotion to Canada and the Empire."[35] Anthems, standing to attention, and flag raising were to be strictly followed by both teachers and pupils although problems with exactly how to fly and salute the flag later resulted in the issuing of amendments.[36] For Empire Day in 1941 teachers were informed that the special topic to be discussed with pupils was "The Empire at War." Included were excerpts from speeches by Winston Churchill and President Roosevelt, quotes from British poets, and descriptions of heroism, all intended to increase loyalty to the empire.[37]

How people in Grunthal reacted to these matters is unclear, but they were probably unwilling to question them. The Department of Education's withdrawal of the teaching certificates of two Mennonite teachers heightened concerns in all Mennonite communities.[38] One certificate was later reinstated when it became clear the teacher was not the author of a pro-Nazi article published just before the war. When the editor of the *Winnipeg Tribune* raised questions concerning the pro-German sympathies of some Mennonite teachers, the Department responded by issuing a statement that "99% of the Mennonite population, both teachers and citizens, are whole-heartedly loyal to British and Canadian traditions." The loyalty of Mennonite teachers was confirmed by school inspectors but somewhat ominously the statement continued that "a very small minority who were otherwise will be dealt with as occasion arises."[39] In effect, all Mennonite teachers were on notice.

Teachers undoubtedly were careful not to express personal opinions other than those required as part of their "patriotic" duties. Certainly nothing was said in a classroom about Mennonite non-resistance. School inspector Herriot may have had entirely innocent intentions when in 1943 he set the children at Spencer School a project to write a composition on "What effect the war has had on our family."[40] The school was situated near Grunthal with a few Russländer pupils whose parents identified with Grunthal, although Herriot does not mention the name of the teacher, Elfrieda Rempel, or the fact that most pupils were Mennonite. Of the six responses Herriot submitted to the *Manitoba School Journal*, only two were published, those by David Heinrichs and Irene Warkentin. Their replies concentrated mostly on prices, better for some items, more expensive for rationed essentials which were difficult to find and purchase. But the compositions avoided sensitive topics beyond one rather obscure final comment that while "our country itself does not fight in the war, it has something to interfere with us even here."[41]

The major problem the people of Grunthal faced with schooling was the constant demand for money from their children, not just because it aided a war they did not wholeheartedly support, but also because it further drained their parents' limited financial resources. Starting with the Children's Ambulance Fund at the start of the war, children were later expected to purchase War Saving Stamps, contribute to the Junior Red Cross, and support a range of other "good causes." While "voluntary," all contributions to War Saving Stamps had to be recorded by the teacher and submitted with their monthly attendance records. The loyalty of schools could thus be scrutinized by officials. They were also made a matter of public record. Throughout the war the *Manitoba School Journal* published extensive lists of schools and the amount of money their pupils contributed to various schemes and Goodwill School was identified as an infrequent contributor. In 1943 a Winnipeg newspaper reported that the school had donated just $36.91.[42] Elsewhere in Manitoba a Mennonite teacher eventually complained about these constant demands in support of war-related schemes insisting they were inconsistent with his non-resistant beliefs. Consequently, he lost his teaching certificate.[43]

It was probably better that Mennonite teachers whose classrooms contained mainly Mennonite children to remain not just true to the tradition of being the "Quiet in the Land," but instead to be the entirely "Silent in the Land." Silence also fell over the use of German outside classes when German and religion were taught. Some school inspectors in Manitoba put pressure on teachers to stop any teaching in German, but this was not so in Grunthal.[44] Mennonite teachers in schools with mainly Mennonite pupils restricted use of Low and High German even in the school yard, a move supported by most in the community. School Inspector Herriot told teachers in Steinbach to "soft-pedal their German language and culture" and he no doubt repeated this advice in Grunthal.[45] Therefore, although there were no official rules on language use, there was also a degree of self-censorship. Older Russländer born in Russia could recall that in 1914 the Russian authorities banned all publication in German, closing Mennonite newspapers and other printing houses. Speaking German in public was also forbidden in wartime Russia and some Mennonites were arrested for using High and even Low German. In Canada during the First World War Mennonites continued to use German but publishing in the language was restricted and publications subject to official censorship.[46] In Grunthal during the Second World War this self-imposed suppression of German had limited influence on the community's use of Low German. The teaching of High German continued in school and in homes where it was considered important; congregational services also continued to be conducted in High German.

In June 1941 Hitler launched his massive surprise military attack on the Soviet Union. His armies made rapid progress and soon reached areas of Ukraine from where most Russländer had emigrated to Canada. Russländer in Canada were not to learn until after 1945 that many Mennonites in Ukraine who had survived Stalin's terror, including relatives, had fallen into German hands where, consistent with racist Nazi thinking they were deemed to be of German descent, provided with a new identity as *Volksdeutsche*, and given preferential treatment over their "non-Aryan" neighbours. But as the Red Army retook the conquered areas in 1943, Mennonites were forced to abandon their settlements and follow the retreating German army westwards.[47] In Canada many Russländer at first were excited by reports of the Nazi invasion. It appeared that Hitler would at last remove the scourge of Bolshevism and its leader, the evil Josef Stalin, as well as, according to Nazi ideology, his Jewish henchmen. A few Mennonites even hoped that if he succeeded, Hitler might permit Russländer to return to their homeland, reclaim their property, and re-establish their way of life. While in hindsight such a notion might appear little more than a fantastic dream, Nazi plans included the colonization of its conquered eastern lands and the establishment of a living space (HG *Lebensraum*) for Germans. Before the war, through reading Nazi propaganda as well as through communication with other Mennonites in Nazi Germany and South America, Russländer Mennonites were aware of the idea of an expanded empire for Germans. What they could not know until after the war, however, was that the invasion of the east, and elsewhere in occupied Europe, would involve the mass murder of millions of people. Only recently has the involvement of a few Mennonites in these events been discussed, but further research is needed on Mennonites under Nazi occupation in Ukraine.[48]

As the German invasion of the Soviet Union began, Hitler had declared war on the United States and the Soviet Union became an ally of Canada, Britain, and the United States against Hitler. For Russländer it had been bad enough watching Hitler cooperate with Stalin in the invasion of Poland in 1939 but now a communist regime was allied with Canada against the German people. As the war progressed and the tide turned against Hitler, Russländer had to endure endless newspaper and radio reports praising victorious Soviet forces and their supreme commander, Stalin, the man responsible for the murder of thousands of their co-religionists and millions of others. The reality of the new situation was brought home to them in 1942 when the Canadian federal and Manitoban provincial governments debated lifting the ban on the Communist Party of Canada and the release of its members held in detention.[49] News of a proposal to lift the ban was not well received by Russländer. Although no reactions from Grunthal are recorded, on the West Reserve Walter Kroeker, a local businessman, telegrammed his local parliamentary member, Howard Winkler, and bluntly told him that a lifting of the ban would "cause a greater exodus" of local Mennonite supporters of the Liberal Party "than any conceivable action on conscription." He continued that unless the Soviets reciprocated and adopted democracy, any "political subservience" to the Soviets "was unnecessary to [the] military alliance." He also suggested that it was "strictly accidental" that "Canadian war interests temporarily parallel Communist interests."[50] Winkler's reply is unknown, but the Liberal Party paid for advertisements in its name to be placed in major Mennonite newspapers explaining in German its position.

Mennonites were not the only Canadians concerned: so too were other politicians, officials, and members of the public.[51] After the ban was lifted, the Communist Party in Canada changed its name to the Labour-Progressive Party of Canada, although members were kept under surveillance. Previously the RCMP had shown a particular eagerness in placing communists under observation and arresting its leaders, but rather less interest in pro-German sympathizers, including Russländer.

In October 1939 an intelligence report noted that while some Mennonites were previously members of the German Bund this was only on "account of their anti-Communistic feelings and not as a result of their pro-Nazi leanings." The report suggested Mennonite religious "tenets" and the group's Russo-German past "weakens the Bund structure."[52] In 1943 the *Monthly Intelligence Report* provided a more detailed account including an analysis of Mennonite history, foundation, and immigration to Canada. It suggested that only a few Mennonites "lean towards Nazism" while a religious condemnation of "totalitarianism and its evil influences" may be "motivated" by "a desire to see Communism crushed" and a belief that only the Nazis could "bring this about." It was therefore "not unnatural that with the Soviets now allied to the United Nations … [a Mennonite minority] might see Nazism in the light of a saviour."[53]

The conflict became truly global once the Japanese attacked Pearl Harbor. The United States, Britain, and its empire, including Canada, now faced war on two fronts. In response the Canadian government planned to expand conscription and make military service overseas compulsory instead of limited to "home defence." As this was a highly sensitive issue in Quebec, the government first decided to hold a nationwide plebiscite on the proposal. It involved a simple yes/no reply to the question: "Are you in favour of releasing the Government from any obligations arising out of any past commitments restricting the methods of raising men for military service?" The word "conscription" was carefully left off the voting paper.[54] Voting took place on 27 April 1942 and the result was that 65.5 per cent voted "Yes" with only Quebec voting "No" (only 27.9 per cent voted "Yes"). In Manitoba the result was an overwhelming "Yes" by 80.3 per cent.

However, the results from Mennonite-dominated voting areas were mixed with higher "No" votes than elsewhere in the province. In Provencher, the electoral district in which Grunthal was situated, more people voted "No" (4,562) than "Yes" (3,210), the only district in Manitoba to vote "No." In the polling station in Grunthal only seven votes were recorded for "Yes" while nineteen were "No."[55] Obviously, turnout on such a sensitive issue was low. The results in areas with high Mennonite populations voting "No" were recognized in a newspaper editorial that blamed "Nazi sympathizers" among their non-British populations and singled out Grunthal as an example of a low "Yes" and high "No" vote.[56]

When Peter Block was informed that his unit was to be posted overseas, he decided he did not want to serve outside Canada and possibly be involved in killing Germans. After a period of leave he failed to return to his unit but was soon picked up by the police. While being transported to a military prison, he escaped by jumping off the train in northern Ontario. Although he injured his leg, he managed to reach Grunthal. From then until the end of the war local people hid him and he did not surrender until the war was over when he was sentenced to a term of imprisonment.[57] But his desertion and official suspicion that he was being hidden in Grunthal altered the tenor of life in the area. Up to then English visitors were rarely seen but now military police and later the RCMP would suddenly arrive in the town unannounced and search surrounding areas for the deserter. The increased police activity in and around Grunthal may have precipitated the break-up of the Grunthal lending library, by then located in Klassen's feed mill. As it included works that might come to the attention of the authorities, it was decided to burn – or by some accounts, bury – all those considered "risky," while others were taken away by individuals and kept, or hidden, in homes. Hitler's *Mein Kampf* survived in a private collection but minus its covers and title page, as some might have considered burning or burying Hitler's testament as sacrilege.

While it might appear that Grunthal was under siege from external forces during the war years, on the economic front the story was very different (see fig. 9.1). The war provided great opportunities for farmers as demand for agricultural produce increased along with higher returns as prices rose.[58] Farm recovery began before the outbreak of war as the country gradually emerged from the Great Depression even if some officials remained cautious about its long-term sustainability. Many attributed improvements in harvest yields in 1936 and 1937 to favourable climatic conditions rather than to overall growth in the province's economy.[59] But the long-term figures suggested a more sustained improvement. Cash incomes from farming in Manitoba that in 1931 had fallen to just $31,785,000, by 1936 had recovered to $47,856,000 and $84,229,000 by 1941. In 1946 after the end of the war incomes had almost doubled to $167, 284,000.[60]

More detailed figures for the East Reserve reveal a similar pattern. These are to be found in the unpublished reports of E.K. Francis who between 1945 and 1946 carried out detailed research on the Mennonites in Manitoba. His carefully tabulated data on all areas of farm life confirms a gradual improvement showing that between 1936 and 1941 average farm values in the East Reserve increased by 18 per cent (from $3,310 to $3,702) and the value of land by 35 per cent per acre (from $17.49 to $24.18).[61] Over the same period the average value of land increased much more rapidly than for buildings and livestock (land by 35 per cent per acre, buildings by just 3 per cent and livestock 17 per

YOUR FARM is the Battlefield
ON THE HOME FRONT...

Fig. 9.1. Wartime advertisement encouraging farmers to increase production. McColl-Frontenac Petroleum Products advertisement encouraging farmers to support the war, one of a number that appeared in the *Steinbach Post* during 1943.

Source: *Steinbach Post*, 1943.

cent). Although 1941 was early in the war years, income from farming, boosted by wartime demand, increased massively. Farm incomes increased by 131 per cent (from $609 to $1,407); this amounted to an increase in returns from one hundred acres between 1936 and 1941 of 170 per cent (from $340 to $919) or per person living on a farm, by 112 per cent (from $105 to $229).[62] The increased investment in farm equipment is illustrated by the rise of 140 per cent in the value of farm implements.[63] In more general terms, Francis states that Grunthal living "standards had increased 100 per cent since the beginning of World War II."[64]

The expansion of agriculture occurred in many forms, stimulated by wartime demand for a range of products which brought the producer good returns.[65] The most important of these remained dairy products, especially butter and cheese. In Manitoba butter production peaked

Table 9.1. Increase in farm values, property, livestock, and income, 1936/1941 in Grunthal

Items increased	1936, $	1941, $	% increase
Value of single farm unit	3,133	3,702	18
Value per 100 acres	1,749	2,418	38
Avg. value 1 acre farmland	7.64	10.28	34.6
Avg. value buildings	900.33	925.18	2.8
Value of implements	236	564	139
Livestock, per farm	547.03	638.39	16.7
Expenditure, per farm	21.05	–	–
Income	609	1407	131
Income per 100 acres	340	919	170
Income per person on farm	105	229	112
Cash profits	398	–	–

Source AM, Francis Mss, MG A55/27; on the obverse Francis wrote "not for publication."

at almost thirty-four million pounds in 1943 compared to an average yearly production of only twenty-four million in the period 1935–9.[66] The average price for milk and milk products in Winnipeg rose from $1.40 per one hundred pounds in 1932–3, to $2.52 in 1943–4.[67] This followed a concerted campaign by the Department of Agriculture to boost production by offering higher returns for these products.[68] In the Hanover area, the value of dairy products increased from $235,810 in 1941 (32 per cent of the total value of farm products), to $517,450 in 1946 (28 per cent of total value).[69] The difference in the value of products indicates increased demand for other goods, particularly sugar beets, hogs, and poultry products, mainly eggs.[70] As butter and cheese prices increased, reaching a high in 1942 and 1943 when production also reached its peak, the government introduced price controls on milk in December 1942 before inflation got out of hand.[71] Wartime reports indicate that the government, while restricting prices, did not want to see levels of production fall. They feared that labour shortages caused by so many men being conscripted would reduce the areas of cultivated land and restrict yields of feed crops and hay that might eventually limit dairy production. The aim was to increase production from almost thirty-two million pounds in 1942 to thirty-five million pounds in 1943 principally by improving farming methods.[72] An absence of mechanical milking machines increased difficulties as cows were still largely milked by hand, overwhelmingly by women and girls.

At the start of the war Grunthal farmers supped milk mainly to City Dairy Ltd. based in Winnipeg which in 1927 had taken over the building previously owned by Johann Braun and Johann Krahn.[73] Grunthal farmers were unhappy with the returns they received for their milk and cream at a time of rising prices so in March 1943 they formed a Grunthal Farmers' Cooperative Dairy Ltd. and bought out City Dairy, which had been producing butter and later cheese.[74] Similar ventures involving dairy products had existed in the area since 1921 when St. Malo established a cooperative cheese factory soon after founding a credit union. Mennonites close to Grunthal began to supply other cooperative dairies first in Niverville in 1940 and in Spencer in 1942. The new Grunthal venture was established with an authorized share capital of $30,000 with each share valued at $10.[75] The cooperative was in addition to the store incorporated under the title of the Grunthal Cooperative Trading Society Ltd., but this was considered by the official registrar of cooperatives in Manitoba, John W. Ward, as a consumer cooperative rather than a producer's cooperative as the Grunthal cooperative factory was a creamery and cheese producer. Not everyone, especially competitors in the region, exactly welcomed the new cooperative, just as some earlier had criticized the cooperative store. The opposition is reflected in letters and reports in the *Steinbach Post*.[76]

Increased demand for other agricultural products, including eggs, was another source of income. Previously laying chickens, like hogs, were kept mostly for home consumption although some enterprising individuals sold eggs in Winnipeg at the height of the Depression. Sugar beet production also received a major boost, especially after 1940 when a new processing plant was opened close to Winnipeg.[77] Although the number of Mennonite growers of sugar beet in Manitoba increased between 1940 and 1945, from 24 per cent to 36 per cent of the total number of producers, few farmers in the Grunthal area participated, as the soils were unsuited to sugar beet growing.[78] But Grunthal people, especially young adults, were involved in sugar beet agriculture in areas over the Red River. It involved hard work, digging, hoeing, weeding, and helping with the harvest before the industry was mechanized.[79] While it paid well, beet work was thoroughly disliked not just because of the heavy labour involved, but also because people were exposed to the heat of summer. Some young people considered that there were better ways to spend a summer, although the camaraderie of the work and the evening activities away from home provided some relief.

During the Depression the need for cash involved making enough to pay taxes and buy the necessities of life. Money could be borrowed through kinship links, if any close relatives possessed any to lend, or obtained at extraordinary rates of interest from the few individuals who somehow had acquired money and hoarded it away. As the economy improved, attention turned to seeking money in order to invest for the future. This usually centred on ways to improve and expand farming, especially the need to buy farm machinery and purchase, lease, or open up new areas of land for cultivation. One way to raise capital was to deal with non-Mennonite financial institutions located in communities in the surrounding area. Some Mennonites in Grunthal had traded with the French credit union in St. Malo before the war. St. Malo's credit union was an initiative of their priest, Father Benoit, who to encourage economic reform among local farmers, had overseen the formation of a "caisse populaire" or "people's bank." This in fact preceded the passing by the Manitoba Legislature in 1937 of an Act enabling credit unions to be formed under the provisions of the Companies Act.[80]

When the St. Malo credit union was recognized as a success, other communities began to follow their lead. In 1941 the Manitoba government encouraged the formation of credit unions and in 1943 the federal government included credit unions as part of its plans for post-war reconstruction.[81] In later listings of credit unions, St. Malo was given the number "1" based on the sequence in which credit unions in other communities were established. St. Pierre was number 6, Altona was 16, Steinbach was 36, and Grunthal was 50. It was in April 1942 that a group met in Grunthal to form a credit union. They carefully signed all the official documents under the watchful eye of Jacob J. Rempel in one of his many roles, this time as commissioner of oaths.[82] Initially ten men joined the credit union, each receiving a single share by depositing sums ranging from just seventy-five cents to $1.[83] The memorandum of understanding specified that members were monthly required to pay twenty-five cents for children aged sixteen and under, and fifty cents for adults. Sums under twenty-five cents could not be deposited although new members could join for a minimum payment of twenty-five cents and any interest on deposits was payable on 31 December. Loans were restricted to members and could not exceed $50. The controlling board of directors was set at seven with a quorum of five to make decisions. It is perhaps not surprising that nearly all the founding members of the credit union were marginal members of the community, Russländer and Kanadier, who had often been excluded from membership in the institutions that controlled key areas of the community. All shared a desire to better themselves, none were Schönfelder, and half recorded their occupation as farmers and the rest were small businessmen: carpenters, shoemakers, a truck driver, and a clerk in Grunthal. Initially the credit union's office was in the carpentry workshop of J.F. Krahn.[84] The formation of the credit union was greeted with suspicion if not hostility by key figures in the community and a number thought it would soon fail. But it did not fail even though, given the backgrounds of its early members, there were initial difficulties in the keeping of accounts and dealing with the legal requirements involved in running a credit union.[85] In time, however, its membership and assets steadily increased despite continued insinuations that it had failed or was about to fail.

The presence of small businessmen at the credit union's founding reflected the continued growth of local businesses in the town that prospered as farmers received better returns for their produce. One aspect of this was increased mechanization of farming as tractors began to supplement and eventually replace horses. On the prairie tractors had been involved in cultivation for a long time, first steam-powered, later diesel and petrol-driven, but the latter were more common in developed areas of the East Reserve. Such tractors, however, were heavy and cumbersome especially when equipped with iron-rimmed wheels. They were also expensive. Improved, lighter, more powerful, and more manageable machines equipped with rubber tires eventually started to appear.[86] In 1936 there were 81,657 tractors in the prairie provinces; by 1941 the number had risen to 112,624 and shortly after the end of the war in 1946, 151,161.[87] As the price of such machines became cheaper some Grunthal farmers purchased their first tractor, especially as factories in the United States and Canada, expanded to produce military machines, with the coming of peace shifted production to domestic goods. Purchasing a tractor involved a large investment and, in many cases, it was bought on credit. Local dealers such as John D. Warkentin and Ted Chornoboy (fig. 9.2) turned to selling tractors as well as motor vehicles, eventually establishing dealerships with companies who provided credit deals to any farmer wishing to purchase their machines.

Tractors therefore made farming more profitable than in the past and it soon became clear they could pay for themselves through expanded cultivation. They not only made a farmer's own work more efficient, but could also earn money through custom work. Russländer farmers discovered that even Kanadier farmers were willing to pay them to cultivate existing land as well as to help open new areas for cultivation. Some Mennonites also did custom work for Ukrainians. As mechanization increased local blacksmiths initially adapted old farming equipment originally intended for use with horses. In time, however, such equipment was abandoned in favour of new modern commercial products specifically designed for work with tractors.[88] And completely new machinery followed, such as binders with combines. Blacksmiths in Grunthal were still in demand, however, as the new equipment was easily damaged, especially when used on the region's stony fields. The most notable blacksmith in the Grunthal area was a Kanadier, David F. Toews, who

Fig. 9.2. Chornoboy's tractor dealership in Grunthal. The Ukrainian Chornoboy family's mechanic business in Grunthal moved into tractors during the Second World War and flourished, as this photograph from 1956 shows.

Source: The *Carillon* Archives, Steinbach, Manitoba.

also pulled teeth and cut hair.[89] Stationary tractors, when properly connected, could also be used to power other machinery but further west where wheat and other grain crops were grown, there was an established tradition of custom work using large, steam-powered tractors. Adventurous young Mennonites from Grunthal and surrounding areas sometimes travelled westwards during the harvest season to work with such machines although it was hard, uncomfortable work given the heat and skin irritations caused by blowing chaff.

Established businesses in New Grunthal also prospered in the improved economic conditions during the war, particularly Guenther's Red and White store. In 1937 Frank Guenther finally moved his family out of the store and into a newly built house. In 1941 a new store was begun in a greatly expanded building which was completed just after the war. This included a lunch counter that further enhanced the store's reputation as a centre for local farmers and other visitors who came to town to do business. Several other businesses were established or expanded, most on the main street. One other major change that occurred during the war years involved the departure in 1944 of "Kaiser" Rempel for Virgil, Ontario. Here he purchased a fruit farm for

$10,000 or $12,000, according to some in Grunthal. The reasons given in Grunthal for his move vary. Some say it was a decision made over concerns for the health of one of his children while others point to his failure as a farmer. Another explanation is that his income began to fall as he no longer received an additional income from the National Trust and had to give up the truck paid for by the Trust as by the 1940s most Russländer had purchased their farms. In Virgil, Rempel became involved with the local credit union but never held as central a role in the community as he had in Grunthal. Rempel's role in the CMBC was also on the wane and in 1946 it finally cleared all the travel debts still outstanding.[90]

By the time Rempel left Grunthal it was clear to any Russländer that Nazis would be defeated and worse, as the Soviet army was rapidly advancing towards Germany and eventually would seize its capital, Berlin. The Nazi empire was collapsing and with it any hope that Russländer would ever regain their lost lands in Ukraine. Once again little is said in the Mennonite press that might indicate Mennonite attitudes to these events. But in the late 1940s a Russländer historical series was established, the Echo-Verlag, overseen and published by Arnold Dyck in a series of volumes devoted to the Mennonite settlements in Russia before the revolution and leading Mennonite figures. For Russländer, their Russian world now lay in the past.[91] As Russländer turned to writing accounts of their pasts, they still had to come to terms with their lives in Canada and face the future. They owned their land and properties, were largely free of debt, and had money. But would the end of the war mean an end of prosperity as it had after the First World War? Would the economy slip back into another economic depression? Or would the progress that had begun before the war and that had been boosted by the demands of the war, continue?

Chapter Ten

Post-War Prosperity

The headline of the 9 May 1945 edition of the *Steinbach Post* announced in German *"The War in Europe is over."* Beneath the headline another notice appeared in English, "Now Thank We All Our God ... with heartfelt gratitude ... for Peace in Europe and the Dawn of Peace in the whole world. Let us Rededicate ourselves to so Live that the Peace may be Enduring." The notice, undoubtedly sponsored by the Steinbach business community as their names followed, was carefully arranged in the form of a "V" for victory. At the base of the "V," as if adding support to the secular world of commerce, were the words "REEVE and COUNCILLORS of the R.M. of HANOVER." Business was never far from the thoughts of leaders of the Steinbach community and no doubt they hoped that peace would bring continued prosperity. God was called on only once, in the headline, and then only indirectly as the first line is from a well-known hymn in German, *"Nun danket alle Gott."* None of Steinbach's many churches endorsed the statement.[1]

The war intensified moves towards controlled economies in Canada and elsewhere to meet the demands of the global conflict. Those involved, however, also had to look ahead. In 1944 representatives of Allied governments met at the Bretton Woods Conference in New Hampshire to establish the foundations for a post-war international order. This included establishing an International Bank for Reconstruction and Development, more commonly known as the World Bank. Planning had begun earlier in the war but the conference brought together representatives of many countries, including Canada.[2] During the war the Canadian federal and provincial governments also started to plan the direction the country might take once Germany was defeated and peace returned. During the war the federal government produced several pamphlets on this topic in *Canadian Affairs* and a series directed at men and women serving in the armed forces under the heading *Looking Ahead*.[3]

Even before the outbreak of war, plans to rebuild the Canadian economy were formulated, influenced by policies pursued in other Western countries stimulated by new economic thinking on the role of government in economic affairs. In Manitoba such planning also began prior to the war and continued during the war when a Post-War Reconstruction Committee was established under the chairmanship of the premier. Several specialist reports written by experts in different fields were published by the provincial government.[4] The most important area investigated involved ambitious plans for the electrification of the province. In Manitoba the issue of farm electrification had been on the agenda of government officials for a long time and the Post-War Reconstruction Committee recommended priority be given to an expansion of electrical power beyond Winnipeg into rural areas.[5] Shortly after peace was declared, the premier of Manitoba, Stuart Garson, wrote to W.L. Mackenzie King, the prime minister of Canada, regarding the province's reconstruction plans and the role of provincial and federal governments in its funding. In a list of priorities, he identified farm electrification as the most important (fig. 10.1).[6]

The bureaucrats in Winnipeg examined how farm electrification had been implemented in the United States, as some neighbouring states had legislated farm electrification in the 1930s. The files of the planning commission contain a number of pamphlets and reports of United States schemes for rural electrification and illustrations from these were sometimes copied by the Manitoba Power Commission into information distributed to its farmers.[7] Trials were conducted in Manitoba in 1943 and 1945 by the commission to test the willingness of farmers to contribute to the cost of expanding the network and purchasing a range of electrical products, not just those useful for farming, but also any intended for domestic use. Farmers were invited to local meetings, shown a film, and given a pamphlet and a survey form to complete.[8] The survey results indicated an eagerness to be connected to the power network but less willingness to sign contracts. This may reflect that mostly men turned up to the meetings and were more interested in the use of electricity in farming operations than their wives, who could be shown the benefits of installing electricity in the home. In response, the commission arranged for separate approaches to be made to women to reveal the range of domestic labour-saving appliances available when a household was connected to the grid.[9] The federal government in Ottawa identified the broader importance of electrification in its own planning commission's report that spoke of "the intangible benefit of

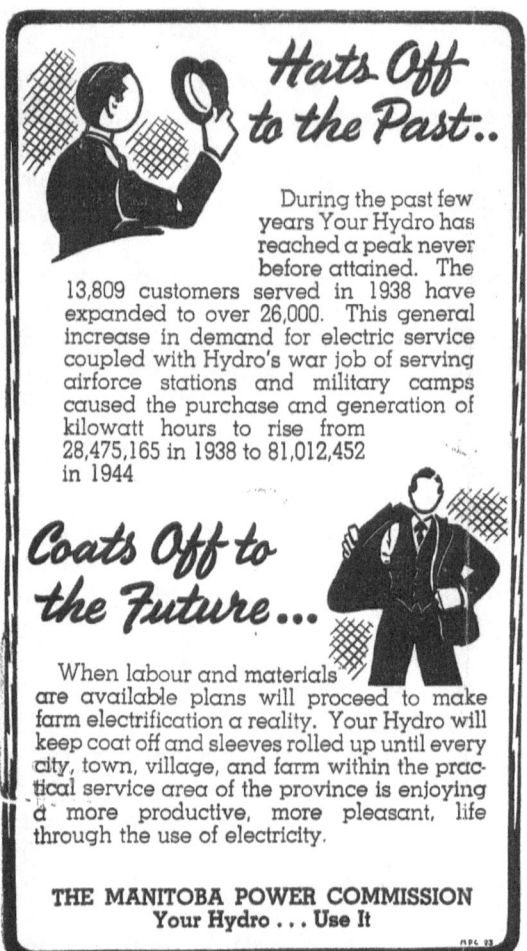

Fig. 10.1. Advertisement promoting electrification. In 1945 the Manitoba Power Commission intensified its campaign to extend the electrical supply (Hydro) network into southern Manitoba, including the Grunthal area. Local newspapers carried advertisements, reports, and photographs of the electricity (Hydro) lines being installed, often by Mennonite linesman employed by the power commission.

Source: *Steinbach Post*, 25 July 1945.

rural electrification through its contribution to the physical and social well-being of the community."[10]

The Manitoba Power Commission's 1945 report *Power for Manitoba Farms* noted that farmers in rural areas of the RM of Hanover were to be included in its survey for future expansion of the network. Electricity in Steinbach as a private venture had existed in a limited way since 1914 and in 1938 the supply was expanded in agreement with the town's board until bought out by the power commission in 1943.[11] Grunthal and its surrounding district were recognized in official notices as possessing a "progressive community" and consequently work to connect the district began in 1946/47 in the second round of special government funding intended to expand the network.[12] In January 1947 a newspaper report stated that Grunthal residents were "at last enjoying city conveniences after a long time waiting."[13] Most rural areas were connected the following year or at least by 1948, with only outlying areas waiting until the early 1950s to finally be linked to the network.

Increased demand soon required the power commission to increase the voltage level and build new transmitting and receiving stations.[14] To undertake this project, large teams of workers were set to work erecting poles, stringing lines, and connecting houses and farm buildings. Several locals found employment on the initial construction and continued as employees of the commission as lines needed to be maintained, while secondary industries such as plumbing, carpentry, and appliance servicing brought additional employment opportunities. To save money some farmers thought they could do the final connections to homes and barns themselves but all they achieved was to put their families at risk of electrocution. Some even managed to kill some of their cows.

The arrival of electricity also witnessed the development of businesses, particularly milk factories. Since the first factory was founded in the 1890s, dairy factories in Grunthal had come and gone.[15] Manitoba Cooperative Dairies was founded in 1921 and established its own production plants in Brandon (1927) and Dauphin (1929).[16] The St. Malo cheese factory was a branch of the Cooperative Industries of St. Malo Ltd.[17] At the end of the war the Grunthal farmers' cooperative venture, established with such high hopes during the war, proved too undercapitalized to expand its plant and meet the increasing supply of milk produced from surrounding farms. It also lacked the infrastructure to market its products efficiently. The cooperative did attempt to sell butter under the brand name "Green Valley," but this failed to increase revenue.[18] It was rumoured that the initial shareholders lost money,

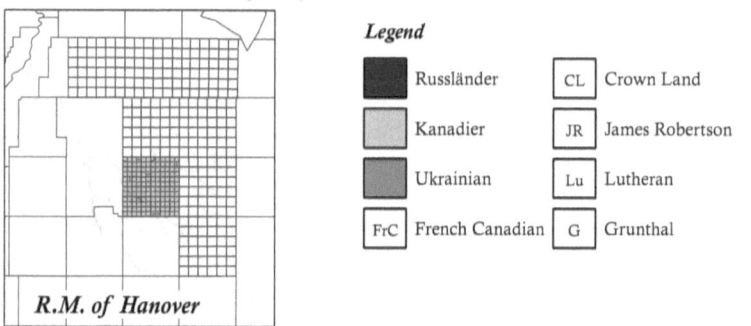

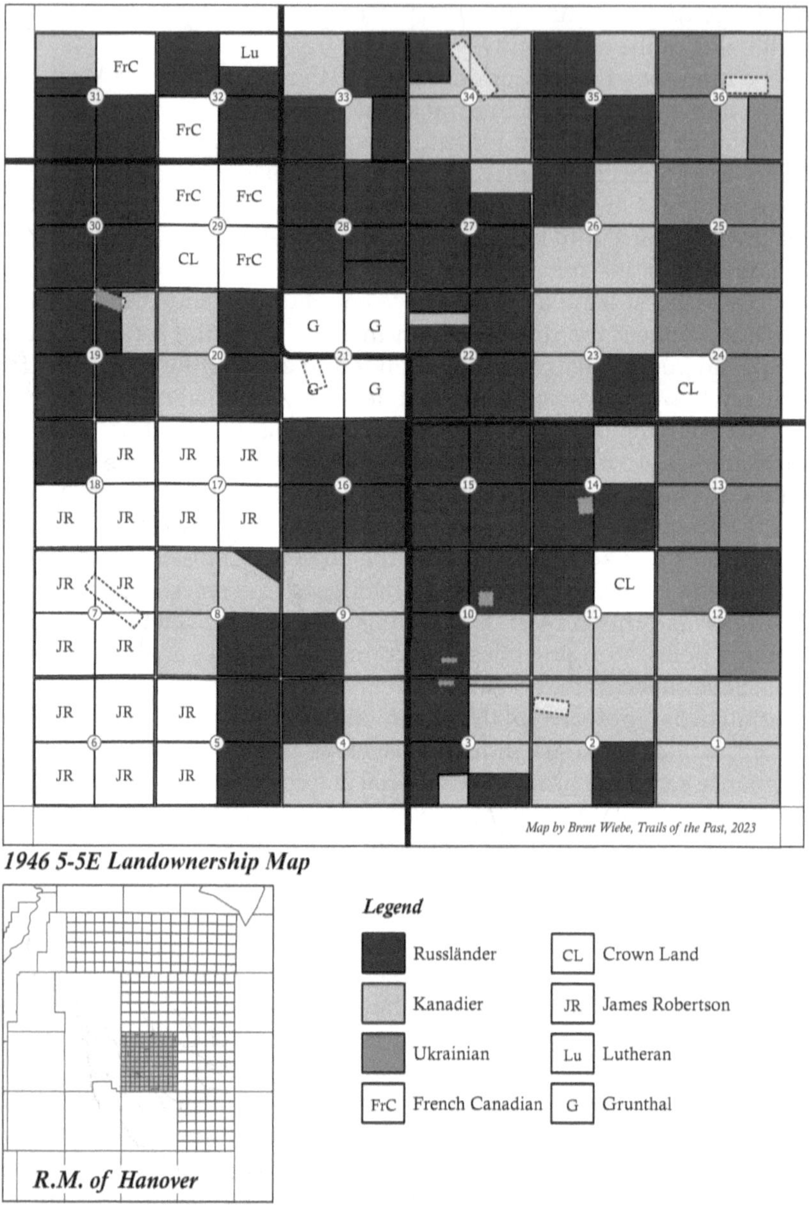

1946 5-5E Landownership Map

Map 10.1. Landownership in 5–5E, 1946. From tax records of the RM of Hanover.

Sources: Map by Brent Wiebe, *Trails of the Past* (2023). Contains information from the Government of Manitoba, licenced under the OpenMB Information and Data Use Licence (Manitoba.ca/OpenMB).

reinforcing Russländer suspicions that cooperatives were risky ventures with hidden socialist aims.

It therefore came as a relief when in 1946 the cooperative was sold, "lock stock and barrel" as one report stated, to a major producer of dairy produce, Kraft Foods Ltd. of Montreal. The new owners invested heavily in the business, building a new factory at a cost of $50,000 with a processing plant and a deep well to obtain water. Unlike earlier dairy ventures, the factory specialized in cheese production and to produce high-quality cheese the latest technology was installed, including ten-thousand-pound cheese vats. By the early 1950s the factory was processing sixty thousand pounds of milk daily from farmers in the surrounding region.[19] It was so successful that within a few years the plant needed to expand. The arrival of Kraft and the modernization of the factory transformed the town of Grunthal as well as the lives of farmers in surrounding areas who supplied the milk.[20] Locals found employment in the factory at levels of remuneration previously unknown in the district. In 1956, however, the Kraft factory, which was not getting the returns it expected, was sold to Modern Dairies Ltd. owned by J.W. Speirs of St. Boniface and became part of its Medo-Lands enterprise.[21] They restructured the factory to produce skimmed milk powder used in a wider range of products including butter and even ice cream.[22]

The Kraft factory took milk but only extracted the richer cream to make cheese. The whey was returned to the farmer who used it to feed hogs. But as Medo-Lands processed more of the milk, on many farms hog numbers declined. On-farm butchering and the secular Mennonite "ritual" of processing hog meat, including the much-loved farmer sausage (LG *Foarmaworscht/Reatjaworscht*), became less common. Instead of the pig-slaughtering bee (LG *Schwienschlachte/Schwienstjast*) a ritual once accompanied by alcohol, it was increasingly left to butchers who slaughtered hogs and other animals, sometimes on the farms of their owners, with the carcasses then taken away for final processing.[23] Some meat and meat products were then sold on while a portion was returned to the farmer and kept in the freezer, another benefit of electrification.

Not all dairy farmers supplied factories with milk as there was still a profit to be made in Winnipeg through selling fresh milk. Once the Piney Highway was opened in 1937 milk was supplied to Winnipeg by truck and in the same year the Manitoba government introduced the Milk Control Act to regulate the supply and price of "bulk milk"[24] To supply milk a producer first had to obtain a contract from one of the companies that held a quota to supply milk to the city. In 1938 the average monthly quota allowed for the greater Winnipeg area was 6,500 lbs; by 1955 it was 8,800 lbs, and by 1968, 22,600 lbs.[25] The entire system was regulated by the Milk Marketing Board which kept a close watch on the quantities of seasonal supply, the quality of the milk, and the prices charged to consumers.[26] This was in contrast to the supply of milk to the local factory which at first was largely unregulated.

Initially milk for Winnipeg was supplied in cans that had to be kept cool either by setting them in cold water or by having well water pumped over them until they were collected by local transfer trucks. The cans bore the identification of the farmer and the name of the city dairy to which they were to be delivered. Later, cans were reloaded onto larger vehicles for transport to the city. At first electrification assisted with the cooling but only through powering cooling water pumps. In 1955 there were twenty-nine milk shippers to Winnipeg who supplied 232,800 pounds of milk.[27] The entire process was laborious and it was not until the early 1960s that cooling tanks were introduced and a revolution in milk handling began.[28]

In Grunthal three different models of tanks were sold through the Grunthal Feed Service, which had already diversified its milling business into selling a wide range of dairy equipment; their advertisements for pumps, piping, and barn conversions appeared in the local newspaper.[29] The installation of the new milk tanks on farms was followed by the arrival of refrigerated milk tankers, although the first farmer to install a bulk milk tank in the region was not a Mennonite but Gus DePape, a person of Walloon descent.[30] As early as 1959 in Grunthal some transfer drivers gained qualifications to drive the new tankers and Klassen's feed mill began to offer bulk milk coolers for sale.[31] The arrival of milk tankers, the installation of refrigerated milk tanks on farms, and later the ability to pump milk improved the quality and distribution of liquid milk. In 1960 just eight tankers served 122 producers in the area that supplied milk to Winnipeg but by 1962, sixteen trucks served 460 producers and carried 72 per cent of the town milk supply.[32]

There was also increased rationalization of production and distribution. Across Manitoba bulk tankers and the requirement on farmers to install cooling tanks reduced the number of suppliers to Winnipeg from 1,300 in the early 1950s to just 678 in 1963.[33] In Grunthal it was mainly Russländer who continued to supply town milk, for detailed records had to be kept and quality strictly monitored. A Grunthal driver who had picked up cans and later driven a tanker, pointed out that of the eight farmers from whom he collected cans, only two were Kanadier, one a Chortitzer, and the other Bergthaler, and both continued to supply town milk once tanks were installed.

The more commercially focused dairy industry, however, was also making use of other scientific advances in milk production, the most

Fig. 10.2. Joseph LaFrance, agricultural advisor. LaFrance was involved with the improved breeding program for milk cows. His work extended right across the southeastern region of Manitoba and he was greatly respected by dairy farmers for using his knowledge to increase the quality of dairy milk cows and for promoting the dairy industry for Mennonite and non-Mennonite farmers.

Source: The *Carillon* Archives, Steinbach, Manitoba.

important of which was the innovative work of the agricultural advisor in St. Pierre, Joseph LaFrance (fig. 10.2).[34] In 1945 he established the Rat River Artificial Breeding Centre, the first such venture in Manitoba connected with local herd improvement associations.[35] Although it began in St. Pierre in 1947 with French farmers, ten Grunthal farmers soon joined the St. Pierre program and by 1948/49 over a thousand cows in the district were included in the scheme.[36] Using a range of strategies, such as employing better breeding bulls, keeping careful records on each cow, culling poor producers, and looking at the best range of feeds, LaFrance greatly increased milk and butter fat output (see table 10.1). A 1953 report showed that offspring of cows of the better breeding bulls increased milk production by an average of 56 per cent and butterfat by

Table 10.1. Increases in production following artificial breeding scheme in St. Pierre, 1947–52

Herds, cow numbers, and production	1947	1948	1949	1950	1951	1952
Number of herds	25	27	25	23	14	17
Number of cows	414	409	369	332	208	284
Average milk production	8,521	9,438	9,917	10,331	10,506	10,855
Average fat prod. per cow	296	315	331	334	359	399

Source: *Dairy News*, no. 4 (April 1953), 2; Dairy Scrapbooks, Department of Agriculture, AM GR 7777.

84 per cent. The same report gave the following figures indicating how the program quickly produced impressive results, increasing yields while reducing herd size.

What the figures do not reveal is that the farmers most eager to learn from LaFrance were Mennonites, especially around Grunthal, as the number of milk cows fell in St. Pierre in the early 1950s as dairying declined in the area.[37] When LaFrance left to take up a new position as chief of agricultural services for Manitoba in 1960, it is not surprising that his farewell was hosted in Grunthal as their dairy farmers had been the principal benefactors of his skill and knowledge.[38]

By 1962 the dairy farmers who were members of the Grunthal Herd Improvement Association had twenty-two herds on test with 487 cows, of which 314 had completed their lactation and produced 3,063,612 lbs of milk with 113,256.1 lbs of butterfat.[39] Producing this quantity of milk was a complicated process for man and beast. With electrification, vacuum milking during the early 1950s gradually replaced hand milking but the milk was still pumped into a bucket and then poured into cans. The early equipment was clumsy and complicated to use. Maintaining consistent pressure was one of the main problems, as were the cups needed to fit on the cows' teats. When the cans were replaced with large tanks the pipes were often found to be inflexible. However, the use of milking machines and the installation of tanks increased the number of cows that could be milked daily on farms from about ten to fifteen to around thirty, thereby also increasing production and returns.

Larger herds meant more feed was required. Some farmers continued to depend on hay while others planted crops including alfalfa and maize to convert into silage. As the growing season on the prairies is short, cultivating feed crops required intense effort. Planting started soon after spring arrived and harvesting finished before winter set in, when cows had to be brought under cover and watered and fed through the long winter months. In the early days straw and dung were cleared from barns by pitchfork and only later regularly deposited into the open by a mechanical chain where it quickly froze. In spring the snow melt and defrosting of the soil brought additional challenges as before seeding the frozen manure had to be spread on fields and ploughed in as fields were prepared for cultivation.

Dairying, however, was neither the only form of making money from farming nor for dairy farmers was it always their sole source of income.[40] Livestock, which included beef and hogs, was also an important source of income and, although to a lesser extent, so were eggs. Eggs had long provided an easy source of income. Unlike before the war when individuals peddled them around Winnipeg, now eggs were marketed in bulk. They were supplied through an egg-grading station located in Grunthal where they were first checked for freshness by candling and then graded, requirements imposed on producers in 1940 by the provincial authorities.[41]

In order to supplement his income, Peter H. Janzen, a dairy farmer, built a large egg-producing chicken run and also worked in town in various managerial positions.[42] On areas less suitable for extensive dairying, mixed farming continued. Peter Klassen, noted for growing watermelons and thus nicknamed *Arbuse* (Watermelon) *Klosse*, was described by one newspaper account as an "intrepid horticulturalist" and told the reporter, "God intended for people to live in a garden environment, that is why he first placed them in the Garden of Eden."[43] His friend, Peter D. Thiessen, was less blessed. In 1954 Thiessen appealed against taxes imposed on his farm claiming that his house, buildings, and his production of sugar beets, potatoes, and eggs had been incorrectly assessed as they were not for commercial sale. He lost his appeal.[44]

The expanded economic activity in and around Grunthal required the town and its environs to be better connected to markets, especially Winnipeg and, although only a few would openly admit it, Steinbach. In the post-war period Steinbach was promoted by Manitoba development agencies and saw its population almost double from 1,900 to 3,739 between 1946 and 1961.[45] From its foundation the East Reserve lacked a direct train connection although in 1878 a line was built through Niverville which became a supply centre for Mennonite settlers.[46] Kanadier communities kept themselves apart from railroads that during the nineteenth century became central places closely tied to the economic development of the prairies. Most important prairie towns were located at key junctions of the rail network; rail junctions were essential in the growth of their rural hinterlands. As none of the Mennonite settlements on the East Reserve were directly connected to a rail network, they relied on roads to link them with railheads and therefore reach major markets. But often these roads were unimproved and in spring and fall frequently turned into quagmires and became impassable. Even in good weather owners of cars in Grunthal were advised to have their vehicles checked over by a mechanic before embarking for Winnipeg.

The importance of major road connections in Manitoba involved not just Canada-wide links but also routes southward to and from the United States border. With the advent of the age of the motor vehicle in the United States, massive road construction had been underway for years and the attraction for Manitoba's provincial government involved the movement of goods and tourists. Plans for a road link southeast to Minnesota from east of Grunthal had been worked on since the Depression. The major post-war argument, however, involved the construction of a more direct route south from Winnipeg to Emerson on the North Dakota border. The issue was whether a new highway was to be built west or east of the Red River. If it went east of the river, it would favour Grunthal, and this proposal was supported by the Steinbach business community and others in the southeast. The road would follow a route via St. Anne's Road, through St. Vital, and then south close to Otterburne, Arnaud, Dominion City, and on to the border at Emerson. Supporters of the eastern route were backed by their member in the Legislative Assembly, Edmond Prefontaine. In Steinbach a Piney Highway Association (*Piney Hochweg Organisation*) was formed and during 1946–7 meetings were held that included representatives from Grunthal.[47] But in 1948 the government announced that the highway was to be constructed west of the Red River. The one piece of good news was that a secondary, all-weather highway would also be built from St. Pierre to Emerson.[48]

For the people of the Grunthal area the issue now became how the town and surrounding districts could get better, improved roads to connect with Steinbach, St. Pierre, and other local towns as well as Winnipeg. Steinbach was rapidly becoming the motor-dealer centre of the region, even attracting buyers from Winnipeg who travelled there to get a special deal on an automobile.[49] Every year the government announced its annual program of road building, road improvements, and highways, and each year the RM of Hanover sent resolutions to government on the issue.[50] In Grunthal, government announcements were carefully studied but in comparison with neighbouring centres it seemed their town was becoming increasingly isolated.[51] In 1960 local residents began a campaign to get other connections added to the annual road building program including a Grunthal/Sarto link to St.

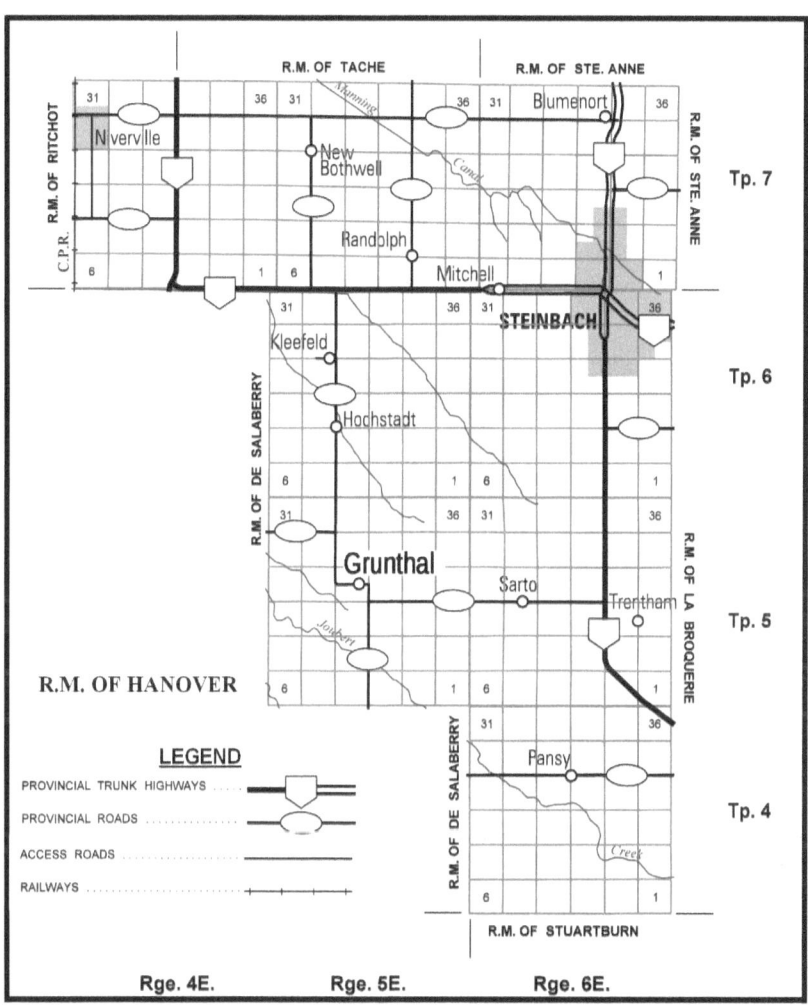

Map 10.2. Road system, RM of Hanover.

Sources: Based on Government of Manitoba maps and adapted by Ernest N. Braun.

Pierre. The different proposals and their supporters and detractors created a problem for the local member of the Legislature, Edmond Prefontaine, as at the previous election campaign had been fought largely over the issue of roads.[52] Eventually, however, the campaigners succeeded.[53] In the long term, roads proved a mixed blessing for communities (see map 10.2). Roads that eased the transportation of produce such as milk, butter, and cheese also allowed residents to venture further afield. Small businesses depended on local customers but as prosperity increased, residents could shop in larger centres, including Steinbach and Winnipeg, where stores carried a greater variety of goods, often at lower prices. A bus service replaced the established transit systems while individuals with cars and trucks could go as far as Winnipeg to shop and return with ease in less than a day.

The improvement and promise of an expanded road network reached across the prairies, creating less dependence on passenger trains. Census returns showed that in 1936 there were 21,293 trucks on farms in the prairie provinces, down slightly from 21,517 in 1931, undoubtedly because of the Depression. In 1941, however, the figures had recovered to 43,363 and by the end of the war in 1946 to 56,177. Post-war prosperity soon increased the number of trucks to 113,512 in 1951.[54] A survey of transportation in Manitoba published in 1938 showed there to be 439 passenger cars and 134 "motor trucks" registered in Hanover, fewer cars than the 706 in the major Mennonite municipality of Rhineland over *jant-sied*, on the "other side" on the West Reserve, but roughly the same number of trucks, 133.[55] Rhineland, however, had easier access to a railway than Hanover. The vehicle figures available for Grunthal provide numbers for both cars and trucks together. In 1943 Grunthal had 156 vehicles, compared to Steinbach with 417; Giroux, 177; Chortitz, 70; Kleefeld, 83; and Niverville, 100.[56]

Contemporary reports, however, even speak of farmers trading in cars for trucks, just another reflection of their increased incomes.[57] Many of the cars had been purchased second-hand, had been in use since the 1930s, and were now in poor condition. In Grunthal a car and truck wrecking business was established to break down vehicles, sell the body work, and where possible store spare parts to help maintain a rapidly aging fleet. But its owner refused to help maintain Model T Fords as he considered them yesterday's technology. New and second-hand trucks and cars were sold and serviced by the garages established before and during the war. Some flourished into the post-war period by diversifying into a range of other vehicles and farm machinery. Others sold products connected with the growing dependence on motorized farm machines and automated equipment.

In the mid-1950s the Chornoboy garage became a Volkswagen dealership, about the same time Jake Banmann started selling the Beetle, or "Bug," as the vehicle was known across North America. The car was favoured in part because of its German origin and continued as part of Chornoboy's business until 1976. The number of tractor agencies increased from the original Warkentin's Allis-Chalmers and

Chornoboy's International Harvester to others in and beyond Grunthal, enabling farmers to purchase new and second-hand models. One farmer purchased a John Deere Model D from a supplier in St. Pierre, and another a Case tractor from Steinbach. Later the Cockshutt-Oliver dealer in Grunthal was Steve Block, whose main supplier was the Neufeld Brothers' garage in Chortitz. Diedrich Heese bought a large Oliver model for the threshing business he developed doing custom work in and around Grunthal. Kanadier, along with Ukrainians, were usually hired to assist with ploughing, grain and alfalfa harvesting, and threshing. Workers were paid in cash no doubt to avoid paying taxes and employers meeting their obligations.

Until the post-war period most Mennonites still lived in houses erected by Kanadier when they first settled in the area. In and around Grunthal these were poorly constructed and insulated against Manitoba's harsh winters. Like their predecessors discovered in the 1870s, Russländer found prairie winters much colder than the Russian steppe. Gaps around windows and in walls had to be insulated with little more than rags and paper; toilets were located outside the house as were the washing facilities for cleaning clothes; wells were also situated outside and water was carried into houses and barns while wells would freeze over in really cold weather. Stoves kept the house warm but were fuelled by cordwood. Bathing and laundry in winter were restricted as water first had to be boiled, and wet bedding and clothing could not easily be hung outside to dry. Women milked cows in cold barns while cream, butter, and the essential baking of bread and cooking was done by women at home, aided by daughters.

In the post-war years a building boom began and as early as 1949 people started to relocate into new houses at first built mainly along Grunthal's main street.[58] The new houses possessed basements often dug out by hand with walls constructed initially from cinder blocks and later with poured concrete.[59] The rest of the house was constructed of wood from lumber mills in Steinbach with new windows, again supplied from Steinbach by Loewen Windows. The construction workers, however, were mainly locals and from 1958 H.T. Friesen supplied lumber from a local yard. On farms much better and more secure water supplies were obtained by digging new wells or improving existing wells through lining them with concrete cribbing pipes. This was work carried out by a local contractor, C.F. Neufeld, who also constructed the cribbing pipes.[60] Well water was pumped to the surface by electric pumps and connected to houses and barns. Toilets in houses now flushed and eventually were connected to proper sewage systems first installed in the town and later in surrounding farms. Farmers who were not connected installed a system of septic fields, large areas located underground filled with stones where the sewage settled and into which effluent water was pumped from a tank.

Post-war prosperity altered the rhythm of life for both men and women. Because of the introduction of new technologies and better housing, the position of women in households changed radically. This had been foreseen in a government report on the benefits of reconstruction that suggested the benefit of modern technology would include:

> the elimination of laborious tasks which necessarily form part of the routine of rural women's work [for example] three constantly recurring tasks, sheer drudgery as such disappears through the use of electrical power for cream separators, churns, and power-washers to take care of the heavy, grimy, weekly accumulation of laundry ... [with the benefit of the] consequent release of energy and time for cultural and social interests and activities.[61]

In houses rooms could be centrally heated from a basement furnace. Kitchens were equipped with electric stoves and sockets to power a range of modern kitchen aids.[62] Laundry could now be done with a washing machine and in winter dried in electric dryers. For women the laborious daily task involved in bread production could be replaced or at least reduced by purchasing freshly baked bread and even cakes from Friesen's bakery after it opened in Grunthal in 1946. At first the bakery produced just six loaves a day but within a year it made one hundred loaves and following its expansion in 1966, it was producing one thousand loaves daily, along with buns, cakes, and pies.[63]

A range of other foodstuffs other than just dry ingredients for cooking could be purchased in Grunthal's stores. This included frozen goods to be stored, along with meat from their own farm, in household freezers which, with refrigerators, improved food preservation. Guenther's store sold a range of electrical goods and appliances for domestic use in homes.[64] These included vacuum cleaners and electric sewing machines which helped women reduce time spent on routine tasks. Eventually all members of the family could enjoy television. When Guenther's store displayed the first television models in their store window in the late 1950s it attracted the attention of many but there were also mutterings of disapproval from some in the community. Soon, however, televisions were installed in most Grunthal homes and opened new ways of accessing the wider world including "worldly" entertainment. In these ways and others, the interiors of homes were changed in structure and content beyond recognition from those before the war. The impact of many of these innovations eased women's lives and social life at home was transformed for the entire family.

In the town new streets were established, named after trees: Oak, Ash, Pine, along with a Church Avenue. New house lots were laid out and in 1961 it was reported that whereas these once sold for $100 each, they now cost between $300 and $500.[65] Even so, in the 1950s another study reported there were still "many vacant areas" giving the centre of town "a casual rural atmosphere," while trails on the north side "of main street" led off to a "haphazard collection of houses built in the 1930s." Beyond, in a "more formal residential area … laid out since the war," the bush pressed in "on both sides of these developments."[66] As the town grew, vacant areas were developed, as old businesses expanded or moved into new premises while other concerns took over old buildings or erected new ones. As the town took on a new significance the old agricultural village established by the original Kanadier began to vanish as its old houses were removed, abandoned, or demolished. This was clearly a new town developed principally by Russländer. E.K. Francis reported in 1945 that of the town's "population of 212, 119 were *Russländer*, 73 Kanadier Mennonites, there were 2 Ukrainian families (8 persons) and one French (12 persons)."[67]

The range of businesses now included not only garages selling cars, trucks, tractors, and farm equipment, but also older businesses that prospered after war's end. Retail and grocery stores developed new ways to attract consumers and especially to take a share of the farmers' increased incomes. The most successful retail centre continued to be Guenther's Red and White Store where its founder Franz Guenther now was ably assisted by some of his sons. They brought a new vision to retailing, beginning by holding a clearance sale of stock accumulated by their father for his "general store." During the sale they managed to dispose of most of the dated goods including boxes of old-fashioned high laced leather shoes to local Hutterites who no doubt took their bargains back to their unsuspecting wives and daughters. The original Guenther store, already expanded to create a "supermarket" atmosphere, in 1961 was remodelled once more and now sold a greater range of fresh and frozen products, hardware, shoes, and clothing, as well as a range of electrical appliances.[68] This proved so successful that in November 1963 a brand new "7000 square feet shopping centre" claimed to be the "biggest grocery, hardware, appliance store in southern Manitoba" replaced the old store which had been remodelled just two years earlier.[69] The new post-war economic conditions favoured private enterprise like Guenther's store and reduced further the ability of the Grunthal Cooperative to compete. After struggling on, it finally closed in 1955.⁷⁰ The reasons for its failure later given around Grunthal are contradictory. Instead of admitting that economic conditions had changed with greater competition, the inevitable small-town rumours suggested everything from a failure of management to even corruption.

In 1948, as well as the dairy factory, there were roughly sixteen businesses listed in an article on Grunthal. These included three garages, two blacksmiths, the feed mill, a bakery, a woodwork shop, an implement shop, a second-hand furniture shop, the egg-grading business, and even a watch repair shop. A joke published in 1947 in the local newspaper mocking Grunthal's attempts to expand its economic base claimed that Mennonites in the town had signed an agreement to supply "buttonholes" for overalls to be shipped in a fleet of trucks to a cloth factory in St. Pierre.⁷¹ Of course there was no factory, and the holes were as vacuous as any major industrial base other than the dairy factory in Grunthal. Instead, most businesses were "service" industries. The post office, however, expanded to include a daily mail delivery service and the transfer service was supplemented by the daily bus service to and from Winnipeg that passed through Grunthal.⁷² Over the following years articles in the local newspaper charted the progress of businesses in the town and in 1959 reported the founding of a new service enterprise, the Rainbow Inn, subsequently destroyed by fire in 1965. The reports, however, say little about other ventures that failed.⁷³ Some reports, particularly those published at the start of each new year, have an air of boosterism about them. Indeed, one published in 1946 written by a "Grunthalbooster," also ridiculed contemporary plans for the expansion of the community.⁷⁴ But there is little doubt that the town continued to prosper, drawing in custom from local Mennonites as well as from further afield, particularly from surrounding Ukrainian districts.

The town's progress was aided by the creation of a Grunthal Town Board and a Grunthal Chamber of Commerce although it is often difficult to differentiate them as in early reports the board is referred to as the "Grunthal Board of Trade."⁷⁵ A post-war report noted that while "Grunthal has not yet been incorporated it has been organized to some extent" and town "affairs, generally, are in the hands of an elected Town Board of three members." The members' powers were "limited" but extended "to such matters as town planning by issuing permits, construction and sidewalks, etc."⁷⁶ Later reports speak of a "village council" and a "Town Board" that corresponded to a "town council in some places" with "a mayor, assistant mayor and town secretary to administer the affairs of the growing town." E.K. Francis writing in the late 1940s noted that a local board of trade was making "a strong bid for incorporation of the place which may in time develop into a small town."[77] A by-law (#421) of the Hanover council of February 1946 established Grunthal as an unincorporated Village District following a petition of a "majority of ratepayers."[78]

The "Board of Trade" appears to be what was later referred to from the early 1950s as a "Chamber of Commerce" consisting mainly of town business owners with a few local farmer members.[79] In many ways the chamber of commerce resembled bodies already established in St. Pierre and Steinbach. The St. Pierre body had existed in principle since 1936 but only operated from 1947, the same year the town contemplated applying for incorporation.[80] The Grunthal Town Board and Chamber of Commerce promoted developments in similar ways to the corresponding organizations in Steinbach and St. Pierre.[81] They reached agreement with the "Grunthal Sports Association" "to organize and promote sports activities" in the community.[82] As the chamber's president described it in 1959, the aim was to:

> bring to the community progress and greater prosperity ... to help the community in its efforts to make this district an even better place where more and more of our young people may find a fuller and more satisfactory life, a place of which every right-thinking citizens [sic] may well be proud.[83]

The chamber of commerce lobbied the province on the need for highways while the town board organized the sealing of roads through the town, curbing, the installation of street lighting (agreed to by the Hanover Municipal Council in 1951), water supply, and a sewage system. The town board also worked with the municipal council on the upgrading of services with a municipal fire truck served by the Grunthal Volunteer Fire Brigade and stationed in Grunthal after 1971.

By the early 1960s to supplement the electrical supply (Hydro), natural gas became available to provide an alternative source of energy.[84] Increasingly the Grunthal community was connected to the rest of the province by energy supplies, roads, and social and cultural services. These were part of the Canada-wide economic development of post-war rural communities that benefited Mennonites in places other than just Grunthal.[85] The people of the Grunthal district, however, could justly look back on the post-war years as a period of progress and steady growth.[86] How much the town grew is indicated by the number of taxpayers on the municipal council rolls (table 10.2).

The sustained prosperity of the Grunthal community can also be assessed by the success of the Grunthal Credit Union. Despite rumours and reports to the contrary, the credit union continued to flourish,

Table 10.2. Number of taxable landholders in Grunthal town according to Hanover municipal records, 1938–70

Year	No.
1938	14
1940	31
1942	36
1944	34
1946	41
1948	63
1950	57
1952	61
1954	63
1956	77
1958	76
1960	92
1962	?
1964	129
1966	122
1968	116
1970	147

gaining new members and increasing the size of its deposits. In 1948 a claim that it was in financial difficulties was rebutted by its president.[87] In 1953 the credit union's assets had increased to $12,500 but dropped in 1956. Soon after, however, its assets recovered, reaching $40,300 by 1958 and more than doubling by 1961 to $90,700. Growth afterwards was considerable and in 1964 its assets stood at $313,400.[88] By 1974 they were estimated at just under $2 million.[89] Moreover, the credit union offered new, modern financial services such as a life insurance scheme in 1958 and a chequing system in 1962. Membership expanded to include many of its original sceptics and a varied clientele of Russländer, Kanadier, and even non-Mennonites.

In an unpublished account of Grunthal written after the war, E.K. Francis described Grunthal as "a small rural trade centre: [with a] lack of good communications" but with "a wide under-developed hinterland" that drew its trade "from the backwoods as far as 15 miles to the Southeast and the South." This included Mennonites, Ukrainians, and even customers from neighbouring French parishes. Francis noted that the "business centre properly speaking has grown up a short distance from the old village (which is almost deserted since the exodus to Paraguay ... [of Kanadier])." The new town of Grunthal was situated at "the crossing point of the Winnipeg and Steinbach roads with a third connection to the New Barkfield area."[90] Based on research a decade later the geographer John H. Warkentin described Grunthal as "still the leading centre of the southern part of the [East] Reserve." This was despite the post-war growth of other urban areas nearby, especially Steinbach, which had drawn Grunthal's Ukrainian customers away from their town. However, Warkentin suggested Grunthal had recovered from such changes, finding new customers among other Ukrainians in the Rosa area, and he expected Grunthal and its local businesses to continue to prosper. While Grunthal was located "in the midst of bush country and away from through highways," the town "definitely [has] ... the qualities of an independent regional capital" and had "risen above the stereotyped pattern of the usual rural prairie trading town in both appearance and atmosphere," possessing "a fresh naivete which is never found in even the smallest centre located on a railway."[91] These post-war comments by outsiders indicate how Grunthal had become a more integrated community attracting people from the surrounding Mennonite and non-Mennonite farmers and associated businesses. Divisions, however, remained.

Chapter Eleven

A United and Divided Community

Increased post-war prosperity in and around Grunthal continued the move towards a more integrated community of Russländer, Kanadier, and non-Mennonites, at least in economic matters. The remnants of the original village of Grunthal were fast disappearing as many of its remaining houses from the first days of settlement were either moved or pulled down. Gnadenfeld's inhabitants were now part of the extended Grunthal community and its name was relegated to yet another historical village of the East Reserve. The new town of Grunthal, created mainly by Russländer, was now the central place of the immediate district and its main thoroughfare was paved, the sidewalks concreted over, and even an improved ice rink built.[1] But well into the 1950s the town buildings remained little more than facades. New shopfronts were often placed over older structures and only a few stores were newly built, such as Guenther's store. An aerial view of the town published in 1962, but probably from a few years earlier, shows a scattering of houses with large empty sections even along both sides of the main street.[2] However, the town and surrounding district were growing fast as the combined activities of a local town board and the chamber of commerce advantaged not just the town, but also the district's community.

A directory from 1962 giving the names and contact details of town officials provides a list of the most prominent members: the president of the chamber of commerce, the mayor, members of the town board, the principal of the collegiate, and the fire chief and his assistant.[3] In some matters, however, the interests of farmers living on their sections and business leaders living in town did not always coincide. This was perhaps a reflection of the usual town versus country conflict, or more correctly the pretensions of the leaders in town over the views of more cautious farmers accustomed to the ups and downs of farming. While the town's business community hoped Grunthal ultimately would be able to compete with other towns on the East Reserve and eventually rival Steinbach, the Reserve's increasingly central place, farmers wanted to grow the agricultural base of their immediate district rather than to be exploited by local businessmen.

Differences in vision can be seen in 1951 when a few Grunthal farmers became involved with the Manitoba Farmers Union (MFU), the same year the chamber of commerce is first mentioned in local reports.[4] The Farmers Union was based on others in Alberta and Saskatchewan that initially were linked with local cooperative movements but in the post-war world had adopted strategies from organized labour unions concerned with industrial issues. The manifesto of the MFU made such a connection clear: farming was a business from which farmers received insufficient recognition and rewards for their contribution to the economy. The time had arrived for farmers to unite, organize, and act together in order to obtain "more equitable returns" for their produce "so a higher standard of living, and a greater sense of security may result."[5] Grunthal farmers certainly attended an MFU meeting in Winnipeg and there are reports that they even formed a "local" along with others in the region.[6] But after these initial reports nothing further is said about their involvement. One reason may be that Mennonites, especially Russländer, were deeply suspicious of trade unions, which they associated with communism. Another reason may be that the MFU was dominated by grain-growing farmers, particularly wheat producers, while Grunthal farmers were mainly concerned with dairy production and did not share many concerns of other MFU members. For Grunthal people, "community" was centred on the town and its growing hinterland, not matters further west on the prairies, even if Mennonite farmers on the other side of the Red River were engaged in the commercial production of grains and other crops not produced around Grunthal.

Several other farming and related organizations linked to non-Mennonite bodies had existed since the 1930s, mostly dominated by Russländer. One of earliest was Kiwanis, founded in the United States around 1915. Kiwanis claimed to focus on the "human and spiritual" instead of the "material values of life." Other aspects of its aims, however, sound rather un-Mennonite, such as its intention to develop "a more intelligent, aggressive, and serviceable citizenship" that included "patriotism."[7] During the pre-war years such aims were probably better suited to Russländer than Kanadier so when in 1933 members of the Winnipeg Kiwanis Club "motored down" to Grunthal to judge agricultural production they met on a Russländer farm.[8] Contacts continued with further visits, principally for children to establish clubs devoted to calves, chickens, and potato production in line with the aim of helping youth develop into useful, productive adults.[9] Russländer were probably eager to improve young people's interest in agriculture in order to keep them busy, rather than to develop the kind of values Kiwanis encouraged. Undoubtedly, Russländer considered children's values to be better encouraged at home, in the classroom, and in Sunday Schools.

Mennonites were also unwilling to form other youth groups such as the Scouts and Girl Guides because these were viewed as semi-military organizations connected with non-Mennonite churches. After the war Grunthalers became involved with another organization, now known as 4-H Clubs but at first as Boys and Girls Clubs, established in 1913 in Roland, a largely English farming district of Manitoba. The clubs flourished from the 1930s onward and became a national organization with the support of provincial governments and federal authorities; in 1952 the name 4-H Clubs was adopted from the United States.[10] The aim of 4-H clubs was to improve farming and homemaking skills by "Learning to Do by Doing." Members had to pledge their "Head to clearer thinking, my Heart to greater loyalty, my Hands to larger service, and my Health to better living, for my Club, my Community, and my Country." Presumably making a pledge was not considered to be swearing an oath, something else Mennonites rejected. Several clubs under the 4-H banner were founded in Grunthal from the late 1940s onward but some lasted for only a short time, such as the Automotive Club, Tractor Club, Potato Club, and Garden Club. Two, however, lasted much longer, especially the Grunthal Dairy Calf Club that mainly involved boys, and the girls' sewing club founded around 1952 in association with the school.[11] Girls of Russländer descent were prominent in the Clothing Club but the Dairy Club included some Kanadier.

In 1955 a Grunthal Horticultural Society was established, an innovation encouraged by the agricultural advisor Joseph LaFrance, who also helped to promote the 4-H Dairy Calf Club. Those involved in the Horticultural Society included Russländer and Kanadier as well as Ted Chornoboy's Ukrainian wife, Luba. Not only were garden plants grown under its auspices, but members were also taught flower arranging and plant decoration as well as how to produce a range of preserves. Eventually the results of all these activities culminated in displays exhibited at a community event initially known as Achievement Day but later as the Fair.[12] Here products and animals were displayed and judged, and awards presented. As the event grew larger a parade passed through town led by the Greenvalley Riders Club, whose members later competed in horse races. The Fair became an annual event that involved

Mennonites and non-Mennonites from the surrounding area of southeastern Manitoba, the wider involvement being reflected in the renaming of Grunthal for a short period when the *Gruen* in the town's name became the English "Green."[13]

With the growth of wider community activities, women increasingly took on roles outside their congregations which for Russländer women meant associating with non-Russländer. Those Mennonites involved in competitions associated with the Fair and other community events drew on skills developed in established domestic practices including bread making and cake baking. The preserved fruit and vegetables essential for the long winter months were now displayed at community events along with examples of sewing, although the latter no longer involved producing the plain dress of their ancestors except when the aim was to dress up for pageants and parades in the style many believed Mennonite pioneers had worn. Some younger women attempted to reproduce contemporary clothing in the latest fashions of the more "worldly" society to be displayed in fashion parades, with elaborate hairdos to match. These activities were also associated with the 4-H Clubs where children and young women organized a Sunshine Clothing Club and their activities extended beyond Grunthal as members entered competitions in Steinbach.[14] In 1959 older Russländer women, most of them married, formed a Grunthal branch of the Women's Institute with more "advanced" sewing courses. Its activities expanded to raise funds for local sports teams and provincial charitable organizations.[15] The town council encouraged the Institute as one of its roles in promoting the town and district.

As well as activities connected with agriculture, there was much else to keep locals involved and occupied as a community in Grunthal's post-war world. Compared with the pre-war period, youth of Grunthal in the late 1940s and into the early 1950s were growing up with a wide range of opportunities to keep them, their parents, their grandparents, and in fact the entire community entertained when everyone was not hard at work. By these means parents hoped to keep young people's minds and bodies busy when not in school or under parental supervision helping in the family business, on the farm, or in the kitchen. Youth needed to be kept clear of the dangerous temptations that came with growing up without risking their salvation and naturally the embarrassment of their parents, other relatives, and the community.

Another strategy was to get young people involved in sports because, as one report with reference to Grunthal and southeastern Manitoba put it, "Individual differences are forgotten when it comes to sports."[16] Several different sports were available, but the main choices were baseball in summer and ice hockey in winter. The latter was by far the most important as in summer there was less free time due to the short growing season that demanded everyone, young and old, be involved in farm work. In contrast, the long winter months provided ample time for sport. Ice hockey in prairie communities, as historian Gerald Friesen has noted, "is associated with the equality and autonomy and agency ... that originated in children's experience on ice ... [i]t also has overtones of class mobility, opportunity, escape from the ordinary, and challenging winters." He further suggests that "hockey belongs with the autonomous world of children's play, where rules are shaped by children's movement and children's bargaining, and where the only legislation that matters is the decree of the group."[17] And of course, winning also matters.

Although Kanadier were aware of the sport in Canada, they rarely permitted their children to become involved. Even in Russia, however, some Russländer knew how to skate when rivers and ponds froze in winter, but this was a form of individual entertainment rather than organized sport.[18] It appears that ice hockey was the other activity besides football that the first Kanadier teacher the Russländer encountered in Grunthal permitted pupils to indulge in. The teacher's interest in football might also account for the formation of a Grunthal Football Club that played St. Pierre in May 1931, but interest in football was short-lived.[19] Under teacher David P. Heidebrecht physical education, including sports, was part of the official school curriculum and could also be organized by the children themselves during break times. School reports speak not only of ice hockey but also volleyball and even ping-pong as popular activities. Outside school it was shopkeeper Guenther who really encouraged ice hockey, in part to keep his sons entertained but also because he genuinely enjoyed watching it and rarely missed a game. In time the family had the making almost of a hockey team. Guenther built an ice rink behind his store so his boys could practice when not helping in the store. In 1934 a newspaper report noted a rink had been built but no club had yet been formed.[20] In other areas around Grunthal a rink could easily be built by flooding a patch of ground while "horses supplied the pucks, free and ample."[21] In later years a proper rink was built near the Medo-Land plant and the dairy company helped pump water to flood it.[22]

Ice hockey is a rather odd choice of sport for non-resistant Mennonites, a fact that has not gone unnoticed by later commentators.[23] This is somewhat supported by contemporary reports of matches in and around Grunthal in which several injured players had to be ferried to hospital in Steinbach and even Winnipeg.[24] Letter writers argued over

Fig. 11.1. The Grunthal Red Wings Hockey Team, 1950.
Source: Photograph courtesy of Margaret Wiens, Grunthal.

who was to blame for the fights that occasionally broke out, usually between opposing Mennonite teams. These could involve pushing, punching, and even use of hockey sticks. One report of a fight between Grunthal and Steinbach players blamed the latter who it claimed, "tried to play dirty hockey."[25] But ice hockey helped unite the community, players, coaches, managers, and, of course, spectators, Russländer and Kanadier (fig. 11.1). Despite often freezing weather practically all male and some female community members would attend matches to cheer on their team.

The Grunthal hockey team adopted the name Grunthal Red Wings and played in the Carillon League for the Prefontaine Cup, which they won in 1951. Soon the team recruited members from other communities like St. Pierre and joined the Manitoba Junior B Playdowns, defeating teams from other areas of southern Manitoba. Gradually the team entered other competitions and the Grunthal team and individual players gained a reputation for success. With both senior and junior teams involved, any winners appeared in group photographs with their trophies proudly displayed. One player who started his career in ice hockey with the Grunthal team and went on to play for national hockey teams was Ken Block, son of the businessman Steve Block.[26] But the major team on the East Reserve remained Steinbach, Grunthal's bitter rival in business and sport. It is ironic therefore that Ken Block is often identified as from Steinbach. Other extremely talented players emerged in Grunthal but for various reasons were unable to pursue hockey careers. Grunthal was also successful in baseball, playing in various local and provincial championships.

In the post-war world, there were other activities of a more non-resistant nature open to young and old in Grunthal that did not risk life and limb. In the spring of 1956 work was begun on the construction of an auditorium, a grand, single-arched structure built on what was called a Quonset style. It was forty by eighty feet and could hold up to five hundred people. Financing came from members of the community, each of whom paid $100 for a share, $25 initially and the remainder to be paid over the next three years. The labour involved in its construction came mainly from the community, saving an estimated $2,000 of the final cost of $6,500. It was hoped that the entire community would continue to contribute to its maintenance and upkeep.[27] Although a community project for all Grunthal's people, leading Russländer obviously considered that it was built on their initiative as an account of its construction eventually appeared in the history of the Elim congregation.[28] When the congregation's building burned down, its services were held in the auditorium and it was also used by school classes as new school buildings were built. The major purpose of the auditorium, however, was to have a central place for music concerts outside the meeting houses of the separate congregations, to stage drama, and hold other community events. For many years these events were held but never in one purpose-built location, but instead in basements of meeting houses or machine sheds on farms when couples married. Cultural activities had also occurred in Warkentin's garage, but only once it was cleared out and cleaned. The need for a permanent community building like the auditorium for musical performances and other cultural activities was clear (fig. 11.2).[29]

Choirs and other forms of musical performance were well developed in Russia before immigration and were later gradually introduced in Canada, especially in Winnipeg once the Russländer became more established. The repertoire was often mixed and could include religious and classical music performed by choirs, string quartets, and even a small orchestra.[30] Similar activities occurred in Grunthal but on a much smaller scale, though for a time a brass band existed. The driving force behind these musical activities came from within the Russländer congregation and from the school, especially the Russländer teachers who

Fig. 11.2. Opening the Grunthal Auditorium with music, 1956. The one-hundred-member choir and orchestra outside the new Grunthal community auditorium. The new auditorium was used for a number of community events including musical events and drama performances. Some of the plays were in Low German, written and published by the Russländer Arnold Dyck, who for a number of years lived in Steinbach and often visited Grunthal. When the Elim Church building burned down the auditorium was used by the Russländer congregation for worship.

Source: The *Carillon* Archives, Steinbach, Manitoba.

encouraged some Kanadier and especially Russländer pupils. Musical activities required practice and demonstrated the benefits of experiencing the power of music for combined groups, whether singing or playing instruments. Membership in musical groups linked schools and different congregations in the district, helping to forge a sense of common identity. Additionally, young people could even travel outside their region and meet other young people, sometimes joining them to perform in larger choirs. Singing also connected members from different generations. Sometimes some directors favoured sacred music and pieces from the past but most experimented with new material, secular and sacred, to satisfy the demands of younger members and themselves. Even choir performances linked to religious events became more varied in content and drew on people and groups from outside the Russländer community. Songfests (HG *Sängerfeste*) were held, as in 1959 when choirs from Arnaud and Grunthal united to sing at the morning service under Grunthal's choir director, John Driedger, and a poem was read by a Mennonite from Niverville. In the afternoon four choirs combined under the direction of a guest conductor, the Reverend George Dugard of Steinbach and Winnipeg, who also sang a solo. Dugard was renowned for his contributions to church music and was associated with the Winnipeg Bible Institute as well as being a voice teacher and choir director in the 1950s at the Steinbach Bible Institute. There he founded a sacred music society, and his daughter married a Mennonite.[31]

The other major cultural activity associated with the auditorium involved drama presentations, mostly in Low German. The performance of works in Low German written by Mennonites, and also a few by non-Mennonites such as Fritz Reuter, dated back to Russia. In 1958 Jacob H. Block presented a reading in Low German in the auditorium but whether it was his own work or from another source is unknown.[32] Mennonites greatly enjoyed such Low German readings, and it is difficult to overemphasize how much Low German, spoken widely in the community, provided a bridge between Kanadier and Russländer. Arnold Dyck, who for many years edited the local newspaper the *Steinbach Post* (later *Die Post*) and several cultural journals, told stories that were popular with older Russländer, but Kanadier and younger Russländer who attempted to read his works struggled with the Low German, unaccustomed as they were to seeing their essentially spoken patois transferred onto a page of text.

But presentations of Low German as drama were entertaining, although there were other complications. Some plays had originally been written in Late Imperial Russia but sometimes rewritten for Russländer communities in Canada, such as Jacob H. Janzen's *De Bildung* (*Education/Enlightenment*), performed in Grunthal in 1946.[33] Other dramas, although written in Canada, drew on aspects of life in Russia before the revolution that were therefore known only to older immigrants. Probably the most important of these, also performed in Grunthal, were the dramas of Arnold Dyck, particularly his *Wellkoam op'e Fortstei* (*Welcome to Forestry Service*) and another, *De Opnom* (*The Reception Room*). They were comedies and to a certain extent could entertain both Russländer and Kanadier, mainly because they were well written.[34] They were performed in successive years in Grunthal, 1951 and 1952.[35] Other comedies were on themes that both Kanadier and Russländer had experienced in Canada, such as *Onsi Hendritj Ditje* (*Our Henry Dycks*), a portrayal of the

Depression years written by J.J. Enns of Ontario.[36] A serious drama on Mennonites escaping Soviet oppression, *Ut bewegte Tiede (Out of Turbulent Times)*, was produced in 1959 but the performance apparently was not well attended.[37] Whether this was because the community preferred comedy or because such a serious topic meant more to Russländer than to Kanadier, who may have stayed away, is unclear. On the other hand, some Russländer also may not have wished to be reminded of such traumatic events in a drama.

Essential to the development of community sport and cultural activities was the Goodwill School but following the departure of Heidebrecht in 1942, teaching in the school became less coordinated. New Russländer teachers from within the community trained in Winnipeg and returned to the district, including the daughters of John G. Peters, manager of the Grunthal Cooperative. They, however, taught elementary level classes, which fits with the post-war period trend of an increasing number of female teachers, a trend found right across the Manitoba elementary school system. The Department of Education believed many young women would eventually marry and leave the teaching profession, so they were predominantly employed as elementary teachers while men were employed to teach higher level, secondary classes as qualified males were viewed as career teachers in Manitoba. Mennonites, however, were noted for the number of males seeking careers in teaching at all levels.[38]

As the community had envisioned when Heidebrecht was still teaching, the Grunthal school should grow to instruct its intelligent students, mainly Russländer, to Grade 12. The one problem that remained was that only Steinbach High School taught to this level and therefore Grunthal students wishing to pursue higher education in Winnipeg first had to pass Grade 12 by attending the Steinbach school. Grunthal Russländer parents considered it would be much better if Grunthal could build its own high school, attract first-class male teachers, and graduate its own youth to higher levels of education. The construction of the new building before the war had been a positive development, but it soon proved far too small to house the growing enrolments or the increase in the number of parents who wished their children to further their education and even become teachers. To achieve the goal of a new high school Russländer first needed to form a Grunthal School Board although the war had delayed plans in this direction. The community could achieve little while the school remained under the control of the official trustee in Winnipeg and although the community had formed a local committee to report to the trustee, it was not autonomous. In 1942 the committee reported that it had not met since 1939 when no minutes had been kept, perhaps because of the outbreak of war.[39] One of the many aims of the post-war provincial government was to improve education and after lobbying by the Grunthal community, an independent local school board was finally established in June 1949.

The new board's membership were all Schönfelder: Johann F. Warkentin, Johann D. Warkentin, and George J. Rempel, the son of Jacob J. Rempel.[40] In the same year the Hanover municipality proposed to Grunthal ratepayers that it create a debenture debt of $6,500 to erect and equip a new school, and approved a decision to support the construction of a two-room school, a proposal that was passed by thirty-eight votes to two.[41] The community, or at least the Russländer community, received support in its effort to take control of schooling and improve the level of instruction but this required finding suitable teachers. First, the community required a new principal for the planned high school, preferably an experienced male Russländer. After Heidebrecht departed, a brother of Jacob J. Rempel, Peter J. Rempel, was employed as principal until 1948. During his tenure, teaching to Grade 11 began but the school was only recognized as a "continuation school" and in 1943 the school inspector reported he could not find a suitably qualified person to teach at this level.[42] While well-connected to the Schönfelder group, Peter Rempel was considered an outsider as he had converted to the Mennonite Brethren. Therefore, he was unacceptable to the community, including his relatives, and did not worship in Grunthal but instead at the Mennonite Brethren church in Steinbach. The next principal, Cornelius Van Thiessen, was better qualified and experienced but as he had served in the armed forces during the war many also considered him unacceptable. After his departure in 1951 he was followed by Harvey Van Penner from Steinbach, whom many considered a disaster as principal. What the school and community really needed was an experienced Russländer teacher and one person in their district stood out: the teacher at the nearby Montezuma School, Cornelius (Neil) G. Unruh.

Unruh had been born in Russia, in the village of Waldheim in the Molochna Colony. Just five years after immigrating to Canada he graduated from the normal school in Winnipeg in 1930 and would later earn Bachelor of Arts and Bachelor of Education degrees from the University of Manitoba. Through the Depression and afterwards he taught at several rural schools that enrolled English and Mennonite pupils.[43] Initially he was rejected as a suitable choice for the Grunthal post for his alleged "communist" sympathies because he was a member and strong supporter of the Manitoba Teachers' Society, considered by many as a workers' union in all but name. The society had existed as a teachers' federation since 1919, a tumultuous time of labour unrest in Winnipeg with which its formation was tangentially connected, but the organization was only constituted as a society under an Act of the Legislature in 1942.[44] Membership was automatic but not compulsory which meant teachers had to opt out of being members, but well over 90 per cent remained.[45] In 1951 the Hanover Mennonite school boards met in Steinbach to discuss the new wage schedules proposed for rural teachers and also changes to the Manitoba Labour Relations Act that permitted teachers to negotiate their wages and conditions with their employers. While members of the boards accepted the new schedule, they rejected any idea of "bargaining" with teachers as an organized body. "To most of the Mennonite trustees," it was reported, "the word 'union' is tantamount to Communism."[46] This was a view not uncommon among other Mennonites with regard to labour unions.[47] A separate body, the Hanover Trustees' Association, was formed and demanded the status quo from teachers, each board settling matters individually with their teachers.

Following the passage of the Act in 1942, the renamed Manitoba Teachers' Society gained the right to negotiate wages on behalf of its members and the trustees discovered local teachers were highly compliant and although society members, they agreed in the first instance not to use provisions of the Labour Relations Act and to resolve conflicts with their local boards.[48] However, Unruh was elected to the society's executive and chaired the "ethics committee," which promoted conservative values.[49] As well as being allegedly a communist through his role in the Teachers' Society, Unruh was also a member of the Mennonite Brethren, unwelcome in Grunthal. But he was also a nephew of the highly respected Professor Benjamin H. Unruh, well known to Russländer for his work in Germany before and after the Second World War. More importantly, Neil Unruh was fully qualified to teach Grades 11 and 12 and could promote a range of cultural activities close to the hearts of Russländer: music, literature, and drama. An added advantage was that he had a large family with extremely talented sons and daughters who would add prestige to the new school. But Unruh was a strict disciplinarian used to having his own way as master of a single-room classroom in a more compliant community than Grunthal. Eventually Unruh was hired by the Grunthal Board as principal of the new school from 1953 but remained an "outsider" in the community on the grounds of his religious affiliations and a lack of kinship connections in an increasingly interrelated community. Unruh and his family worshipped in the Mennonite Brethren church in Steinbach, but they also participated in activities of the Elim congregation.

The other person appointed to teach Grades 9 and 10 soon after Unruh's arrival was another experienced teacher, Peter J.B. Reimer.[50] Reimer was not a Russländer but a Kanadier from Steinbach, a person of Kleine Gemeinde ancestry, and a minister in its successor organization, the Evangelical Mennonite Church. At first sight this again was an odd choice: another outsider in the Grunthal community by faith and background. He was, however, married to a non-Kleine Gemeinde, a Chortitzer woman with connections to Kanadier around Grunthal. Reimer was highly intelligent, well qualified, and able to teach High German. He was to remain in Grunthal for fourteen years, moving into town and becoming widely respected in the community. Other teachers were hired by the board as the school expanded. A young Mennonite who arrived in Canada in the post-war immigration from Europe, Paul Neustaedter, was appointed in 1955 to teach at levels below Reimer. He was selected by the Grunthal School Board after being interviewed in Low German at the normal school in Winnipeg where he agreed to teach German and religion (in German) before and after school and to set up a "shop" to instruct boys in woodwork. For the latter work he negotiated an additional payment outside the schedule, an indication that the board still acted unilaterally when it hired new teachers, a practice Unruh disagreed with as it occurred without the approval of the Teachers' Society.

The impact of the new teaching staff on teaching was almost immediate as students in higher-level classes graduated with excellent results. Through community efforts and student fundraising the school purchased new resources although when some were later transferred by the district board to the elementary school without consultation, Reimer wrote to the local newspaper in protest.[51] Unruh introduced innovations such as interest groups to promote activities outside class time and organized school councils for different age groups that gave young people a voice in how the school was run. Musical concerts involving choirs and an orchestra of strings and later brass, combined with plays and literary performances, created a new cultural atmosphere. Moreover, young people from the school represented Grunthal outside the district in music and creative activities in Steinbach and in other areas of Manitoba.

In 1958 in the Manitoba Legislature the local member for Carillon, Edmond Prefontaine, described the school:

> Grunthal has a three-room high school. It is manned by possibly the best three high school teachers that I have ever known. Two of them are married men, dedicated men to teaching, doing a wonderful job. I have

attended two of their graduation exercises of number 12 students, speaking to the people there. These men have homes in the village of Grunthal – they are perfectly satisfied, the locality has made enormous sacrifices to pay them decent salaries.[52]

To those of the greater Grunthal community, however, the school and education in general remained primarily a Russländer affair. Although the school included Kanadier and even Ukrainian students, most did not progress to the higher classes but instead left school early to work on farms or assist in family businesses. Another indication of how much schooling was viewed as a Russländer concern is reflected in the annual yearbook, *Green and Gold*, produced by the graduating class from the early 1950s. It included a notice of congratulation to graduates written in High German by the Elder of the Elim congregation while the other congregations in Grunthal were not represented, perhaps because they had so few members graduating from the upper classes, and it was accepted that this was just another Russländer display of their dominance.

The disconnection between education and a united sense of community was also reflected in the major educational reforms debated and implemented in Manitoba in the 1950s and 1960s. Here the differences in the Hanover district between Kanadier and Russländer and town and country were starkly revealed. Calls for reform in the structure of school districts, the curriculum, and in other educational matters had begun before the war and were renewed once the war ended as provincial governments proposed changes to education.[53] In April 1945 the idea of creating larger school units in a process widely known as "consolidation" was debated in the Manitoba Legislature. Edmond Prefontaine opposed the creation of larger secondary school administrative units, as they "would place an unfair financial burden on the strong municipalities."[54] The government was forced to compromise and consequently an experiment in consolidation was initiated in the Dauphin area while in 1950 the Department of Education "accelerated" moves to support schools that offered students an opportunity to progress to Grades 11 and 12.[55]

The Minister of Education declared the experiment to establish larger administrative units a success, but school trustees in the Rhineland, a district dominated by Mennonites, condemned the idea and instead asked for locally managed, improved schools that were well equipped.[56] The debate continued for a number of years until in 1957 the Liberal government in power established a Royal Commission on Education whose brief included an embrace of consolidation or the creation of larger administrative units.⁵⁷ The commission accepted submissions and took evidence from interested parties, including two from Mennonite organizations involved with higher educational issues, the Mennonite Collegiate Institute in Gretna and the Manitoba Mennonite Educational Committee in Winnipeg. Both submissions, dated November 1957, along with the commission's notes and questions posed by the commission's chair at public hearings, are preserved in the Archives of Manitoba and indicate possible cooperation between the Mennonite organizations in drafting their submissions. The report's final suggestion included a recommendation to create larger school divisions with separate boards.⁵⁸ The boundaries of the proposed new divisions were to be formed on the recommendation of a separate boundary commission, but their number was estimated as between fifty to sixty across the entire province.

The member for Carillon, Edmond Prefontaine, speaking in the Legislature singled out Grunthal as an example of a place that would be disadvantaged by the formation of larger educational areas. He understood that a boundary commission might consider placing Grunthal with St. Pierre but "because of cultural and social relationships" Grunthal was more likely to be included with Steinbach. Sending their students to Steinbach when they were already well-served by their own school was unnecessary as the members of this

> ... little community will and possibly rightly so say we are supplying a good high school in Grunthal, we're against being included into a division which might force our high school to disappear. Our children might be transported by bus morning and night to Steinbach. Our children are ours, they're getting a good education and we want to stay out.

Although unwilling to oppose all the Royal Commission's recommendations, Prefontaine expressed concerns about proper representation for a place like Grunthal if they were included in a larger division.⁵⁹

Before any final decision could be made, a referendum on the boundary commission's recommendations was put to the people of Manitoba in early 1959. A notice of the referendum providing dates, places, and the names of returning officers, (Peter H. Janzen in Grunthal), appeared in the local newspaper.⁶⁰ Over one hundred thousand Manitobans voted, resulting in a margin of seven to three voting in favour of the proposed new divisions, but the proposal did not find favour in the two areas with large Mennonite populations, Rhineland and Hanover which along with two other rural municipalities, Boundary and Stanley, rejected them.⁶¹ In Hanover the figures were 991 for and 1,093 against consolidation, a close-run result. A closer examination of the rejection in what would become the Hanover Secondary School Division reveals underlying differences between Kanadier and Russländer and between rural and semi-urban districts over issues around schooling and education in general (see table 11.1).[62] A contemporary report on the results not only gives figures for Hanover but also the percentage of possible voters who cast a vote. This reveals a very low turnout, just 37 per cent across the proposed area. In Steinbach only 30 per cent turned out and it would have been even lower had not a group of "volunteers," noticing that by 4:00 p.m. only 16 per cent had voted, driven around town with a "mobile public address system" encouraging people to get out and vote. In Grunthal the highest turnout, at 48 per cent, was recorded for Hanover, most probably Russländer.[63] But overall, the result in Hanover was a rejection of the proposal to form larger educational districts. A Winnipeg newspaper reporter interviewed the principal of the Steinbach Collegiate, Nick Toews, who confirmed that it was conservative Mennonites who had swung the vote against acceptance of the recommendations, as they "feared government control of their children's education." Leading Mennonites from the West Reserve confirmed this view.[64]

Soon after the February referendum a seventeen-man delegation from Grunthal, Niverville, and Steinbach approached the Minister of Education and requested a second vote be taken. They pointed out that only 19 per cent of ratepayers in Hanover had voted and suggested that the reason for this was probably that many non-voters had assumed the decision would "carry." They were sure that a second vote would bring out more voters in favour of the proposal. This rather disingenuous suggestion failed to recognize the division in the area between conservative, mostly rural voters, and progressive "town" voters. In the case of the "urban" areas of Grunthal and Niverville, most Mennonites were Russländer whereas rural areas had a majority of Kanadier. Russländer were a minority in Steinbach, but here many Kanadier were progressives, especially about education. The minister did not initially agree to the request.[65]

A campaign to gather support for a new vote was mounted and it was pointed out to ratepayers that if changes were not made school taxes would increase and that Grunthal's Goodwill School District had already increased its levy from 41.5 mills to 61 mills, meaning that a farm assessed at $1,000 now had to pay an extra $19.50 a year. The proposals of the Royal Commission would provide grants that would decrease school levies. Accompanying this note in the local newspaper was a request for people to sign a petition requesting a new vote.[66]

Table 11.1. Selected referenda results for forming new Secondary School Division No. 15 in 1959

Location	27 February 1959		6 November 1959	
	For	Against	For	Against
Spencer	11	36	20	21
Kleefeld	20	116	43	56
Randolph	25	81	15	92
Blumenort	8	127	3	140
Landmark	35	65	55	65
New Bothwell	11	112	7	112
Grunthal	113	24	149	15
Steinbach	478	123	184	166
Niverville	85	65	112	27

Source: Schellenberg, *Schools – Our Heritage*, 269.

The campaign, which required 40 per cent of voters to request a new vote, was successful and the minister finally agreed to it in November. Ahead of the vote the Grunthal School Board posted an appeal in the local newspaper urging all ratepayers to vote for the proposed unitary plan. It gave several reasons why people should vote in favour, stressing especially its provision of a better future for "our youth."[67]

In many ways the result of the second vote again confirmed the divide in the larger community and was very similar to the first (see table 11.1). The overall turnout in conservative areas remained low with most rejecting the proposal. However, with more progressives voting for the proposal than against (1,512 to 872), in the second round this proved sufficient for the proposal to be accepted. The second round turnout in Grunthal was higher than in the first with more in favour than against. Here at least, the Russländer had asserted themselves and showed a continued support for higher education even if in Steinbach far fewer people participated, perhaps because there was no one with a public address system to get them out to vote.

The implementation of the Royal Commission's report, the formation of new divisional boundaries, and the creation of a new Board of Education were not the end of efforts to reorganize education in the province. The 1959 Report of the Royal Commission recognized that the objections of some communities to larger areas and consolidation of schools were based on a desire to preserve rural schools as well as religious and ethnic factors. But it was also pointed out that their recommendations applied only to secondary schooling and local autonomy could continue in elementary schooling.[68] Russländer interest in improving and extending educational reform in Grunthal continued through the early 1960s as the provincial government indicated further changes were to come. This culminated in an announcement in 1967 that a new scheme was planned to cover all schools from elementary to secondary level. It is not surprising that when this occurred many of the old divisions between conservative rural and progressive urban Mennonites re-emerged. Among the government proposals was the establishment of unitary school divisions that would entail the closure of small, mostly rural schools that usually taught the lower levels, and an expansion of larger schools, such as that in Grunthal, which could teach pupils from elementary through to secondary levels. Such a move required major changes to funding and better resourcing of schools, including the construction of new buildings. It would also need a reorganization of school boards that would better represent community interests and demonstrate greater responsibility to government.

Once again, the government put the proposal to a referendum and once more in the Hanover District the number opposed to change (1,336) outnumbered those in favour (922). The results for the mainly Mennonite areas indicate a divide like in 1959 between mainly conservative rural communities of mostly Kanadier, and towns with progressive Mennonites, including Russländer-dominated Grunthal. Other factors were also involved in some communities, such as the loss of a local school, the need to transport children to another centre, and the potential for local businesses to lose customers to other centres where children were schooled. This time Steinbach strongly supported the proposal because their community stood to gain through any concentration of educational resources and because it was a growing business centre.

The overall rejection of the proposal, however, again mostly limited to Mennonite-dominated areas of the province, was not the end of the matter. As in 1959, sections of the progressive Mennonite and non-Mennonite communities demanded a second referendum. This time the progressives succeeded by 1,802 to 1,794. Once again Grunthal played a major role in getting the town and people in their district to cast a vote. In the end the result in Hanover was extremely narrow: a margin of just eight votes. Those opposed to the proposal attempted to get the result overturned. Their efforts focused on the Grunthal vote where it was claimed irregularities had occurred on polling day. Those opposed to the outcome and responsible for the claim met in New Bothwell, a clear indication that the opposition came from more

Table 11.2. Selected referenda results for forming Unitary School Division No. 15 in 1967

Location	10 March 1967		15 December 1967	
	For	Against	For	Against
Spencer	19	60	–	–
Kleefeld	33	88	120	94
Randolph	24	93	33	96
Blumenort	37	120	26	76
Landmark	19	128	30	175
Bothwell	7	145	14	165
Grunthal	127	77	241	177
Steinbach	436	238	902	423
Niverville	113	125	166	176

Source: Schellenberg, *Schools – Our Heritage*, 270.

conservative Mennonites. A judge in St. Boniface heard the accusations and dismissed them all.[69]

As well as differences of opinion over school reform the other important source of division in Grunthal and surrounding areas concerned religious affiliation. Distinctions between Mennonites and non-Mennonites were obvious. Non-Mennonites included Catholic, Ukrainian Orthodox, and Ukrainian Catholic churches but these were insignificant when compared with the differences between Mennonite congregations. Descendants of the original Chortitzer congregation established by the 1874 immigrants were scattered in the district around Grunthal and continued to meet either in schoolhouses or in their own meeting houses, one located in the village of Chortitz and another in Grunthal.[70] The Russländer congregation's first meeting house was replaced in 1949 by a new building as post-war economic conditions improved (see fig. 11.3.a). It was constructed mostly by volunteer labour but burned down in 1961, destroying most of its contents, and was quickly replaced by a new, modern building (fig. 11.3).[71] The Bergthal congregation which began to arrive in the 1930s initially met in schoolhouses but in 1939 a building was constructed with help from Bergthalers from the West Reserve close to Spencer North School.[72] In 1949 the building was raised onto a newly dug out basement and enlarged with an addition. Eventually the Bergthaler Church proved too small, so a new building was constructed in Grunthal. A newcomer to Grunthal, the Evangelical Mennonite Brethren began to operation in the district during the 1950s and eventually built a church in Grunthal in 1964/65.[73] Most of its members were from a Kanadier background but a

(a)

(b)

Fig. 11.3. Later Elim churches that served the Russländer community. Pictured are two of three churches that have over time been used by the Russländer congregation in Grunthal between 1949 and the present. The present church was built in 1961 after the second building burned down: (a) Second Elim Church, Grunthal in 1957, and (b) New Elim Church, Grunthal c. 1961. Russländer immigrants either purchased existing places of worship from other religious groups or built or renovated other buildings especially in rural areas. As their populations grew and their members became more prosperous larger buildings were constructed, often with basements equipped with resources to serve the membership on Sundays and to hold other events such as weddings and funerals.

Sources: (a) *The Canadian Mennonite* collection/Mennonite Archives of Ontario; (b) Mennonite Heritage Archives, Winnipeg (492–743).

few Russländer associated with the Mennonite Brethren joined because the church practised baptism by immersion. Later other congregations were founded with Mennonite and non-Mennonite members including the Grunthal Abundant Life Fellowship Inc. and the Grunthal Christian Fellowship Tabernacle.

Such a proliferation of congregations, especially in and around a relatively small district like Grunthal, while confusing to outsiders, is easily understood by Mennonites as they have long recognized that the boundaries of faith and practice must be carefully policed. Since the sixteenth century, Mennonite and closely related groups have proliferated because of separations due to persecution and migration as well as external influences and these different pasts have created varied groups. And last, but not least, internal schisms have divided Mennonites.[74] While members of different Mennonite congregations and even non-Mennonites have associated in secular activities, in religious matters different Mennonite congregations have preferred to remain separate. Grunthal was not unique in establishing and maintaining such divisions. In 1965 Professor Jack Thiessen, raised in Grunthal, gave a talk on "Steinbach Philosophy."[75] He recalled how, in 1948, an attempt was made to organize a *Sängerfest* in a central Steinbach church that would include members of different Mennonite congregations:

> One church dropped out because the choir proposed to sing an English number. One group dropped out because there were German numbers on the program. Another church dropped out because of a [music] director, another because the choir had a piano and they believed that was sinful, and another because the choir proposed to sing in four-part harmony, which to them was also sinful.

The reference to a choir intending to sing in four-part harmony suggests a Russländer choir was to be involved, most likely from either Elim or Steinbach.

One issue held in suspicion by members of the different congregations in and around Grunthal involved courtship and marriage between Mennonites from different congregations. A few such unions did occur but then one partner usually had to agree to leave their congregation and join that of their partner. It was usually the wife who made this move even if non-religious kinship interactions were maintained into the succeeding generation. Similar marital connections between Mennonites and non-Mennonites, however, were almost impossible until more recent times. A Ukrainian growing up in a Mennonite community like Grunthal, who attended a largely Mennonite school, played games with other Mennonites, and even learned to speak Mennonite Low German, was told that he should not look at Mennonite girls and certainly not entertain any thoughts of courtship that might lead to marriage.

Within the Russländer community, however, some aspects of the relationship between religious observance and social practices changed, especially those concerned with marriages and funerals. In the past these occasions were only weakly connected with religious observance and instead more connected with marking the passage through the life course of all in the community. Only baptism involved a religious ritual held in the meeting house, but marriages and funerals, considered worldly, were marked with minimal ritual and not held in the meeting house but instead in the yards of one of the families involved. Both marriages and funerals were "celebrated," although in different ways. However, some in the community, particularly ministers, believed these celebrations needed to be curtailed, especially those associated with marriage. So in time, marriages and funerals were moved from homes into the meeting house, under the oversight of ministers and deacons.

Today a phone call or message announces a death and local radio stations carry regular notices. Most people in the congregation and others from the community attend the service in the meeting house where the body is usually displayed in an open coffin. One descendant of a Russländer suggested ironically the display was only so people could ensure the deceased is dead. Following the service most of those attending share food and coffee in the basement of the meeting house prepared by the congregation's women. Only relatives and close friends accompany the deceased to the cemetery. Marriages, however, show the most change. Gradually weddings became limited to those the couple and their parents invited whereas once all members of the congregation attended marriages without an invitation. But gradually, especially after marriages moved into the meeting house, only those invited proceeded to the wedding lunch. In this manner the former sense of unity among Russländer weakened, especially among members of the younger generations. Marriage ceremonies might now involve Mennonites of different groups as well as non-Mennonite friends, work mates, and neighbours especially where today marriages involve individuals of non-Mennonite backgrounds.

In the post-war world as the Grunthal community became focused on developing the town, its community expanded to include surrounding areas inhabited by Mennonites and non-Mennonites with whom Grunthal people traded, played sports, and attended school. In one way it was a united community but in others old markers of separation continued to divide people. Within the town and its adjacent district, Russländer remained dominant, but they had never been fully united and now there were signs of change. A crucial factor was time itself. The initial adult cohort that was aged over twenty when they immigrated in the 1920s was growing old. While at the time of immigration this cohort may not have been the same age, they possessed shared experiences if not in exact detail. But many older immigrants died before the Second World War, often without having adjusted to the new country, and with only a limited knowledge of English and Canadian ways. The members of the generation who increasingly controlled affairs in the post-war world were often younger immigrants even though they might have been born in Russia or Soviet Ukraine. Some had immigrated as small children and did not share the memories of Russia and experiences of their parents. Over 50 per cent of Russländer who arrived in Canada in 1924, the year when the majority of Schönfelder immigrated, were aged under twenty and more than half of these were under ten years of age.[76] The younger generation were more skilled in the English language and in Canadian ways than their parents. The post-war world, however, was a time of change not just for Canada, but also for the members of the Grunthal community as different generations began to succeed each another.

Chapter Twelve

Generational Transition and Succession

In time as their populations aged all Russländer communities faced issues associated with the succession of younger generations. After immigration all Russländer were primarily focused on how to rebuild communities sufficiently prosperous that they and successive generations could not just maintain their faith and identity, but also be able grow and succeed in a rapidly changing world. This required finding ways to hold onto successive generations so essential for the continuance of Mennonite life. Successful young Mennonites, trained in English with High German merely as a second language, would progress to higher education located outside their home communities and after graduating would often seek employment outside the Mennonite world. The type of success Russländer hoped for the next generation could have negative consequences for the first generation of immigrants. This raised the related issue of who was to care for the aging population of Russländer when their young people, increasingly socially mobile, lived away from home.

To complicate matters further, many elderly people lived longer than in the past. In Canada the next generation at first could do little to help more elderly Russländer who had immigrated with little or no financial resources and had had insufficient time to accumulate capital to support themselves once they retired. When they immigrated a number, however, possessed cultural capital developed mostly through the education received in Imperial Russia, but for many in Canada this proved of little value as it took a long time to rebuild even the basics of their lives. An entire generation of Russländer grew old and exhausted long before a degree of prosperity returned. Also, many younger Russländer, born in Russia or in the years immediately following immigration, never received the benefits of the type of education their parents had received in their old homeland. Consequently, they struggled to fulfil their parents' hopes of reconstructing anything resembling the lost Russian Commonwealth in Canada and found it difficult if not impossible to meet their parents' hopes of doing so. The burden of fulfilling the task thus largely fell on the second or third generation of the descendants of Russländer born in Canada, whether they liked it or not. Many of these later generations were torn between trying to meet the expectations and dreams of parents and grandparents or creating new lives for themselves. In time some came to doubt the increasingly unrealistic expectations of the older generation as they themselves neared retirement.

Two old people's homes (HG *Altenheim*) were founded in Molochna, Russia, prior to the First World War and some Russländer in Grunthal undoubtedly knew of their existence.[1] Old people's homes also existed elsewhere in North America, including some in Canada associated with Bergthal congregations on the West Reserve.[2] In December of 1957 a group from Grunthal visited a home for old people in Winkler, a town with a mixed Mennonite and non-Mennonite population.[3] In the past, a member of the "village council," J.W. Peters, was reported to have said, "people had spent their lives in the community and worked hard to build it up, yet when it comes time to enter honourable retirement and have a hard-earned rest, they were forced to move to some distant place far from friends and kinsfolk, simply because there was no place in the locality where they could go."[4] J.J. [Baker] Friesen and a committee of eight proposed the establishment a similar home in Grunthal and the proposal received widespread support.[5] Later in the year a decision was made to go ahead with the idea.[6] This involved establishing an incorporated society, a board of directors, and a committee to oversee the construction of a suitable complex and organize fundraising events.[7] In 1960 the Manitoba Minister of Health officially opened the first complex, named the Menno Home.[8] It cost $93,000, a sum beyond the imaginings of most Grunthal Russländer just twenty years earlier, but now built largely through funds raised within the community with additional support from a government grant and loan.[9] A women's committee, which included representatives of all three major congregations, the Spencer Bergthal, the Chortitzer, and the Elim congregations, was established to look after "the needs and wants" of the residents.[10]

In the post-war world generations of Russländer men and women experienced change in different ways. For women change occurred mainly in the domestic sphere as labour-saving technology gave younger, educated Russländer women greater opportunities to play an increasing role in congregational and community activities.[11] Within the Elim congregation the new generations formed their own women's groups. Elim's first women's group, the Tabea Verein, was eventually disbanded but before this occurred another body, the Maria Martha Verein, was formed in 1948 and in 1975, the Elim Ladies Auxiliary.[12] In this way each generation of women asserted their independence from the male-controlled congregational council.[13] The Auxiliary prepared coffee with refreshments following weekly congregational worship and also after funerals and other events. In a world where men controlled the congregation, these informal gatherings provided an important outlet for women, but they also reflected the women's experiences of growing up outside a male-dominated Russländer world, especially as the post-war expansion of schooling presented girls with a wider range of opportunities than had existed before the war.

Unlike many older Kanadier, Russländer parents favoured higher education for sons and daughters. Intelligent girls could progress to the higher grades and after graduating some attended the normal school in Winnipeg, after 1958 called the Manitoba Teachers' College. Following a year's training they mostly found employment in local rural schools, if possible close to Grunthal. Here they taught in small, one-room classrooms but only until they married, as teaching was considered an occupation for unmarried women and only a few pursued it as a long-term career. At least three of the daughters of the shopkeeper Johann G. Peters, Margaret, Mary, and Jessie, trained as teachers in the late 1940s, progressing from rural schools to teach at the elementary level in Grunthal. For many years at least two remained unmarried, and all eventually marrying much later than most women of their generation. Despite the limitations placed on females regarding pursuing teaching as a career, several young females from Grunthal and surrounding areas trained and became teachers from the 1950s onward. The largest number were of Russländer descent although a few Kanadier from more progressive families also became teachers.

The training and experience as teachers increased women's desire to be more involved in their communities and congregations. In the Elim congregation women played important roles in Sunday School teaching and during the 1970s were even permitted to attend general membership meetings of the Elim congregation, roles that had previously been the exclusive domain of men.[14] A response to a 1993 questionnaire seeking information for a history of the Manitoba Mennonite Conference elicited a response from Elim on women's role in the congregation. The response suggested that only in 1977 were women first permitted to vote at congregational meetings. In 1977 they were also permitted to be a chairperson, deaconess, treasurer, secretary, worship leader, Sunday School leader, choir director, and *Vorsänger*, but were not permitted to be a lead minister, assistant minister, or lay minister.[15] This response reveals a rather conservative congregation where men basically remained in control.

More progressive policies were pursued regarding schooling. The Grunthal School Board set to work to plan the construction of a new high school to accommodate the increasing number of students desiring to progress to higher grades. As enrolments increased, more teachers were also required. Following the 1959 *Report of the Royal Commission on Education*, additional classrooms and teaching resources were needed but these were slow to materialize, along with any increase in funding. This situation was eased by the promise of additional grants following the drawing up of new boundaries for the newly established Hanover School Division. As the money was to be paid annually the funding was spread over several years.[16] The newly constructed high school was at first named the Goodwill Collegiate but subsequently renamed the Grunthal Collegiate in November 1961. The term "collegiate" covered only the higher-level classes while the lower school covering grades one to eight retained the name Goodwill School.[17] Use of the term "collegiate" provided the upper school with status, as in Hanover only Steinbach possessed a collegiate, while the oldest and most prestigious Mennonite institution, the Mennonite Collegiate Institute in Gretna, had long used the title. A new building for the Grunthal Collegiate was constructed in 1961 with six classrooms, a science laboratory, and a small gymnasium. When the Collegiate took possession of the new building, elementary classes moved to the old building. In the upper school each grade had a teacher with the principal, at least under Unruh, responsible for the highest. In 1961 there were seventy-two students in the upper school: Grade 9 had twenty-three students; Grade 10, twenty-two; Grade 11, fourteen; and Grade 12, thirteen.[18]

Grunthal had come a long way since the first days of Russländer settlement when all that existed was a one-room classroom and most students did not even reach Grade 9. The new school buildings boosted the profile of the community and helped keep many of its youth focused and busy. Sport and other recreational activities in school and in the community were ways of controlling the young as they advanced towards adulthood. The graduating class was given additional responsibilities that included production of the glossy yearbook with text as well as school photographs paid for by Grunthal and even Steinbach businesses whose advisements appeared at the back of each issue. The photographs show very adult-looking graduands: young men in dark suits and bow ties and women in stylish frocks. For the graduation ceremony the top class later adopted American degree–like dress with mortar boards. The local newspaper also carried reports of successful senior year students with studio photographs.

But behind all this was an uneasy sense that there were more problems in the post-war world than before the war with the transition to adulthood. Continued attendance at school still identified maturing pupils as "children," especially while they remained at home. As the time spent in school was extended, pupils reached puberty and were in close contact with the opposite sex. This brought new concerns, real or imagined, to parents and the community. To older Russländer the threat of the natural attraction of young people to each other added to fears of the loss of High German and continuance of their faith among the younger generation. In 1959 the principal of the high school, C.G. Unruh, acting in his other role as president of the Grunthal Chamber of Commerce, hinted at these problems:

> Many of our young people are continuing to put forth a great deal of effort in undesirable directions and much of this is due to a lack of youth leadership. Guiding them in a constructive program of sports activities therefore must continue to be a responsibility of the community as much as it is its responsibility to create deterrents to the undesirable escapades of some misguided individuals.[19]

Unruh was pointing out that not just teachers were responsible for the discipline of young people, but also the community and in particular, parents. Everyone had an interest in ensuring the younger generation grew up to be responsible individuals, members of the community, and, following baptism, obedient members of the congregation. But what might Unruh have been referring to when speaking of "undesirable escapades" and "some misguided individuals"? One possibility may have been when a student climbed the school flagpole and tied a dead cat to it before school began, when the national flag had to be raised as required by the Department of Education. It was a troublesome period of transition for a community concerned with achieving a successful and responsible transition of the young into adulthood.

While several young people who graduated successfully from Grade 12 went on to higher education, those who left school earlier worked on the family farm, in family-owned businesses, and sometimes in low-paid occupations. Where employment was within the family business, the nature of the work created a clear sense of continuity to their way of life. Those who graduated from high school and pursued further qualifications experienced a marked discontinuity from the lives of their parents and grandparents. Higher education and better employment opportunities often took young people away from Grunthal into worlds and experiences of which members of the older generation had little knowledge. Some young people would not return except for occasional visits while a very few vanished completely, only to reappear briefly many years later only to disappear once again, a pattern not restricted to Grunthal. Not every second-generation Russländer in Grunthal was able to move easily between the different worlds of language and culture associated with Russian/Mennonite/German on one hand and English/Canadian on the other. But some remained grounded in a distinctly Mennonite sense of being and belonging while also being able to successfully participate in the wider world. Two examples of second-generation Grunthal Mennonites who went on to higher education in Canada and Germany are therefore instructive.

The first is Abraham Johann Friesen, born not in Canada but in Russia in 1919.[20] In pre-revolutionary Russia his family had been private landowners in Schönfeld but at the time of his birth they must have been living as refugees elsewhere. The family immigrated quite late to Canada in 1927 as most Schönfelder arrived in 1924, but eventually they settled among fellow Schönfelder in Grunthal. Educated in Grunthal and the Steinbach High School, Friesen was subsequently employed in several occupations in Manitoba and other prairie provinces, including as a printer. He produced two small literary works written in High German with Grunthal given as the place of publication, *Prost Mahlzeit!* (*Good Health!*), and a play, *Gott grüsse dich!* (*God Greets You!*), reflecting at first sight the influence of Arnold Dyck, whose writings at that time were very popular among Mennonites.[21] At the time Friesen's work received little notice in the Mennonite world, least of all in Grunthal. The play was apparently never performed either in Grunthal or elsewhere although a Mennonite secular magazine published a short note on the work.[22] Professor Watson Kirkconnell of the University of Toronto, an expert on Germanic languages who regularly reviewed literary works by "new" Canadians, was also positive about *Prost Mahlzeit!*, which he described as an account of an elderly, tyrannical Mennonite male dominating a meal table.[23] However, a leading Mennonite educator condemned Friesen's work as unsuitable for young readers because it misrepresented Mennonites to non-Mennonites.[24]

Shortly after publishing his works Friesen set out to gain higher qualifications in Germany, first at Göttingen University and then in Mainz. He eventually earned a PhD with a thesis on two obscure seventeenth-century German writers of drama and then taught in several universities in the United States and Canada before being appointed to a chair in German at the University of New Brunswick. Here he married a non-Mennonite born in Germany and they raised three sons. Friesen published few academic works but contributed to newspapers and journals, often in the form of poetry written under the pseudonym "Karlo." Some of his writings can be found in Mennonite collections and late in life he published a book under his own name.[25] Friesen's works, however, remained clearly in the Germanic tradition and reflect the influence over young Mennonites by grandparents and parents born in Russia. Friesen, however, seems to have had little impact in Grunthal once he moved away and mainly maintained contacts with members of his family who continued to live in the town.

The other figure was quite different. Jack [Johann] Thiessen was born in Manitoba in 1931 in Gnadenfeld, the small community close to Grunthal which was eventually incorporated into Grunthal's expanding town. Unlike the Friesen family, the Thiessens were from Khortitsa, and they too had immigrated relatively late to Canada, in 1926. Thiessen's mother had been a member of the Mennonite Brethren, an extremely rare religious affiliation in the Grunthal area. Thiessen's father was a colourful character in and around Grunthal and young Thiessen grew up on the fringes of the more established Schönfeld-dominated world. In Gnadenfeld he had numerous opportunities to associate with Kanadier and other Khortitsa immigrants. The latter were led by Wilhelm Sawatzky, who would have preferred to see a separate Russländer community develop in and around Gnadenfeld and in closer affiliation with Kanadier than existed in Schönfelder Grunthal. The predominant language Thiessen grew up with was Mennonite Low German, spoken by his parents and local Kanadier. This was not the High German favoured by Abraham Friesen's Schönfelder family even though in everyday discourse almost all Grunthalers used Mennonite Low German.

Thiessen performed well at school and completed his final year in Gretna, not Steinbach. Afterwards he entered the University of Manitoba and later studied in Germany, eventually earning a PhD from the University of Marburg/Lahn on the subject of Mennonite Low German.[26] Thiessen's published doctorate was the first of a series of academic papers that would culminate in his magnum opus, a dictionary of Mennonite Low German published in revised editions between 1999 and 2018.[27] After a period of teaching, research, and administration at the University of Winnipeg, Thiessen became an independent scholar. Like Friesen, Thiessen also published literary works but unlike Friesen, his extensive oeuvre includes contributions in Low German and English as well as several translations.[28] Some of his literary writing relating to Mennonites might best be termed risqué, at least for Mennonites of a sensitive and moralistic turn. But some of his work merely drew on and extended the rich oral tradition of storytelling in the rich, colourful language of Mennonite Low German. While Friesen moved away from Grunthal to the Maritime provinces leaving his Mennonite roots behind, Thiessen maintained a close connection with fellow Mennonites, particularly around the area in which he was raised. Sometimes his presence delighted local Mennonites and occasionally it shocked others. However, while little is known about Friesen as he belongs to the "lost" second generation of Grunthal Russländer, everyone knew or had heard about Thiessen. He returned to his community, rejoined the Elim congregation, and after his death in 2022 was buried in the Grunthal cemetery.

During the early years of post-war prosperity, Russländer and their older children took advantage of the new economic conditions by expanding farms, establishing new enterprises, or diversifying existing businesses. Inevitably, however, the time arrived when everyone had to face the decision about whether to either transfer their concerns to another generation or to sell out altogether. If passed on or sold to a younger family member, those who took over had to accept the responsibilities involved. Sometimes the process was far from orderly due to the different ages of those involved, particularly when members of the older generation had to face the decision in changed economic circumstances. For those who were older at the time of immigration the challenge of succession occurred before the full benefits of post-war prosperity took effect. But even after prosperity came after the war, some first-generation owners were only too willing to transfer enterprises after many years of labour and struggle.

Others, however, were more reluctant to release their control. Often these were the more entrepreneurially minded Russländer eager to continue expanding their enterprises by purchasing additional land or developing their businesses in town. In these cases, sons and daughters were expected to continue to work for them, as employing outside labour was more costly. Children were expected to work for their bed and board, occasionally even after they were married and had started to raise a family. Individuals in such situations, particularly males, were referred to as still being "under their father's thumb." To gain full independence, they had to wait for their father to die or become incapacitated before they could inherit a farm or business. Even then, the assets might be distributed among family members, creating years of debt. As a Mennonite Low German saying expresses it: *One will get a buttered slice,/And one a chicken dice;/That is good, that is good,/We're heirs, no time for crying.*[29]

In Grunthal it is sometimes claimed that "only the dumb one" inherited the farm as educated sons and daughters sought a future elsewhere. An examination of several cases of those who inherited the family farm or business might suggest there might indeed be a correlation between succession and educational achievement. But marks in school in no way suggest a lack of intelligence even if this could be confirmed with any degree of certainty. The reality was that not everyone responded well to schooling and some preferred to leave school as early as possible and to work for their living. At least one Grunthaler who progressed to university and successfully took up teaching as a career, gave it all up and took up farming as he enjoyed the work and in doing so, he was able to adopt a lifestyle less stressful than managing a school.

The age of the next generation who assumed the responsibilities of succession, not to mention the number of children who might wish to take over a farm or business or receive their share, varied from family to family so it is difficult to generalize on succession. It is also difficult to obtain exact details of inheritance as these frequently concerned agreements, made before the death of the owners of properties, that remained private and that do not appear on probate documents. In such cases private agreements were agreed between the parties involved, not foreign "English" law, at least to the point where titles to land and businesses had to be formally registered. In one case an owner-farmer decided when he turned sixty to make an agreement with one of his sons to sell him the farm for a sum of $25,000. The son lacked sufficient capital to purchase the farm outright, so it was agreed he pay $100 a month for five years towards the agreed sum; his father continued to hold the deeds to the farm while the son worked for him but received a share of the farm's income to make the payments and support the son's family. After five years when the father reached sixty-five, a respectable "retirement" age and the son had paid $20,000, the father agreed that the son was "now the boss" and their management roles were reversed. Succession had been achieved in stages along with the transfer of property well before the father's demise. The son was now in total control of the farm and immediately set to work to modernize it, devoting his attention to herd improvement for increased milk production and abandoning his father's attempts to develop a small-scale egg-producing enterprise.

Owners of established businesses in town faced similar problems as they grew older. In the large Guenther's store some of the sons helped their father for several years until in 1956 he sold the business to two sons, Art and Eddie, and then retired, at least in principle.[30] Before the war Franz Guenther had built a highly successful business out of a general store serving the needs of the local community in and around the town. People who needed everyday items but did not want to travel to stores in Steinbach or even Winnipeg, came to purchase the few household items rather than risk the roads to more distant locations. To meet their requirements Guenther carried a broad range of items but in the post-war world his sons modernized the business.

By 1956 the premises were in urgent need of remodelling, businesses practices required modernizing, and the brothers had found a new wholesale supplier, Ray Desjardins of Western Grocers.[31] A new seven-thousand-square-foot "shopping centre" was built in 1963 and Eric, another brother who was an accountant, joined his brothers. The "grand" reopening was marked by articles in the local newspaper on the store and its history.[32] It was reported that people had come from "all over the surrounding district: St. Pierre, St. Malo, Otterburne, Niverville, New Bothwell, Steinbach, Sarto, Pansy, Roseau River, Stuartburn, Tolstoi, and even Winnipeg" along with a few from west of the Red River. The crowd was estimated to be over a thousand people but whether they came to purchase anything or just to win the "special" prizes on offer, drawn over three nights, is unclear.[33] One thing that is certain, however, is that the emergence of a different generation of entrepreneurs marked a new beginning in retail shopping in Grunthal.

There were also other changes associated with the transfer of farms and businesses to the new generation. In terms of residence several options were available to new owners: they could remain in the original building, move into an existing annex, or into a newly constructed modern house, the latter especially favoured by those with growing families. Building a new house meant parents could remain in their old, familiar homes although if their children had left the area, the building might prove too large for a couple or a single person. Alternatively, they could build a new, smaller home nearby or move into a newly built home in Grunthal town on a site they might have purchased earlier when new streets and house plots were laid out. After 1944 ownership of more than one piece of property or site in Grunthal itself increased steadily. In 1944 just six people owned multiple properties or plots in Grunthal town, but by 1950 this had increased to eleven; by 1956 the figure was twenty and by 1964 it was over forty when, according to municipal records, four to eight properties were listed under a single name.[34] This growth may reflect people purchasing sites in the town to move onto after they had given up farming or for children and other relatives. All these options contributed to the "building boom" in Grunthal reported in the local newspaper in the early 1960s (see map 12.1).[35]

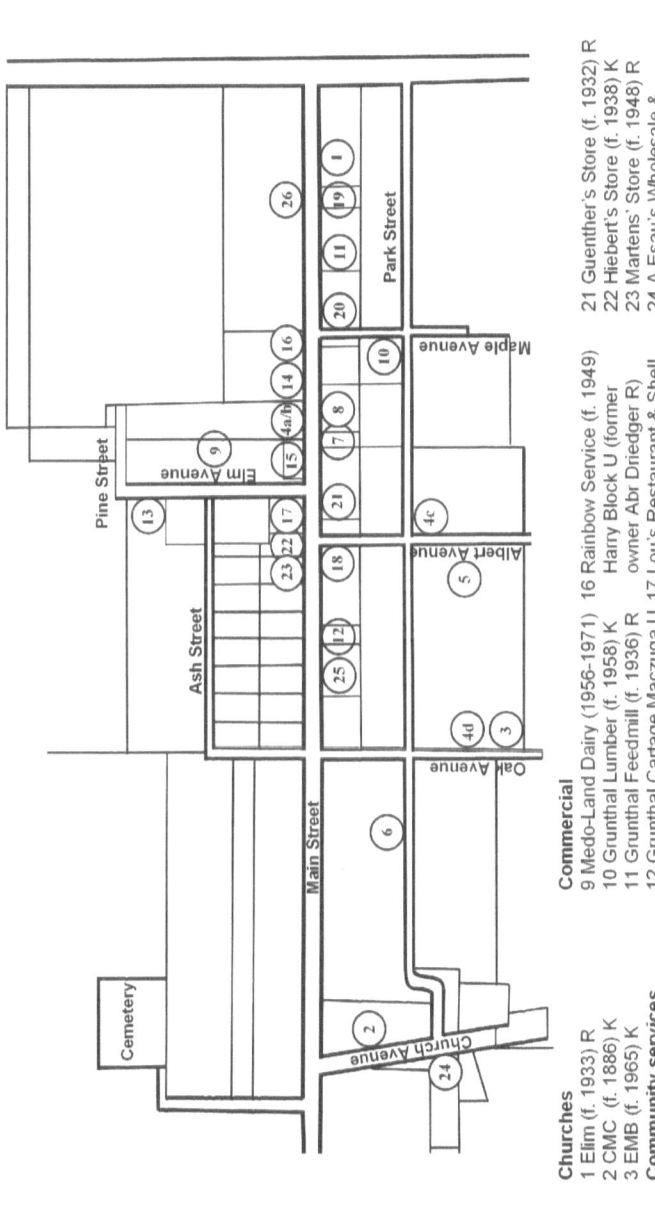

Map 12.1. Plan of Grunthal township, 1967.

Note: K = Kanadier; R = Russländer; U = Ukrainian.

Source: Map by Ernest N. Braun.

Fig. 12.1. Elder J.J. Enns and his wife Anna (Rempel), 1942. Johann J. Enns (left) and his wife Anna (Rempel) (right) in 1942 shortly before he was elected Elder of the Elim congregation. Enns was a pious man and was first elected a minister of the Elim congregation in 1927 and was elected the Elder of the congregation in 1943, a position he held until his death. He was the first Schönfelder and Grunthal resident to hold the post of Elder as previously the congregation had been served by Elders of other congregations. In a way, this was a sign of the independence and maturity of the congregation and their place in the community.

Source: Mennonite Heritage Archives, Winnipeg (677–99).

An alternative for retired people was to leave Grunthal entirely and move to Steinbach or Winnipeg, especially if one of their offspring was living in these places. Others, attracted by warmer climes, could move even further to Ontario or British Columbia. The latter was especially popular.

An important aspect of retirements, whether or not they involved a move away from Grunthal, concerned changes in the structure of power and influence in the community. In principle the Elim congregation was led by Johann J. Enns until his death in 1966 (see fig. 12.1). The pretentions of Grunthal Russländer for its congregation had seen Enns ordained as Elder in 1943. In Russia in the decades before the revolution many younger Elders were drawn from the ranks of highly educated teacher-preachers, especially in the major congregations. This practice continued in Canada after immigration: the Elder of the Winnipeg Schönwiese congregation, Johann Klassen, was highly educated and a leader in Manitoba in various Canada-wide conferences. There were also other Elders, many of whom had been ordained in Russia, who were active leaders and equally well-educated. In comparison, Grunthal's Elder was not nearly as highly educated although he studied religious texts assiduously. He also played only a minor role in the wider Russländer world of religious leaders. Other Elim ministers and deacons, like their Elder, were unpaid and possessed a limited or no theological training. They came from different backgrounds and held contrasting religious views, often expressed in their sermons. Some ministers adopted the safer, well-established practice of reading from old sermon texts, either their own or written by others. But one well-educated minister, Wilhelm J. Peters, who resettled from Crystal City in the Chortitz area, joined Elim as a minister in 1934 and expressed views unfamiliar to most people in the congregation. Peters had been ordained in Khortitsa in 1920 before immigrating to Canada but in Russia had experienced a religious conversion after attending a revival meeting led by a non-Mennonite German evangelist, Professor E.F. Stroeter.[36]

Even after Elim had an Elder of their own and a full complement of elected ministers and deacons, the congregation did not always achieve a sense of unity, peace, and tranquility. As in many Mennonite congregations, accession to office involved a degree of politics as candidates had to put their names forward for vacant positions and present themselves before a congregational meeting. Behind the scenes ahead of the voting there was often informal lobbying and not all who wished to be chosen succeeded. In the early years of the formation of the congregation, for instance, J.J. Rempel failed to find support in a religious role. Other ministers sometimes desired not to continue in office, especially as they grew older. Some members announced openly their objections to the outcome of voting and to the choice of certain individuals and demanded that this be recorded in the minutes. In the post-war world there was increased dissatisfaction with Elder Enns's leadership. He was considered weak and certain members disliked the way he acted towards them. He was also not in the best of health. In March 1949 matters came to a head at a congregational meeting that dragged on for three days.[37] A proposal was put forward to appoint two people who were not ministers, Jacob Block and Jacob Schapansky, to assist Enns but the motion was lost by a vote of thirteen to twenty-three. Instead, it was decided that leadership should come from the ministers and when this was voted on in two further rounds, Minister Heinrich A. Warkentin received the highest number of votes – twenty-eight to just eleven for another minister, Abram H. Froese.

Warkentin was appointed for three years as "leader." He proved highly effective at bringing most members together even if a few remained opposed to him. As well as holding Sunday services and chairing meetings, ministers also had pastoral duties which some managed better than others. Warkentin only moved into Grunthal in 1944 after farming in St. Elizabeth in Manitoba and was not a Schönfelder but before immigration came from the Khortitsa-linked settlement of Grünfeld. Appointed as a minister in the Reinland Congregation in 1926, he was popular with many in Grunthal but his position as lead minister was challenged in 1952 as his three-year term ended. The matter was put to a vote and as a compromise Enns was recognized as Elder of the congregation and Warkentin continued as leader after receiving the highest number of votes. In 1955, after another three-year period had passed, Warkentin was re-elected unopposed. However, the leadership issue was raised again in 1957 as Warkentin's health began to fail and early in 1958 his ill health resulted in another challenge.

Dietrich Heese, who chaired a number of these meetings, appears often to have opposed Warkentin's efforts, which were supported by other progressive ministers and laypeople to promote a more inclusive congregation, especially for younger members. Heese himself was younger than the existing ministers so his reasons for opposing Warkentin and the others are unclear. But he was conservative, promoted High German, and may have harboured a desire to play an even greater role in the congregation. In later years he acted as a correspondent on Elim's affairs with *Der Bote*, played a central role in organizing the Grunthal history book, and wrote an account of Elim's history.[38] When Warkentin died in 1959, Enns resumed his position as Elder and leader but in December 1961 announced his resignation due to old age. His resignation was on condition that the position of leader be assumed by Nick A. Janz, a younger minister.[39]

Like Warkentin, Janz only arrived in Grunthal in the 1940s when he purchased a farm on the edge of town. His brother John had already settled in the Neu-Bergfeld area south of Spencer and joined the Spencer Bergthaler Church. Only in 1947 did John transfer his membership to Elim after purchasing a farm nearer Grunthal. He eventually became the congregation's business administrator and assisted in rebuilding of the meeting house after it burned down in 1961. The brothers were very different in temperament. Nick Janz was conservative, his brother more liberal, active on the board of the cooperative, and a founding member and keen supporter of the credit union. Eventually he also served as the Dairy Herd Improvement Association for Grunthal and the surrounding district.[40] The election of Nick Janz in 1959, first as a minister and later as leader of the congregation, was in many ways unusual as he had immigrated from Siberia. Mennonites from Siberia were often viewed as poorly educated by Mennonites from southern Russia and his late immigration from the Soviet Union aroused suspicions among those who immigrated earlier. Some Janz family members had been associated with the Mennonite Brethren in Russia and this merely increased suspicion of the family in Grunthal. In the post-war period, however, Nick Janz developed an impressive dairy farm although after he retired from farming, he established a somewhat bizarre personal zoo, later called the Cottonwood Corner Game Farm, with bison and even a caged African lioness. Although largely self-taught, Nick Janz possessed excellent personal and organizational skills. Older people sometimes spoke of him as their "Elder" although his proper title was "Lead Minister." His lack of education, however, meant that the High German of his sermons was coloured by Low German expressions, a not uncommon occurrence for Kanadier and even Russländer ministers.

The Elim congregation's conservatism meant it was extremely slow in adjusting to changes occurring in conferences and congregations across Canada after the Second World War.[41] The founding of the Canadian Mennonite Bible College in Winnipeg in 1947 resulted in a new generation of young people educated in theology and other subjects by instructors drawn from both Russländer and Kanadier communities. Although at first teaching emphasized High German, use of English gradually increased and in 1964 the College became an approved teaching centre of the University of Manitoba. The College received financial support from the Elim congregation and some of its young people attended. Qualified graduates started to be appointed to congregations, supplementing or replacing aging unpaid ministers. Gradually nonprofessional ministers drawn from within a congregation were phased out. More significantly the insistence on High German in conference addresses, notices, and congregational reports diminished after the 1960s although not without resistance from some quarters.

In Elim the views of its congregational leaders extended beyond the conservative opinions and disagreements of its largely untrained lay ministers. In January 1969 the congregation debated whether they wished to continue with a *Vorsänger* guiding the congregation in hymn singing. This position was filled usually by election but in many other Russländer congregations the position had gradually been phased out as choirs, pianos, and other musical instruments were introduced. The role of *Vorsänger* had begun to change in Russia before immigration as choirs became increasingly sophisticated.⁴² Following a debate it was declared that the Elim congregation "desired" to continue with the practice but then the placement of the *Vorsänger* became an issue. Some older people complained that although "repositioned" closer to the congregation, they were uncertain "if it belongs this way" as at times, "we feel like we are singing alone." The congregation decided that they should retain the existing system although a piano had been installed and a choir formed.⁴³

A more pressing matter concerned the transition from High German to English in worship services. The transition proved very slow in Elim with worship still held in High German well after other congregations had introduced either a mixed English/German service or separate English and German services at different times on Sundays. The issue of how to transition from German to English in worship remained a problem for aging Russländer in both General Conference and Mennonite Brethren Russländer communities.⁴⁴ If there were two services, older Russländer worshipped at the German service, but as the ranks of elderly worshippers were thinned by death, illness and in some cases, dementia, German services ceased. The *Yearbook* of the Conference of Mennonites in Manitoba indicates that the transition to English occurred in some congregations at least ten years earlier than in Elim. In 1965 the conference's *Yearbook* appears in German and English for the first time; in 1968 the minutes of the conference are bilingual and from 1969 they are all in English. The *Yearbook* of the conference in Canada began to publish some reports in English as early as 1955 and by 1969 they were mostly in English with a few reports in English and German persisting until 1971/72.

In all Mennonite communities in Manitoba children were schooled in English and High German was available in the curriculum as a second language. Efforts were made to encourage parents to choose High German as the second language for their children to learn rather than another language, such as French. The benefits of choosing German were highlighted in Mennonite newspapers which noted that High German was closer to English than French or any other language. Additionally, it was argued that older people who knew German could help children acquire the language and finally, by learning High German there were opportunities for children to expand their knowledge of Mennonite history.⁴⁵ However, in Grunthal Low German was the language of many homes, Kanadier and Russländer, but increasingly this was mixed with English especially when children were speaking with adults. Although children could understand some of what their parents and grandparents said in Low German, they rarely used the language among themselves, preferring English instead.

However, Sunday School instruction in Elim continued in High German much longer than was either sensible or practical. While the Conference of Canada continued to produce study material for Sunday Schools in High German and English, most younger grandchildren of Russländer, including those in Elim, struggled with services and published material in German. Teachers in Elim who tried to introduce English in Sunday School, especially those in charge of the younger grades who were often young mothers, were reprimanded.[46] In 1961, in answer to a questionnaire requesting an evaluation of the Conference of Mennonites in Manitoba Summer Bible School's program, Grunthal's minister A.H. Froese replied in German and English that many parents did not want their children to attend. He considered a possible reason for their unwillingness was because the school was taught exclusively in English and went on to suggest that if material in German was included, parents might permit their children to attend.[47] The language issue emerged in Elim once again in 1969 during discussions over whether more English might be permitted in the congregation but any idea that it be introduced was rejected in spite of a division of opinion on the matter. The main objector to any use of English was Dietrich Heese.[48] It was not until the early 1970s that some English was introduced but only as part of a combined German and English service.[49] The statutes of the Elim congregation, first drawn up in 1927 and later revised, were eventually translated into English only in 1979 and it was not until 1982 that young people were permitted to use English instead of German when reading the catechism in preparation for baptism.[50]

The language issue in Elim, a desire to preserve High German thought to be essential for the continuance of the Mennonite faith and identity, was part of a larger struggle over the issue that occurred in other Russländer communities in Canada where the first generation of immigrants of the 1920s held onto power. It was particularly in the postwar period that the need for a transition of power between generations became apparent. Many older Russländer believed that the knowledge and use of High German had declined because people did not want to appear pro-German by speaking it openly. But concerns over the use of High German and discussions on the need to preserve the language for future generations had been a constant theme among Russländer since the very first years of settlement in Canada.[51] Newspapers carried regular articles on the issue while teachers' and religious conferences received reports and positional documents on similar themes. After the war Heinrich Dyck and Victor Peters founded a new journal, the

Mennonitische Lehrerzeitung (1948–50), later renamed the *Mennonitische Welt* (1950–2), to promote Mennonite culture among teachers and especially the use of High German. The articles included some written by non-Mennonites with rather dubious pre-war connections with Nazi organizations. Neither journal succeeded as English-language publications steadily replaced them.[52]

Although the journals ceased publication, concerns over the German language did not go away. In 1952 a "Mennonite Society for the Fostering of the German Mother Tongue" (*Mennonitische Verein zur Pflege der deutschen Muttersprache*) was established in Manitoba through the efforts of the former principal of the Mennonite Collegiate in Gretna, Gerhard H. Peters, a somewhat controversial figure.[53] The idea was met with great enthusiasm by many older Russländer and soon branch societies were established in Mennonite communities from British Columbia to Ontario. Peters requested support from elders and leaders in every Mennonite community and congregation.[54] To attract as many members as possible the cost of membership was set at just $1.00, provoking a response from J.J. Hildebrand who argued this was demeaning because even a watermelon cost only $2.00. The title and stated aims of the *Verein* were primarily secular and none of its founders were ordained ministers. However, its aims played on the connection between German and religion and it soon received support from numerous Russländer ministers and even some older Kanadier religious leaders eager to retain the association between High German and the Mennonite faith. A major problem soon emerged, however, which involved what exactly constituted the Mennonite "mother tongue." Was it High German or Low German, especially when English was the language of so many Mennonite homes? This point was raised by the influential Mennonite leader, C.F. Klassen, in response to the *Verein*'s insistence that "mother tongue" referred only to High German.[55]

By remaining separate from religious conferences, the organization's programs avoided the kind of direct conflict between secular and religious views of Mennonite identity that had existed before the war. As the *Verein*'s aim was to maintain knowledge and use of German rather than to directly promote faith, secular German language books were ordered from Germany. Unlike in the pre-war years these reflected post-war German culture purged of Nazi ideas. The *Verein*'s community library was established in private homes and some of its leading members, especially in Winnipeg, included individuals who were once eager supporters of the now discredited Nazi regime. At least one, Dr. Walter Quiring, had served during the war in administrative roles in the eastern lands conquered by the Nazi forces.

Despite his dubious record, Quiring immigrated to Canada after the war and in 1952 joined the editorial board of the *Mennonitische Welt* and eventually became editor of *Der Bote*, the leading Russländer newspaper.[56] In spite of the opening of German-language schools and the promotion of a range of cultural activities, the *Verein*'s greatest supporters belonged to the passing generation of Russländer. Their descendants were more attracted to English and English literature than to German. But the holding on to German, for religious and cultural reasons, helped create a period of confusion between first-generation Russländer and succeeding generations who wished to express themselves in Canadian English, one language of the country most identified with.

During Heidebrecht's time teaching at the school most Russländer adults in Grunthal hoped he would establish competence in High German among his pupils and foster an appreciation of German literature. But neither wish was fully realized. Unruh and Reimer, as his most significant successors, were chosen not just because they were competent teachers, but also because they could maintain High German. However, Low German continued to be used in social situations while High German remained restricted to worship services on Sundays and the second language learned in classes at school. During the war when teaching High German was restricted, little was done to maintain formal instruction in the language even if some parents put greater effort into using it at home. The coming of peace, however, gave the community an opportunity to reassess the language situation, including considerations of the role of language in being Mennonite while also developing a future for their children in the largely English-speaking world beyond the community. A proper balance was needed between acquiring English, learning German, and using the latter in the congregation, community, and at home. The issue became more critical as the number of pupils entering the school system again put pressure on school resources. The promise that the *Verein* could assist in the maintenance of High German attracted several Russländer in Grunthal who joined the organization and sent their subscriptions to Winnipeg in the year it was founded (table 12.1).

How many maintained their membership and continued to pay annual subscriptions is unclear despite its low fee. The large number of November enrolments may be because they submitted their applications together, thereby saving on postage and the cost of individual money orders. But it might also indicate a degree of social pressure to be involved as well as a genuine concern over the continuation of High German. Many older Grunthal people continued to subscribe to

Table 12.1. Grunthal Russländer enrolled in the *Mennonitische Verein zur Pflege der deutschen Muttersprache*, 1952

Month enrolled	People enrolled
September	A.P. Martens
October	Elder J.J. Enns; John G. Peters (with wife and three children)
November	D.D. Enns, John S. Martens, Abram N. Esau, John F. Warkentin, H.H. Unger, A.B. Krahn, P.H. Janzen, Jakob A. Martens, Abram Driedger, John J. Friesen, Jacob J. Schellenberg
December	John D. Warkentin; D.D. Warkentin

Source: "Mennonite German Language Society," MHA 4147 (4), Membership Ledger.

German-language newspapers and magazines, Mennonite and non-Mennonite. Elim had an "official" correspondent with *Der Bote* which occasionally published reports on the congregation although obituaries, with a life history, appear to have been the major responsibility. At the same time the original immigrants, and especially from the younger generation, subscribed to English newspapers: *The Carillon*, the *Winnipeg Tribune*, and the *Winnipeg Free Press*, as well as a range of other English magazines.[57]

The transitions and succession between older and younger generations in the post-war world were made more difficult as a younger generation moved into higher education and new employment opportunities in non-Mennonite society. At a teachers' conference in Springstein, Manitoba, held in August 1950, David H. Paetkau presented a paper for discussion that asked, "Why Are We Losing Our Youth and How Can We Counteract This Loss?"[58] Paetkau, born in Russia in 1903, had trained as a teacher in Ekaterinoslav during the troubled years of the Russian Civil War. He immigrated to Canada in 1926, and eventually found employment in the prestigious German-English Academy in Rosthern, Saskatchewan, where he was recognized as a noted music teacher and compiler of Mennonite music.[59] The question Paetkau raised in 1950 reveals how some leaders thought about the issues even if he, like others, had few answers. "For us Mennonites" he began,

> ... the problem is doubly difficult. We have been put down in a new home, a new culture, and we have not yet been able to rest; instead, we are in the middle of the process of assimilation. Our youth are also in a strange environment and trying to find themselves.

While Paetkau wanted to maintain the Mennonite faith, keep youth committed to the beliefs of their ancestors, and at the same time proficient in High German, he recognized that they were increasingly living in the "world," not separate from it. They were drawn to other educational institutions and away from Mennonite-German centres of education which were based around religious study.

If the young wanted to be teachers, nurses, doctors, scientists, and even pursue academic careers, they had to attend English-speaking training centres and universities and later be employed in situations where German was of little or no use. Paetkau also was aware that some young Mennonites who had studied beyond their communities wished to marry partners from outside the Mennonite world, often "English," without knowledge of High German. Even if partners were willing to be baptized and become Mennonites, the continued use of German as the only language of worship resulted in them and their partner eventually leaving Mennonite congregations. And in cases where some Mennonites only spoke English, he reminded his listeners, "it is no good to brand ... [them] as black sheep." As most of his audience had been born, raised, and educated in Russia, Paetkau could refer back to different issues Mennonites faced before immigrating to Canada. Whereas in Russia "a [Mennonite] girl would rather stay a young maiden for 100 years than marry a 'Russian,' in Canada this was now a thing of the past."[60] In Russia, the religious attitude of Mennonite youth towards the Orthodox Church had been clearly demarcated, but in Canada "we are dealing generally with Protestant tendencies with which we fundamentally agree." Most importantly, however:

> Canada is not a land of privileges; we are all the same in a democracy. Our children do not want to be special, to be spoiled; we just want to be Canadians. And everyone being the same is inconsistent with a claim to a special status.

Paetkau clearly recognized that the old and especially the younger generation were now facing a series of contradictions in a rapidly changing world. The most important of these concerned what it meant to be Canadian.

Chapter Thirteen

Becoming Canadian

"This is my country, but it was never my father's." The speaker was an elderly Mennonite who was born in Russia but immigrated as a young child in the 1920s and spent most of his life in Grunthal. The contrast between generations in a new land could not be more starkly stated. It is similar in many ways, however, to the experiences of Ukrainians who immigrated to Canada following the Second World War and their descendants. The immigrant generation would remain in enforced exile, with thoughts fixated until their dying days on another place and a way of life. In contrast their sons and daughters adjusted to the country they now considered home and in turn their own children became proud Canadians.[1] So it was for the Mennonite speaker as one son became a respected teacher and the other a government minister in the provincial legislature. While such attitudes were not the same for all immigrants and some adjusted better than others to life in Canada, there are other indications that the lost world of pre-revolutionary Russia continued to dominate the lives of the first generation of Russländer immigrants.

When this generation approached the end of their lives, a number of picture books were published with photographs devoted mainly to the world of pre-revolutionary Russia.[2] The editor of one collection was Gerhard Lohrenz, Elder of a Winnipeg congregation, who from the 1960s on led sixteeen or seventeen tours to the Soviet Union that included many Russländer.[3] And as Russländer began to die, their obituaries often included accounts of their lives in Russia but little was said of their working lives following immigration in spite of most having spent more time in Canada than in Russia

When in 1967 the first-generation immigrant Jacob H. Block published his thirty-five-page booklet on Grunthal's history, his foreword suggested it was a "contribution" to mark Canada's centennial of nationhood. He also suggested he and his family, connected with Grunthal for twenty-two years, had "deep roots in its sandy, stony ground" and were "so closely associated with Grunthal and its inhabitants, it has become our home." Block's small work, however, was written in German and printed in archaic German Gothic font.[4] In 1974 when a much larger account of Grunthal and its past was published, it was in English, not German. The book was dedicated to two Kanadier business pioneers, Johann Braun and John Krahn, who had "built so much," and whose enterprises were founded prior to the Russländers' arrival. The dedication encouraged the town's younger generation to follow in their "footsteps" and to look forward, "unafraid, never once glancing back except to meditate and give thanks to God for giving us the opportunity to live in this big, beautiful land, and for FREEDOM." Unfortunately, the foreword also claimed that it was written to celebrate the one hundredth anniversary of the "first" settlement of Mennonites in Canada, not just in Manitoba. This regrettably overlooked the fact that many Ontario Mennonites had settled long before Mennonites arrived from Russia, or that Ontario Mennonites had assisted those who immigrated during the 1870s and the 1920s.[5]

It was not just Russländer who were muddled about the past. In 1967, John H. Menzies contributed the regular school inspector's comments to the Grunthal Collegiate yearbook, noting that 1967 was a "dramatic year for Canadians" as Canada's Confederation was one hundred years old and "the settlement dates back three and one-half centuries, during which time the founding peoples, first the French, and then British, then both together, then with people of other origins have co-existed and co-operated."[6] There was no mention of Indigenous peoples, and Mennonite histories of Hanover and Grunthal published soon after also say nothing about the previous inhabitants of the land before Mennonite settlement began. Both, however, contain passing references to Métis who were involved in a confrontation with officials showing Mennonite delegates from Russia possible sites for settlement in the 1870s.[7]

Following the Canadian Centennial of 1967, Manitoba celebrated the century of its own foundation in 1870. In July 1970 Queen Elizabeth II, accompanied by the then Prince Charles, briefly visited Steinbach where the chairman of the Ministerial Association spoke on "the biblical basis for the Mennonites' support for the monarchy."[8] The royal party then proceeded in a motor convoy to St. Pierre and on their way passed through Sarto and Grunthal. Unlike Sarto, Grunthal residents were honoured when, according to the official itinerary, the "royal cavalcade" would proceed with a "slow drive" through the town.[9] On the day "thousands" of local people lined the main street standing beneath lamp posts bedecked with Canadian and Manitoban flags.[10] Later, in

August, another celebration with decorated floats followed the route of the Queen's fleeting visit and a special "Centennial Thanksgiving Day" was held in the auditorium led by ministers of the four main congregations with choir singing followed by a brief presentation on Anabaptist and Mennonite history.[11] The parade of floats highlighted local businesses and community organizations and was followed by a number of events, including a cow-milking contest and a centennial costume competition with participants dressed as First Nations maidens and nineteenth-century Mennonite pioneers.[12] Truly, Grunthal Mennonites were now integrated, however oddly, into the culture of Manitoba and Canada.

The late 1960s and early 1970s proved a busy time for celebration for Canadians and for Mennonites. In 1972 the Elim Congregation decided to mark the forty-fifth anniversary since its foundation with a publication outlining its history with photographs of its current members.[13] To mark the centenary of the first Mennonite settlement in Manitoba in 1874, Mennonites in Winnipeg and elsewhere organized elaborate programs.[14] In 1974 the Elim congregation held a service to recognize the centenary of Mennonite settlement in Manitoba. Its correspondent took the opportunity to remind readers that it was also fifty years since the first Russländer arrived in Canada even if the truth was that the first Russländer had arrived in 1923 while Grunthal's Schönfelder mostly immigrated in 1924.[15] In 1977 the fiftieth anniversary of the establishment of the Elim congregation was marked by a thanksgiving service. In his account Dietrich Heese gave a more accurate account of the Russländer immigration, noting it began in 1923, as he related more to Khortitsa people, many of whom arrived before those from Molochna.[16]

Before the various centennial celebrations occurred an increasing number of new symbols began to reflect the growing sense of Canadian nationalism. The new flag design with a maple leaf was adopted on 15 February 1965, replacing the British Union Jack on a red ensign and a shield enclosing the arms of Canada's provinces.[17] This did not occur without considerable debate and controversy across Canada, especially among those of British descent and military veterans. But there are few signs of any opposition in Grunthal or indeed among any Mennonites, Russländer or others.[18] The local Steinbach English-language newspaper published a letter of protest but it was written by a non-Mennonite, most likely of British descent.[19] While individual provinces kept or designed their own flags, the new national flag was instantly recognizable and helped identify the nation in dramatic fashion.[20] In 1967 Queen Elizabeth II visited Canada as the country celebrated the centenary of Canadian confederation and in Grunthal the centennial float carried

Fig. 13.1. Grunthal Centennial Parade float, 1967. The 1967 Canada Centennial celebration with float decorated with the new Canadian flag and carrying the Grunthal queen, Melita Driedger.

Source: Courtesy of Melita Ennis.

Grunthal's own queen sporting a large decorative representation of the new flag (fig. 13.1). In 1980 Canada adopted "O Canada" as its national anthem, already the de facto anthem for many years, having been used during the 1939 royal tour of George VI. Provincial law in Manitoba required elementary and secondary schools to sing the national anthem as the national and provincial flags were raised so there was no way a new generation of Canadians, Mennonite and non-Mennonite, could resist the changing face of Canadian nationalism. Federal and provincial governments also developed political programs to encourage the development of nationalism, thereby shaping the destiny of future generations.

Older Russländer had first-hand experience living under different rulers and regimes and had directly experienced some of the major political events of the twentieth century, including war, revolution, migration, exile, and economic depression. At the start of the century, they were Russian citizens, then Soviet citizens, and finally Canadian citizens. When they entered Canada, it was part of the British Empire but a country with a high degree of political autonomy, an elected federal parliament, and provincial legislatures. In Canada the Russländer had come to terms with a new political order and quite early they had few objections to being involved in politics, local or otherwise. As most became citizens, they registered as voters and consequently their names appear on voters' lists for municipal, provincial, and federal elections. Candidates in provincial and federal elections were mostly associated with political parties and the apparent long-time Russländer support for the Liberal party began to change.[21] Russländer started to examine more closely the policies and performance of other parties, and their voting patterns becomes more varied.[22] The change in voting patterns was complicated by a proliferation of political parties, some with candidates possessing recognizable Mennonite surnames.[23] Older Russländer now had to decide whether to remain loyal to a particular party, represented by a non-Mennonite candidate, or to vote for another party with a Mennonite-named candidate. A further problem presented itself where the Mennonite candidate was either of Russländer or of Kanadier descent.

In federal elections the percentage of Mennonites voting in Grunthal gradually increased from a wartime low of just 34 per cent in 1940, to 40 per cent in 1945, and to over 60 per cent in 1949. It then dropped to just to 37 per cent in 1953, possibly because of Canada's involvement in the Korean war (1950-3) supported by a Liberal government. The number voting then increased to 60 per cent in 1957 and rose again to over 70 per cent in all the elections that followed (1958/1962/1963) until 1965 and 1972 when the turnout dropped back into the 60 per cent range.[24] It is impossible from these results to differentiate between Russländer and Kanadier voters in the Grunthal area, but it is safe to assume that more Russländer than Kanadier voted. A comparison between Russländer-dominated Grunthal with the village of Chortitz, where most voters were conservative Kanadier, supports such an assumption. In 1940 only 16 per cent of Chortitz voters cast a vote and in 1945 only 9 per cent, while turnout remained under 50 per cent until 1974, when 63 per cent voted.

Support for different political parties in the Grunthal area varied, with votes first given to the Liberals or conservative liberals and even Social Credit, but eventually, like in most of Manitoba's rural communities, the Progressive Conservatives. Equally important is the lack of support shown for more "socialist" parties, especially the New Democratic Party (NDP), where the Mennonite vote for the latter was mostly an urban phenomenon. Figures for turnout in provincial elections are unavailable but is safe to assume they followed those for federal elections. Elections for positions in the municipality were not based on an allegiance to a particular political party but concerned local issues and a desire for each ward to select a councillor who was "one of their own."

The selection of a reeve, however, could reveal regional politics across the municipality. A good example occurred in 1947 when elections for reeve were held. It was a three-way contest between candidates from the three centres of Steinbach, Niverville, and Grunthal and focused on issues such as roads and ditches and how assessments were calculated for local taxes. According to a local newspaper report a "political campaign was mounted," particularly in Grunthal where their candidate was Ted Chornoboy, the Grunthal businessman of Ukrainian descent. He eventually received 281 (91 per cent) of the votes cast in Grunthal, gaining 293 votes of the 364 registered voters in the town and immediate area. He also received support from Sarto voters, 81 per cent or 175 votes from 216 cast from a total of 312 registered voters. Chornoboy therefore won by 706 votes to 567 over his rival from Steinbach, J.R. Barkman.[25] Eventually Grunthal Russländer of the next generation would be elected as reeve and for a time they dominated the leadership of the municipality.

Younger Mennonites responded positively to the post-war sense of being Canadian that involved a gradual decline in the Anglo-focused culture. Many first-generation Russländer had difficulties identifying with pre-war English-dominated culture even though, from afar, many admired some of its aspects such as its emphasis on education and culture. Many Kanadier, especially conservative groups, however, wished to remain apart from any identification with the "English" (LG *Enjlisch*) but the attitudes and opinions of Russländer were more complex. In Late Imperial Russia most Mennonites identified as loyal subjects of Russia's rulers and were willing to learn Russian and adopt some aspects of Russian culture. But they were unwilling to be entirely Russianized.[26] This involved a strategy of remaining Mennonite: a strategy easier to achieve in Russia's multinational empire, despite the threat of Russian nationalism.

But Canada was different. Its political institutions and its legal system, and even its culture, especially in Western Canada, had been transferred from Britain and outside Quebec, English was the major language. In the early years following immigration, Russländer were expected to adopt the English language and assimilate to "English" (i.e., British) culture. "English" was the common term used by Mennonites and non-Mennonites in Canada although the term "British" might better reflect the identity of settlers from the United Kingdom, even though the more inclusive term itself has a complex history in Britain and its colonies.[27] Eager to take advantage of opportunities in Canada,

Russländer quickly acquired the English language and where it was to their advantage, British ways. But they also did not want to lose their identity and faith, closely based around the German language. So, the Russländer dilemma was how to become *like* the British but not to become *totally* "English" in the process.

The generation schooled in Manitoba before and during the Second World War experienced an educational system that emphasized Canada's place in the British Empire.[28] After the war, however, this gradually began to change and a greater emphasis on Canada as an independent nation with its own history was introduced to schools, although not without considerable debate.[29] The same occurred with the introduction of Canadian literature where the earlier emphasis had been on British writers.[30] As "being English" was increasingly replaced by "being Canadian," Mennonites responded.[31] The enactment of the Canadian Citizenship Act in 1946 took effect on 1 January 1947 and was the first major step towards the creation of a separate Canadian legal identity, although in Canada most Russländer had been British subjects since the 1930s. The two Grunthal Russländer who had failed to register as British discovered they could not receive Canadian social benefits until they became Canadian citizens. But the days of Britishness in Canada were numbered.[32]

In a statement to the Canadian House of Commons on 8 October 1971, Prime Minister Pierre Trudeau announced that from now on multiculturalism would be official government policy. The move was intended to provide official recognition of the cultural contributions to Canada of the country's diverse ethnic groups and preserve the cultural freedom of all those who identified with an ethnicity. As proposed, the policy of multiculturalism was based on recommendations of an earlier Royal Commission on Bilingualism and Biculturalism.[33] Appointed in 1963, the commission was to examine the existing state of bilingualism and biculturalism in Canada and work towards developing an equal partnership between English-speaking and French-speaking Canadians. It was originally established by the Liberal government headed by Prime Minister Lester B. Pearson, who also indicated an eagerness to create a unified Canadian identity by promoting the new flag and national anthem. The Royal Commission took submissions from groups across Canada and was also instructed to consider the cultural contributions of ethnic groups other than English-speaking and French-speaking communities. Many of these other cultural groups expressed a concern that the commission's mandate to examine the contributions of all groups had been ignored during the enquiry. The commission therefore attempted to address these concerns in their fourth and final report where they recommended that minority groups be given greater recognition and support to preserve their languages and cultures.[34]

Several "cultural" Mennonite groups, dominated by Russländer, made written submissions to the Royal Commission and spoke with the commissioners. No submission was made, at least directly, by a Mennonite congregation or collectively by the Manitoba or other Canadian conferences. A brief, however, was prepared by something that called itself a Winnipeg branch of the "Mennonite Society for the Promotion of the German Language in Canada," along with a Vancouver sister organization, the "Mennonite German Language Society."[35] Another submission came from a body calling itself the "Canadian Mennonite Association" based in Altona, Manitoba. A final submission was from a body called the "Manitoba Mennonite Trustee Association and Manitoba Mennonite Educational Committee" which gave its postal address as Winkler, Manitoba.[36] The submission from Winkler may have involved a local Mennonite Brethren congregation whose members were embroiled in a bitter dispute over continued use of German in congregational affairs, particularly religious services, a dispute that threatened a schism.[37] On the other hand the Altona and Winkler submissions might also have involved the business leader A.J. Thiessen, who had attempted to enter politics and was interested in school reform.[38] No organization from the East Reserve where Grunthal was located submitted a brief, perhaps because the area lacked a united body to address concerns on the issue.

The leaders of the Winnipeg "Mennonite Society for the Promotion of the German Language" claimed the organization had been founded with the "aim ... to help young Mennonites to become real bilingual Canadians." By bilingualism they meant English and their "chosen" language, High German, which was their "cultural heritage" as Mennonites. The major issue stressed in other Mennonite submissions involved the teaching of German in schools, a matter that had been highlighted long before the Royal Commission was established and that had been included in the earlier submissions to the Manitoba provincial Royal Commission on Education.[39] Another submission was made in 1965 by something called the "Canadian Mennonite Association" in Winnipeg but exactly what this was and who it represented is unclear. It may have been associated with the *Mennonitisches Bildungsinstitut*, founded in 1958 and later renamed the Westgate Mennonite Collegiate in Winnipeg, primarily a Russländer initiative linked to two influential Mennonite congregations in Winnipeg.[40] The Mennonite request to the 1960s Royal Commission on Bilingualism and Biculturalism by the Winnipeg *Verein*, however, extended beyond Winnipeg with an insistence that each school district be permitted to decide on which language it would teach as a second language. French was clearly not viewed as an appropriate second language to be taught in schools where most children were Mennonite.

When the commission's reports reached the federal Canadian Parliament and Senate the relationship between language and culture shifted from two languages and two cultures towards multiculturalism while leaving the issue of bilingualism versus multilingualism unresolved. The final outcome in 1971 of the drive to resolve the thorny problem of English versus French Canada and meet the demands of other ethnic communities, was to stress the bilingual nature of the country while promoting culture with the policy of multiculturalism. The latter recognized that the linguistic diversity of the population could be acknowledged as just another aspect of culture and dealt with under the aegis of multiculturalism. All official documents along with a host of other notices now had to be in both English and French. Other languages now became invisible while other cultures, or at least a selection of "traditions," could be exhibited in new ways.

The view that the commission had failed to notice the wider cultural diversity of Canada, referred to as the "third element," was recognized especially by those of Ukrainian descent such as the noted linguist Thomas M. Prymak and Senator Paul Yuzyk.[41] Yuzyk had carried out research with Ukrainians at the same time that E.K. Francis studied Mennonites, both funded by the Manitoba Historical Society, a point he acknowledged. Yuzyk first expressed his views in an address to the Senate, later included in a scholarly article responded to by other scholars.[42] Yuzyk noted that at the start of the century those of British descent constituted just under 60 per cent of Canada's population, the French just over 30 per cent, while the rest were 12 per cent. By 1961, however, those of British descent were only 44 per cent, the French remained at 30 per cent, but the rest had more than doubled to 26 per cent.[43] Canada was now a multicultural nation.

Manitoba was slow to follow the federal government's lead and its first piece of legislation on multiculturalism was the Manitoba Intercultural Council Act of 1984, amended in 1992. It stated that the "Legislative Assembly" recognizes "that Manitoba's multicultural society is not a collection of many separate societies, divided by language and culture, but is a single society united by shared laws, values, aspirations and responsibilities." In this single, united society "persons of various backgrounds have the freedom and opportunity to express and foster their cultural heritage … to participate in the broader life of society" but on condition that they "abide by and contribute to the laws and aspirations that unite society."[44] The right to be different therefore has limitations and being a loyal Canadian who recognizes the laws of the land in which they live takes precedence over cultural roots to another country or ethnic group. Citizenship is paramount.

One positive result of multiculturalism as official policy was government support for a wide range of "ethnic" activities. Various groups who could lay claim to an ethnic heritage could expect support from government grants aimed at cultural activities such as singing and dancing, often in what were assumed to be national folk costumes from their "homelands," the serving of ethnic foodstuffs, and other aspects deemed "cultural." Many of these have been displayed at folk festivals such as Folkorama in Winnipeg where Mennonites have a pavilion but without the alcohol included by some other ethnicities.[45] University programs have been established to further teaching and research on ethnic groups where academics can draw on research funding; journals and books on ethnic themes have been supported. A veritable industry has come into existence subsidized by governments, federal and provincial. The aim is to allow everyone to be different if the differences focus on a limited range of common, non-controversial activities unlikely to foster discord, such as singing, dancing, costume, crafts, and food. In this way difference can be managed within an all-embracing system and help establish a unified Canadian nationalism.

Mennonites initially had some difficulty in fully accessing these benefits. While they could be redefined as an ethnic group in the new environment, their primary claim to identity was religion, at least for a majority. Unfortunately, emphasizing religion as a cultural difference was not something promoted by official multiculturalism as religious differences have a long history of division, discord, and violence. A Mennonite ethnicity centred on religion was further complicated by the fact that Mennonites obviously were internally divided by religious differences. They were a bewildering patchwork of people, some the result of varied migrations to Canada at different times and from different homelands. But these religious differences could also be a result of a long history of internal division and schism.

Another significant problem associated with identifying with a "Mennonite" ethnicity in Canada was that most Mennonites had few "folk" customs or practices, especially when compared with many other richly endowed ethnic groups. Mennonite singing consisted predominantly of religious hymns, not folk songs, even if communities did possess rhymes and folk songs, but these were only recited or sung in private. A few Mennonites, Kanadier and Russländer, even played musical instruments such as fiddles at social gatherings, but never combined religious hymns with folk ditties. Kenneth Peacock recorded some folk songs, mostly Kanadier, in southern Manitoba in the early 1960s before multiculturalism became official policy and a German folklorist made another study of Saskatchewan Mennonites; these were followed by more detailed Mennonite studies.[46] There were also the circle "dances" (HG *Schlüsselbund*) of young people at weddings and other gatherings that some claimed were just "games," not dancing, especially when they were condemned as such.[47] Mennonite opinion, seriously and non-seriously, is that "Mennonites don't dance." In private, however, several risqué jokes are told of immoral acts being mistaken for dancing. Dancing is supposedly "forbidden" along with "playing cards, fashionable clothes, movies and most other forms of entertainment."[48]

There was also an absence of Mennonite dress to display at ethnic events to mark their distinctiveness, even if a few studies suggest otherwise.[49] At the time Russländer immigrated many conservative Kanadier still wore plain dress as a sign of humility. This was not, however, the practice in Russia before 1914 although the wearing of dark clothing, especially at Sunday services, was a personal choice but not a necessity. This did not prevent some older Russländer women from judging what younger women wore, as in the case where one younger married woman was presented with a piece of material to cover a cut-away area beneath her neck that the gift-giver considered "too exposed." The recipient refused to wear it and just put it in a drawer. In everyday attire, however, Russländer and Kanadier Mennonites' dress was very similar to non-Mennonites. The only way Mennonites could dress up in "ethnic" attire was to assume the clothes some believed may have been worn at the time of the 1870s immigration. Even in the 1870s, however, the dress of Mennonite immigrants was not dissimilar from that of many other new agrarian immigrants of the time and eventually most settlers adjusted their clothes to local conditions.

While Mennonites could not take full advantage of the opportunities multicultural programs offered as a single ethnic group, collectively they had long been recognized as distinct and identified as one of Western Canada's "ethnic" communities long before multiculturalism was official policy. The use of the term "ethnic" appears in popular and academic studies dating back to before and shortly after the Second World War.[50] Before multiculturalism emerged, the Mennonite Heritage Village was established outside Steinbach in 1967 with all the trappings that identified Mennonites as one of Canada's, and especially Manitoba's, distinctive pioneer immigrant settler groups. A chair in Mennonite studies was established in 1978 at the University of Winnipeg, funded by government and Mennonite donors. Mennonite works written by Mennonite academics, local Mennonite historians, and especially literary works by poets and novelists all benefited from ethnic support programs that helped fund their publication. Royden Loewen's book on Blumenort was assisted with a grant provided by the Minister of State for Multiculturalism, as was my own despite me not being a Canadian citizen.[51]

Although there is little evidence that following the implementation of official bilingual and multicultural programs either people or organizations in Grunthal drew directly on the funds, the community undoubtedly entered into the spirit of multiculturalism. One example is the expansion of the annual fair which in more recent years has also received support and recognition as a multicultural event.[52] Mennonite publications such as the Conference of Mennonites in Canada's *Canadian Mennonite* and the more secular magazine *Mennonite Mirror* carried advertisements from the Canadian government that promoted multicultural initiatives. The Mennonite Literary Society published *Mennonite Mirror*, funded in part by the Manitoba Arts Council and the Canadian government's multicultural programs. It published essays, reports, and reviews mostly in English, but a few in High and Low German. Both *Mennonite Mirror* and *Canadian Mennonite* were subscribed to by Mennonites in Grunthal and Elim supported the Mennonite Conference that produced *Canadian Mennonite*. Copies of the *Mirror* with the names and addresses of Grunthal residents eventually found their way to the town's thrift shop.

Even before the Royal Commission on Bilingualism and Biculturalism began its work, some Mennonites had argued for a combination of multilingualism and multiculturalism.[53] The very idea of *Bi*lingualism and *Bi*culturalism conflicted with the experience of older Russländer born and raised in Russia where *multilingualism* and *multiculturalism* existed across Russia's ethnically diverse empire. For Russländer the experience of a multilingual and multicultural world continued after immigration to Canada, as they read, wrote, and spoke High German, most spoke or understood Mennonite Low German, and they acquired English. In Grunthal some immigrants mastered English more quickly than others and older Russländer never became entirely competent in the language, a situation hampered because they had settled in an area where Mennonite Low German was the main means of communication. Women, especially older married women, were disadvantaged as they had fewer opportunities than their husbands to interact with English speakers. In Grunthal older Russländer could communicate with their Ukrainian neighbours despite differences in speech; some Russländer had mastered it as a first language from their Ukrainian nursemaids. The children and grandchildren of first-generation Russländer, however, were exposed to English through schooling and soon adapted to spoken and written English even if, as in Grunthal, they at first learned the language mainly from Russländer teachers trained in Canada for whom English was also a second language. It was for this reason that for some time the English spoken by young people in Grunthal possessed a distinctiveness recognized by more fluent English-speaking Mennonites from more integrated Kanadier communities like Steinbach. Al Reimer from Steinbach, whose father taught in Grunthal, recalled playing hockey for Steinbach against Grunthal and claimed he could easily recognize his opponents by their English accents that he attributed to Heidebrecht's influence.[54]

By the 1970s younger Mennonites, including those from around Grunthal, were not bilingual in French and English. Even when older Grunthal people talked with neighbours who spoke Manitoban French, they conducted conversations in English, as their neighbours could also speak English. In later years a few ambitious young people sought to learn French in the hope of getting a position in the public service where a degree of proficiency in both languages was an advantage. But most Mennonites of the younger generation stood clearly on the English side of Canadian bilingualism. This also meant that, despite the concerted efforts of the older generation to encourage both English and High German among the younger generation, their attempts failed. In Grunthal Mennonite Low German persisted longer than High German but only as a spoken language. Gradually, however, young people found that although to a degree they could understand Mennonite Low German conversations between parents and grandparents, they could not easily reply in the language. It was little used among people of their own generation apart from a few words or phrases occasionally dropped into English conversations. Mennonites, including those in and around Grunthal, have become increasingly monolingual in English. This did not mean that Mennonites in Grunthal felt themselves to *be* English, as for older people, especially Kanadier, to become English had always possessed the negative sense of surrendering one's faith and becoming worldly. No such negativism applied to the French (LG *Fraunzeesisch, Fraunzoos*), presumably because no Mennonite could conceive of becoming a French Canadian.[55]

Mennonites born in Canada to the first generation of Russländer immigrants, however, could identify with post-war developments in the formation of a Canadian identity. Becoming Canadian, though, meant a great deal more than just the recognition of the changing symbols of Canadian nationalism and the adoption of Canadian English. It implied a willingness to participate in Canada's political system and a greater involvement in Canadian society beyond the Mennonite world. Not all the fears of loss and assimilation held by many first-generation Russländer or earlier by Kanadier came to pass. Mennonites remained "Mennonite" but not always in quite the same way as understood by earlier generations in Grunthal or elsewhere. Being Mennonite, however, came to mean many things, especially for younger, educated Mennonites who attended centres of higher education in Winnipeg and elsewhere. The idea of being Mennonite included expanding the understanding of the Mennonite past beyond the time when their ancestors had immigrated to Russia. It now extended back to the Reformation and the Anabaptist foundations of the Mennonites. This involved not just a greater awareness of "origins," but also a call for a "rediscovery" of the "vision" of the Anabaptists and its application to contemporary life. An American Mennonite historian, Harold S. Bender, first used the term "Anabaptist Vision" in 1944 and subsequently it was adopted by Mennonite scholars and younger laypeople.[56] But different generations in Grunthal tended to look to different pasts. Older Russländer looked to a lost Russian past in the Old World, Kanadier to the 1870s immigration to Canada, pioneer settlement, and lives disrupted by later events. Younger generations from both groups looked to an Anabaptist/Mennonite past and future and could even think globally to Mennonite groups established through evangelical activity in various parts of the world.

Other factors have continued to influence Mennonite historical understanding. Because of the large-scale exodus of Kanadier Mennonites in the 1920s, their relations and descendants who remained in or returned to Canada developed a transnational world that runs north and south from Canada to South America, often helped by those to the south continuing to hold Canadian passports.[57] Russländer in Canada developed a distinctly west to east orientation that extends across Canada from British Columbia, where many settled or retired to, across the prairie provinces to Ontario. While a few Russländer had connections with Mennonites in the United States, there are also people of similar post-Russian Revolution and post-Second World War backgrounds living in Paraguay and Brazil. However, few connections were maintained with these communities especially beyond the first generation. The kind of kinship connections and return movements for visits and work that have been maintained between by Kanadier in Canada and those in Mexico and Paraguay do not exist for the descendants of Russländer.[58] Mennonites who have left the Soviet Union or its successor states after the 1970s, known as *Umsiedler* or *Aussiedler*, "resettlers," have mostly remained in Germany and had limited contact with the descendants of Russländer in Canada.[59]

Another aspect that has influenced Canadian Mennonite identity has involved the growing independence of a distinctly Canadian Mennonite "Church Conference" from its former relationship with Mennonites in the Unites States. This developed into separate organizations, a Mennonite Church Canada, and a Mennonite Church USA, distinct from the earlier North American Mennonite Conference. For Canadian Mennonites this was a response to a much wider political separation from its United States neighbour, a separation that is in many ways illusory. Canada, economically and culturally, has been increasingly dominated by its neighbour as Canada's ties with Britain faded as the empire was replaced by a much weaker commonwealth following the Second World War. As the Canadian prime minister Pierre Trudeau famously noted about its neighbour in 1969, Canada was like a mouse "sleeping with an elephant."[60] What is true for Canada as a whole is also true for many aspects of Mennonite life in Canada, including in Grunthal.

For some Grunthal people, however, the "elephant" that lies just south of the town still has advantages. Much of the local hog production is sold in the United States, along with other produce. Moreover, its southern neighbour can be easily accessed through the crossing point at Emerson where, as Canadian citizens, Grunthal Mennonites can easily come and go although few venture further into the United States except for vacations. The main attraction is the nearby settlements in North Dakota, popular with Mennonites and other Manitobans because they sell a range of cheap consumer goods.[61] Something else that has attracted Russländer and Kanadier Mennonites from Grunthal is North Dakota's liquor stores that sell beer and spirits more openly than in Manitoba where, in the tradition of a frontier society, severe restrictions long existed on the sale of alcohol even if these have been relaxed in recent years.[62] For some time, alcohol in Manitoba was controlled by the provincial government, sold only from its outlets that were staffed by its employees. After 2003 alcohol could be served with meals in restaurants in Steinbach and in 2008 its first liquor store opened. Grunthal people can also purchase alcohol legally in Sarto or St. Pierre but at higher prices than in the United States.

A major influence on expanding Mennonite views and understanding of the world beyond their communities was through reading newspaper reports. In Grunthal Russländer read mostly Mennonite German-language newspapers, but also some English newspapers from Winnipeg. In 1946 the local *Carillon* newspaper began publication and soon replaced the German language *Die Steinbach Post* (from 1963, *Die Post*) and rapidly became the most widely read paper in Hanover. Another German newspaper published in Steinbach beginning in

1977, *Die Mennonitische Post*, was supported by the Mennonite Central Committee but was mostly intended to serve Mennonite communities in Latin America.[63] Eventually, as the ability to read High German declined with the passing of the first generation of Russländer, the *Canadian Mennonite* replaced *Der Bote*.[64] Mennonite and non-Mennonite newspapers from the United States were not subscribed to, especially by Russländer. Other forms of communication took time to develop. Radio reception without a short-wave receiver remained poor in Grunthal until the 1950s when AM broadcasts could be received including those from Canadian national stations. At the same time several independent radio stations, some broadcasting from Winnipeg, were established. Eventually Mennonite-owned stations were also founded, many of which carried religious messages, sacred music, and news from Mennonite communities. Notices of the death of locals were of particular importance for a people closely connected by kinship and where deaths were often sudden and attendance at funerals almost obligatory. These southern Manitoba Mennonite radio stations had a major influence on Mennonite community life but also on religious identity, often introducing evangelical influences uncommon before they started to broadcast.[65]

In the postwar Mennonite world, modern communication and consumer society brought messages of religious hope and gratification in the form of instant salvation, and in particular to rural and urban Mennonite communities in Manitoba. In the 1950s Steinbach became a centre of a religious crusade led by a Mennonite preacher from Virginia, George R. Brunk II.[66] He spent three weeks in the town, nightly addressing crowds seated in his big tent, row upon row. The tent and Brunk's luxurious aluminum touring caravans resembled a travelling circus but without acrobats, tamed animals, and obvious clowns, although no one appears to have noted the similarity at the time. Like any ringmaster, Brunk collected large sums of money from collections to cover his "expenses." In earlier years Steinbach had experienced evangelical revivals led by American preachers whose messages caused conflict within Kleine Gemeinde congregations, but nothing like Brunk's crusade.[67] One Russländer born and raised in Steinbach later described the revival meetings as having "all the charm and subtlety" of one of Hitler's Nuremberg rallies, a somewhat ironic statement as in the 1930s at least one Russländer businessman from Winnipeg attended and reported favourably on Hitler's 1938 rally.[68] More than a few Russländer and Kanadier from Grunthal and its surrounding areas attended Brunk's meetings but later one Russländer claimed that few responded to the "call" to walk up to the front to seek forgiveness for their sins and declare their conversion. Instead, they insisted they attended merely "to see what all the fuss was about." If this was so, it did not reflect the impact Brunk had on East and West Reserve Kanadier where many were deeply affected, and their experiences helped break the link between generations, long-established religious beliefs, forms of worship, and the authority of Mennonite ministers.[69]

Television would further increase the reach of American evangelists, beamed right into people's homes through signals broadcast from Canadian and US stations. But these new modes of communication also gave access to other forms of entertainment, particularly sports. Grunthal Mennonites, like all Canadians, could now watch national sports live, especially hockey, basketball, and baseball.[70] These sports were broadcast across North America as Canadian teams played in Pan-American leagues. Other North American entertainment practices in Grunthal, distinctly un-Mennonite in terms of either faith or culture, were reflected in activities such as bingo nights, in spite of Mennonite religious objections to gambling.[71] The 4-H Sewing Club held a Halloween party with members dressed in homemade fancy costumes depicting Little Red Riding Hood, a gypsy, a clown, a pirate, and even a lady dressed as a figure from the Roaring Twenties – a time when the first generation of Russländer ladies could not have been involved.[72] Another cultural factor was the promotion of Mennonite foodstuffs, as "ethnic" food was promoted by the Canadian federal policy of multiculturalism. "Mennonite foods" began to appear in shops, supermarkets and even in a Mennonite-themed restaurant, "d'8 Schtove," that later closed. Mennonite cookbooks, however, have continued to flourish, both in print and available online. They have even been the subject of academic study.[73] Less attention has been paid, however, to the gradual adoption of a wide range of North American foodstuffs in Mennonite households, many of which have replaced established Mennonite dishes. Grunthal has even had a Chinese restaurant with takeout.

Another cultural influence of North American origin concerns the adoption of English naming practices, mainly involving personal names. Mennonites have long drawn on personal forenames from the Bible with a few German and Russian names. It was also an established practice to transfer names between generations with the first son named after the grandfather, the second after the maternal grandfather. For females the first daughter was named after the maternal grandmother and the second after the paternal grandmother. A statistical survey of the 1924 cohort of immigrant Russländer, which would include most of Grunthal's Schönfelder settlers, provides data on naming. Almost 34 per cent were called either Johann (18 per cent) or Jakob (16 per cent), and although in Late Imperial Russia some families began to adopt Russian names, usually derived from members of the imperial household such as Nikolai (4 per cent), these are uncommon. Other names are Germanic in origin, with Heinrich the most popular (14 per cent) along with Gerhard (8 per cent), but there are also a few named Franz (4 per cent) or Wilhelm (3 per cent). Female names are more varied: 52 per cent are named Maria (21 per cent), 17 per cent Katherina, and 14 per cent Helena. These are followed by Margaretha (8 per cent), Anna (8 per cent), and Elisabeth (7 per cent). These six constitute 74 per cent of all female names.[74] In Russia a Russianized transliteration of forenames also developed. In some cases, Johann became Ivan; Bernhard, Boris; Dietrich, Dmitri, and so forth. It also became very common to use the Russian patronymic system where the father's forename became the basis for the middle name for both males and females. So, if the father's name was Johann, it was Russianized as Ivanovich for males (as in Nikolai Ivanovich) and for females (Katherina Ivanova), the suffix indicating female gender. Russian diminutives could also be used. For instance, Nikolai (Nicholas) became Kolya, Alexander became Sasha. Such changes were mainly limited to the very late period of imperial rule but were especially common among highly educated, often estate-owning and urban Mennonites who resided away from the main areas of Mennonite settlement.

In Canada, especially around Grunthal, when Russländer immigrated they discovered a different system of naming among Kanadier, especially regarding middle names, a subject often neglected by Mennonite genealogists who mostly concentrate on surnames.[75] While Kanadier still drew mainly on the Bible for forenames, the middle name, or more precisely a letter, indicated the family name of the mother. So, in the case of a person called Abraham B. Klassen, the "B" indicated that the mother's surname might be Braun. As Canadian English came into greater use even established forenames began to alter. Abraham became Abe; Jacob, Jake; John, Johnny; Nikolai, Nick, and so on. In some families biblical, German, and Russian names were replaced by new British and North American names. J.J. Rempel gave one son the name George although this might have been derived from Gerhard or even the German name Georg. But given Rempel's eagerness to take advantage of the benefits Canada had to offer, it might have been chosen because the ruling English monarch at the time was George V. Also, and somewhat predictably, Franz Guenther, pioneer of Grunthal's integration into Canadian life and ways, quite early gave most of his sons names like Arthur, Eric, and Edward (Eddie). Significantly, no Kanadier or Russländer, despite their near neighbours, resorted to French or Ukrainian forenames. No one was called Pierre, Jacques, or Etienne, nor were any named Bohdan, Oleh, or Yaroslav.

Place names were also Anglicized. As Grunthal expanded, new streets were given English, not German, names. When the school district centred on Grunthal grew, the Grunthal Collegiate increasingly drew in students from beyond town and in 1971 its name was changed to Green Valley School.[76] The Centennial Park in Grunthal established to mark the 1967 and 1970 Canadian and Manitoba centennials was also named Green Valley. In post-war German-language sources the umlaut in Grunthal (Grünthal) was occasionally used but in English-language sources was dropped. Somewhat ambiguously Jacob Block indicated the umlaut in the title of his history of Grunthal as "Gruenthal" but dropped this spelling throughout the text. Early in 1963, however, a more radical suggestion for Grunthal's name was proposed when a popular Winnipeg radio station, CKY, apparently with the approval of provincial officials, formulated a plan to encourage economic progress in Manitoba.[77] This involved the station "adopting" a town and promoting it over the airwaves. Eventually twenty-six town mayors were invited to submit proposals as to why their towns should be selected, with a suggestion that the selected town might promote tourism through the radio station encouraging visitors to participate in local events. In turn this would encourage tourism in the province and help communities develop any existing facilities. Of the mayors who responded three communities were selected: Binscarth, La Riviere, and Grunthal, arranged in that order. If the first community selected rejected the offer following a vote of local taxpayers, the offer would then be made to the next so Grunthal would have the chance only if the other communities rejected the offer.

In the event, both Binscarth and La Riviere taxpayers rejected the proposal mainly because it came with strings attached. To gain the benefits of the offer the selected community was required to change its name to "Seekaywye," a phonetic form of the station's call letters, CKY. Opposition to the idea of a name change, however, came not just from within the two communities, but also from others in Manitoba. The Manitoba Historical Society was particularly vocal in its opposition with some members even suggesting that the proposed name had an "obscene" meaning in Ininew, an Indigenous language, although this was denied by the scheme's promoters. Provincial officials who first had supported the idea suddenly changed their minds when the Canadian Permanent Committee on Geographical Names intervened. It was pointed out to the Manitoba Minister of Municipal Affairs that the suggested change contravened their rules, namely that any place name "construed as advertising a particular commercial or industrial enterprise" was not permitted. Taxpayers in Grunthal therefore never got a chance to vote on the proposal or reap the benefits if they had approved it. Contemporary newspaper reports suggest there was support for change from sections of the community, particularly the town council and chamber of commerce. It was argued that the development of a Grunthal sports complex and other projects would benefit from "a little plugging from the radio station" and this would extend beyond Manitoba across North America, "continent-wide." The mayor, Steve Block, suggested there was a "general feeling" in town in favour of the scheme but only if local voters agreed.[78] What is remarkable about the alleged enthusiasm to drop the German name of Grunthal, one assigned by the original Mennonite settlers to Manitoba in 1878, is that the town's commercial leaders, dominated by Russländer and their descendants, appeared willing to sacrifice the past to the commercial benefits of North American capitalism. It might also have shown there were things worse than losing an umlaut from the community's name or translating it from German into "Green Valley."

Conclusion

The Past in the Present

Today the differences between Mennonites of the two major immigrations of the 1870s and 1920s, once expressed by the terms Kanadier and Russländer, have weakened and virtually disappeared among many of their descendants. In other ways, however, aspects of their pasts continue into the present. In the past, however, outsiders have sometimes been unwilling to predict that Mennonites in this area of Canada would still exist today. In 1936 the general editor of a series of books on Canadian "group" settlements in western Canada, W.A. Mackintosh, said Mennonites, and other ethnic communities formed "cultural islands" that hoped to "preserve their religion and their ways of life." While these "peculiar peoples" had "made important material and spiritual contributions to the wider community," he suggested their way of life "retarded the progress of assimilation." C.A. Dawson, the author of one of the books in the series, suggested that by the early 1930s Mennonites were "unconsciously" undergoing a "process of absorption" into Canadian society. Although he believed assimilation was inevitable, Dawson recognized that it was "impossible at present" to predict if it would "be complete 50 years hence, 100 years, or more."[1]

Dawson is not the only person to predict the end of Mennonite communities, especially seeing the general decline of many rural communities. Around 1976 the Planning Branch of the Manitoba Department of Municipal Affairs published a background report on the future of the RM of Hanover, an area with a large Mennonite population.[2] It noted that since 1946 the municipality had experienced a decrease in population, especially among the age group fifteen to thirty-four, due mainly to outmigration and this included those aged twenty to thirty-four, the major child-bearing cohort necessary to ensure the future population and economic development of the municipality. A closer examination of population figures for Hanover over a longer period time, however,

Table C.1. Hanover RM population, 1921–2021

Year	Population
1921	4,795
1931	5,833
1941	8,190
1951	6,570
1961	6,771
1971	6,237
1981	7,428
1991	8,905
2001	10,789
2011	14,026
2021	17,216

Source: "Manitoba Communities: Hanover (Rural Municipality)," Manitoba Historical Society, revised 7 May 2023, http://www.mhs.mb.ca/docs/municipalities/hanover.shtml.

Table C.2. Population of Grunthal district and town, 1951–71

Year	Grunthal district (incl. town)	Grunthal town
1951	887	256
1961	825	287
1966	1,020	431
1971	1,057	483

Source: Manitoba, *Rural Municipality of Hanover: A Background Report into Development and Growth Potential*, 11.

leaving aside the anomalous wartime years, indicates that, except for the early 1970s, the municipality's population has increased, and from the 1980s onward recovered (table C.1).

When the figures are examined more closely, the early declines occurred mainly in the rural areas while the population of towns has increased. This was particularly marked in the municipality's major towns: Steinbach, incorporated in 1951, and Niverville, incorporated in 1971, but also for the unincorporated town of Grunthal and its surrounding district where the population increased (table C.2).

While no separate figures for Kanadier and Russländer are available, the first generation of Russländer remained dominant in the town and district until around 1970, a fact that can be attributed to their social and

Table C.3. Elim membership, 1946–2020

Year	No. of members
1946	199
1950	227
1965	277
1975	226
1985	211
1995	195
2000	184
2020	137

Source: Jacob J. Enns, Marlene Epp, and Richard D. Thiessen, "Elim Mennonite Church (Grunthal, Manitoba, Canada)," Global Anabaptist Mennonite Encyclopedia Online, June 2021, https://gameo.org/index.php?title=Elim_Mennonite_Church_(Grunthal,_Manitoba,_Canada)&oldid=172374. See Appendix 1 for slight variation in numbers.

cultural skills and to demographic factors: Russländer simply outnumbered Kanadier. After 1980 there are indications Russländer were losing their advantage as the population of both the town and its surrounding district increased. The strategy of the first Russländer immigrants to build a community was inconsistent with sustaining it for future generations. The central contradiction in the Russländer vision of community was one that extended back to the final years of the Mennonite Commonwealth in Russia. This involved the maintenance of an essentially rural base while also encouraging the new generation to obtain higher educational qualifications than their parents. This strategy included an assumption that the future generation would return home and help develop a more complex and wealthier Mennonite community.

The result of this strategy translated to Canada by the immigrants of the 1920s, especially in rural areas, was the loss of a community's most talented youth who sought opportunities in the non-Mennonite world, often in urban centres. While some from the next generation might be tempted to return, there were insufficient opportunities to hold them all in rural areas. Subsequent generations were even less likely to return and settle. The impact of the Russländer community-building contradiction can be seen in the decline of membership in Elim's congregation (table C.3 and appendix 1). However, in recent years some descendants of Russländer have chosen to reside in Grunthal and commute to work in Winnipeg or larger towns in the Hanover region and therefore they have maintained their membership in Elim. Overall, however, the congregation's membership has fallen.[3]

Table C.4. Bergthaler membership, 1965–2000

Year	No. of members
1965	70
1975	99
1980	105
1985	151
1990	160
1995	152
2000	146

Source: Marlene Epp and Alf Redekopp, "Grunthal Bergthaler Mennonite Church (Grunthal, Manitoba, Canada)," Global Anabaptist Mennonite Encyclopedia Online, July 2020, https://gameo.org/index.php?title=Grunthal_Bergthaler_Mennonite_Church_(Grunthal,_Manitoba,_Canada)&oldid=168947.

Although exact statistics are lacking, an examination of records of the Elim congregation suggests there has also been a steady decline in family size in younger members of the congregation, a pattern already underway in Russia and among progressive Mennonites in the United States and probably Canada.[4] This pattern is associated with what is known as the demographic transition where an increase in the age of marriage, use of contraception, and increases in the number of educated women with careers has resulted in smaller families. In Grunthal, descendants of Kanadier simply outbred Russländer. Unlike the Elim congregation, until recently the Grunthal Bergthaler congregation grew in membership (table C.4).[5] In part this was due to Bergthaler families having more children than second-generation Russländer but in recent years the size of the Bergthaler congregation has stabilized, partially because the size of families has fallen from about five children in the 1960s, to four in the 1970s, and more recently to three or fewer.[6] The largest Bergthaler family in recent times contained fourteen children, which may have encouraged some descendants of Russländer to refer disparagingly to Bergthaler vehicles driving around Grunthal as "Bergthaler baby wagons."

Another significant factor of the increased Kanadier presence in Grunthal is that fewer have moved away from the district when compared with descendants of Russländer. One result is that the descendants of Kanadier are taking back the town and its surrounding area, a process that began in the 1960s as the first generation of Russländer born in Canada grew to maturity.

Today there are several religious groups in Grunthal besides the Elim and Bergthaler, some with members of Kanadier descent and a few with Russländer. These include the Christian Mennonite Church, abbreviated to the CMC Church of Grunthal, formerly known just as the Chortitzer Church, and another with "Mennonite" still in its title, the Grunthal Evangelical Mennonite Brethren, consisting mostly of people of Kanadier descent.[7] Other religious groups no longer identify as Mennonite in a strictly religious sense, including the Grunthal Christian Fellowship, the Graceway Church, and the Abundant Life Fellowship. The membership of the last three is unclear, although it is rumoured to be small. Not all have websites, and few appear interested in the past, concentrating instead on the present and future. Elim Church has a sophisticated website containing a detailed history of the congregation, memoirs of some founding members, and an explanation of the church's traditions.[8] The past is certainly in the present.

While the religious allegiance of Grunthal churches may be divided, other more secular activities appear to be united and to have moved into the internet age. The website of the business community contains a few historical details on education, medicine and dairying, ice skating and restaurants, in that order. It does not, however, speak of Russländer or Kanadier and says little on religion.[9] A Wikipedia entry gives a description of the town's location with a brief history giving a link to the 2021 Canadian census.[10]

Do census returns provide an accurate account of either Grunthal's present or its past? One problem is the way the census categories are constructed. Previous census results, some which are available online, can reveal something about Grunthal's past but not in any detail. The entry "Grunthal" refers only to the Local Urban District of Grunthal, not its rural hinterland that instead is included in the Hanover Municipality. According to the latest census, the population of the Urban District in 2021 had increased by 6.1 per cent since 2016, from 1,640 to 1,782 inhabitants.[11] Other comparisons between the censuses of 2016 and 2021, however, are difficult because the categories used to gather information in the two censuses are markedly different. In 2016 any reference to Mennonites is entirely absent in terms of either ethnicity or religious affiliation. In fact, no data on religion was collected in 2016. In 2021, however, Mennonites were included in the section "Ethnic or cultural origin for the population in private households" (see table C.5). The number of replies for "Mennonite" recorded for Grunthal, as with the returns for neighbouring Hanover and Steinbach, is probably too small. The category "origin" presented respondents with a range of options but unlike "Mennonite," it included categories mostly associated with nation states. For Mennonites an association of identity with a nation state historically has been a matter of controversy, especially for Russländer. Moreover, confusion as to the meaning of "cultural origin" when associated with identity undoubtedly resulted in some Mennonite replies contributing to any of the following responses: German (18 per cent), Russian (10 per cent), Ukrainian (9 per cent), and Dutch (2 per cent). Younger Mennonite respondents, no longer dreaming of former homelands and lost identities, might have chosen Canadian (18 per cent).

A related area of confusion for Mennonites were questions concerning language, especially when related to Mennonite Low German (see table C.5). Respondents were asked whether a language was considered the "mother tongue," whether it was the primary language spoken at home, at work, or if the respondent just had "knowledge" of it. The latter is very vague as for younger Mennonites many things might be included, ranging from a limited understanding of spoken Low German, to an inability or unwillingness to speak the language. It might also include just a basic awareness of the language. Unlike the general category "Mennonite," the questions on language were grouped under confusing headings. Most Mennonites do not associate the main headings "Saxon" and "Franconian" with the Low German they either speak or know. The subcategories offered, which included both Plautdietsch and Low German, might also have presented difficulties as a comparison of Grunthal responses with rural Hanover and urban Steinbach might suggest (table C.5). However, the fact that Low German is mostly spoken by older Mennonites is probably reflected in the figure of 84 per cent of respondents who reported they used English at home, whether Mennonite or non-Mennonite.

Questions related to religion might seem the most obvious other place to identify Mennonites in the census. Although no questions on religion were included in the 2016 census, questions had been included in earlier censuses. The Canada-wide Household Survey of 2011 also asked questions about religion but unfortunately the data was not broken down beyond the level of province and major metropolitan areas. Steinbach, however, was surveyed although any Mennonite response was included not by name but under the general category, "Other Protestants."[12] In 2021 "Mennonite" was not included as a category under religion. but was included under the category "specific Anabaptist groups, denominations, or traditions, not included elsewhere (e.g., 'Hutterite')."[13] Mennonite respondents were presented with no alternative, but "Anabaptists" may have chosen to mark this box. Most Mennonites in Grunthal and the district would have recognized the term,

Table C.5. Results of the 2021 Canadian census using categories presented to respondents in three Mennonite population areas of southeastern Manitoba

Locations as defined by the census	Ethnic or cultural origin in private households: "Mennonite"		Mother tongue: "Low Saxon – Low Franconian languages"		Religious affiliation: "Anabaptist" ("Mennonite" not presented as an option)	
	Total no. respondents	%	Plautdietsch totals (%)	Low German totals (%)	Total no. respondents	%
Grunthal town (pop. 1,782)	625	35%	180 (10%)	95 (5.3%)	190	11%
RM Hanover (pop. 17,216)	4,625	27%	350 (2%)	1,320 (8%)	1,745	10%
Steinbach city (pop. 17,589)	3,485	20%	1,095 (6%)	175 (1%)	1,705	10%

been aware of its use by historians of the Reformation and modern Mennonite theologians, and heard it referred to by ministers (but little else). The term "Anabaptist" is rarely used in everyday discourse in Grunthal, so this past does not exist in the present, except of course at census time. The number of people who identified with this term in Grunthal was considerably lower than those who identified as Mennonite in the ethnic and origin category. A similar disparity occurred in the returns for Hanover and Steinbach (see table C.5).

However, to understand the present one has to understand the past. Official surveys and websites apparently are unable to even identify Grunthal's Mennonites, least of all to explain their varieties in the small town or its surrounding countryside. Grunthal is a town still located in a predominantly Mennonite area, built and then rebuilt by Mennonites of different migrations although the rebuilding was achieved not just by Mennonites, but also by non-Mennonites. The rebuilding that occurred from the late 1920s on, however, was dominated by one group, the Russländer who today go unmentioned by name in current official and unofficial sources. It was accomplished with a speed that is apparent to those who understand the past. How else can the enigmatic words of one elderly Kanadier Mennonite be understood, "What Russländer achieved in thirty years, has taken Kanadier over one hundred years"?

Appendix One

Elim Congregation Statistics

Table A.1. Elim congregation, 1927–75 (selected statistics)

Year	Members	Families	Total*
1927	136	–	–
1930	181	78	407
1934	206	113	490
1936	177	85	419
1939	202	71	462
1940	216	80	469
1943	229	92	486
1944	194	90	470
1946	196	87	475
1947	207	89	479
1950	244	103	495
1960	271	–	–
1965	272	–	–
1970	266	–	–
1975	226	–	–

* Baptized and unbaptized members.

Appendix Two

Agreement with the Intercontinental Company over Land on East Reserve

June 30th, 1926[1]

The Intercontinental Company, Ltd.
Winnipeg, Man.

Dear Sirs, –

We understand that you have for sale about 45,000 acres of farm lands together with chattels thereon, located approximately as follows: –

(a) In what is known as the East Reserve, South East of the City of Winnipeg, and East of the Red River, in the Province of Manitoba.

4,000	Acres in Township	No 4.
14,000	"	No 5.
8,000	"	No 6.
7,500	"	No 7.
5,000	"	No 8.

(b) 5,200 acres in the Province of Saskatchewan, in the vicinity of Lost River, and 1,400 acres in the vicinity of Herbert.

We agree to find Russian Mennonite farmers who will purchase all of these lands and chattels under the following conditions:

All purchased [lands and chattels] will be made under crop sales contract, in form approved by this Board [the Canadian Mennonite Board of Colonization].

A schedule of prices will be presented to us by you with the understanding that we will have the right to re-arrange such schedule upon a basis which in our judgement better represents the proportionate value of the farms and chattels offered, it being understood, however, that any re-arrangement of such schedule shall total the same figure as the total on the list furnished to us, it being further understood that the average price of all the lands purchased (including the chattels) shall approximate thirty-two dollars and fifty cents ($32.50) per acre. A commission of two and a half percent (2.5) of the principal amount of the sales made under contracts on the above lands and accepted by you will be paid by you to this Board in the following manner: –

On or before March 1st, each year, a sum will be paid equal to ten per cent (10%) of the amount paid on the principal amount owing under such contacts during the period commencing the previous March 1st, until the commission due has been fully paid; provided, however, that no such payment in any one year shall exceed five thousand dollars ($5,000.00). First payment [is] to be made [on] March 15th, 1928.

You will advance to us five hundred dollars ($500.00) on receipt of this letter, and will further advance one thousand dollars ($1,000.00) upon commencing to carry out the memorandum as outlined in this letter, and twenty-five hundred ($2,500.00) dollars shall be paid in four (4) weeks from the date of commencement of operations without any obligation on our part to submit [a] detailed statement of expenses.

If for any reason the matters herein set out are not completed by either party, the above advances shall be retained by the Board in full satisfaction, and the Company shall have no right to the return of any moneys advanced by it; otherwise such advances shall be treated as advance payments on commission. All such advances shall be considered as advance payments on commission unless the commission earned shall not equal the amount of such advances, in which case the Company shall have no claim against the Board.

You will give to this Board written evidence of commission due, in accordance with the terms hereof, in the form of commission contracts. The Board will assign to you as collateral to secure such advance, commission contracts as above described to an amount equal to at least three times the amount of such advances.

The Company shall be under no obligation to execute contracts unless [by] August 31st, 1926, contracts for sale covering ninety per cent (90%) of the lands hereby offered for sale shall have been offered to the Company by the Board, signed by the prospective purchaser and by the guarantors in connection therewith, as provided for below.

Possession of farms shall be given to each individual purchaser or purchasers as soon as possible after contracts have been signed, but not later than February 1st, 1927. All purchasers who have signed contracts on or before August 31st, 1926, shall be given a definite notice on or before August 31st, 1926, whether the Company will complete the contract and endeavour to give approximate date of possession.

The Board will see its best efforts to sell the farms to experienced farmers, of good type, and you shall have the right to interview any of the prospective purchasers, and, if, in your judgement, any prospective purchaser is not suitable, you shall have the right to reject him and we will attempt to find another in his stead.

The purchasers in groups of from four (4) to ten (10) according to the best interests of the vendor and purchasers will jointly and severally guarantee their respective obligations.

It is understood that in all cases where the Canadian Mennonite's farm is taken over including the chattels, that is, farms [sic] animals, machinery and household equipment, such unit shall be sold as it exists and additional equipment that you agree to supply as part of Schedule "A" attached, in the Province of Manitoba. In cases where the farm is listed without chattels, we both shall co-operate in preparing a list of the chattels required, which shall be furnished by you at cost, and said cost shall be added to and included in the sales contract but shall not increase the approximate cost of the total block. We retain the right to re-arrange equipment on these farms where in some cases one farm is short and another farm is overstocked, in order to equalize the services according to the operation of each individual farm.

The method of procedure will be approximately as follows:

You will furnish a list and description of the lands and selling prices of the same, also submit tentatively a grouping arrangement which you have prepared.

We will prepare a schedule and regrouping which in our judgement is more suitable.

We will not send anyone onto these farms for inspection purposes or sales until notified by you that we may do so.

We will both then co-operate in the matter of showing the land and closing the contracts.

It is further agreed that if any buildings now located in the village of Schoensee will be required to be moved on to say any particular parcel of land, the Company shall do this at its own expense and cost of same shall not be an extra charge to the purchaser.

In each case where an unequipped farm is being offered for sale, a definite schedule of equipment is to be presented to the purchaser and the price is to include the price of land and equipment.

Yours very truly

Chairman [David Toews]

Notes

Introduction

1 Peters, "The Forgotten Immigrants"; Adolf Ens, personal communication.
2 Birdsell, *The Russländer.*
3 M. Redekop, *Making Believe.*
4 Barber and Watson, *Invisible Immigrants*; Barr, *Swedes in Canada.*
5 Ross, *Communal Solidarity.*
6 C. Redekop, *Mennonite Society*; Driedger, *Mennonites in the Global Village*; R. Enns, "From Generation to Generation?"
7 Jack Thiessen, "Grünthal."
8 F.H. Epp, *Mennonites in Canada, 1786–1920*, chs. 8 and 9.
9 Peters, "The Forgotten Immigrants."
10 S. Klassen, "Recruits and Comrades," 6.
11 S. Klassen, "Recruits and Comrades," 33.
12 Craft, *Breathing Life into the Stone Fort Treaty.*
13 Craft, *Breathing Life into the Stone Fort Treaty.*
14 For more on the negative impact of colonization on the lives of Indigenous people, see Carter, *Aboriginal People*; Daschuk, *Clearing the Plains.*
15 Adolf Ens, *Subjects or Citizens?*, ch. 1; on similar doubts concerning Icelandic immigrants, see Eyford, *White Settler Reserve.*
16 Jack Thiessen, *Mennonite Low German Dictionary*, 106–7.
17 Kuzina, "Mennonites and Aboriginals"; on the impact on Métis, see G.J. Ens, "The Manitoba Act."
18 J. Wiebe, "On the Mennonite-Métis Borderland," 115.
19 J. Wiebe, 113–14.
20 Canada, Indian Claims Commission, Purdy, Bellegarde, and Holman, *Roseau River Anishinabe First Nation.*
21 Theologians have recently explored Russländer accounts of trauma in their past and how this may have influenced their ability to show empathy

276   Notes to pages 8–10

with the experiences of Indigenous peoples. See Kampen, "The Spectre of Reconciliation."
22 F.H. Epp, *Mennonite Exodus*.
23 H. Paetkau, "A Struggle for Survival"; H. Paetkau, "Separation or Integration?"
24 H. Paetkau, "Russian Mennonite Immigrants."
25 Baar, "Patterns of Selective Accentuation."
26 Jones, "Grounding Diaspora in Experience."
27 Jenna Klassen, "She Brought It to Canada in 1926."
28 *Grunthal History 1874–1974*; an earlier German account is Jacob Block's *Beitrag zur Geschichte Gruenthal's*.
29 R. Wiebe, "Tombstone Community"; R. Wiebe, *Of This Earth*; Kroeger, *Hard Passage*.
30 *Elim Gemeinde Grunthal, Manitoba*.
31 Elim Mennonite Church of Grunthal, *Our Walk With God*.
32 *Chortitzer Mennonite Conference, 1874–1990*; J.D. Klassen, *The 45 Year History of Grunthal Bergthaler Mennonite Church*.
33 Stoesz, *A History of the Chortitzer Mennonite Church*.
34 Francis, *In Search of Utopia*; J.H. Warkentin, *The Mennonite Settlements*.
35 A. Warkentin, *Reflections on Our Heritage*; Penner, *Hanover: One Hundred Years*. The West Reserve was divided between the RMs of Rhineland and Stanley; G.J. Ens, *Volost and Municipality*.
36 Epp-Thiessen, *Altona: The Story of a Prairie Town*; M. Neufeld, *Prairie Pioneers: Schönthal Revisited*; on Winkler, adjacent to the Reserve but important to Mennonites, see Werner, *Living between Worlds*.
37 Zacharias, *Reinland: An Experience in Community*; Gerbrandt, *Adventure in Faith*.
38 W. Friesen, "A Mennonite Community in the East Reserve"; Braun and Klassen, *Historical Atlas of the East Reserve*.
39 Loewen, *Blumenort*; Loewen, *Family, Church, and Market*; Loewen, *Diaspora in the Countryside*; and his numerous articles and essays; on Steinbach, see Ralph Friesen, *Between Earth and Sky*.
40 *Working Papers of the East Reserve*; J. Dyck, *Historical Sketches of the East Reserve*; Ens, Braun, and Fast, *Settlers of the East Reserve*; Fast, *Gruenfeld (now Kleefeld)*.
41 Voisey, "Rural Local History and the Prairie West"; Voisey, *Vulcan*.
42 Sylvester, *The Limits of Rural Capitalism*; Dick, *Farmers "Making Good"*; Loewen, "On the Margin or in the Lead"; and Loewen, "Beyond the Monolith of Modernity."
43 Lehr, *Community and Frontier*; Swyripa, *Storied Landscapes*; Eyford, *White Settler Reserve*.
44 Marshall, *Cultivating Connections*.

45 Hillary, "Definitions of Community"; Clark, "The Concept of Community"; a more recent overview is Blackshaw, *Key Concepts in Community Studies*.
46 Tönnies, *Community and Civil Society*.
47 Jack Thiessen, *Studien zum Wortschatz der kanadischen Mennoniten*; Jack Thiessen, "History of Mennonite *Plautdietsch*"; Jack Thiessen, "A New Look at an Old Problem"; R. Epp, *The Story of Low German & Plautdietsch*.
48 Weaver-Zercher, *Martyrs Mirror: A Social History*.
49 H. Rempel, *Kjenn jie noch Plautditsch?*; Thiessen, *Mennonite Low German Dictionary*. I am grateful to Jack Thiessen and Ernest N. Braun for discussions on the meaning of "community" in Mennonite Low German.

1. Russia and Canada: The Consequences of the First World War

1 Loewen and Nolt, *Seeking Places of Peace*; Steiner, *In Search of Promised Lands*.
2 Günther, Heidebrecht, and Peters, *"Onsji Tjedils"*; A. Reimer, *"Sanitätsdienst* and *Selbstschutz"*; L. Klippenstein, *Peace and War*.
3 D. Rempel, "The Mennonite Commonwealth in Russia"; Urry, *None but Saints*; L.G. Friesen, *Mennonites in the Russian Empire*.
4 Urry, "Mennonite Economic Development."
5 G.J. Ens, *Die Schule muss sein*.
6 F.H. Epp, *Education with a Plus*.
7 D. Rempel, "The Mennonite Commonwealth in Russia"; Urry, "The Cost of Community"; Urry, "The Mennonite Commonwealth in Imperial Russia Revisited."
8 Urry, "Prolegomena to the Study of Mennonite Society."
9 L.G. Friesen, "Mennonites in the Russian Revolution of 1905"; Urry, *Mennonites, Politics, and Peoplehood*, ch. 5; L.G. Friesen, *Mennonites in the Russian Empire*, 168–76.
10 A. Friesen, *In Defense of Privilege*, pt. 3; Urry, *Mennonites, Politics, and Peoplehood*.
11 D.G. Rempel, "The Expropriation of the German Colonists in South Russia"; A. Friesen, *In Defense of Privilege*, ch. 10.
12 A. Friesen, *In Defense of Privilege*, pt. 4; L.G. Friesen, *Mennonites in the Russian Empire*, 178.
13 Adolf Ens, *Subjects or Citizens?*
14 Millman, *Polarity, Patriotism, and Dissent*.
15 Adolf Ens, "The Conspiracy That Never Was"; for an alternative view, see Hamm, "Revisiting the Canadian *Privilegium*."
16 J. Wiebe, "On the Mennonite-Métis Borderland," 115.
17 Carr-Stewart, "A Treaty Right to Education."

18 Morton, *Manitoba: A History*, 350–3, 361; Francis, "The Mennonite School Problem in Manitoba"; Francis, *In Search of Utopia*, 175–6, 179–86; F.H. Epp, *Mennonites in Canada, 1786–1920*, ch. 14; Janzen, *Limits on Liberty*, ch. 5; Adolf Ens, *Subjects or Citizens?* 62–6, chs. 4 and 6; Sneath, "Whose Children Are They."
19 M.W. Friesen, *Neue Heimat in der Chacowildnis*, 173.
20 F.H. Epp, *Mennonites in Canada, 1920–1940*, 122, table 15; M.W. Friesen, *Kanadische Mennoniten bezwingen eine Wildnis*, 17–18.
21 Engelstein, *Russia in Flames*.
22 Gerwarth, *The Vanquished*, especially ch. 7.
23 Töws, *Schönfeld: Werde- und Opfergang*, unpublished English translation in the Rare Books Collection of the MHA; Cherkazainova, "Shenfel'dskaya volost'"; see also Tiessen, *The Schoenfelder Russlaender*.
24 Töws, *Schönfeld*, 24–6; Cherkazainova, "Shenfel'dskaya volost'."
25 Emmons, "The Peasant and the Emancipation."
26 Carl Driedger, Winnipeg, conversations with author, 1974. Also conversations with other older Schönfeld residents.
27 T. Rempel, *Letters of a Mennonite Couple*.
28 L.G. Friesen, "Mennonites in the Russian Revolution of 1905."
29 Urry and Helmut-Harry Loewen, "Protecting Mammon."
30 V. Peters, *Nestor Makhno: The Life of an Anarchist*; J.B. Toews, *Czars, Soviets and Mennonites*, ch. 6; S. Patterson, *Makhno and Memory*. Makhno may have been abused by a Schönfeld Mennonite landowner (Cherkazainova, "Shenfel'dskaya volost'," 59n21).
31 Toews, *Mennonites in Ukraine*, 11–20; G. Doerksen and J. Driedger, early 1920s, "Die Schoenfelder Gemeinde," A.A. Friesen Papers (MLA 60–9), Mennonite Library and Archives (partial English translation in Toews, *Mennonites in Ukraine*, 9–11); Schroeder, *Miracles of Grace and Judgement*; Cherkazainova, "Shenfel'dskaya volost'," 58–60.
32 Toews, "The Origins and Activities of the Mennonite *Selbstschutz*; A. Reimer, "*Sanitätsdienst* and *Selbstschutz*"; Klippenstein, *Peace and War*, ch. 7; contemporary and later accounts in Toews, *Mennonites in Ukraine*, 92–107.
33 C.P. Toews, *The Terek Settlement*; Martin, "The Terekers' Dilemma.".
34 Schroeder, *Miracles of Grace and Judgement*, 114–16; J.B. Toews, *Czars, Soviets and Mennonites*, 92; Dyck, Staples, and Toews, *Nestor Makhno and the Eichenfeld Massacre*.
35 Lohrenz, *Zagradovka: History of a Mennonite Settlement*, ch. 8; Neufeld (Navall), *A Russian Dance of Death*, pt. 2.
36 J.P. Dyck, *Troubles and Triumphs, 1914–1924*; Baerg, *Diary of Anna Baerg, 1916–1924*.
37 Schroeder, *Miracles of Grace and Judgement*; Rempel with Rempel Carlson, *A Mennonite Family in Tsarist Russia*, pt. 5.

38 *Die Mennoniten-Gemeinden in Russland.*
39 F.H. Epp, *Mennonite Exodus*, ch. 5.
40 Goerz, *Memrik: A Mennonite Settlement in Russia*, 82–6.
41 Urry, "After the Rooster Crowed"; Martin, "The Russian Mennonite Encounter with the Soviet State," 15–22; L.G. Friesen, *Mennonites in the Russian Empire*, 196–201, 206–9.
42 Kulischer, *Europe on the Move*, chs. 3 and 4; Marrus, *The Unwanted*, especially ch. 2.
43 Gatrell, "Refugee History and Refugees in Russia."
44 Stead, "Canada's Immigration Policy," 61.
45 F.H. Epp, *Mennonite Exodus*, 94–5, 101–5; F.H. Epp, *Mennonites in Canada, 1920–1940*, 154–6.
46 A few individuals found their way abroad before 1923, some returning to Germany with German troops in 1918; others who had served in the White Army fled to Constantinople or North Africa, and later entered the United States and Canada. See I. Epp, *Constantinoplers*.
47 Appeal to all Schönfeld refugees signed by Gerhard Dörksen, Johann Driedger, and Johann Enns (*Flüchtlinge*), 7 April 1924, Petershagen, Molochna; Herbert P. Enns Collection, Mennonite Archives of Ontario, Conrad Grebel University College, Waterloo, Hist. Mss. 1.118.
48 Felshtinsky, "The Legal Foundations of the Immigration and Emigration Policy of the USSR."
49 F.H. Epp, *Mennonite Exodus*, chs. 16–17; F.H. Epp, *Mennonites in Canada, 1920–1940*, ch. 7.
50 C.P. Neufeldt, "The Flight to Moscow, 1929"; E. Warkentin, "The Mennonites before Moscow"; Savin, "The 1929 Emigration of Mennonites from the USSR."
51 *Canadian Annual Review of Public Affairs* (1923), 269; *Canadian Annual Review of Public Affairs* (1933), 449.
52 H.L. Dyck, "Collectivization, Depression, and Immigration."
53 C.P. Neufeldt, "Through the Fires of Hell"; J.A. Neufeld, *Path of Thorns*; Beznosov, "Kulak, Christian, and German."
54 F.H. Epp, *Mennonite Exodus*, pt. 6.

2. Russländer Find Homes

1 Thompson, *The Harvests of War*.
2 G. Friesen, *Canadian Prairies*, ch. 14.
3 Urry, *None but Saints*, chs. 11, 13; Adolf Ens, "Mennonite Education in Russia."
4 "Zum diamenten Jubiläum der Kanadischen Konfederation," *Bote*, 15 June 1927, 3; Jakob P. Penner, "Die Konstitution Kanadas," *Bote*, 22 June 1927, 3; Jacob P. Penner, "Wie Canada sich entwickelt," *Bote*, 29 June 1927, 2–3.

5 GAP, "Mennoniten-Wanderungen," *Nordwesten*, 10–17 March 1926, 1.
6 NC [Nikolai Classen], "Canada oder Russland? (Von einem Neueinwanderer aus Russland)," *Nordwesten*, 3 November 1926, 1.
7 Adolf Ens, *Becoming a National Church*.
8 Peters, "The Forgotten Immigrants."
9 F.H. Epp, *Mennonite Exodus*, ch. 7; F.H. Epp, *Mennonites in Canada, 1786–1920*, 311–12; 351–3. On Toews and CMBC, see Klaassen, *"The Days of Our Years"*.
10 Urry, "David H. Epp: Intellectual, Spiritual, Cultural Leader"; and Urry, "Dietrich Heinrich Epp: First Editor of *Der Bote*."
11 Loewen and Urry, "A Tale of Two Newspapers"; for a general insider history of the MBs, see J.A. Toews, *A History of the Mennonite Brethren Church*.
12 Jenna Klassen, "She Brought It to Canada in 1926."
13 F.H. Epp, *Mennonite Exodus*, 210–14; H. Paetkau, "Russian Mennonite Immigrants," 81–2.
14 F.H. Epp, 214–17.
15 Kelley and Trebilcock, *The Making of the Mosaic*, ch. 5.
16 Francis, *In Search of Utopia*, 203.
17 Stead, "Canada's Immigration Policy," 59, 61.
18 F.H. Epp, *Mennonite Exodus*, ch. 9.
19 On the impact of the revolution and its aftermath on the Russian aristocracy, see Smith, *Former People*.
20 E.K. Francis, "Escape from the Red Paradise," ch. 12 from a draft of *In Search of Utopia*, 19, AM, Ms. MG9, A55–20.
21 P. Rempel, "Ein Ueberblick über die Siedlungsmöglichkeiten"; F.H. Epp, *Mennonite Exodus*, 186–8.
22 "Eine Einwandererstatistik," *MR*, 22 April 1925, 5, 8.
23 F.H. Epp, *Mennonite Exodus*, 188–9.
24 F.H. Epp, 189–94.
25 H.C. Enns, "An die gewesenen Glieder der Kirchengemeinde zu Schönfeld."
26 J.J. Enns, "Zu Hause."
27 F.H. Epp, *Mennonites in Canada, 1920–1940*, 448–50; see also R.C. Neufeldt, "We Are Aware of Our Contradictions."
28 [Letter from Westbourne dated 7 May 1925,] *Nordwesten*, 13 May 1925, 5.
29 John A. Driedger and George J. Rempel, conversations with the author, 1989/90.
30 H. Enns, "Abraham P. Nachtigal's Experiences on a Farm."
31 [Letter from Westbourne dated 19 July 1925,] *Nordwesten*, 29 July 1925, 7.
32 A.D. Warkentin, "Kurzer geschichtlicher Ueberblick ueber das Entstehen und die ersten 50 Jahre der Mennonitengemeinde Glenlea," *Bote*, 20 April 1976, 3, 5.

33 Fisher, "(Trans)planting Manitoba's West Reserve."
34 F.H. Epp, *Mennonites in Canada, 1920–1940*, ch. 3.
35 *Gnadenthal, 1880–1980*; for Rhineland, see Zacharias, *Footprints of a Pilgrim People*.
36 J.H. Warkentin, *Mennonite Settlements*, 156–60; J. Dyck, "Alt-Bergfeld," 48.
37 On details of costs and profits, see W.H. S[mith], "Corporación Paraguaya," 718.
38 Quiring, "The Canadian Mennonite Immigration," 36; Fretz, *Pilgrims in Paraguay*, 16; Eicher, *Exiled Among Nations*, 80.
39 Francis, *In Search of Utopia*, 193.
40 Kleinpenning, *The Mennonite Colonies in Paraguay*, 5.
41 Adolf Ens, *Subjects or Citizens?* 214, table 19; Ens notes that figures given for Mennonite emigration to Latin America vary.
42 Bender, "Intercontinental Company, Limited."
43 Jacob J. Rempel, "Grunthal, 1926–1974," unpublished manuscript, c. 1974.
44 Report of the Winnipeg Office of the Canadian Colonization Association to the Directors of the CPR, 5 August 5 1926, CPR Papers 1886–1958, Ms. 2269, Box 82, File 646, Glenbow – Alberta Institute Archives.
45 Figures from the Company's letter to David Toews of the MBC, 13 May 1930, CMBC Papers, Vol. 117, No. 58, MHA.
46 "Report of our investigation ... Winnipeg Office of the Canadian Colonization Association," 21 June 1926, 3, CPR Papers, Ms. 2269, Box 82, File 646, p. 2, Glenbow – Alberta Institute Archives.
47 P. Klassen, *The Mennonites in Paraguay*, 60.
48 Report of the Winnipeg Office of the Canadian Colonization Association to the Directors of the CPR, 18 and 21 June 1926, 3, CPR Papers, Ms. 2269, Box 82, File 646, Glenbow – Alberta Institute Archives.
49 David Toews, draft of letter to the Intercontinental Company Ltd., 26 June 1926, in Frank H. Epp Papers, *Mennonite Exodus* research notes, ch. 20, Hist. Mss. 1–26, 6, Mennonite Archives of Ontario, Conrad Grebel University College, Waterloo. Final letter dated 30 June in CMBC Files, Vol. 1171, No. 58, MHA.
50 "Zur Klärung der Sache," *Bote*, 18 August 1926, 2–3.
51 Reports of the Winnipeg Office of the Canadian Colonization Association to the Directors of the CPR, 5 August and 6 November 1926, CPR Papers, Ms. 2269, Box 82, Files 646–7, Glenbow – Alberta Institute Archives.
52 Braun, *A Biography of Peter A. (1890–1971) and Lena (1893–1991) Braun*, 11; Heese "Farms: Memories."
53 J. Dyck, "Alt-Bergfeld," 48; Penner, *In Search of Our Heritage*.
54 J.H. Warkentin, *Mennonite Settlements*, 11–14; 18–20, 22, 25–7.
55 Quoted in J.H. Warkentin, *Mennonite Settlements*, 19.
56 A. Dyck, *Collected Works*, vol. 3.

57 J.H. Warkentin, *Mennonite Settlements*.
58 Sawatsky, "The Control of Social Space in Mennonite Housebarns."
59 J.H. Warkentin, "Mennonite Agricultural Settlements"; J.H. Warkentin, *Mennonite Settlements*; Braun and Klassen, *Historical Atlas of the East Reserve*, 186–9.
60 G.W. Sawatzky, "Landwirtschaftliche Ausstellung," *MR*, 10 October 1928, 4.
61 RM of Hanover, Tax Records for 1926/27.
62 Braun and Klassen, *Historical Atlas of the East Reserve*, 176.
63 Jacob J. Rempel, "Grunthal, 1926–1974."
64 J.J. Rempel, "Erinnerung aus meiner Dienstzeit" and "Erinnerungen aus den Jahren 1914–1918." These have been edited in Günther, Heidebrecht, and Peters, *"Onsji Tjedils"*, 224–36, and are given in English in Jacob Rempel, *Consider the Threshing Stone*.
65 Thiessen, *Mennonite Low German Dictionary*, 246; 344; 471.
66 Sawatzky, "Landwirtschaftliche Ausstellung," 2.
67 Franz (Frank) Steingart, interview, recording by Ellen Baar, Brock University, Archives and Special Collections; Mennonites of Niagara: pioneers. SPCL FC 3140.8 M45 B374 1977 and Mennonite Archives of Ontario, Conrad Grebel University College, Waterloo, Russian Mennonite Immigrants Oral History Project, cassette tapes recorded 1976–8 by Henry Paetkau and Stan Dueck.
68 C.F. Klassen, letter to CMBC, 14 October 1931, in CMBC Papers, Vol. 1313, No. 875, MHA.
69 "Landwirtschaftliche Ausstellung in Grünthal," *SP*, 24 September 1930, 5.
70 J.H. Warkentin, *Mennonite Settlements*, 161–2.
71 G.G. Kornelsen, "Ostreserve Nachrichten," *SP*, 6 June 1928, 6.
72 G.G. Kornelsen, "Ostreserve Nachrichten," *SP*, 20 June 1928, 4.
73 Sawatzky, "Landwirtschaftliche Ausstellung."
74 J.H. Warkentin, *Mennonite Settlements*, 119–25.
75 A. Reimer, "Introduction" to *Koop enn Bua tus*, in A. Dyck, *Collected Works*, 3:360.
76 A. Dyck, "Koop and Bua Go Travelling," 72.
77 Sawatzky, "Landwirtschaftliche Ausstellung"; R.M. Scott, "Grunthal Settlers Learn Mixed Farming," *MFP*, 24 October 1931, 4; reprinted as "Die Ansiedler bei Grünthal lernen die gemischte Wirtschaft," *Bote*, 7 November 1931, 4. The report might be associated with immigrant community competitions of the time: see James Urry, "A Forgotten Encounter."
78 Braun, *A Biography of Peter A. (1890–1971) and Lena (1893–1991) Braun*, 13.
79 Rempel, *MR*, 10 July 1929, 4.
80 Scott, "Grunthal Settlers Learn Mixed Farming."
81 J.H. Warkentin, *Mennonite Settlements*, 122, table 8.

82 P.K. Ketler [Letter from Grunthal of 12 December 1928], *SP*, 19 December 1928, 6.
83 P.K.K. [Letter from Grunthal of 22 October 1928], *SP*, 31 October 1928, 1.
84 Sawatzky, "Landwirtschaftliche Ausstellung in Grünthal," *MR*, 10 October 1928, 1; also in *SP*, 17 October 1928, 1; shorter version in *Bote*, 18 October 1928, 2–3.
85 J.J. Rempel, "Wie bessert man die Viehbestand auf der Farm?" *MR*, 24 July 1929, 4; also in *SP*, 7 August 1929, 1; see also *MR*, 10 July 1929, 4.
86 *Bote*, 11 June 1930, 3; 16 July 1930, 4; the representatives were J.J. Friesen, H.P. Wiens, and W.W. Sawatzky.
87 Scott, "Grunthal Settlers Learn Mixed Farming."
88 Letter dated 7 May 1930, CMBC Records, MHA Box 1171, No. 58.
89 Fisher, *Robert D. Fisher Manual of Valuable and Worthless Securities*, 77.
90 Intercontinental Company Ltd. to holders of farm lien bonds, 28 March 1933, CMBC Records, Vol. 1171, File 57, MHA.
91 D. Toews, "Immigration und Nothilfe," 69.
92 F.H. Epp, *Mennonite Exodus*, 301–4; F.H. Epp, *Mennonites in Canada, 1920–1940*, 369–70; Bender, "Intercontinental Company, Limited."

3. The Bases of Community

1 T.D. Regehr, "Mennonite Change"; Buhr, "Pursuit of a Vision."
2 J. Friesen, *The Glenlea Mennonite Church History*; N. Driedger, *The Leamington United Mennonite Church*.
3 Group and leader's list in B.B. Janz to A.A. Friesen, B.B. Janz Papers, Box 1, CMBC, Winnipeg, originally in the A.A. Friesen Archives, Mennonite Library and Archives.
4 P. Dyck, *Orenburg am Ural*.
5 Penner, *The Story of Aunt Erna*; Penner, *In Search of Our Heritage*.
6 Obituary of Abraham Peter Janz, *MR*, 23 February 1955; Obituary of Elzabeth (Schmidt) Janz, *MR*, 11 August 1971.
7 Nick Janz, conversation with the author, 1974.
8 David H. Epp and Richard D. Thiessen, "Heese, Heinrich (1787–1868)," Global Anabaptist Mennonite Encyclopedia Online, November 2010, https://gameo.org/index.php?title=Heese,_Heinrich_(1787–1868)&oldid=145436.
9 G.K. Epp, "Urban Mennonites in Russia"; Urry, "Growing Up with Cities"; Huebert, *Mennonites in the Cities of Imperial Russia*.
10 *Bote*, 6 May 1925, 4; Dietrich Heese, conversations with the author, 1989/90.
11 F.H. Epp, *Mennonite Exodus*, 185–6; M. Epp, "The Mennonite Girls' Home"; F.E. Klippenstein, "Doing What We Could."

12 J. Friesen, *Against the Wind*, 31–8.
13 P. Dyck, *Orenburg am Ural*.
14 Thiessen, *Mennonite Low German Dictionary*, 300, 312.
15 Peters and Thiessen, *Mennonitische Namen/Mennonite Names*.
16 J.J. Hildebrand to J. Winfield Fretz, 10 May 1938, in J.W. Fretz Fonds, Hist. Mss. 1.24, Mennonite Archives of Ontario, Conrad Grebel University College, Waterloo.
17 Francis, *In Search of Utopia*, 212; draft in AM, Mss. MG9, A55–20.
18 Thiessen, *Mennonite Low German Dictionary*, 102, 189, 238.
19 Novakampus, *Kanadische Mennoniten*; quoted in Gerbrandt, *Adventure in Faith*, 292.
20 Francis, *In Search of Utopia*, 212.
21 Howell and Klassen, "Contrasting du/Sie patterns," 70.
22 G.G. Kornelsen, "Ostreserve Nachrichten," *Post*, 18 September 1929, 8, and 18 October 1930, 8; Peter B. Harder [Letter dated 14 November], *Post*, 27 November 1929.
23 Urry, "Time and Memory," 7–8.
24 Thiessen, *Mennonite Low German Dictionary*, 262. *Trü* means "marriage, trust, fidelity"; *Trüa* means "sorrow, grief, sadness," and has several variants.
25 Thiessen, *Mennonite Low German Dictionary*, 131–2, 479; Judith Klassen, "Music, Mimesis, and Modulation ," 422–31.
26 M. Epp, *Mennonite Women in Canada*.
27 Andersen, "Métis."
28 Thiessen, *Mennonite Low German Dictionary*, 153, 392.
29 D.F. Plett, *Saints and Sinners*.
30 Hiebert, *The Holdeman People*.
31 Loewen, *Family, Church, and Market*, esp. ch. 10.
32 Anecdotal accounts of differences between East and West Reserve Mennonites deserve further study.
33 Elsie Janzen, "Grunthal History," *CN*, 17 September 1967; Werner, "More than Just a Business."
34 Chiel, *The Jews in Manitoba*, 58.
35 "Wann he eenem Jud bedreeje well, mott he ver Freestetj oppstoahne. Wann he eenem Monist bedreeje well, bruckt he goar nicht schlope gohne" (Thiessen, *Mennonite Low German Dictionary*, 502).
36 Budnitskii, *Russian Jews*; Kellogg, *The Russian Roots of Nazism*.
37 Robinson, *A History of Antisemitism*.
38 Wagner, *Brothers Beyond the Sea*, 104–5.
39 Lehr, *Community and Frontier*.
40 Belton, "German in Our Schools," 262.
41 Johann Driedger, conversations with the author.
42 Thiessen, *Mennonite Low German Dictionary*, 86, 203, 217, 382.

43 Urry, "Of Borders and Boundaries," 503.
44 Thiessen, *Mennonite Low German Dictionary*, 358.
45 Thiessen, 68, 81.

4. Re-establishing Institutions

1 Urry, "The Cost of Community."
2 In Russia the Khortitsa Colony included the village of Chortitza, Nieder Chortitza, and Insel Chortitza, and others. Kroeker, *First Mennonite Villages*.
3 Braun and Klassen, *Historical Atlas of the East Reserve*.
4 Urry, *None but Saints* on the earlier Flemish/Frisian distinction.
5 "Klassen" in A. Warkentin, *Who's Who among the Mennonites, 1937*, 83; "Aeltesten J.P. Klassen," *Gruess Gott! Rundschreiben der Schoenwieser Gemeinde* 58 (June 1947): 1–3.
6 "Etwas zum Nachdenken," *MR*, 22 April 1925, 2.
7 Adolf Ens, *Becoming a National Church*, ch. 2.
8 F.F. Enns, *Elder Enns*, 66.
9 Jack Thiessen, *Predicht fier haite*.
10 "Korrespondenzen," *Nordwesten*, 29 July 1925, 7.
11 "Protokoll einer Vorberatung mennonitische Immigranten verschiedner Gruppen in Manitoba zwecks Gründung einer Gemeinde organisation am 28 Juni 1925, in der Zionskirche zu Winnipeg," *MR*, 15 July 1925, 12; "Protokoll der Beratung der Vertreter der in Manitoba angesiedleten Gruppen der Mennoniten-Gemeinden (eingewanderten in dem Jahren 1923–1925), am 29 September 1925, in der Reformierten 'Zionskirche' in Winnipeg, Man," *Bote*, 14 October 1925; also in *MR*, 4 November 1925, 1–2; Meeting with J.J. Enns in attendance, *Bote*, 17 March 1926, 3.
12 Enns's accounts of the Grunthal congregation's foundation appear in different places but vary: Enns, "Historisches Material der Gemeinde Elim zu Grunthal Manitoba 1927–1952"; Enns, "Historisches Material der Gemeinde Elim zu Grunthal Manitoba 1927–1952/Historical Notes of the Grunthal Church from the Period 1927–1952," in *Grunthal History 1874–1974*, 69–74; Elim Mennonite Church, *Our Walk with God*, 10–14; Wiens, "The History of the Elim Mennonite Church" and G. Friesen, "Elim Mennonite Church of Grunthal: Historical Update." Surviving documents held by the Elim Church do not always correspond with these later accounts.
13 On the complex history of North American Mennonite conferences, see Edmund G. Kaufman and Henry Poettcker, "General Conference Mennonite Church (GCM)," *Global Anabaptist Mennonite Encyclopedia Online*, November 2009, https://gameo.org/index.php?title=General_Conference_Mennonite_Church_(GCM)&oldid=174932.

14 "Gemeindeorganisation," *Bote*, 9 March 1927, 3.
15 *Bote*, 12 September 1928; J. Enns et al., *Dem Herrn die Ehre; Jubilate: 60 years First Mennonite Church*, ch. 2.
16 Grunthal Church Meeting Book, Grunthal, 19 June 1927; original minutes in "Protokol. Der allgemeinen Bunderberatung der Gemeinde in 'Elim' zum Gruental am 19. Juni 1927," Abraham Gerhard Peters Fonds, Waterloo Historical Mss, 1.91.1 Mennonite Archives of Ontario, Conrad Grebel University College, Waterloo.
17 "Ein Tag der Tag," *Bote*, 17 August 1927, 2; Enns's later account omits J.J. Rempel and H.J. Enns, who died in 1928, from the *Vorsänger* list.
18 See *Elim Gemeinde*, 23–4; Elim Mennonite Church, *Our Walk with God*, 16.
19 Grunthal Church Meeting Book, Grunthal.
20 Benjamin Ewert, "Die neue Mennonitenansiedlung bei McCreary, Man.," *Bote*, 22 August 1934, 2.
21 F.H. Epp, *Mennonites in Canada*, 252, for similar problems in other Russländer communities.
22 Meeting Protokoll, Johann Jakob Enns Papers, Vol. 2400, MHA.
23 Bückert Papers, April and September 1933, Vol. 300, MHA; I am grateful to Anna Ens for drawing my attention to these.
24 A.A. Peters to J.J. Enns, 15 February 1934, and Heinrich Olfert to J.J. Enns, December 1935 and January 1936, Enns Papers, Vol. 2400, MHA; Johann P. Bückert to David Toews on the McCreary controversy, February 1936, Bückert Papers, Vol. 300, MHA. See also, Zacharias, *Footprints of a Pilgrim People*, 81–2.
25 F.F. Enns to J.J. Enns, March to June 1933, with J.J. Enns's draft replies, Enns Papers, Vol. 2400, MHA.
26 Meeting Protokoll, 23 April 1933, Enns Papers, Vol. 2400, MHA.
27 Meeting Protokoll, November 1933, Enns Papers, Vol. 2400, MHA.
28 David Fast, conversations with author, 1974.
29 *Elim Gemeinde*, 27.
30 David Fast to J.J. Enns, J.J. Enns Papers, Vol. 2400, MHA; the issues involved remain unclear.
31 Unruh, *Die Mennonitische Bibelschule*.
32 F.H. Epp, *Mennonites in Canada, 1920–1940*, 557–8.
33 Letter, J.H. Enns Papers, Vol. 2400, MHA.
34 Abraham Gerhard Peters Fonds, Mennonite Archives of Ontario, Conrad Grebel University College, Waterloo.
35 F.H. Epp, *Mennonites in Canada, 1920–1940*, 459–61.
36 On Reuter readings in Russia, see Rempel with Rempel Carlson, *A Mennonite Family in Tsarist Russia*, 73, 225.
37 H.H. Epp, "The Khortitsa 'Naturschutzverein.'"
38 *Gesangbuch zum gottesdienstlichen und häuslichen Gebrauch in den Mennoniten-Gemeinden Russlands*, and the *Choralbuch* of Heinrich Franz.

39 Berg, *From Russia with Music*.
40 Berg, "Music among the Mennonites in Russia."
41 Letkemann, "The Hymnody and Choral Music of Mennonites in Russia."
42 G.G. Kornelsen, *SP*, 17 June 1936; "Sängerfest Held at Grunthal on Sunday," *WFP*, 17 June 1936, 8.
43 Jacob H. Block "Die Feuerversicherung in der Ansiedlung Grünthal, Man.," *Bote*, 14 February 1934, 1–2.
44 *SP*, 28 February 1934.
45 "The Grunthal 'Beerdigungs Kasse,'" in *Grunthal History 1874–1974*, 77–8.
46 Toews, *Mennonites in Russia*, 398.
47 Meeting of July 1928, *Bote*, 12 September 1928, 1; F.H. Epp, *Mennonites in Canada, 1920–1940*, 239, 267; M. Epp, *Mennonite Women in Canada*, 132–7.
48 Bestvater, "Der Tabea Naeverein," 40–2; Elim Mennonite Church, *Our Walk with God*, 80–1.
49 Urry, "A Forgotten Encounter."
50 Lena Rempel, "Unser Nähkursus," *Bote*, 30 March 1932, 1.
51 Bestvater, "Der Tabea Naeverein," 40; Elim Mennonite Church, *Our Walk with God*, 80.

5. Schools and Education

1 Urry, "The Snares of Reason."
2 Cherkazianova, "Mennonite Schools and the Russian Empire.".
3 Urry, *None but Saints*, esp. ch. 9.
4 Urry, *Mennonites, Politics, and Peoplehood*, 103.
5 Adolf Ens, "Mennonite Education in Russia."
6 Sudermann, "My First Journey as Deputy in South Russia."
7 Adolf Ens, "The Conspiracy that Never Was."
8 Francis, *In Search of Utopia*, 161–5; Jake Peters, *Mennonite Private Schools*.
9 Anderson, *The Education of the New-Canadian*, 76.
10 Gregor and Wilson, *The Development of Education in Manitoba*, chs. 3–5.
11 Adolf Ens, *Subjects or Citizens?* ch. 4.
12 F.H. Epp, *Mennonites in Canada, 1786–1920*, 338–42; G.J. Ens, *Die Schule muss sein*, ch. 1.
13 For Russländer the term Old Colony indicated Khortitsa but not for Kanadier Reinlander.
14 Unruh, "A History of the Goodwill School District"; Schellenberg, "Goodwill: School District No. 1967," in *Schools – Our Heritage*, 67–76.
15 Healey, "Quakers and Mennonites."
16 Francis, *In Search of Utopia*, 181–6; F.H. Epp, *Mennonites in Canada, 1786–1920*, 354–7; Adolf Ens, *Subjects or Citizens?* 116–30, with a list of new districts in Hanover at 129, table 6.

17 A. Friesen, "Emigration in Mennonite History," 57–8.
18 Petition of Chortitzer of the Niverville area, January 1920, quoted in A. Friesen, "Emigration in Mennonite history," 64–6.
19 Official Trustee, School District Correspondence, Department of Education, GR 1630, 1922, AM.
20 Official Trustee, School District Correspondence, Department of Education, GR 1630, 5, 1923, AM; *MFP*, 22 June 1925.
21 P. Dyck, "Education in Steinbach"; "Steinbach: School District No. 65," in Schellenberg, *Schools – Our Heritage*, 214–25. Friesen, *Between Earth and Sky*, 461–8.
22 Letters to the School Trustee, Official Trustee Correspondence, Department of Education, RG19 F2 Box 9, AM; Official Trustee, School District Correspondence, GR 1630, 1925, AM.
23 Official Trustee, School District Correspondence, Department of Education, GR 1630, 1922, AM.
24 Report, 4 May 1928, School District Correspondence, Department of Education F-Granv. GRI, AM.
25 Official Trustee, School District Correspondence, Department of Education, GR 1630, 1925, AM.
26 Discussions with Mennonites who attended the school at this period.
27 Official Trustee, School District Correspondence, Department of Education, GR 1630, 1921, AM.
28 Unruh, "A History of Goodwill School District," 37.
29 Unruh, "A History of Goodwill School District," and discussion with Warkentin's former pupils.
30 School District Correspondence, Department of Education, 1927, Eve-Granv. GRI, AM; School District Correspondence, Department of Education, 1928, Eve-Granv. GRI, AM.
31 Council Minutes, 1 August 1927, Office Papers, RM of Hanover.
32 School District Correspondence, Department of Education, 1929, AM.
33 Tomlinson was suspended in 1941 after irregularities were found in his accounts; later found guilty of failing to keep proper records, although acquitted of fraud, he was sentenced to six months in prison. Tomlinson Court Case Records, Department of Education, GR 1660, AM.
34 G.G. Kornelsen, "Ostreserve Nachrichten," *SP*, 24 January 1931, 8.
35 Block, *God's Footprints*.
36 Block was a friend of the writer and publisher Arnold Dyck.
37 Heidebrecht, *Ein holperiger Lebensweg*; autobiographical "Lebenslauf" in his obituary, *Bote*, 19 October 1988, 6.
38 Töws, *Schönfeld*, 96; translated in Toews, *Mennonites in Ukraine*, 24.
39 Heidebrecht, "Über meine Arbeit auf Reesor, Ont."; Heidebrecht, *Ein holperiger Lebensweg*, ch. 10; Dennis, *Memories of Reesor*.

40 Council Minutes, RM of Hanover, 8 September 1931.
41 A. Reimer, "The War Brings Its Own Conflict," 15.
42 Anna Heidebrecht Obituary, *MR*, 17 April 1968, 11; David Heidebrecht Obituary, *Bote*, 19 October 1988, 6.
43 Heidebrecht, *Ein holperiger Lebensweg*, 94; it was actually nearer $80.
44 Heidebrecht, 102–3.
45 Heidebrecht, 109.
46 Calculated from School District Correspondence, Department of Education, AM.
47 Letters of 5 October with approval on 16 October, School District Correspondence, Department of Education, G-Hy, 1935, GI, AM.
48 Heidebrecht, "Plain Mathematics."
49 School District Correspondence, Department of Education, Fe-Gy, 1934, AM.
50 Unruh, "A History of Goodwill School District," 24.
51 Inspector Herriot's Report, School District Correspondence, Department of Education, G-Hy, October 1935, AM.
52 School District Correspondence, Department of Education, G-J, 1936, AM, for blueprints of the new school; on the fire, see Unruh, "A History of Goodwill School District," 26.
53 School District Correspondence, Department of Education, G-J, 1936, AM.
54 Daily Registers of School District of Goodwill No. 1967, 1938/39–1939/40, MHA.
55 Daily Registers of School District of Goodwill No. 1967, 1942–3, MHA.
56 Manitoba, *Report of the Department of Education. Year Ending June 30th, 1931*, 22.
57 Accounts of the Secretary-Treasurer, Goodwill School Division No. 1967, for 1920–37, MHA; Daily Registers of School District of Goodwill No. 1967, 1941–2.
58 School Districts Correspondence, Department of Education, Gavr-Gypsumville, 1931, Far-Graysville, 1933, AM.
59 Heidebrecht, *Ein holperiger Lebensweg*, 98.
60 Report of Herriot, School District Correspondence, Department of Education, 1932, F. Grea-, GRI, May 1932, AM.
61 School District Correspondence, Department of Education, G-Hy, GI, 1935, AM.
62 Heidebrecht, *Deutsches Sprachbuch*; Heidebrecht, *Ein holperiger Lebensweg*, 95–7.
63 Peter Braun, "Die deutsche Sprache," *Bote*, 9 May 1928, 1; P[eter]B[raun], "Sprachliche Ungezogenheiten," *Bote*, 19–26 June 1929, 2.
64 J.N. Ediger, "Warum die Pflege der hochdeutschen Sprache für unser Volk hier in Amerika so wichtig ist," *MR*, 18 September 1929, 4–5; C.H. Friesen, "Haltet fest an der Muttersprache," *MR*, 1 August 1934, 2.
65 "Zur 'Pädagogischen Ecke,'" *Bote*, 23–30 April 1930; T. Warkentin, "Mangelndes Volksbewusstsein," *Bote*, 8 January 1936, 3.

66 Heidebrecht, *Ein holperiger Lebensweg*, 102–3.
67 Schellenberg identified Heidebrecht as "D.H. of Grünthal," "Was du tun willst, das tue bald!" *Bote*, 11 July 1934, 2–3; also in *SP*, 25 July 1934, 2.
68 Heidebrecht, *Ein holperiger Lebensweg*, 109.
69 CMBC Files, Vol. 1275, File 633.
70 G.J. Ens, *Die Schule muss sein*; F.H. Epp, *Education with a Plus*.
71 V. Peters, "The Immigrant."
72 [Arnold Dyck,] "Die Manitoba Schulwoche," *SP*, 22 October 22, 1931, 3.
73 Ankli, "Farm Income on the Great Plains," 100–1.
74 P. Dyck, "Education in Steinbach," in A. Warkentin, *Reflections on Our Heritage*, 290–2.
75 Heidebrecht, *Ein holperiger Lebensweg*, 107.
76 SE5–6–5E, see "Historic Sites of Manitoba: Gravel Ridge School No. 2285 (RM of Hanover)," Manitoba Historical Society, revised 22 November 2020, http://www.mhs.mb.ca/docs/sites/gravelridgeschool.shtml; Margaret [Peters] Franz, discussions with the author.
77 Heidebrecht, *Ein holperiger Lebensweg*, 107.

6. Debts, Depression, and a New Grunthal

1 Safarian, *The Canadian Economy*; Berton, *The Great Depression*, 9.
2 Marchildon, "Introduction," *Drought and Depression*.
3 G. Friesen, *The Canadian Prairies*, ch. 13; Wiseman, "The Pattern of Prairie Politics."
4 Knight, *Interim Report and Findings of the Economic Survey Board of Manitoba*, 1:46; Grant, Davidson, and Chernick, *Agricultural Income*, 52, table 16.
5 Grose, *Industrial Resources of Manitoba*, 37; Ankli, "Farm Income on the Great Plains," 101n36, with other provincial figures.
6 Grant, Davidson, and Chernick, *Agricultural Income*, 74, 86.
7 Unemployment assistance figures from Pearson, *Provincial Finance in Manitoba*, 11, 13.
8 Knight, *Interim Report*, 2:274.
9 F.H. Epp, *Mennonite Exodus*, 211, 286; F.H. Epp, *Mennonites in Canada*, 383.
10 *Canadian Annual Review of Public Affairs* (1933), 449.
11 F.H. Epp, *Mennonite Exodus*, 210–12, 214–17.
12 See F.H. Epp, 289–94.
13 D.D. Rempel, "The Wonderful Ways of God," 10.
14 F.H. Epp, *Mennonite Exodus*, 283; 288, table 6.
15 Klassen is remembered mainly for his work with post–Second World War refugees rather than his earlier CMBC activities; Klassen and Klassen, *Ambassador to His People*; G. Rempel, "Cornelius Franz Klassen."
16 F.H. Epp, *Mennonite Exodus*, 286.
17 F.H. Epp, 290–2; reports in CMBC Papers.

18 C.F. Klassen to the Board, 14/15 October 1931, CMBC Papers, Vol. 1313, No. 875, MHA.
19 CMBC Papers, 1194, No. 186 and 1294, Box 775, MHA.
20 Klassen, letter dated 15 October and form, CMBC Papers, Box 1298, No. 803, MHA.
21 CMBC Papers, Box 1294, No. 776, MHA.
22 CMBC Papers, Box 1297, No. 797, MHA.
23 CMBC Papers, Box 1296, No. 788, MHA.
24 F.H. Epp, *Mennonite Exodus*, ch. 18.
25 Figures from F.H. Epp, *Mennonite Exodus*, 276, table 4.
26 Osokina, *Stalin's Quest for Gold*.
27 List in *MR*, 1 May 1929, 7; *Bote*, 1 May 1929, 1–2.
28 Report, CMBC Papers, Box 1294, No. 775, MHA.
29 "Landwirtschaftliche Ansiedlung in Grünthal," *SP*, 27 September 1933, 2.
30 Correspondence, Steinbach File, CMBC Files, Vol. 1182, MHA.
31 A. Warkentin, *Reflections on Our Heritage*, 225–9.
32 Pauls, *Bethesda: The First Fifty Years*.
33 F.H. Epp, *Mennonite Exodus*, 308–11.
34 A.J. Dueck, *Concordia Hospital*.
35 Johann Enns [Letter from Grunthal], *MR*, 22 August 1928, 8.
36 Ronald Friesen, *Pioneers of Cheese*, 174–7.
37 Gray, *The Winter Years*.
38 "The Cordwood Industry," in *Grunthal History 1874–1974*, 175–7.
39 "'Momento mori.' Zwei Todesfall in Grünthal," *MR*, 22 March 1939, 9; his nickname, (LG *Missionär* Wiens), was because it was suggested he stole ("took") valuables, just as visiting missionary preachers collected ("took") money for their cause.
40 P.A. Thiessen [Letters from Grunthal], *Nordwesten*, 10 June 1931, 5; 6 January 1932, 5; a Russländer, Thiessen sold the *Nordwesten* in Grunthal.
41 G.M. Neufeld [Letter from Grunthal], *SP*, 27 February 1929, 5; G.G. Kornelsen, "Ostreserve Nachrichten," *SP*, 24 January 1934, 5: 8; B.W. Funk [Letter from Gnadenfeld], *SP*, 4 November 1936, 5.
42 Peter G. Funk [Letter from Grunthal], *SP*, 12 November 1931, 4; P.A. Thiessen [Letters from Grunthal], *Nordwesten*, 6 January 1932, 5; G.G. Kornelsen, "Ostreserve Nachrichten," *SP*, 24 January 1934, 8; *SP*, 7 February 1934, 8.
43 *Grunthal History 1874–1974*, 30–5, and contemporary newspaper accounts.
44 "Canadian Industrial Exhibition," *The Grain Growers' Guide*, 26 July 1911, 8; [Advertisement with Braun endorsing the Midget Flour Mill,] *The Grain Growers' Guide*, 16 October 1912, 21.
45 "Doktor Peters gestorben," *SP*, 18 January 1928, 6; M.W. Friesen, *Neue Heimat in der Chacowildnis*, 298–9.
46 *Grunthal History 1874–1974*, 82–5.
47 Elsie Janzen, "Grunthal History," *CN*, 17 September 1967, 5.

48 Johann U. Peters [Letters], *SP*, 17 May 1916, 2; 11 October 1916, 2; 19 May 1917, 2.
49 Francis, *In Search of Utopia*, 226–30; Werner, "Sacred, Secular and Material."
50 G.M. Neufeld [Letter from Grunthal], *SP*, 27 February 1929, 3.
51 J.J. Friesen [Letter from Neu-Bergfeld], *SP*, 3 April 1935, 4.
52 Vogt, *The Steinbach Saga*, 63, fig. 5.5.
53 B.W. Funk [Letter from Gnadenfeld bei Grunthal], *SP*, 27 May 1936, 3; "Guenther's," *Grunthal History 1874–1974*, 131–3; Eddie and Eric Guenther, discussions with the author.
54 Council Minutes, December 1931, RM of Hanover.
55 "Ein Beobachter" [Grunthal], *SP*, 10 December 1931, 8; J.F. Warkentin, "Postal Service"; "Postdienst" in Block's *Beitrag zur Geschichte Gruenthal's*, 28; on Hiebert's job loss, G.G. Kornelsen, "Ostreserve Nachrichten," *SP*, 1 August 1934, 8.
56 Peter Voth [Letter from Grunthal], *SP*, 22 November 1933, 5; G.G. Kornelsen, "Ostreserve Nachrichten," *SP*, 14 February 1934; Kornelsen, *SP*, 11 July, 1934, 8.
57 "Grunthal," Archives: Post Offices and Postmasters, Government of Canada, updated 20 July 2023, https://recherche-collection-search.bac-lac.gc.ca/eng/home/record?app=posoffposmas&IdNumber=13411.
58 Warkentin, "Memoirs." Unpublished typescript in the author's possession.
59 G.G. Kornelsen, "Ostreserve Nachrichten," *SP*, 11 July 1934, 8.
60 "Grunthal Feed Mill," in *Grunthal History 1874–1974*, 134–5; and Vernon Wiebe, conversations with the author.
61 This was the case for David and Margaretha Warkentin; see M. Warkentin, *Descendants of Jacob Heinrich Thiessen*, 72–5.
62 "Grunthal Garage," in *Grunthal History 1874–1974*, 136; and John D. Warkentin, conversations with the author.
63 B.W. Funk [Letter from Gnadenfeld], *SP*, 27 May 1936.
64 "Chornoboy Farm Equipment," in *Grunthal History 1874–1974*, 138–40; Gary Chornoboy, discussions with the author.
65 B.W. Funk [Letter from Gnadenfeld], *SP*, 17 July 1935, 3.
66 J.J. Friesen [Letter from Neu-Bergfeld], *SP*, 3 April 1935, 4.
67 J.J. Braun [Letter from Grunthal], *SP*, 17 June 1936, 2–3.
68 Resolution No. 9, 7 May 1935; Resolution No. 13, 2 July 1935; Council Minutes, RM of Hanover Papers.
69 Collector's Rolls, RM of Hanover.
70 C.H. Friesen, "The Formation of the Bergthaler Church."

7. Old World and New World Politics

1 Urry, *Mennonites, Politics, and Peoplehood*.
2 Urry, *None but Saints*, ch. 6.

3 Urry, "The Mennonite Commonwealth in Imperial Russia Revisited."
4 F.H. Epp, *Mennonite Exodus*.
5 Urry, *Mennonites, Politics, and Peoplehood*, ch. 5; A. Friesen, *In Defense of Privilege*.
6 Urry, *Mennonites, Politics, and Peoplehood*, ch. 6.
7 *MR*, 3 February 1926; "Bericht über die Versammlung der Neu-Eingewanderten von Manitoba am 20 und 21 Juni 1928 in Winnipeg," *MR*, 11 July 1928, 5; Gerhard Sawatzky, *Nordwesten*, 11 July 1928, 8.
8 Rempel, "Wie verbessert man den Viehbestand auf der Farm?"
9 "Eindrücke von der Provinzial-Delegierten-Versammlung der seit 1923 in Manitoba eingewanderten Mennoniten am 18. und 19. Juni d[iesem] J[ahre] in der Zionskirche der Mennonitengemeinde Winnipeg," *MR*, 9–23 July 1930, 7.
10 "Protokoll der 6. Provinzialen Vertretversammling der Mennoniten Manitobas im Bethaus zu Gruenthal, 29–30. Juni 1933"; printed copy in B.J. Schellenberg Collection, Vol. 549, xx 3, MHA.
11 *SP*, 25 May 1933; "Protokoll der 6. Provinzialen Vertretversammling ... "
12 Esau, "Establishment, Preservation and Legality."
13 Adolf Ens, *Subjects or Citizens?* 66–7.
14 J. Dyck, *Oberschulze Jakob Peters*; A. Warkentin, *Reflections on Our Heritage*, 57–8, 60.
15 Adolf Ens, *Subjects or Citizens?* 67–74; Goldsborough, *With One Voice*.
16 A. Warkentin, *Reflections on Our Heritage*, ch. 5; Penner, *Hanover: One Hundred Years*, pt. 1.
17 On Braun see K.J.B. Reimer, "Johann Braun."
18 The first "record book" of council members in the RM of Hanover Office starts in 1927.
19 Council Minutes, 27 March 1927, RM of Hanover.
20 Council Minutes, 5 March 1930, RM of Hanover.
21 Council Record Book, 28 February 1933, RM of Hanover; Wiebe's place of residence varies in different records.
22 [Letter from Chortitz,] *Nordwesten*, 7 December 1932, 5.
23 A. Warkentin, *Reflections on Our Heritage*, 60–2.
24 *Nordwesten*, 13 January 1932, 5.
25 A. Warkentin, *Reflections on Our Heritage*, 60–1; Penner, *Hanover: One Hundred Years*, 173–4.
26 Loewen, *Diaspora in the Countryside*.
27 Stoesz, *A History of the Chortitzer Mennonite Church*, 163.
28 A. Warkentin, *Reflections on Our Heritage*, 274–7.
29 A. Warkentin, 278–9.
30 Dueck, "Mennonite Federal Electoral Behaviour," 27, 65; Buhr, "Pursuit of a Vision," 196–7.
31 I am grateful to Michael Coulson, Professor Emeritus of the Department of Geography, University of Calgary, for the rolls and details of federal election results from the National Archives in Ottawa.

32 Dueck, "Mennonite Federal Electoral Behaviour," 59; but see Buhr, "Pursuit of a Vision," 197–8, for attitudes in Coaldale, Alberta, before the emergence of Social Credit.
33 Entz, "Der Courier" and "Der Nordwesten," in *The Multilingual Press in Manitoba*.

8. Conflicted Identities

1 Urry, "Gender, Generation and Social Identity."
2 J.B. Toews, "Russian Mennonites and *Allianz*"; D. Sudermann, "*Allianz* in Ukraine."
3 Urry, *Mennonites, Politics and Peoplehood*, 122–4; A. Friesen, *In Defense of Privilege*, pt. 2.
4 J.H. Janzen, "The Activities of the K.f.K in Russia."
5 A. Reimer, "The Print Culture of the Russian Mennonites."
6 Kappeler, *The Russian Empire*; Schmaltz, "What's in a Name?"
7 L.G. Friesen, *Mennonites in the Russian Empire*, 163–8.
8 Urry, "The Russian Mennonites."
9 F.H. Epp, *Mennonite Exodus*, 43.
10 J.P. Dyck, *Troubles and Triumphs, 1914–1924*, 54; entry of 18 September 1918.
11 These included North America, Mexico, and Australia.
12 "A Few Thoughts on the Emigration Question," in Toews and Toews, *Union of Citizens of Dutch Lineage*, 358; the author is misidentified as P. Baerg: see A. Friesen, "Wrong Author Attributed."
13 "Some Observations Concerning the Current Situation of the Mennonites in Russia and the Prospects of Emigration," in Toews and Toews, *Union of Citizens of Dutch Lineage*, 348, 352, 355.
14 Figures in F.H. Epp, *Mennonites in Canada*, 327.
15 P. Klassen, *The Mennonites in Paraguay*, ch. 12; Thiesen, *Mennonite & Nazi?*; Eicher, *Exiled Among Nations*, ch. 3.
16 J.P. Klassen, "Dem Deutschen Volk," *MR*, 26 March 1930, 2–3; a poem with the same title by P.P. Isaac appeared in *MR*, 23 July 1930, 5.
17 "Faschismus und Bolschewismus im Kampf," *MR*, 22 February 1928, 3.
18 [Editorial,] *MR*, 4 February 1931, 11.
19 B.H. Unruh, "Um die deutsche Sache," *MR*, 17 February 1937, 4; Unruh was active in politics after 1917, later a representative of the CMBC in Germany, and became a supporter of the Nazi regime, a move that compromised his post-war relations with Mennonites. See Neufeldt-Fast, "Benjamin Unruh."
20 Goossen, *Chosen Nation*, ch. 5.
21 Eric Hobsbawm, *Uncommon People*, ch. 22, "Jazz Comes to Europe."
22 *Bote*, 6 November 1935, 5.

23 "Das Sängerfest in Grunthal, Man.," *SP*, 26 July 1939, 6; the term was used to describe Jazz in Nazi Germany: Dümling, "Reine und unreine Musik."
24 Urry, "A Mennostaat for the Mennovolk?"; Urry, *Mennonites, Politics, and Peoplehood*, 196–9.
25 Hanebrink, *A Specter Haunting Europe*.
26 H. Loewen, "Mennonites, National Socialism and Jews."
27 Keiter, *Russlanddeutsche Bauern*.
28 Details on individual record cards including comment by C.F. Klassen on Isaak, CMBC Records, 1932, MHA.
29 T.D. Regehr, "Walter Quiring."
30 F.H. Epp, *Mennonite Exodus*, 320–3; F.H. Epp, *Mennonites in Canada*, 517–29.
31 Goossen, "Terms of Racial Endearment."
32 Gesche, *Kultur als Instrument der Aussenpolitik*; Wagner, *Brothers Beyond the Sea*, ch. 2.
33 See Ross, "A Contribution to the Study of *Völkische Ideologie*," 15; it was later renamed the *Verband der Russlanddeutschen*.
34 D[ietrich]. H. Epp, "Das Zentrale Mennonitische Immigrantenkomitee," *Bote*, 21–8 July 1948, 2, 3.
35 Urry, "The Reading Worlds of Russlaender and Kanadier," 133–8.
36 Ross, "A Contribution to the Study of *Völkische Ideologie*," 116–22.
37 Wagner, *Brothers Beyond the Sea*, ch. 3.
38 Urry, *Mennonites Politics and Peoplehood*, 236–7.
39 On Nazi racial categories involving "Frisians," see Beyen, "A Tribal Trinity."
40 Schröder, *Russlanddeutsche Friesen*; G. Rempel, "Heinrich Hajo Schroeder."
41 A.B. D[yck], "Bücherbesprechung," *Mennonitische Volkswarte* 6, no. 2 (June 1936): 9
42 F.H. Epp, "An Analysis of Germanism"; F.H. Epp, *Mennonite Exodus*, 320–5.
43 J.J. Hildebrand, "Printing News Articles against the Germans," *WFP*, 15 June 1935, 8.
44 B.B. Janz, "Kommt Menno Simons unter die Nationalsozialisten," *MR* and *Bote*, 26 December 1934, 1; "Bin ich Nationalsozialist? Bewahre," *MR* and *Bote*, 11 January 1939, 1; the latter was originally published in an English-language newspaper in Lethbridge, Alberta.
45 Goosen, *Chosen Nation*; Kobelt-Groch and von Schlachta, *Mennoniten in der NS-Zeit*.
46 Walter Quiring, "Adolf Hitler über die Kirchen in Deutschland," *Bote*, 9 October 1935, 4; Thiesen, *Mennonite and Nazi?*, 158; P. Klassen, *Die Deutschvölkische Zeit*; Eicher, *Exiled Among Nations*.
47 D. Bergen, *Twisted Cross*.
48 G. Neufeld [Letter], *MR*, 16 December 16, 1936, 4.
49 Otto Dyck, discussions with the author in British Columbia.

50 "A Grunthal Farmer in No Man's Land," *CN*, 8 December 1961, section 3, 1–2.
51 Adolf Ens, "Becoming British Citizens." On the United States, see Juhnke, *A People of Two Kingdoms*; R. Loewen, "American Nationalism."
52 For Manitoba, see Anna Ens, *In Search of Unity*, 43–5.
53 F.H. Epp, *Mennonites in Canada*, especially ch. 9; Dueck, "Evangelical Mennonite Brethren."
54 Steiner, *In Search of Promised Lands*.
55 Jack Thiessen, *The Eleventh Commandment*, 64, 66.
56 "Zur 'Pädagogischen Ecke,'" *Bote*, 20 April 1930, 2.
57 T. Warkentin, "Mangelndes Volksbewusstsein," *Bote*, 8 January 1936, 3.
58 Peter Braun, "Die Deutsche Sprache," *Bote*, 9 May 1928, 1.
59 D[ietrich] E[pp], "Religion und deutsche Sprache in Schule und Haus," *Bote*, 6 December 1928, 1.
60 J.H. Janzen, *Lifting the Veil*, 70–1; Urry, "Growing Up with Cities," 140–1.
61 J.H. Janzen, "Plautdietsch."
62 Peter Block, discussions with the author.
63 "Adam, where are you? (*Adam, wo best Du?*)" Jack Thiessen, *The Eleventh Commandment*, 75.
64 G.J. Ens, *Die Schule muss sein*, ch. 8.
65 G.H. Peters, "Wie begegnen wir der Gefahr der Entfremdung der deutsch-mennonitischen Jugend?" *Bote*, 4 September 1935, 1–2; Walter Quiring, "Wie packen wir's an?" *Bote*, 16 October 1935, 1; Gerhard Töws, "Wenn wir geeint und treu zum Werke gehn," *Bote*, 13 November 1935, 2.
66 P.J. Sawatzky, "Nachklänge vom Grigorjewer Tage auf Starbuck, Man., am 17. Juli 1938," *MR*, 24 August 1938, 1; also published in *Bote*, 24 August, 13.
67 G.G. Schmidt, "Kurze Mitteilungen über die in Canada lebenden Tereker," *MR*, 20 July–10 August 1938; Schmidt, "Die Zusammenkunft der Tereker," *Bote*, 13 July 1938, 2; Schmidt, "Einige Angaben ueber die Tereker Siedlung," *Bote*, 27 July 1938, 5.
68 Jacob Block, "Achtung! Schlachtinger und Baratower!" *SP*, 15 March 1939, 2; Block, "Baratower und Schlachtinger," *MR*, 12 April 1939, 2; Block, "Bekantmachung," *Bote*, 31 May 1939, 4. A reunion to mark the twentieth anniversary of Russländer immigration was held during the Second World War; see F.F. Sawatzky, "Die Baratow-Schlachtinger Fest, abgehalten in der Kirche zu Gnadenthal bei Plum Coulee, Man. am 20. Juni 1943," *SP*, 14 July 1943, 2.
69 K. Fast "An alle Schönfelder," *Bote*, 19 January 1938, 3; *Bote*, 9 February 1938, 3; *Bote*, 13 April 1938, 4; *MR*, 13 April 1938; K. Fast "An alle Schönfelder," *MR*, 3 and 20 August 1938; *Bote*, 28 September 1938, 3.
70 Töws, *Schönfeld*; K. Fast "An alle Schönfelder!" *MR*, 8 February 1939, 7; *Bote*, 15 February 1939, 2; *MR*, 2 June 1939, 2.

71 Töws, *Die Heimat in Flammen*; Töws, *Die Heimat in Trümmern*.
72 Töws, *Schönfeld*, 4.
73 "Das Sängerfest in Grunthal, Man.," *SP*, 26 July 1939, 6.
74 Erenberg, *The Greatest Fight of Our Generation*.

9. The War Years

1 Dederich Navall, Altadena, CA, to David Toews, Rosthern, SK, 27 June 1935, Mennonite Board of Colonization Papers, Vol. 1177, File 99, MHA.
2 John Giesbrecht [Letter to the editor], "Communists and Nazis," *WFP*, 25 February 1939.
3 J.J. Hildebrand, "Suggestions of Disloyalty Resented by Mennonites," *WFP*, 25 February 1939, 14; and earlier in the *WFP*, "The Lost Ten Tribes in the Far East," 24 March 1934, 18; "Our Flag Is One Thing, Our Race Is Another," 27 November 1937, 24.
4 "Hitler Salute: Local German Hail Rebirth of Fatherland under Fuehrer," *WFP*, 30 January 1939, 1.
5 Urry, *Mennonites, Politics and Peoplehood*, 236–7.
6 "Adolf Hitlers Reichstagsrede im Wortlaut," *MR*, 10 May 1939, 12; on the speech, see Mommsen, "Hitler's Reichstag Speech."
7 Urry, *Mennonites, Politics, and Peoplehood*, 203.
8 A.B. Wiebe to Howard Winkler, 23 December 1940, 3 February 1941, Howard W. Winkler Papers, MG 14, B. 44, File 3, 3882, 3886, AM.
9 Letter from Howard Winkler, 22 May 1940, Winkler Papers, PAM MG 14, 64 File 2, AM.
10 Plumptre, *Mobilizing Canada's Resources*, 30.
11 Byers, "Mobilising Canada."
12 Stacey, *The Arts of War and Peace*, 630; J.A. Toews, *Alternative Service*, 34. On general Canadian policies, see M.D. Stevenson, *Canada's Greatest Wartime Muddle*.
13 *SP*, August 1940, 3, and others.
14 Martens "Accommodation and Withdrawal"; Fransen, "As Far as Conscience Will Allow"; T.D. Regehr, *Mennonites in Canada*, pt. 2: "The Crucible of War." On Canadian experience in general, see Keshen, *Saints, Sinners, and Soldiers*.
15 See, for instance, Jacob Rempel, *Consider the Threshing Stone*, ch. 2.
16 A.J. Dueck, "Making a Case for Non-combatant Service."
17 C. Stoesz, "Are You Prepared to Work in a Mental Hospital?"; also, C. Stoesz, "The Creation of an Identity."
18 Canada, *National Registration Regulations 1940*.
19 Canada, *National Registration Regulations 1940: Instructions for the Use of Deputy Registrars*, 10–11.

20 Canada, *National Registration Regulations 1940: Instructions for the Use of Deputy Registrars*, 11.
21 H.R. Reimer addressing members of Kleine Gemeinde descent, "Registration," *Christlicher Familienfreund*, August 1940, 1–3.
22 B.B. Janz, "The Mennonites: Mostly of Dutch Origin," *MR*, 31 July 1940, 5–6 (repr. from the *Lethbridge Herald*).
23 A. Friesen, *In Defense of Privilege*, especially ch. 13.
24 Johann G. Rempel, "Die Frage Nummer Acht," *MR*, 4 August 1940, 3; also in *Bote*, 14 August 1940, 2, with subsequent discussion in H.P. Toews, "Zu unsere Geschichte," *MR*, 18 September 1940, 4–5.
25 "Puzzles in Racial Origin Are Set for 'Canadians' in National Registration," *Toronto Telegram*, 10 August 1940; J.V. McAree, "Puzzles Presented by the Registration," *Globe and Mail*, 4 September 1940; Editorial, *Toronto Telegram*, 13 August 1940.
26 Letter, *MR*, 8 August 1940; T.D. Regehr, *Mennonites in Canada*, 47–9; R.C. Neufeld, "Tolerant Exclusion."
27 Ryder, "The Interpretation of Origin Statistics," 473–4.
28 Canada, *Defence of Canada Regulations*, 13.
29 J.G. Rempel, *Katechismus in der Wehrlosigkeit*.
30 Reddig, "Judge Adamson Versus the Mennonites I."
31 *Bericht ueber die Sitzung von Vertretern de Mennonitengemeinden im westlichen Canada, abgehalten in der Kirche der Ersten Mennonitengemeinden zu Saskatoon, Sask., am 29. Januar 1942*, 7; printed copy in Military Service, 1322, 1942–3, MHA.
32 G. Dueck, *Chortitzer Mennonite Conference*, 48–50; cutting listing Bergthalers, *SP*, 4 October 1944, in the Benjamin Ewert Papers, 543 (File 44), MHA; Neufeld, *Mennonites at War*, 99, 102, 103, 105, and 112.
33 T.D. Regehr, "Lost Sons"; on enlistments see also Dirks, "War Without, Struggle Within."
34 Questionnaire in J.J. Hildebrand Papers, 3308, File 72, MHA.
35 *Patriotic Exercises (Prescribed by the Advisory Board of the Department of Education)* [1941], given to teachers; these amended existing 1938 regulations.
36 "Minister's Page," *Manitoba School Journal* 4, no. 1 (1941): 3.
37 Province of Manitoba, Department of Education, *Empire Day, May 23, 1941*.
38 J.J. Bergen, "The World Wars and Education."
39 "Minister's Page," *Manitoba School Journal* 2, no. 4 (1939): 2; the *Winnipeg Tribune*'s editorial, "The Mennonites and Canada," *WT*, 17 November 1939, was republished in the same issue.
40 "A Wartime Project," *Manitoba School Journal* 7, no. 6 (1944): 16, 22.
41 Irene Warkentin, *Manitoba School Journal* 7, no. 6 (1944): 22.
42 *Winnipeg Evening Tribune*, 29 March 1943, 18.
43 J.J. Bergen, "My Experience as a Conscientious Objector," 1, 3–5.

44 J.J. Bergen, "The World Wars and Education," 162.
45 A. Reimer, "The War Brings Its Own Conflict," 15.
46 F.H. Epp, *Mennonites in Canada*, 392–4; Healey, "Quakers and Mennonites," 231; Entz, "The Suppression of the German Language Press"; on Canadian policies in both wars, see Martin and Adam, *Sourcebook of Canadian Media Law*.
47 Goossen, *Chosen Nation*, ch. 6; Klets, "Caught between Two Poles"; Urry, "Mennonites in Ukraine during World War II."
48 G. Rempel, "Mennonites and the Holocaust"; Jantzen and Thiesen, *European Mennonites and the Holocaust*.
49 For Manitoba, see Perrun, *The Patriotic Consensus*, ch. 1; for all of Canada, see Frazer, "From Pariahs to Patriots," 19–21.
50 Telegram dated 22 July 1942, Howard W. Winkler Papers, MG 14 B44, Box 2, File 2, AM.
51 Whitaker, "Official Repression of Communism."
52 Kealey and Whitaker, *R.C.M.P. Security Bulletins: The War Series*, 38; Williams, "Placing 'Rights and Liberties in Pawn,'" 81.
53 Kealey and Whitaker, *R.C.M.P. Security Bulletins: The War Series, Part II*, 88 (11 March 1943); Urry, *Mennonites, Politics, and Peoplehood*, 338n34.
54 Granatstein, *Conscription in the Second World War*, 43.
55 *WT*, 28 April 1942.
56 Editorial: "Manitoba's 'No' Vote," *WT*, 1 May 1942.
57 Block, *God's Footprints*, 22–5.
58 Fowke, "Economic Effects of the War."
59 Grant, Davidson, and Chernick, *Agricultural Income*.
60 Grose, *Industrial Resources of Manitoba*, 37; Grant, Davidson, and Chernick give slightly different figures as does *Historical Statistics of Canada: Section M: Agriculture Canada*, but not outside an acceptable range; "Section M: Agriculture," Historical Statistics of Canada, Statistics Canada, https://www150.statcan.gc.ca/n1/pub/11-516-x/sectionm/4057754-eng.htm.
61 Francis first published much of the data in "The Adjustment of a Peasant Group," and later in *In Search of Utopia*, ch. 9.
62 Hanover figures in J.H. Warkentin, *Mennonite Settlements*, 242; in 1936 the figure for Grunthal is the same but in 1941 it is lower, at $670.
63 E.K. Francis Mss, MG A5/27, AM; also "Report Submitted to the Historical & Scientific Society of Francis," 1945/47, MG A55/9, table 31. Francis's figures were probably collated from census data.
64 Francis Mss, MG A55/9, AM.
65 Ronald Friesen, *When Canada Called*, ch. 6.
66 Britnell and Fowke, *Canadian Agriculture in War and Peace*, 290, table 22.
67 Milk Control Board of Manitoba, *Annual Report*, 1950, 6 gives figures for 1932–3 to 1949–50.

300 Notes to pages 172–8

68 See Manitoba, Department of Agriculture, *Butter Rationing* in Dairy Scrapbooks, 1033–47, GR 7777, AM.
69 Penner, *Hanover: One Hundred* Years, 65.
70 Comparative figures for different product receipts in 1944–5 in Patterson and Trevor, *The Dairy Farm Business in Manitoba*, 31.
71 Britnell and Fowke, *Canadian Agriculture*, 290, table 22.
72 Manitoba, Department of Agriculture, *Butter Rationing*.
73 Ronald Friesen, *Pioneers of Cheese*, 174–84.
74 *Grunthal History 1874–1974*, 125–6.
75 Register of Co-operatives, Co-operative Services Branch, Agriculture and Immigration, 1916–49, G 2479, GR 3718, AM; Ronald Friesen, *Pioneers of Cheese*, 179.
76 A.A.M. Schroeder [Letter], *SP*, 3 February 1943, 5; G.G. Kornelsen, "Ostreserve Nachrichten," *SP*, 17 March 1943, 4.
77 S. Hiebert, *Growing Sugar in Manitoba*.
78 J. Friesen, "The Manitoba Sugar Beet Industry," 194, table 17.
79 John J. Kornelsen, "Beet Hoeing," in *Grunthal History 1874–1974*, 186–8.
80 Gauthier, *De la table de cuisine à la rue principale*.
81 Ward, *Join Your Credit Union*; Canada, Advisory Committee on Reconstruction, *I. Agricultural Policy*, 36–3.
82 Grunthal Credit Union Office, "Application for Letters Patent of Incorporation of a Credit Union Society under the 'Companies Act,'" 18 April 1942; and "Letters Patent of Incorporation of Grunthal Credit Union Society Limited under the 'Companies Act,'" 29 April 1942.
83 Named in official documents and "Grunthal Credit Union," *Grunthal History 1874–1974*, 142.
84 "Grunthal Credit Union," *Grunthal History 1874–1974*, 143.
85 *Memoirs of John F. Warkentin*." Unpublished manuscript in the author's possession.
86 Ankli, Helsberg, and Thompson, "The Adoption of the Gasoline Tractor"; Shepard, "Tractors and Combines."
87 Britnell, "Perspective on Change," 439, table 2.
88 MacPherson, "Better Tractors for Less Money."
89 *Grunthal History 1874–1974*, 116.
90 F.H. Epp, *Mennonite Exodus*, 344–6.
91 Urry, "Time: The Transcendent and the Worldly," 24–6.

10. Post-War Prosperity

1 *SP*, 9 May 1945, 1.
2 Rasmussen, "Canada and Bretton Woods"; Lamoreaux and Shapiro, *Bretton Woods Agreements*.

Notes to pages 179–84   301

3 "Reconstruction," Wartime Canada, 2023, https://wartimecanada.ca/categories/reconstruction.
4 Joseph Henry Ellis, *Manitoba Agriculture and Prairie Farm Rehabilitation Activities* (1944); Eric W. Thrift, *Town and Country Post-War Planning* (1944); W. Morton, *Local Government Reorganization* (1945).
5 Manitoba, *A Farm Electrification Programme*; "Manitoba's Blueprint for Power," 6–8.
6 Stuart Garson to Mackenzie King, 30 August 1945, Interim or Immediate Post War Projects, Post War Planning, F0081, Box 2, AM.
7 U.S. Department of Agriculture, *A Guide for Members of REA Cooperatives*; Manitoba Rural Electrification, Post War Planning, F0081, Box 4, AM.
8 Manitoba Power Commission, *Power for Manitoba Farms*; examples in Manitoba Rural Electrification, Post War Planning, F0081, Box 4, AM.
9 Manitoba Power Commission, *Report of the Farm Electrification Test,*, 8–12.
10 Canada, Advisory Committee on Reconstruction, *VI. Post-War Problems of Women*, 20.
11 "History of Local Light and Power," *CN*, 1947, 25, December progress edition.
12 Manitoba Hydro, *A History of Electric Power in Manitoba*, 30, https://www.hydro.mb.ca/corporate/history/history_of_electric_power_book.pdf.
13 *CN*, 30 January 1947, 7.
14 "Grunthal and Piney Now Become New Hydro Centres," *CN*, 8 May 1954, 1; "10 Record Breaking Years for the M.P.C," *CN*, 29 April 1955, 1.
15 *Grunthal History 1874–1974*, 124–31.
16 Hull, *The History of Co-operation*, 15–16.
17 Ward, *The Organization and Operation of a Consumer's Cooperative*, 46.
18 *CN*, 27 August 1948, 6.
19 Killick, *Manitoba Dairying*, 139; see also *Modern Refrigeration* 56 (1952), 48. Killick was the Dairy Commissioner for Manitoba.
20 "Kraft Plant at Grunthal, 'Canada's Finest,'" *CN*, 27 August 1948, 6; "Grunthal Plant Holds Open Day," *CN*, 27 July 1951, 3; *Grunthal History 1874–1974*, 127; see also Ronald Friesen, *Pioneers of Cheese*, 180–1.
21 *Dairy News*, no. 11 (15 November 1956); Dairy Scrapbooks, Department of Agriculture, GR 7777, AM.
22 *CN*, 2 May 1958, 17; *Grunthal History 1874–1974*, 127–31; Ronald Friesen, *Pioneers of Cheese*, 182–3.
23 Thiessen, *Mennonite Low German Dictionary*, 225, with relevant LG ditty.
24 J.H. Warkentin, *Mennonite Settlements*, 237.
25 Killick, *Manitoba Dairying*, 175.
26 Killick, 171–6.
27 J.H. Warkentin, *Mennonite Settlements*, 238.
28 "Milk Handling Undergoes a Revolution," *CN*, 19 August 1960, 4–5.

29 *CN*, 2 May 1958, 19; *CN*, 3 October 1958, 11; [Advertisement for tanks,] *CN*, 31 July 1959, 12.
30 *CN*, 15 March 1959, 8; *CN*, 27 March 1959, 11; Wes Keating, "If It's New and for Dairy, Gus DePape Will Have It," *CN*, 28 June 1972.
31 On training, *CN*, 15 March 1959, 8; Klassen advertisement, *CN*, 27 July 1959, 1.
32 Milk Control Board of Manitoba, *Annual Report*, (1960), 6 and *Annual Report* (1962), 6.
33 Milk Control Board of Manitoba, *Annual Report* (1963), 5.
34 On LaFrance (1902–89) see "LaFrance, Joseph," Manitoba Agricultural Hall of Fame, 2016, http://www.manitobaaghalloffame.com/ahofhonourroll/la-france-joseph/.
35 Typescript paper on Manitoba artificial breeding, Dairy Scrapbooks, Dairy Section, Department of Agriculture, 1947–53, GR 7777, AM; "Artificial Insemination Helps Upgrade Dairy Herds," *CN*, 22 June 1962, section 4, 1.
36 *Dairy News*, no. 19 (August 1947); *Dairy News*, no. 14 (March 1947); Dairy Scrapbooks, Department of Agriculture, GR 7777, AM.
37 *Dairy News*, no. 70 (1951), 5; Dairy Scrapbooks, Department of Agriculture, GR 7777, AM.
38 "Farewell for Lafrance at C. of C. Banquet," *CN*, 10 June 1960, 5; see also earlier recognition, "Community Honors Jo Lafrance on 25 Years of Agricultural Service," *CN*, 29 March 1957, 14.
39 "Grunthal Cows Produce 3,063,612 Lbs. of Milk," *CN*, 13 April 1962, section 2, 5.
40 J.H. Warkentin, *Mennonite Settlements*, 241; the figures for Hanover in 1936/41 are different in Francis, "The Adjustment of a Peasant Group," 225, table 5.
41 *Grunthal History 1874–1974*, 141.
42 J.J. Braun, "Grunthal," *SP*, 8 June 1949, 5.
43 *CN*, 13 February 1947, 2.
44 Maybank J., in matter of the Municipal Act and the assessment appeal of Peter D. Thiessen, Assessment and Appeals, Municipal Board, AM.
45 Manitoba, Department of Industry and Commerce, *Facts about Steinbach*; Loewen, *Diaspora in the Countryside*, 59.
46 Braun and Klassen, *Historical Atlas of the East Reserve*, 98–9.
47 *SP*, 14 August 1946; undated *WT* cuttings, 5738, Roads 1, 1939–47; 5739, Roads 2, 1948–9, UofM Archives; "Grunthal Group Urges East Road," *WFP*, 6 November 1947, 5.
48 Provincial Engineers 1948 report given to the Minister of Public Works, AM; "10 Year Roads Record Unequalled in Southeast," *CN*, 2 April 1956, 1, 31.
49 T.D. Regehr, *Mennonites in Canada*, 159–62.
50 "Fully Confident that Road Will Be Constructed," *CN*, 7 August 1959, 1.

Notes to pages 188–94   303

51 "Roads Open Up the Land," *CN*, 7 September 1967, centennial edition, in the section covering the period 1946–54.
52 "Sarto-St. Pierre Road Still Up in the Air," *CN*, 31 July 1959, 1; "Grunthal Road Need Draws Fire from Grit," *WT*, 5 February 1960, UofM Archives, WT Files 5742 Roads 1956–61.
53 "Sarto-Grunthal to Get Thru Highway," *CN*, 5 August 1960, 1; "Road Crews Begin Much-Needed Work," *CN*, 26 August 1960, section 2, 3; "Grunthal District Celebrates Completion of New Highway," *CN*, 2 December 1960, 1.
54 Britnell, "Perspective on Change," 439, table 2.
55 Dillabough, *Transportation in Manitoba*, 82.
56 Notes to *In Search of Utopia*, ch. 13, Francis Mss, MG A 55 ISU, AM.
57 *CN*, 10 February 1950, 1.
58 *CN*, 6 June 1949, 5.
59 Warkentin, *Descendants of Jacob Heinrich Thiessen*, 74.
60 *CN*, 24 August 1956, 6.
61 Canada, Advisory Committee on Reconstruction, *VI. Post-War Problems of Women*, 20–1.
62 Manitoba Power Commission, *M.P.C. Appliance Catalogue*, 8.
63 "Grunthal: A Tour of the Town," *CN*, 7 September 1967, section 3, 10, centennial edition.
64 Advertisement for appliances, *CN*, 13 February 1959, 6.
65 "Grunthal Enjoys Building Boom," *CN*, 2 June 1961, section 2, 4.
66 J.H. Warkentin, *Mennonite Settlements*, 253.
67 Francis original manuscript of *In Search for Utopia*, c. 1951, AM, MG9, A55, 645–6.
68 "Guenther Bros. Open New Store," *CN*, 2 June 1961, section 3, 4.
69 "Guenther Bros. Store is Nearing Completion," *CN*, 15 November 1963; "Business Had Start in 'Dirty Thirties'" and "Guenther Bros. Grand Opening," *CN*, 29 November 1963, section 3, 4; *Grunthal History 1874–1974*, 131–3.
70 D.J. Rempel "Recollections of the Formation of the Grunthal Co-op Store," *Grunthal History 1874–1974*, 122–4.
71 *CN*, 24 October 1947, 1.
72 "Grunthal: A Thriving Country Village," *CN*, 27 August 1948, 6.
73 *Grunthal History 1874–1974*, ch. 15 on businesses in Grunthal in 1974.
74 "A Grunthalbooster," "This Is Grunthal," *CN*, 7 March 1946, 1; "A Picture Story of Grunthal" [feature article with advertisements for local businesses], *CN*, 24 August 1956; "Personalities That Help to Make Grunthal Tick," *CN*, 29 March 1957, 13; "Grunthal Planning for 1959," *CN*, January 1959, 13; "Grunthal Plans Big for the Year Ahead," *CN*, 26 February 1960, 1–2.
75 *CN*, 18 April 1946, 4.
76 "Grunthal: A Thriving Country Village"; *Grunthal History 1874–1974*, 113 uses the same wording.

77 Francis c. 1947/48 in his "Report to the Historical Society of Manitoba," Ms. MG A 55/29, p. 700, AM.
78 Minutes, 1 February 1946, RM of Hanover, copy supplied by Eddie Guenther.
79 Elsie Janzen, "Grunthal Looks Back on 15 Years of Progress," *CN*, 19 January 1962, 3; *Grunthal History 1874–1974*, 115.
80 Jolys and Côté, *Pages de souvenirs et d'histoire*, 266–77, 326.
81 *CN*, 26 January 1951, 7.
82 Early 1950s copy of *Constitution* provided by Eddie Guenther.
83 "Grunthal C. of C. Reviews '58 Seeks New Prospects for '59," *CN*, 16 January 1959, 12; the president was the principal of the school, C.G. Unruh, hence the reference to "young people."
84 "Natural Gas for Grunthal," *CN*, 24 November, 1961, 1.
85 See T.D. Regehr, *Mennonites in Canada 1939–1970*, pt. 3.
86 Janzen, "Grunthal Looks Back on 15 Years."
87 J.A. Martens [Letter], *CN*, 3 September 1948.
88 Figures supplied by the Grunthal Credit Union Society Limited from a 1964 report and confirmed by contemporary newspaper reports: *CN*, 7 February 1958, 7; "Grunthal Credit Union Assets are Doubled," *CN*, 19 September 1958, 12.
89 *Grunthal History 1874–1974*, 143.
90 Manuscript of Francis, *In Search of Utopia*, c. 1951, PAM, MG9, A55, 645–6, AM.
91 J.H. Warkentin, *Mennonite Settlements*, 252–3.

11. A United and Divided Community

1 *CN*, 16 January 1959, 13; "Grunthal Chamber [of Commerce] Repairs Skating Rink," *CN*, 31 October 1958, 10; "Grunthal [Town Board] Holds Annual Meet," *CN*, 8 February 1963.
2 *CN*, 22 June 1962, section 5, 3; aerial photograph, cover of Block's *Beitrag zur Geschichte Gruenthal's*.
3 *CN*, 13 April 1962, section 2, 5.
4 *CN*, November 1951, 5.
5 United Farmers Union, *Manifesto*, 5.
6 "Farmers' Union Movement Gains Momentum in the South East," *CN*, 11 April 1952, 1.
7 "Our Values," Kiwanis International, 2018, https://www.kiwanis.org/about/values.
8 "Grunthal Better Farming Contest Winners Announced," *WFP*, 7 September 1933, 1; "First Kiwanian Better Farming Competition Held," *WFP*, 13 September 1933, 10.

9 "Agricultural News: Boys and Girls Start 16,500 Chicks," *WFP*, 3 June 1935, 13; "[Winnipeg Kiwanis] Hold Agricultural Fair at Grunthal," *WFP*, 24 September 1937, 15.
10 See history of the Canadian movement at "History," Manitoba 4-H Council, 2022, http://www.4h.mb.ca/history.
11 *Green and Gold of 1955*, 31; *CN*, 29 March 1957, 18.
12 "Grunthal 4-H Club Holds Annual Achievement Day," *CN*, 4 June 1954.
13 *Grunthal History 1874–1974*, 155–70 with numerous photographs.
14 *Grunthal History 1874–1974*, 155–9, with photographs.
15 *Grunthal History 1874–1974*, 191–3.
16 "Grunthal: A Thriving Country Village," *CN*, 27 August 1948, 8.
17 G. Friesen "Hockey and Prairie Cultural History," 220, 219.
18 M. Penner, "Die neue Maedchenschule," 38.
19 P. Thiessen [Letter from Grunthal dated 1 June 1931], *Nordwesten*, 10 June 1931, 5.
20 *SP*, January 1934.
21 Jack Thiessen "The Plot of Despair," 44–5.
22 *CN*, 16 January 1959, 13.
23 "Should Mennonites Boycott Hockey?" *CM*, 13 November 2000; for a Mennonite Brethren view of competitive sports in general, see Jake Suderman, "I've Got Game But Is It a Gift from God?" *Mennonite Brethren Herald*, 15 December 2006.
24 *CN*, 21 February 1946, 3; *CN*, 22 January 1960: *Grunthal History 1874–1974*, 199–201.
25 Steve Bisson, "Letters, Grunthal," *CN*, 26 January 1951, 1.
26 *Grunthal History 1874–1974*, 203–4.
27 "Grunthal Building Community Hall," *CN*, 29 June 1956, 1; on the final cost, see Janzen, "Grunthal Looks Back on 15 Years"; also, *Grunthal History 1874–1974*, 78–81; the building was later used as the town's fire station.
28 *Elim Gemeinde*, 57–9.
29 *Grunthal History 1874–1974*, 78–9.
30 B. Klassen, *Da Capo*.
31 *CN*, 14 August 1959, 12.
32 *CN*, 27 November 1959, 12.
33 *CN*, 21 February 1946, 4; Janzen, *Lifting the Veil*, 70–1; on Janzen, see H. Paetkau, "Jacob H. Janzen."
34 A. Reimer, "Derche bloom Räde."
35 *Grunthal History 1874–1974*, 80.
36 *CN*, 2 May 1958, 19; H. Paetkau, "Low German Drama," 28.
37 *CN*, 16 January 1959, 13.
38 Bruno-Jofré and Ross, "Decoding the Subjective Image," 576.

39 Minutes of meetings of the local committee, February 1942, Annual Reports from Goodwill School 1940–9, Department of Education, AM.
40 Minutes of meetings of the local committee, June 1949, Annual Reports from Goodwill School 1940–9, Department of Education, AM; *CN*, 17 June 1949, 5.
41 Notice to ratepayers, *CN*, 3 December 1948, 2; results: *CN*, 3 June 1949, 2.
42 Minutes of meetings of the local committee, November 1943, Annual Reports from Goodwill School 1940–9, Department of Education, AM.
43 Unruh obituary, *WFP*, 9 February 1995, 7.
44 See Aivalis, *Winnipeg 1919*, intro., for literature on the strikes.
45 Chafe, *Chalk, Sweat, and Cheers*, 123, 157.
46 "Trustees Accept Wage Schedule; Reject Negotiation Clauses," *CN*, 6 February 1951, 1.
47 Janis Thiessen, *Not Talking Union*.
48 *CN*, 16 March 1951, 1.
49 *CN*, 5 October 1951, 1.
50 Hildebrand, *Upholding the Old*.
51 *CN*, 9 February 1962, section 2, 1.
52 Manitoba, *Legislature Debate*, 30 October 1958, Vol. 1, No. 6a, 9.
53 Buri, *Between Education and Catastrophe*, intro.
54 *WT*, 5 April 1945.
55 *WT*, 30 May 1950.
56 *WT*, 8 May 1950; 2 December 1950; Rhineland's condemnation, *WT*, 21 December 1950.
57 Buri, *Between Education and Catastrophe*, ch. 9.
58 Manitoba, *Report of the Royal Commission on Education*, ch. 2.
59 Manitoba, *Legislature Debate*, 30 October 1958, Vol. 1, No. 6a, 9.
60 *CN*, 13 February 1959, 15.
61 Peter Desbarats, "Roblin Victory in Big Approval," *WT*, 28 February 1959.
62 Schellenberg, *Schools – Our Heritage* and an earlier draft dated 4 November 1982, Vertical Files, MHA, and contemporary newspaper reports.
63 "Southeast Divisions Turn Down School Propositions," *CN*, 16 March 1959.
64 Ross Henderson, "Reasons Behind the Rejection," *WT*, March 1959, undated cutting in UofM *WT* Files, 2757; Gregor and Wilson, *The Development of Education in Manitoba*, 123, quoting the *Red River Valley Echo*.
65 "Request for 'Second Chance' on School Vote Turned Down," *CN*, 13 March 1959, 1; also, *WT*, 13 March 1959, UofM *WT* Files, 2757.
66 "Notice to the Ratepayers Residing in the Proposed School Division of Hanover No. 28," *CN*, 8 May 1959, 15.
67 *CN*, 30 October 1959.
68 Manitoba, *Report of the Royal Commission on Education*, 23.
69 Schellenberg, *Schools – Our Heritage*, 261–2.

70 Stoesz, *A History of the Chortitzer Mennonite*.
71 Janzen, "Grunthal Looks Back on 15 Years," 3.
72 Gerbrandt, *Adventure in Faith*, 238–40.
73 *Grunthal History 1874–1974*, 68–77; R. Reimer, *Grunthal E.M.B. Church*.
74 M. Reimer, *One Quilt, Many Pieces*, ch. 15.
75 "Professor Takes Look at 'Steinbach Philosophy,'" *CN*, 19 April 1965, 1.
76 28.2 per cent were aged zero to ten years and 24.4 per cent were aged eleven to twenty: "Eine Einwandererstatistik," *MR*, 22 April 1925, 5.

12. Generational Transition and Succession

1 Urry, "The Cost of Community," 37.
2 Andrew R. Shelly, and Tilman R. Smith, "Homes, Retirement and Nursing," Global Anabaptist Mennonite Encyclopedia Online, revised 15 January 2017, https://gameo.org/index.php?title=Homes,_Retirement_and_Nursing&oldid=143601.
3 *CN*, 12 August 1960, section 3, 2–3.
4 "Approval Given Old Folks' Home," *CN*, 5 June 1959, 14.
5 "Grunthal Planning for 1959," *CN*, 16 January 1959, 13.
6 *Grunthal History 1874–1974*, 87–8.
7 *CN*, 27 November 1959, 12.
8 *CN*, 28 August 1960, 1.
9 *CN*, 26 August 1960, 1.
10 *CN*, 22 January 1960.
11 Epp, *Mennonite Women*; O.D. Regehr, "From Refugee to Suburbanite."
12 *Elim Gemeinde Grunthal*, 40–2; Elim Mennonite Church, *Our Walk with God*, 80–4.
13 Elim Mennonite Church, 81.
14 Elim Mennonite Church, 65.
15 [Response from Grunthal,] Supplemental Questionnaire, History Project by Anna Ens, Conference of Mennonites in Manitoba, 4577–26, MHA.
16 Schellenberg, *Schools – Our Heritage*, 72–3.
17 Franz, "Grunthal's Schools," 96; Franz taught in the elementary school for many years.
18 Figures in Schellenberg, *Schools – Our Heritage*, 73.
19 C.G. Unruh, "Grunthal C. of C. Reviews '58 [and] Seeks New Prospects for '59," *CN*, 16 January 1959, 13.
20 A.J. Friesen (1919–2011), son of Johann and Anna (Driedger) Friesen and a younger brother of John (Baker) Friesen; *Descendants of Cornelius Friesen*, 127–8.
21 A.J. Friesen, *Prost Mahlzeit!*; A.J. Friesen, *Gott grüsse dich!*
22 D. Sch[ellenberg?], "Das Neue Buch," *Mennonitische Welt*, October 1952.

23 Kirkconnell, "New-Canadian Letters," 436; he described the play as "spirited."
24 D.H. Paetkau, *Warum verlieren wir unsere Jugend?*
25 In Epp and Wiebe, *Unter dem Nordlicht*, 65–74; A.J. Friesen, *Aus Gottes linker Hand*.
26 "Grunthal Student Goes to Germany," *CN*, 19 August 1955, 1.
27 Jack Thiessen, *Studien zum Wortschatz der kanadischen Mennoniten*; the dictionary was first published in Steinbach, then by the University of Wisconsin Press in 2003; the latest edition by "The Friends of Jack Thiessen" was published in New Bothwell in 2018; Considine, "Mennonite Low German Dictionary."
28 His translations into Low German of classic works included Saint-Exupéry's *The Little Prince*, Busch's *Max and Moritz*, and Lewis Carroll's *Alice's Adventures in Wonderland*.
29 "Eena oaft en Stetj Bottabroot,/De aundre oaft en Heenafoot;/Daut ess goot, daut ess goot,/Woa wie uck waut oawe" (Jack Thiessen, *Mennonite Low German Dictionary*, 498).
30 *Grunthal History 1874–1974*, 133.
31 "Guenther Bros. Open New Store," *CN*, June 1961, section 3, 4.
32 "Guenther Bros. Store Is Nearing Completion," *CN*, 15 November 1963, section 3, 4; "Business Had Start in 'Dirty Thirties,'" *CN*, 29 November 1963, section 3, 4; "Guenther Bros. Grand Opening," *CN*, 29 November 1963, section 3, 4.
33 "Guenther Bros. Grand Opening," *CN*, 29 November 1963, section 3, 4.
34 Figures based on Hanover Municipal Council taxation records; not all are consistent.
35 "Grunthal Enjoys Building Boom," *CN*, 2 June 1961.
36 On Stroeter see J.B. Toews, "The Calm before the Storm."
37 Elim Congregation Meeting Books, Book 2, 39–43, held by the congregation, and Microfilm 186, MHA.
38 Heese, "Ein Bericht zum 50. Jubilaeum."
39 *Grunthal Gemeindeblatt*, 24 December 1961, 2388-02, MHA.
40 Nick and John Janz, conversations with the author; obituaries in *CN*, 26 July 2002, 4; *CN*, 4 May 2006.
41 Adolf Ens, *Becoming a National Church*; Anna Ens, *In Search of Unity*.
42 Berg, *From Russia with Music*, 15–16.
43 *Vorsänger* Report in Elim Gemeinde Grunthal, *Elim Gemeinde 1969 Jahrbuch*, 6, 2389-05, MHA.
44 Ediger, *Crossing the Divide*; J.A. Loewen "The German Language, Culture and the Faith."
45 "Why Do Mennonite Circles Choose German as a Second Language?" *CN*, 23 October 1959, 3; *CM*, 23 October 1959, 4.

46 "History of Our Church Services and Operations," Elim Mennonite Church, Grunthal, Manitoba, https://www.elimmennonite.org/history/.
47 Correspondence with Congregations S.B.S. Questionnaire 1961, Conference of Mennonites in Manitoba fonds, 615 (24), 28 August 1961, MHA.
48 Elim Gemeinde Grunthal, *Elim Gemeinde 1969 Jahrbuch*, 22–3, 2389–05, MHA.
49 G. Friesen, "Elim Mennonite Church."
50 G. Friesen, "Elim Mennonite Church," 1–2; the first printing, and only in German, was *Statuten der Mennonitengemeinde Elim*; earlier versions not printed and with amendments, are held by the Elim Congregation.
51 G[erhard]. Loewen, "Wie kann man die Sinn fuer das Deutsche unter der Jugend wecken und pflegen (Referat auf der Lehrer-Konferenz zu Steinbach, Man.)," *Nordwesten*, September 1926. Loewen was a popular Mennonite teacher and poet in Russia and Canada: see H. Loewen, "Gerhard Loewen (1863–1946)."
52 T.D. Regehr, *Mennonites in Canada, 1939–1970*, 295–6n21.
53 G.J. Ens, *Die Schule muss sein*, 151–4; T.D. Regehr, *Mennonites in Canada, 1939–1970*, 254, on the circumstances of Peters leaving MCI in 1948; on his attitude to High German before and after the Second World War, see Bergen, "The World Wars and Education," 163–4, 166–7.
54 Peters's letter dated 1 September 1952 outlining the *Verein*'s founding principles along with other material is found in the Board of Colonization Files, 1334 (1020), MHA. The organization's name changed over time; its extensive files are in MHA, 4146–9.
55 Klassen to Peters, May 1953, Mennonite German Society 4147, File 14, MHA Archives.
56 T.D. Regehr, "Walter Quiring."
57 Urry, "The Reading Worlds of Russlaender and Kanadier."
58 First published in *Bote* and separately as a pamphlet: D.H. Paetkau, *Warum verlieren wir unsere Jugen?*
59 D.H. Epp, "David Paetkau – Music His First Love."
60 Wealthy Mennonite men did marry Russian women before the revolution, but it was uncommon.

13. Becoming Canadian

1 Hinther, *Perogies and Politics*, ch. 6.
2 Quiring and Bartel, *Als ihre Zeit erfüllt war*, translated in, *In the Fullness of Time*; and Gerhard Lohrenz, *Heritage Remembered*.
3 John J. Friesen, "Lohrenz, Gerhard (1899–1986)," Global Anabaptist Encyclopedia Online, 1989, https://gameo.org/index.php?title=Lohrenz,_Gerhard_(1899–1986)&oldid=143052.

4 Block, "Vorwort" to *Beitrag zur Geschichte Gruenthal's*, 2.
5 *Grunthal History 1874–1974*, "Dedication," iv; "Foreword," iii.
6 *Green and Gold: Grunthal Collegiate 1967/68*, 3.
7 A. Warkentin, *Reflections on Our Heritage*, 18; *Grunthal History 1874–1974*, 17; L. Driedger, "Native Rebellion and Mennonite Invasion"; L. Klippenstein, "Manitoba Métis and Mennonite Immigration"; Giesbrecht, "Métis, Mennonites and the 'Unsettled Prairie'"; J. Wiebe, "On the Mennonite-Métis Borderland."
8 *CN*, 3 June 1970, 1.
9 *CN*, 3 July, 1970; map of route: "Royal Tour," *CN*, 8 July 1970, 1.
10 [Report by correspondent of the Elim congregation], *Bote*, 20 October 1970, 7.
11 Martin Durksen, "Grunthal feiert Centennial-Dankgottesdienst," *Bote*, 1 September 1970, 6–7.
12 *Grunthal History 1874–1974*, 224–6; "1970 Manitoba Centennial as celebrated in Grunthal," 223–32; on Hanover celebrations, including Grunthal, see Penner, *Hanover: One Hundred Years*, pt. 6.
13 [*Elim Gemeinde*; announcement by J.J. Friesen], *Bote*, 6 July 1971, 12.
14 Jeremy Wiebe, "Performing Ethnicity."
15 J.F. Warkentin, *Bote*, 16 July 1974.
16 Heese, "Ein Bericht zum 50. Jubilaeum."
17 Patterson, "The Red Ensign."
18 Johnson, "The Last Gasp of Empire"; Igartua, *The Other Quiet Revolution*, 175–92.
19 Henry T. Boaler [Letter from Otterburne], *CN*, 1 January 1965.
20 Grebstad, "The Flag of Our Fathers?"
21 Urry, *Mennonites, Politics and Peoplehood*, 208–9.
22 T.D. Regehr, *Peace, Order & Good Government*.
23 Feigert, *Canada Votes, 1935–1988*, ch. 10 for Manitoba; Adams, *Politics in Manitoba*; Urry, *Mennonites, Politics, and Peoplehood*, ch. 9.
24 Based on official returns in Canada, Office of the Chief Electoral Officer *Statutory Report of the Chief Electoral Officer of Canada*.
25 *CN*, 17 October 1947, 1; results in *CN*, 31 October 1947, 1.
26 Urry, "The Russian Mennonites," 31–2.
27 Colley, *Britons*.
28 Bruno-Jofré, "Citizenship and Schooling in Manitoba."
29 Osborne, "Teaching History in Schools."
30 Harker, "Canadian Literature in Canadian Schools."
31 Igartua, *The Other Quiet Revolution*; Buckner, "Canada and the End of Empire."
32 Champion, *The Strange Demise of British Canada*.
33 Conway, "From Britishness to Multiculturalism."
34 Canada, *Report of the Royal Commission on Bilingualism and Biculturalism*.

35 *Brief submitted to the Royal Commission on Bilingualism and Biculturalism. By the Mennonite Society for the Promotion of the German Language in Canada*, Winnipeg, 1964, typescript in the University of Winnipeg Library – F 1035 M4M4; Haque, "Multiculturalism, Language, and Immigration Integration," 221n1, cites a version in the papers of the Commission in Library and Archives Canada.
36 *Brief, Manitoba Mennonite Trustee Association and Manitoba Mennonite Educational Committee*, Winkler, Manitoba, 1964.
37 Ediger, *Crossing the Divide*, ch. 5.
38 Stoesz, "Abraham J. Thiessen"; Urry, *Mennonites, Politics, and Peoplehood*, 225.
39 J.N. Neufeld, "Why Not Two Languages?" *CM*, 10 April 1959, 2, with extensive subsequent correspondence between April and June; George Doerksen, "Manitoba Educational Thrust," *CM*, 25 April 1958, 1, 8; "Education Briefs Ask – Strengthen Religion, Language Instruction," *CM*, 13 February 1959, 1, 11 (with submissions); D.K. Duerksen, "Why Do Mennonite Circles Choose German as a Second Language?" *CN*, 23 October 1959, 3; also in *CM*, 23 October 1959, 4.
40 Janis Thiessen, *Necessary Idealism*.
41 Prymak, "The Royal Commission and Rudnyckyj's Mission."
42 Yuzyk, "Canada: A Multicultural Nation"; Rose et al., "Discussion of Senator Yuzyk's Paper"; Yuzyk briefly responded in "Reply, Rather than Retort."
43 Karpiak, *Senator Paul Yuzyk, 1913–1986*; his address contained more detailed figures.
44 *The Manitoba Multiculturalism Act*, C.C.S.M. c. M223, https://web2.gov .mb.ca/laws/statutes/ccsm/_pdf.php?cap=m223.
45 Smucker, "Faith Versus Culture?"
46 Peacock, *Twenty Ethnic Songs*, 48–62; V.C. Friesen, *The Windmill Turning*; D.H. Klassen, *Singing Mennonite*.
47 Judith Klassen, "Music, Mimesis, and Modulation."
48 Driediger, *No Dancing God*, 15.
49 Graybill and Arthur, "The Social Control of Women's Bodies"; Epp, *Mennonite Women*, 183–203; L.S. Plett, "Refashioning Kleine Gemeinde Women's Dress."
50 Dawson, *Group Settlement*, pt. 2: "The Mennonites"; Francis, "The Nature of the Ethnic Group"; Francis, *In Search of Utopia*.
51 Loewen, *Blumenort*, v; Urry, *None but Saints*, 4.
52 *Bulletin*, Canadian Ethnic Studies Association 6, (1979), 14; "Agriculture Societies Receive Improvement Grants to Upgrade Exhibition Buildings and Fair Grounds," Government of Manitoba, 29 July 1998, https://news .gov.mb.ca/news/index.html?item=23510&posted=1998-07-29.
53 Haque, *Multiculturalism within a Bilingual Framework*, 99–100.

54 A. Reimer, discussions with the author.
55 Thiessen, *Low German Mennonite Dictionary*, 68, 81.
56 Bender, "The Anabaptist Vision"; Sawatsky, *History and Ideology*, viii.
57 Loewen, *Village among Nations*.
58 Essays on "Return of the Kanadier" *JMS*, 22 (2004); Loewen, *Village among Nations*, ch. 6.
59 Gerhard Hildebrandt, Gerhard Wölk, and Hans von Nissen, "Umseidler (Aussiedler)," Global Anabaptist Mennonite Encyclopedia Online, 1989, https://gameo.org/index.php?title=Umsiedler_(Aussiedler).
60 Granatstein and Bothwell, *Pirouette*, 52.
61 Elvins, "A River of Money Flowing South."
62 "History of Liquor Regulation in Manitoba," *Beer Winnipeg* (blog), April 2016, https://beerwinnipeg.files.wordpress.com/2016/04/liquor-laws-history.pdf.
63 Loewen, *Village among Nations*, ch. 7.
64 Loewen and Urry, "A Tale of Two Newspapers."
65 Jeremy Wiebe, "A Different Kind of Station"; Balzer, "Exploring the Timbre of Mennonite Radio."
66 F.H. Epp, *Revival Fires in Manitoba*; Loewen and Nolt, *Seeking Places of Peace*, 148–9; Nolt, "Activist Impulses," especially 229–32 for the Canadian prairies.
67 Loewen, "Mennonite 'Repertoires of Contention.'"
68 Vogt, *The Steinbach Saga*, 55; C.A. DeFehr, "Meine Reiseeindruecke," *MR*, 6–13 April 1938, 10.
69 M. Redekop, *Making Believe*, 33–9; 183–4; 231–2.
70 Kuffert, *Canada before Television*.
71 *CN*, 15 February 1963, section 3, 4.
72 *CN*, 9 November 1962, section 3, 3.
73 M. Epp, *Eating Like a Mennonite*, ch. 3.
74 "Eine Einwandererstatistik," *MR*, 22 April 1925, 5.
75 But see G. Penner, "Mennonites and Middle Names."
76 *Grunthal History 1874–1974*, 96.
77 Holm, "Name Authorities."
78 "Kay-Wye: Grunthal Leaders Ponder Big Name-Changing Offer," *CN*, 20 March 1964, 1; "Grunthal Awaits Verdict on Its Future as C-K-Y," *CN*, 3 April 1964, 1.

Conclusion: The Past in the Present

1 Dawson, *Group Settlement*, ix, 171.
2 Manitoba, *Rural Municipality of Hanover: A Background Report into Development and Growth Potential*; supplemented by figures from the *Bureau of Statistics for the Census of Canada* for 1976.

3 Another factor is that later descendants of Russländer have left the church completely, especially when they also have married non-Mennonites.
4 P. Redekop, "The Mennonite Family"; on the history of 1874 immigrants to the USA, see Stevenson and Everson, "The Cultural Context of Fertility Transition."
5 A similar pattern could probably be seen in the Chortitzer Church, now the CMC, although no reliable figures are available.
6 Epp and Redekopp, "Grunthal Bergthaler Mennonite Church," give slightly lower figures. The church withdrew from Mennonite Church Manitoba in 2001 and therefore it is not listed on the All Churches of Canada website: "Churches in Grunthal, Manitoba, Canada," All Churches of Canada, 2023, https://grunthal-mb.allcanadachurches.com/church/.
7 These have their own or related websites: Christian Mennonite Conference, http://www.cmconference.ca/; Grunthal EMB Church, https://www.grunthalemb.com/; there is also a Reinland Mennonite Church connected with the town.
8 "History of Elim Mennonite Church, Grunthal," Elim Mennonite Church, Grunthal, Manitoba, https://www.elimmennonite.org/history/.
9 "About Grunthal History," Village of Grunthal, South Eastern MB, 2023, https://www.grunthal.ca/about.php.
10 "Grunthal, Manitoba," Wikimedia Foundation, revised 28 January 2023, https://en.wikipedia.org/wiki/Grunthal,_Manitoba.
11 All figures given for 2016 are from Statistics Canada, "Grunthal [Population centre], Manitoba and Manitoba [Province]," Census Profile, 2016 Census, Statistics Canada Catalogue no. 98–316-X2016001, updated 18 June 2019, https://www12.statcan.gc.ca/census-recensement/2016/dp-pd/prof/details/page.cfm?Lang=E&Geo1=POPC&Code1=1414&Geo2=PR&Code2=46&SearchText=grunthal&SearchType=Begins&SearchPR=01&B1=All&TABID=1&type=0.
12 Statistics Canada, "Manitoba," 2011 National Household Survey: Data Tables, https://www12.statcan.gc.ca/nhs-enm/2011/dp-pd/dt-td/Rp-eng.cfm?LANG=E&APATH=5&DETAIL=0&DIM=0&FL=A&FREE=0&GC=46&GID=0&GK=1&GRP=0&PID=105399&PRID=0&PTYPE=105277&S=0&SHOWALL=0&SUB=0&Temporal=2013&THEME=95&VID=0&VNAMEE=&VNAMEF=.
13 Statistics Canada, "Appendix 2.14, Religions disseminated in 2021, 2011 and 2001," Dictionary, Census of Population, 2021, 26 October 2022, https://www12.statcan.gc.ca/census-recensement/2021/ref/dict/app/index-eng.cfm?ID=a2_14.

Appendix Two: Agreement with the Intercontinental Company over Land on East Reserve

1 CMBC Files, Vol. 1171, No. 58, MHA.

Bibliography

Archival Sources

Canada

Alberta

Glenbow – Alberta Institute Archives, Calgary, Alberta
  Canadian Colonization Association, Reports of the Winnipeg Office
  Canadian Pacific Railway Papers 1886–1958

British Columbia

Mennonite Historical Society of British Columbia, Abbotsford
  David P. Heidebrecht Fonds

Manitoba

Archives of Manitoba
  Advisory Committee on Coordination of Post-War Planning, Files and Reports, 1943–6
  Department of Agriculture and Immigration [later Department of Agriculture]:
    Cooperative Services Branch, Registrar of Cooperatives, Reports, 1916–59.
    Dairy Division, Scrapbooks, 1933–47, 1948–54, 1955–9.
  Department of Education Papers:
    Department of Finance, Post-War Reconstruction Files, 1941–8.
    Francis, E.K. Typescript Report (1947) for Manitoba Historical Society and drafts (1951/54) of *In Search of Utopia*, MG9 A55.
    Miscellaneous Records, School Divisions, 1950–69.

School District Correspondence, Official Trustee Correspondence, 1920–45.
Howard Winkler Papers
Manitoba Assembly, Provincial Election returns, 1922–45
Royal Commission on Education, 1957–8:
    Brief submitted to the Royal Commission on Education by the Manitoba Mennonite Educational Committee, Winnipeg, November 1957.
    Brief submitted to the Royal Commission on Education by the Mennonite Collegiate Institute, Gretna, MB, November 1957.
    Unruh, Cornelius G. "A History of the Goodwill School District, Number 1967." Paper submitted to the University of Manitoba, December 1956. AM, MG9, D15 (since transferred to the University of Manitoba).

Centre for Mennonite Brethren Studies Winnipeg
B.B. Janz Papers
Mennonite Brethren Study Conferences (Study Papers) 1956–present:
Loewen, J[acob].A, "The German Language, Culture and the Faith," A Study Paper Read at the Conference on "Dynamics of Faith and Culture in Mennonite Brethren History," MB Studies Winnipeg, 14–15 November 1966. (3, Box 15, File E)

Elim Church, Grunthal
Congregational Membership Record Book
Minutes of Congregational Meetings

Grunthal
Credit Union:
Application for Letters Patent of Incorporation of a Credit Union Society under the "Companies Act," 18 April 1942.
Grunthal Credit Union Society Limited, Report 1964. (Typescript showing growth of assets, 1943 to 1964.)
Letters Patent of Incorporation of Grunthal Credit Union Society Limited under the "Companies Act," 29 April 1942.

Mennonite Heritage Archives, Winnipeg
Benjamin Ewert Papers
B.J. Schellenberg Papers
Canadian Board of Colonization Papers, 1923–
Conference of Mennonites in Manitoba fonds
Correspondence with Congregations [S.B.S. Questionnaire 1961]
Education Committee Files
Elim Church Register and Records, Microfilm
Friesen, Gerald, "Elim Mennonite Church of Grunthal: Historical Update 1979–1985," Unpublished Essay for Professor A. Ens, Vertical Files
History Project by Anna Ens [Questionnaires to congregations]
J.J. Hildebrand Papers

Johann P. Bückert Papers
John P. Dyck Papers
Johann J. Enns Papers
Peter H. Enns Papers
Manitoba Mennonite Mutual Insurance Company fonds:
  Individual insured inventories by village, 1936–49.
  Lists of policyholders and inventory lists, 1940–1.
Mennonite German Society, 1952–c. 1980
Schellenberg, John K, [Draft of a history of the Hanover School Division,] 4 November 1982, Vertical Files
School Registers and Account Books for Gravel Ridge School, Goodwill School, Spencer School (including Spencer North and Spencer South)
Toews, Gerhard, *Schoenfeld: The Development and Destruction of a German Settlement in the Ukraine*, Translated by Eric Ens in Collaboration with Catherine Kirkland and S. John T. Kirkland, 2000, Rare Book Collection
Wiens, David, "The History of the Elim Mennonite Church," Unpublished Essay for Professor John Friesen and Adolf Ens, March 1980, Vertical Files
ZMIK Papers

Manitoba Legislature Library, Winnipeg
  H.L. Patterson & H.W. Trevor, *The Dairy Farm Business: A Preliminary Report on an Economic Survey of Farms Producing Dairy Products for Sale in Eastern Manitoba ... June 1, 1942 to May 31, 1944*, Typescript c. 1945

Rural Municipality of Hanover Records, Municipal Office, Manitoba
  By-Laws of the Municipality, 1920–37
  Minutes of Council Meetings, 1927–50
  Personal Property Tax Assessments 1940–5
  Petitions to the Councillors, RM of Hanover, 1920–50
  Tax Assessment Rolls, 1921–50
  Tax Collector's Rolls, 1921–50
  Tax Sales Files, 1920–50
Section maps showing landownership in the RM of Hanover, 1926, 1948/49

Ontario

Brock University, Archives and Special Collections
  Steingart, Frank (Franz), Interview, sound recording by Ellen Baar, Mennonites of Niagara: Pioneers, SPCL FC 3140.8 M45 B374 1977.

Mennonite Archives of Ontario, Conrad Grebel University College, Waterloo
  Abram A. Peters Papers
  Frank H. Epp Collection:
    Mennonite Exodus Research Notes.
    Mennonites in Canada Files.

Herbert P. Enns Collection
J.H. Janzen Fonds:
Bestvater, Abram, Franz Guenther, J.J. Rempel, and Frank [Franz] Steingart, interviews recorded 1976–8 by Henry Paekau and Stan Dueck, Russian Mennonite Immigrants Oral History Project.
Janzen, Jacob H., "The Activities of the K.f.K in Russia from the Year 1922 to 1924, A.D.," Unpublished account prepared for C. Henry Smith, Bluffton College, 1928.
Rempel, Jacob J., *Gedanken und Erinnerungen aus den Jahren 1918–1924 von J.J. Rempel, Virgil.*

United States of America

Mennonite Library and Archives, North Newton, Kansas
A.A. Friesen Papers (MLA 60–9):
Doerksen, G. and J. Driedger, "Die Schönfelders Gemeinde," c. 1924. (English translation in Toews, *Mennonites in Ukraine amid Civil War and Anarchy*.)
H.P. Krehbiel Papers, MLA Mss 12, Box 33, Folder 208:
History of the General Conference – Canadian District.
Reply from J.J. Enns on the Grünthal congregation, May 1938.

Other Unpublished Sources

Block, Jacob H. *God's Footprints*. [Mimeographed biography.] Translated by Agnes Dyck. Grunthal, n.d.
Guenther. [Miscellaneous store receipts from the 1930s.] Originals held by E. Guenther.
Klassen, Peter P. [Personal account books, 1941–8.] Copies of exercise books; originals held by Peter Klassen.
Neufeld, Jacob J. *My Childhood in Russia*. [Unpublished notes, 1908–87, in the author's possession.]
Penner, Irma [Wiens]. *In Search of Our Heritage: Prussia to South Russia to Canada. A Journey with the Wiens Family and Janz Family*. Fredericton, NB: printed by the , 2020.
– *The Story of Aunt Erna: Her Childhood in Russia*. Fredericton, NB: printed by the , 2002.
Rempel, Jacob J. "Grunthal, 1926–1974." [Undated typescript headed Virgil, Box 205, Ont. From Henry Rempel, Winnipeg, via David Rempel-Smucker.] N.p., 2004, 7 pp.
Warkentin, John H. "Memoirs." [Undated typescript in the author's possession.] N.p., n.d. 22 pp.

Theses

Buhr, Joanna R. "Pursuit of a Vision: Persistence and Accommodation among Coaldale Mennonites from the Mid-nineteen-twenties to World War II." Master's thesis, University of Calgary, 1986.
Dirks, Nathan R. "War Without, Struggle Within: Canadian Mennonite Enlistments During the Second World War." Master's thesis, McMaster Divinity College, 2010.
Dueck, Theodore J.H. "Mennonite Federal Electoral Behaviour on the West Reserve in Manitoba, 1887–1935." Master's thesis, University of Manitoba, 1987.
Epp, Frank H. "An Analysis of Germanism and National Socialism in the Immigrant Newspapers of a Canadian Minority Group, the Mennonites in the 1930s." PhD diss., University of Minnesota, 1965.
Friesen, Abraham. "Emigration in Mennonite History with Special Reference to the Conservative Mennonite Emigration from Canada to Mexico and South America after World War One." Master's thesis, University of Manitoba, 1960.
Friesen, John. "The Manitoba Sugar Beet Industry: A Geographical Study." Master's thesis, University of Manitoba, 1962.
Jones, Cynthia. "Grounding Diaspora in Experience: Niagara Mennonite Identity." PhD diss., Wilfrid Laurier University, 2010.
Kampen, Melanie. "The Spectre of Reconciliation: Mennonite Theology, Martyrdom, and Trauma." PhD diss., University of Toronto, 2019.
Klassen, Shelisa. "'Recruits and Comrades' in 'A War of Ambition': Mennonite Immigrants in Late 19th Century Manitoba Newspapers." Master's thesis, University of Manitoba, 2016.
Letkemann, Peter. "The Hymnody and Choral Music of Mennonites in Russia, 1789–1915." PhD diss., University of Toronto, 1985.
Paetkau, Henry. "Separation or Integration? The Russian Mennonite Immigrant Community in Ontario, 1924–45." PhD diss., University of Western Ontario, 1986.
– "A Struggle for Survival: The Russian Mennonite Immigrants in Ontario, 1924–39." Master's thesis, University of Waterloo, 1977.
Regehr, Olga Dyck. "From Refugee to Suburbanite: The Survival and Acculturation of North Kildonan Mennonite Immigrant Women, 1927–1947." Master's thesis, University of Manitoba, 2006.
Ross, Gerald G. "A Contribution to the Study of *Völkische Ideologie* and *Deutschtumsarbeit* among the Germans in Canada During the Inter-war Period." Master's thesis, Lakehead University, 1996.
Sawatsky, Roland M. "The Control of Social Space in Mennonite Housebarns of Manitoba (1874–1940)." PhD diss., Simon Fraser University, 2004.

320   Bibliography

Stoesz, Conrad. "The Creation of an Identity: The Conscientious Objector in Canadian Mennonite Memory." Master's thesis, University of Manitoba/University of Winnipeg, 2018.
Warkentin, John. "The Mennonite Settlements of Southern Manitoba." PhD diss., University of Toronto, 1960.
Wiebe, Jeremy. "A Different Kind of Station: Radio Southern Manitoba and the Reformulation of Mennonite Identity, 1957–1977." Master's thesis, University of Manitoba, 2008.

Primary Sources

Baerg, Anna. *Diary of Anna Baerg, 1916–1924.* Edited and translated by Gerald Peters. Winnipeg: CMBC Publications, 1985.
Belton, George R. "German in Our Schools." *Educational Journal of Western Canada* 3 (1902): 262.
"Bericht über die Versammlung der Neu-Eingewanderten von Manitoba am 20 und 21 Juni 1928 in Winnipeg." *MR*, 11 July 1928.
Bestvater, Margareta. "Der Tabea Naeverein." In *Grunthal History, 1874–1974*, 40–2..
Block, Jacob. *Beitrag zur Geschichte Gruenthal's: 1874–1967.* Steinbach, MB: printed by the , 1967.
Braun, Ernest N., and Glen R. Klassen. *Historical Atlas of the East Reserve.* Winnipeg: Manitoba Mennonite Historical Society, 2015.
Canada. *Defence of Canada Regulations.* Ottawa: Government of Canada, 1939.
– *National Registration Regulations 1940.* Ottawa: J.O. Patenaude, 1940.
– *National Registration Regulations 1940: Instructions for the Use of Deputy Registrars and Voluntary Assistant Deputy Registrars.* Ottawa: J.O. Patenaude, 1940.
Canada, Advisory Committee on Reconstruction. *I. Agricultural Policy: Final Report for the Subcommittee,* 16 December 1943. Ottawa: Edmond Cloutier, 1944.
– *VI. Post-War Problems of Women: Final Report for the Subcommittee,* 30 November 1943. Ottawa: Edmond Cloutier, 1945.
Canada, Indian Claims Commission, Shelia Purdy, Daniel J. Bellegarde, and Alan Holman. *Roseau River Anishinabe First Nation: Report on 1903 Surrender Inquiry.* Ottawa: Indian Claims Commission, 2007.
Canada, Office of the Chief Electoral Officer. *Statutory Report of the Chief Electoral Officer of Canada.* Ottawa: Chief Electoral Officer of Canada, [1940–72].
Chortitzer Mennonite Conference, 1874–1990. Steinbach, MB: Chortitzer Mennonite Conference, 2004.
Die Mennoniten-Gemeinden in Russland während der Kriegs-und Revolutionsjahre 1914 bis 1920. Heilbronn am Neckar, Germany: Kommissions-Verlag der Mennonitische Flüchtlingsfürsorge e.v., 1921.

Dillabough, James V. *Transportation in Manitoba*. Winnipeg: Manitoba Economic Survey Board, 1938.
Dyck, Arnold. *Collected Works*. Steinbach, MB: Manitoba Mennonite Historical Society, 1988.
Dyck, John P., ed. *Troubles and Triumphs, 1914–1924: Excerpts from the Diary of Peter J. Dyck, Ladekopp, Molotschna Colony, Ukraine*. Springstein, MB: printed by the editor, 1981.
"Eindrücke von der Provinzial-Delegierten-Versammlung der seit 1923 in Manitoba eingewanderten Mennoniten am 18. und 19. Juni d[iesem] J[ahre] in der Zionskirche der Mennonitengemeinde Winnipeg." *MR*, 9–23 July 1930.
Elim Gemeinde Grunthal. *Elim Gemeinde 1969 Jahrbuch*. Grunthal, MB. [Copy in MHA 2389–05].
– *Elim Gemeinde Grunthal, Manitoba 1927–1972*. Steinbach, MB: Martens Printing for the Grunthal Gemeinde, c. 1972.
– *Statuten der Mennonitengemeinde Elim zu Grunthal*. Winnipeg: Regehr's Printing, 1962. [Translated into English, 1979].
Elim Mennonite Church of Grunthal History Book Committee. *Our Walk with God: 75th Anniversary of the Elim Mennonite Church, Grunthal, MB*. Altona, MB: D.W. Friesen, 2002.
Enns, H.C. "An die gewesenen Glieder der Kirchengemeinde zu Schönfeld, Gouv. Jekater., Alexandrowsk Kr., Süd-Russland." *MR*, 3 June 1925.
Enns, J.J. "Historisches Material der Gemeinde Elim zu Grunthal Manitoba 1927–1952." *Elim Jahrbuch* (1969): 33–42.
– "Historisches Material der Gemeinde Elim zu Grunthal Manitoba 1927–1952/Historical Notes of the Grunthal Church from the Period 1927–1952." In *Elim Gemeinde Grunthal, Manitoba 1927–1972*. Steinbach, MB: Martens Printing for the Grunthal Gemeinde, c. 1972.
– "Zu Hause." *MR*, 3 June 1925.
Epp, Frank H., ed. *Revival Fires in Manitoba: A Report on the Work of Brunk Revivals, Inc., in the Manitoba Communities of Steinbach, Winkler, Altona and Winnipeg, June to September 1957*. Denbigh, VA: Brunk Revivals Inc., 1957.
Fisher, Robert D. *Robert D. Fisher Manual of Valuable and Worthless Securities*. New York: Robert D. Fisher & Company, 1941.
Franz, Margaret. "Grunthal's Schools." In *Grunthal History 1874–1974*, 91–5.
Friesen, Abraham J. *Aus Gottes linker Hand: Stimme eines Irrenden. Gedichte*. Toronto: The German Canadian Historical Association, 1995.
– *Gott grüsse dich!* Grünthal, MB: printed by the , 1952.
– *Prost Mahlzeit!* Grünthal, MB: printed by the ,1949.
Friesen, C.H. "The Formation of the Bergthaler Church of Grunthal." In *Grunthal History 1874–1974*, 74–6.
Friesen, John. *The Glenlea Mennonite Church History*. Winnipeg: Fortress Software, 2002.

Friesen, W. "A Mennonite Community in the East Reserve: Its Origin and Growth." *Papers Read before the Historical and Scientific Society of Manitoba*, ser. 3, no. 19 (1962–3): 24–43.
Grant, H.C., C.B. Davidson, and J.E. Chernick. *Agricultural Income and Rural Municipal Government in Manitoba*. Winnipeg: Economic Survey Board, 1939.
The Green and Gold of 1955. Grunthal, MB: Goodwill School, 1956.
The Green and Gold: Grunthal Collegiate 1967/68. Grunthal, MB: 1968.
Grose, R.E. *Industrial Resources of Manitoba*. Winnipeg: Department of Industry and Commerce, Province of Manitoba, 1954.
Grunthal History, 1874–1974. Grunthal, MB: Grunthal History Book Committee, 1974.
Günther, Waldemar, David P. Heidebrecht, and Gerhard J. Peters, eds. *"Onsji Tjedils." Ersatzdienst der Mennoniten in Russland unter den Romanows*. Yarrow, BC: Columbia Press, 1966.
Heese, D[ietrich W.] . "Ein Bericht zum 50. Jubilaeum der Elim Gemeinde zu Grunthal." *MM* 7, no. 1 (1977): 23–4; also, *Bote*, 18 July 1979.
– "Farms: Memories." In *Grunthal History 1874–1974*, 173–5.
Heidebrecht, D.P. *Deutsches Sprachbuch mit besonderer Berücksichtigung der Rechtschreibung: für die Oberabteilung (etwa sechster, siebenter und achter Grad)*. Gruenthal, MB: printed by the , 1935.
– *Ein holperiger Lebensweg*. Clearbrook, BC: A. Olfert, c. 1979.
– "Plain Mathematics." *The Western School Journal* 30, no. 5 (1935): 141.
– "Über meine Arbeit auf Reesor, Ont." *Mennonitische Lehrerzeitung* 1, no. 4 (1949): 10–13.
Huebert, Helmut. *Mennonites in the Cities of Imperial Russia*. Vols. 1 and 2. Winnipeg: Springfield, 2006.
Hull, John T. *The History of Co-operation in Western Canada*. Winnipeg: The Co-operative Marketing Board, 1930.
Janzen, Jacob H. *Lifting the Veil: Mennonite Life in Russia Before the Revolution*. Edited by Leonard Friesen. Translated by Walter Klaassen. Kitchener, ON: Pandora, 1998.
Kealey, Gregory S., and Reg Whitaker, eds. *R.C.M.P. Security Bulletins: The War Series, No. 1, 1939–1941*. St. John's, NL: Committee on Canadian Labour History, 1989.
–, eds. *R.C.M.P. Security Bulletins: The War Series, Part II, 1942–45*. St. John's, NL: Committee on Canadian Labour History, 1993.
Keiter, Friedrich. *Russlanddeutsche Bauern und ihre Stammesgenossen in Deutschland*. Jena, Germany: Gustav Fischer, 1934.
Klassen, John D. *The 45 Year History of Grunthal Bergthaler Mennonite Church 1936–1981*. Altona, MB: D.W. Friesen, c. 1981.
Knight, Thomas C. *Interim Report and Findings of the Economic Survey Board of Manitoba*. Winnipeg: Economic Survey Board, 1938.

Kornelsen, John J. "Beet Hoeing." In *Grunthal History 1874–1974*, 186–8.
Lamoreaux, Naomi R., and Ian Shapiro, eds. *The Bretton Woods Agreements: Together with Scholarly Commentaries and Essential Historical Documents*. New Haven: Yale University Press, 2019.
Manitoba. *A Farm Electrification Programme: Report of Manitoba Electrification Commission 1942*. Winnipeg: Provincial Government Printer, 1943.
– *Report of the Royal Commission on Education*. Winnipeg, 1959.
Manitoba, Department of Agriculture. *Butter Rationing: More Milk – More Butter*. Publication no. 180. Winnipeg, January 1943.
Manitoba, Department of Education. *Empire Day, May 23, 1941*. Winnipeg, January 1941.
Manitoba, Department of Industry and Commerce, The Bureau of Industrial Development. *Facts about Steinbach: An Industrial Survey of the Town of Steinbach*. Winnipeg, c. 1954.
Manitoba, Department of Municipal Affairs, Municipal Planning Branch. *Rural Municipality of Hanover: A Background Report into Development and Growth Potential*. Winnipeg, Department of Municipal Affairs, Municipal Planning Branch, c. 1976.
Manitoba Power Commission. *M.P.C. Appliance Catalogue*. Winnipeg, c. 1950.
– *Power for Manitoba Farms*. Winnipeg, c. 1943.
– *Report on the Farm Electrification Test*. Winnipeg: Manitoba Power Commission, 1945.
Martin, Robert, and G.S. Adam. *A Sourcebook of Canadian Media Law*. 2nd ed. Ottawa: Carleton University Press, 1994.
Novakampus. *Kanadische Mennoniten*. Winnipeg: Rundschau Publishing House, 1924.
Paetkau, David H. *Warum verlieren wir unsere Jugend und wie koennen wir diesem Verlust entgegenarbeiten?* Rosthern, SK: Der Bote Druckerei, 1950.
Patterson, H.L., and H.W. Trevor. *The Dairy Farm Business in Manitoba 1942–1947*. Ottawa: Government of Canada, Department of Agriculture, 1949.
Pearson, Ralph McN. *Provincial Finance in Manitoba*. Winnipeg: Economic Survey Board, 1938.
Peters, K. *Genealogy of the Schoenwieser Janzens, 1752–1979*. Winnipeg: n.p., 1979.
Plumptre, A.F.W. *Mobilizing Canada's Resources for War*. Toronto: Macmillan, 1941.
Reimer, K.J.B. "Johann Braun – One of the First Businessmen." In *Grunthal History 1874–1974*, 34–5.
Reimer, Richard. *Grunthal E.M.B. Church: 25th Anniversary, 1956–1981*. Grunthal, MB: Grunthal E.M.B. Church, 1981.
Rempel, D.J. "Recollections of the Formation of the Grunthal Co-op Store." In *Grunthal History 1874–1974*, 122–4.
Rempel, Jacob J. *Consider the Threshing Stone: Writings of Jacob J. Rempel a Mennonite from Russia*. Edited by David J. Rempel Smucker. Translated by

David J. Rempel Smucker and Eleanore (Rempel) Woollard. Kitchener, ON: Pandora, 2008.
- "Erinnerung aus meiner Dienstzeit." *Volksfreund*, 1 March 1918, 7–10; 7 March 1918, 3–4.
- "Erinnerungen aus den Jahren 1914–1918." *Mennonitische Volkswarte*, March 1936; April 1936; May 1936. (Edited version in Günther, Heidebrecht, and Peters, *"Onsji Tjedils"*, 224–36.)

Rempel, Johann G. *Katechismus in der Wehrlosigkeit. Nebst kurzen Bemerkungen zu den einzelnen Fragen und Antworten*. Rosthern, SK: D.H. Epp, n.d.

Rempel, Peter. "Ein Ueberblick über die Siedlungsmöglichkeiten für die neu eingewanderten Mennoniten aus Russland." *Der Mitarbeiter*, 17 January 1924.

Rempel, Teodor, ed. *Letters of a Mennonite Couple, Nicolai and Katharina Rempel. Russia: War and Revolution, 1914–1917*. Fresno, CA: Center for Mennonite Brethren Studies, 2014.

Scarrow, Howard A. *Canada Votes: A Handbook of Federal and Provincial Election Data*. New Orleans: Hauser, 1962.

Schroeder, Gerhard P. *Miracles of Grace and Judgement: A Brief Account of the Personal Contacts and Experiences with Some of the Leaders and Followers of the Notorious Makhnovshchina during the Civil War in the Ukraine 1914–1923*. Lodi, CA: printed by the , 1974.

Schröder, Heinrich H. *Russlanddeutsche Friesen*. Döllstädt: Selbstverlag der Verfassers, 1936.

Stacey, C.P., ed. *The Arts of War and Peace, 1914–1945*. Vol. 5 of Historical Documents of Canada. Toronto: Macmillan, 1972.

Toews, David. "Immigration und Nothilfe." In *Bericht über die zweiunddreissigste Allgemeine Konferenz der Mennoniten in Canada*, 65–75. Rosthern, SK: D.H. Epp, 1934.

Toews, John B., ed. *Mennonites in Ukraine amid Civil War and Anarchy (1917–1920): A Documentary Collection*. Fresno, CA: Center for Mennonite Brethren Studies, 2013.

Toews, John B., and Paul Toews, eds. *Union of Citizens of Dutch Lineage in Ukraine (1922–1927), Mennonite and Soviet Documents*. Fresno, CA: Center of Mennonite Brethren Studies, 2011.

Töws, Gerhard. *Die Heimat in Flammen*. Regina: Sonderabdruck aus *Der Courier*, c. 1933.
- *Die Heimat in Trümmern*. Steinbach, MB: Warte, 1936.
- *Schönfeld: Werde- und Opfergang einer deutschen Siedlung in der Ukraine*. Winnipeg: Rundschau Publishing House, 1939.

United Farmers Union. *Manifesto*. Gilbert Plains: MFU, c. 1951.

U.S. Department of Agriculture. *A Guide for Members of REA [Rural Electrification Authority] Cooperatives*. Washington, DC: U.S. Department of Agriculture, 1940.

Ward, John W. *Join Your Credit Union*. Winnipeg: Department of Agriculture, 1941.
– *The Organization and Operation of a Consumer's Co-operative*. Winnipeg: Department of Agriculture, 1941.
Warkentin, A. *Who's Who among the Mennonites, 1937*. North Newton, KS: Bethel College, 1937.
Warkentin, John F. "Postal Service." In *Grunthal History 1874–1974*, 133–4.
Working Papers of the East Reserve Village Histories, 1874–1910. Steinbach, MB: The Hanover Steinbach Historical Society, 1990.

Secondary Sources

Adams, Christopher. *Politics in Manitoba: Parties, Leaders, and Voters*. Winnipeg: University of Manitoba Press, 2008.
Aivalis, Christo. Introduction to *Winnipeg 1919: The Strikers' Own History of the Winnipeg General Strike*, edited by Norman Penner. Toronto: James Lorimer, 2019.
Andersen, Chris. *"Métis": Race, Recognition, and the Struggle for Indigenous Peoplehood*. Vancouver: UBC Press, 2014.
Anderson, J.T.M. *The Education of the New-Canadian: A Treatise on Canada's Greatest Educational Problem*. Toronto: J.M. Dent & Sons, 1918.
Ankli, Robert E. "Farm Income on the Great Plains and Canadian Prairies, 1920–1940." *Agricultural History* 51, no. 1 (January 1977): 92–103.
Ankli, Robert E., H. Dan Helsberg, and John Herd Thompson. "The Adoption of the Gasoline Tractor in Western Canada." In *Canadian Papers in Rural History*, vol. 2, edited by Donald H. Akenson, 9–40. Gananoque, ON: Langdale, 1980.
Baar, Ellen. "Patterns of Selective Accentuation among Niagara Mennonites." *Canadian Ethnic Studies* 15, no. 2 (1983): 77–91.
Balzer, David. "Exploring the Timbre of Mennonite Radio in Manitoba: A Case Study of *The Gospel Light Hour* and *The Abundant Life*." *Conrad Grebel Review* 36, no. 2 (Spring 2018): 133–53.
Barber, Marilyn, and Murray Watson. *Invisible Immigrants: The English in Canada since 1945*. Winnipeg: University of Manitoba Press, 2015.
Barr, Elinor. *Swedes in Canada: Invisible Immigrants*. Toronto: University of Toronto Press, 2015.
Bender, Harold S. "The Anabaptist Vision." *Church History* 13, no. 1 (March 1944): 3–24. https://doi.org/10.2307/3161001.
– "Intercontinental Company, Limited." In *ME*, vol. 3, 43–4. Hillsboro, KS: Mennonite Brethren, 1955.
Berg, Wesley. *From Russia with Music: A Study of the Mennonite Choral Tradition in Canada*. Winnipeg: Hyperion, 1985.

- "Music among the Mennonites in Russia." In Friesen, *Mennonites in Russia, 1788–1988*, 203–19.
Bergen, Doris L. *Twisted Cross: The German Christian Movement in the Third Reich.* Chapel Hill: University of North Carolina Press, 1996.
Bergen, John J. "My Experience as a Conscientious Objector to Participation in Violence and Armed Conflict." *Newsletter of the Mennonite Historical Society of Alberta* 9, no. 2 (2007): 1, 3–5.
- "The World Wars and Education among Mennonites in Canada." *JMS* 8 (1990): 156–72.
Berton, Pierre. *The Great Depression 1929–1939.* Toronto: McClelland & Stewart, 1990.
Beyen, Marnix. "A Tribal Trinity: The Rise and Fall of the Franks, the Frisians and the Saxons in the Historical Consciousness of the Netherlands since 1850." *European History Quarterly* 30, no. 4 (October 2000): 493–532. http://doi.org/10.1177/026569140003000402.
Beznosov, Alexander. "Kulak, Christian, and German: Ukrainian Mennonite Identities in a Time of Famine, 1932–1935." In Friesen, *Minority Report*, 260–86.
Birdsell, Sandra. *The Russländer.* Toronto: McClelland & Stewart, 2001.
Blackshaw, Tony. *Key Concepts in Community Studies.* London: Sage, 2010.
Braun, Walter F. *A Biography of Peter A. (1890–1971) and Lena (1893–1991) Braun.* N.p.: c. 1992.
Britnell, G.E. "Perspective on Change in the Prairie Economy." *Canadian Journal of Economics and Political Science* 19, no. 4 (November 1953): 437–54. https://doi.org/10.2307/138292.
Britnell, G.E., and V.C. Fowke. *Canadian Agriculture in War and Peace 1935–1950.* Stanford, CA: Stanford University Press, 1962.
Bruno-Jofré, Rosa del Carmen, ed. *Issues in the History of Education in Manitoba: From the Construction of the Common School to the Politics of Voices.* Lewiston, NY: Edward Mellen, 1993.
Bruno-Jofré, Rosa del Carmen, and Colleen Ross. "Citizenship and Schooling in Manitoba between the End of the First World War and the End of the Second World War." In *Citizenship in Transformation in Canada*, edited by Yvonne M. Hébert, 112–33. Toronto: University of Toronto Press 2002.
- "Decoding the Subjective Image of Women Teachers in Rural Towns and Surrounding Areas of Southern Manitoba: 1947–1960." In Bruno-Jofré, *Issues in the History of Education in Manitoba*, 569–93.
Bryce, P.H. "The Immigrant Settler." In Kennedy, *Social and Economic Conditions*, 35–44.
Buckner, Phillip A. "Canada and the End of Empire, 1939–82." In *Canada and the British Empire*, edited by Phillip A. Buckner, 107–26. Oxford: Oxford University Press, 2008.

Budnitskii, Oleg. *Russian Jews between the Reds and the Whites, 1917–1920*. Philadelphia: University of Pennsylvania Press, 2012.
Buri, George. *Between Education and Catastrophe: The Battle over Public Schooling in Postwar Manitoba*. Montreal: McGill-Queen's University Press, 2016.
Byers, Daniel. "Mobilising Canada: The National Resources Mobilization Act, the Department of National Defence, and Compulsory Military Service in Canada, 1940–1945." *Journal of the Canadian Historical Association* 7, no. 1 (1996): 176–203. https://doi.org/10.7202/031107ar.
Canada. *Report of the Royal Commission on Bilingualism and Biculturalism. Book IV: The Cultural Contribution of the Other Ethnic Groups*. Ottawa: Queen's Printer, 1969.
Canada, Library of Parliament. *History of the Federal Electoral Ridings 1867–1980: British Columbia, Alberta, Saskatchewan, Manitoba, Yukon, Northwest Territories*, vol. 1. Ottawa: Library of Parliament, Information and Reference Branch, c. 1981.
Carr-Stewart, Sheila. "A Treaty Right to Education." *Canadian Journal of Education/Revue canadienne de l'éducation* 26, no. 2 (2001): 125–43. https://doi.org/10.2307/1602197.
Carter, Sarah. *Aboriginal People and Colonizers of Western Canada to 1900*. Toronto: University of Toronto, 1999.
Chafe, J.W. *Chalk, Sweat, and Cheers: A History of the Manitoba Teachers' Society Commemorating its Fiftieth Anniversary, 1919–1969*. Winnipeg: Manitoba Teachers' Society, 1969.
Champion, C.P. *The Strange Demise of British Canada: The Liberals and Canadian Nationalism, 1964–1968*. Montreal: McGill-Queen's University Press, 2010.
Cherkazianova, Irina (Janzen). "Mennonite Schools and the Russian Empire: The Transformation of Church-State Relations in Education, 1789–1917." In Friesen, *Minority Report*, 85–109.
– "Shenfel'dskaya volost': istoriya vozniknoveniya i ischeznoveniya mennonitskikh poseleniy [Schoenfeld Volost: The History of the Founding and Disappearance of a Mennonite Settlement]." *Modern Studies in German History* (2020): 44–71. https://doi.org/10.15421/312003.
Chiel, Arthur A. *The Jews in Manitoba: A Social History*. Toronto: University of Toronto Press, 1961.
Clark, David B. "The Concept of Community: A Re-Examination." *Sociological Review* 21, no. 3 (August 1973): 397–416. https://doi.org/10.1111/j.1467-954X.1973.tb00230.x.
Colley, Linda. *Britons: Forging the Nation, 1707–1837*. London: Pimlico, 1994.
Considine, John P. "Mennonite Low German Dictionary: A Review Article." Review of *Mennonite Low German Dictionary: Mennonitisch-Plattdeutsches Wörterbuch*, by Jack Thiessen. *JMS* 22 (2004): 247–58.

Conway, Shannon. "From Britishness to Multiculturalism: Official Canadian Identity in the 1960s." *Études canadiennes/Canadian Studies* 84 (2018): 9–30. http://doi.org/10.4000/eccs.1118.

Craft, Aimée. *Breathing Life into the Stone Fort Treaty: An Anishnabe Understanding of Treaty One*. Sakatoon: Purich Publishing, 2013.

Daschuk, James W. *Clearing the Plains: Disease, Politics of Starvation, and the Loss of Aboriginal Life*. Regina: University of Regina Press, 2021.

Dawson, C.A. *Group Settlement: Ethnic Communities in Western Canada*. Toronto: Macmillan, 1936.

Dennis, Hedy Lepp. *Memories of Reesor: The Mennonite Settlement in Northern Ontario, 1925–1949*. Leamington, ON: Essex-Kent Mennonite Historical Association, 2001.

Descendants of Cornelius Friesen. Headingley, MB: The Peter Friesen Family, 1986.

Dick, Lyle. *Farmers "Making Good": The Development of Abernethy District, Saskatchewan, 1880–1920*. 2nd ed. Calgary: University of Calgary Press, 2008.

Driedger, Leo. *Mennonites in the Global Village*. Toronto: University of Toronto Press, 2000.

– "Native Rebellion and Mennonite Invasion: An Examination of Two Canadian River Valleys." *MQR* 46 (July 1972): 290–300.

Driedger, Nicholas N. *The Leamington United Mennonite Church: Establishment and Development, 1925–1972*. Altona, MB: D.W. Friesen, 1972.

Driediger, Ab Douglas. *No Dancing God: Mennonite Stories*. Kelowna: Rutgers Publications, 1998.

Dueck, Abe J., ed. *Canadian Mennonites and the Challenge of Nationalism*. Winnipeg: Manitoba Mennonite Historical Society, 1994.

– *Concordia Hospital: Faith, Health and Community: 75 Years, 1928–2003*. Winnipeg: Concordia Hospital, 2003.

– "Evangelical Mennonite Brethren in Alberta: Bruderthaler or Mennonite Brethren?" *MH* 22, no. 1 (March 1996): 1–2, 8; *MH* 22, no. 2 (June 1996): 6–7.

– "Making a Case for Non-combatant Service: B.B. Janz's Negotiations with the Government during World War II." *JMS* 25 (2007): 107–24.

Dueck, Gustav. *Chortitzer Mennonite Conference: 1874–1990*. Steinbach, MB: Chortitzer Mennonite Conference, 2004.

Dümling, Albrecht. "Reine und unreine Musik. Jazz und jazzverwandtes in der NS-Austellung 'Entartete Musik.'" In *Jazz und Sozialgeschichte*, edited by Theo Mäusli, 47–68. Zürich: Chronos, 1994.

Dyck, Arnold. "Koop and Bua Go Travelling." Translated by Al Reimer. *JMS* 7 (1989): 72–83.

Dyck, Harvey L. "Collectivization, Depression, and Immigration, 1929–1930: A Chance Interplay." In *Empire and Nations: Essays in Honour of Frederic H. Soward*, edited by Harvey L. Dyck and H. Peter Krosby, 144–59. Toronto: University of Toronto Press, 1969.

Dyck, Harvey L., John R. Staples, and John B. Toews. *Nestor Makhno and the Eichenfeld Massacre: A Civil War Tragedy in a Ukrainian Mennonite Village.* Kitchener, ON: Pandora, 2004.
Dyck, John. "Alt-Bergfeld." In *Historical Sketches of the East Reserve 1874–1910: Villages – Biographies – Institutions,* edited by John Dyck, 9–53. Steinbach, MB: Hanover Steinbach Historical Society, 1994.
– *Oberschulze Jakob Peters 1813–1884: Manitoba Pioneer Leader.* Steinbach, MB: Hanover Historical Society, 1990.
Dyck, Peter. "Education in Steinbach." In Warkentin, *Reflections on Our Heritage,* 288–92.
Dyck, Peter P. *Orenburg am Ural: Die Geschichte einer mennonitischen Ansiedlung in Russland.* Yarrow, BC: Columbia Press 1951.
Ediger, Gerald C. *Crossing the Divide: Language Transition among Canadian Mennonite Brethren, 1940–1970.* Winnipeg: Centre for Mennonite Brethren Studies, 2001.
Eicher, John P.R. *Exiled Among Nations: German and Mennonite Mythologies in a Transnational Age.* Cambridge: Cambridge University Press, 2020.
Elvins, Sarah. "'A River of Money Flowing South': Cross-Border Shopping in North Dakota and the Insatiable Canadian Desire for American Goods, 1900–2001." *History of Retailing and Consumption* 1, no. 3 (September 2015): 230–45. https://doi.org/10.1080/2373518X.2015.1134256.
Emmons, Terence. "The Peasant and the Emancipation." In *The Peasant in Nineteenth Century Russia,* edited by Wayne S. Vucinich, 41–71. Stanford: Stanford University Press, 1968.
Engelstein, Laura. *Russia in Flames: War, Revolution, Civil War, 1914–1921.* New York: Oxford University Press, 2018.
Enns, F.F. *Elder Enns: "Ohm Franz."* Winnipeg: Derksen Printers, 1979.
Enns, Herbert, ed. "Abraham P. Nachtigal's Experiences on a Farm in Markham." *Mennogespräch* 10, no. 2 (1992): 14–15.
Enns, J., Abram Vogt, and Johann Klassen, eds. *Dem Herrn die Ehre: Schönwiese Mennoniten Gemeinde von Manitoba 1924–1968.* Altona, MB: D.W. Friesen, 1969.
Enns, Robert. "From Generation to Generation? Faith and Culture in One Russian Mennonite Immigrant Family." *Direction,* pt. 1, 38, no. 1 (Spring 2009): 79–92; pt. 2, 39, no. 2 (Fall 2009): 233–45.
Ens, Adolf. *Becoming a National Church: A History of the Conference of Mennonites in Canada.* Winnipeg: CMU Press, 2004.
– "Becoming British Citizens in Pre-WWI Canada." In Dueck, *Canadian Mennonites and the Challenge of Nationalism,* 69–87.
– "The Conspiracy That Never Was." *MH* 11, no. 3 (September 1985): 1–2.
– "Mennonite Education in Russia." In Friesen, *Mennonites in Russia, 1788–1988,* 75–97.

- *Subjects or Citizens? The Mennonite Experience in Canada, 1870–1925*. Ottawa: University of Ottawa Press, 1994.
Ens, Adolf, Ernest N. Braun, and Henry N. Fast. *Settlers of the East Reserve: Moving In – Moving Out – Staying*. Winnipeg: Manitoba Historical Society, 2009.
Ens, Anna Epp. *In Search of Unity: Story of the Conference of Mennonites in Manitoba*. Winnipeg: CMBC Publications, 1996.
Ens, Gerhard J. *"Die Schule muss sein": A History of the Mennonite Collegiate Institute, 1889–198*. Gretna, MB: Mennonite Collegiate Institute, 1990.
- "The Manitoba Act, the Métis and the Mennonites: A Tale of Two Reserves." *Preservings*, no. 36 (2016): 4–11.
- *Volost and Municipality: The Rural Municipality of Rhineland, 1884–1984*. Altona, MB: The RM of Rhineland, 1984.
Entz, W. "Der Courier." In *The Multilingual Press in Manitoba*, edited by Joyce Bowling and M.H. Hykawy, 101–5. Winnipeg: Canada Press Club, 1974.
- "Der Nordwesten." In *The Multilingual Press in Manitoba*, edited by Joyce Bowling and M.H. Hykawy, 106–10. Winnipeg: Canada Press Club, 1974.
- "The Suppression of the German Language Press in September 1918 (with Special Reference to the Secular German Language Papers in Western Canada)." *Canadian Ethnic Studies* 8, no. 2 (1976): 56–70.
Epp, Dick H. "David Paetkau – Music His First Love." *Saskatchewan Mennonite Historian* 10, no. 1 (April 2004): 20–3.
Epp, Frank H. *Education with a Plus: The Story of Rosthern Junior College*. Waterloo, ON: Conrad, 1975.
- *Mennonite Exodus: The Rescue and Resettlement of the Russian Mennonites since the Communist Revolution*. Altona, MB: D.W. Friesen 1962.
- *Mennonites in Canada, 1786–1920: The History of a Separate People*. Toronto: Macmillan, 1974.
- *Mennonites in Canada, 1920–1940: A People's Struggle for Survival*. Toronto: Macmillan, 1982.
Epp, George K. "Urban Mennonites in Russia." In Friesen, *Mennonites in Russia, 1788–1988*, 239–59.
Epp, George K., and Heinrich Wiebe, eds. *Unter dem Nordlicht: Anthologie des deutschen Schrifftums der Mennoniten in Canada*. Winnipeg: Mennonite German Society of Canada, 1977.
Epp, H.H. "The Khortitsa 'Naturschutzverein' (Society for the Protection of Nature)." In *First Mennonite Villages in Russia, 1789–1943: Khortitsa – Rosental*, edited by N.J. Kroeker, 142–4. Vancouver: printed by the editor, 1981.
Epp, Irmgard, ed. *Constantinoplers: Escape from Bolshevism*. Victoria, BC: Trafford Publishing, 2006.
Epp, Marlene. *Eating Like a Mennonite: Food and Community across Borders*. Montreal: McGill-Queen's University Press, 2023.

- "The Mennonite Girls' Home of Winnipeg: A Home Away from Home." *JMS* 6 (1988): 100–14.
- *Mennonite Women in Canada: A History*. Winnipeg: University of Manitoba Press, 2008.
- "More Than 'Just' Recipes: Mennonite Cookbooks in Mid-twentieth Century North America." In *Edible Histories, Cultural Politics: Towards a Canadian Food History*, edited by Franca Iacovetta, Valerie J. Korinek, and Marlene Epp, 173–86. Toronto: University of Toronto Press, 2012.

Epp, Reuben. *The Story of Low German & Plautdietsch: Tracing a Language across the Globe*. Hillsboro, KS: Reader's Press, 1993.

Epp-Thiessen, Esther. *Altona: The Story of a Prairie Town*. Altona, MB: D.W. Friesen, 1982.

Erenberg, Lewis A. *The Greatest Fight of Our Generation: Louis vs. Schmeling*. Oxford: Oxford University Press, 2006.

Esau, Alvin J. "The Establishment, Preservation and Legality of Mennonite Semi-communalism in Manitoba." *Manitoba Law Journal* 31, no. 1 (2005): 81–109.

Eyford, Ryan. *White Settler Reserve: New Iceland and the Colonization of the Canadian West*. Vancouver: University of British Columbia Press, 2016.

Fast, Henry. *Gruenfeld (now Kleefeld): 1874–1910: First Mennonite Village in Western Canada*. N.p.: printed by the , 2006.

Feigert, Frank B. *Canada Votes, 1935–1988*. Durham: Duke University Press, 1989.

Felshtinsky, Yuri. "The Legal Foundations of the Immigration and Emigration Policy of the USSR, 1917–27." *Soviet Studies* 34, no. 3 (July 1982): 327–48. https://doi.org/10.1080/09668138208411422.

Fisher, Susie. "(Trans)planting Manitoba's West Reserve: Mennonites, Myths, and Narratives of Place." *JMS* 35 (2017): 127–48.

Fowke, Vernon. "Economic Effects of the War on the Prairie Economy." *Canadian Journal of Economics and Political Science* 11, no. 3 (August 1945): 373–87. https://doi.org/10.2307/137402.

Francis, E.K. "The Adjustment of a Peasant Group to a Capitalistic Economy." *Rural Sociology* 17, no. 3 (September 1952): 218–28.
- *In Search of Utopia: The Mennonites in Manitoba*. Altona, MB: D.W. Friesen, 1955.
- "The Mennonite School Problem in Manitoba 1874–1919." *MQR* 27 (July 1953): 204–37.
- "The Nature of the Ethnic Group." *American Journal of Sociology* 52, no. 5 (March 1947): 393–400. https://doi.org/10.1086/220031.

Fransen, David. "'As Far as Conscience Will Allow': Mennonites in Canada During the Second World War." In Hillmer, Kordan, and Luciak, *On Guard for Thee*, 131–49.

Frazer, Chris. "From Pariahs to Patriots: Canadian Communists and the Second World War." *Past Imperfect* 5 (1996): 3–36. https://doi.org/10.21971/P7NK5Z.

Fretz, Joseph Winfield. *Pilgrims in Paraguay: TheStoryof MennoniteColonizationin South America*. Scottdale, PA: Herald, 1953.

Friesen, Abraham. *In Defense of Privilege: Russian Mennonites and the State before and during World War I*. Winnipeg: Kindred, 2006.

– "Wrong Author Attributed to 'Some Thoughts on Emigration.'" *MH* 27, no. 2 (June 2001): 5–6.

Friesen, Gerald. *The Canadian Prairies: A History*. Toronto: University of Toronto Press, 1984.

– "Hockey and Prairie Cultural History." In *River Road: Essays on Manitoba and Prairie History*, 215–29. Winnipeg: University of Manitoba Press, 1995.

Friesen, John, ed. *Against the Wind: The Story of Four Mennonite Villages (Gnadental, Gruenfeld, Neu-Chortitza and Steinfeld) in Southern Ukraine, 1872–1943*. Winnipeg: Henderson Books, 1994.

–, ed. *Mennonites in Russia, 1788–1988: Essays in Honour of Gerhard Lohrenz*. Winnipeg: CMBC Publications, 1989.

Friesen, Leonard G. "Mennonites in Russia and the Revolution of 1905: Experiences, Perceptions and Responses." *MQR* 62 (January 1988): 42–55.

– *Mennonites in the Russian Empire and the Soviet Union: Through Much Tribulation*. Toronto: University of Toronto Press, 2022.

–, ed. *Minority Report: Mennonite Identities in Imperial Russia and Soviet Ukraine Reconsidered, 1789–1945*. Toronto: University of Toronto Press, 2018.

Friesen, Martin W. *Kanadische Mennoniten bezwingen eine Wildnis: 50 Jahre Kolonie Menno ... 1927–1977*. Asuncion, Paraguay: Verwaltung der Kolonie Menno, 1977.

– *Neue Heimat in der Chacowildnis*. Loma Plata, Paraguay: Sociedad Cooperative Colonizadora Chortitzer Komitee, 1997.

Friesen, Ralph. *Between Earth and Sky: Steinbach, the First 50 Years*. Steinbach, MB: Derksen Printers, 2009.

Friesen, Ronald. *Pioneers of Cheese: A Social and Economic History of the Cheese Industry in Southern Manitoba, 1880–1960*. N.p.: printed by the , 2010.

– *When Canada Called: Manitoba Mennonites and World War II*. N.p.: printed by the , 2006.

Friesen, Victor Carl. *The Windmill Turning: Nursery Rhymes, Maxims, and other Expressions of Western Canadian Mennonites*. Edmonton: University of Alberta Press, 1988.

Friesen, W. "A Mennonite Community in the East Reserve: Its Origin and Growth." In *Manitoba Historical Society Transactions*, ser. 3, no. 19 (1962–3), 24–43. Winnipeg: Manitoba Historical Society, 1964.

Gatrell, Peter. "Refugee History and Refugees in Russia during and after the First World War." *Vestnik of Saint Petersburg University. History* 62, no. 3

(September 2017): 497–521. http://doi.org/10.21638/11701/spbu02.2017.305.
Gauthier, Maurice. *De la table de cuisine à la rue principale : 50 ans d'histoire des caisses populaires du Manitoba, 1937–1987*. Winnipeg: Conseil de la coopération du Manitoba, 1989.
Gerbrandt, Henry J. *Adventure in Faith: The Background in Europe and the Development in Canada of the Bergthaler Church of Manitoba*. Altona, MB: D.W. Friesen, 1970.
Gerwarth, Robert. *The Vanquished: Why the First World War Failed to End, 1917–1923*. London: Allen Lane, 2016.
Gesche, Katja. *Kultur als Instrument der Aussenpolitik totalitärer Staaten. Das Deutsche Ausland-Institut 1933–1945*. Köln: Böhlau, 2006.
Giesbrecht, Donovan. "Métis, Mennonites and the 'Unsettled Prairie,' 1874–1896." *JMS* 19 (2001): 103–11.
Giffen, P. James. *Rural Life: Portraits of the Prairie Town, 1946*. Edited by Gerald Friesen. Winnipeg: University of Manitoba Press, 2004.
Gnadenthal, 1880–1980. Winkler, MB: Gnadenthal History Book Committee, 1982.
Goerz, Heinrich. *Memrik: A Mennonite Settlement in Russia*. Translated by Eric Enns. Winnipeg: CMBC Publications, 1997.
Goldsborough, Gordon. *With One Voice: A History of Municipal Governance in Manitoba*. Altona, MB: Association of Manitoba Municipalities, 2008.
Goossen, Benjamin W. *Chosen Nation: Mennonites and Germany in a Global Era*. Princeton: Princeton University Press, 2017.
– "Terms of Racial Endearment: Nazi Categorization of Mennonites in Ideology and Practice, 1929–1945." *German Studies Review* 44, no. 1 (February 2021): 27–46. http://doi.org/10.1353/gsr.2021.0001.
Granatstein, J.L. *Conscription in the Second World War 1939–1949: A Study in Political Management*. Toronto: McGraw Hill, 1969.
Granatstein, J.L., and Robert Bothwell. *Pirouette: Pierre Trudeau and Canadian Foreign Policy*. Toronto: University of Toronto Press, 1990.
Gray, James H. *The Winter Years: The Depression on the Prairies*. Toronto: Macmillan, 1966.
Graybill, Beth, and Linda B. Arthur. "The Social Control of Women's Bodies in Two Mennonite Communities." In *Religion, Dress and the Body*, edited by Linda B. Arthur, 9–29. New York: Berg, 2000.
Grebstad, David W. "The Flag of Our Fathers? The Manitoba Provincial Flag and British Cultural Hegemony in Manitoba, 1870–1966." *Raven: A Journal of Vexillology* 23 (2016): 55–79. https://doi.org/10.5840/raven2016235.
Gregor, Alexander, and Keith Wilson. *The Development of Education in Manitoba*. Dubuque, IA: Kendall/Hunt, 1984.
Hamm, Blake. "Revisiting the Canadian Privilegium: The Lowe Letter, Good Faith, and International Law." *MQR* 94, no. 3 (July 2020): 307–45.

Hanebrink, Paul. *A Specter Haunting Europe: The Myth of Judeo-Bolshevism*. Cambridge, MA: Harvard University Press, 2018.
Haque, Eve. "Multiculturalism, Language, and Immigration Integration." In *The Multiculturalism Question: Debating Identity in 21st-Century Canada*, edited by Jack Jedwab, 203–23. Montreal: McGill-Queen's University Press, 2014.
– *Multiculturalism within a Bilingual Framework: Language, Race, and Belonging in Canada*. Toronto: University of Toronto Press, 2012.
Harker, W. John. "Canadian Literature in Canadian Schools: From the Old to the New Internationalism." *Canadian Journal of Education* 12, no. 3 (Summer 1987): 417–27. https://doi.org/10.2307/1495233.
Healey, Robynne Rogers. "Quakers and Mennonites and the Great War." In *Canadian Churches and the First World War*, edited by Gordon L. Heath, 218–40. Cambridge: Lutterworth, 2014.
Hiebert, Clarence. *The Holdeman People: The Church of God in Christ, Mennonite, 1859–1969*. South Pasadena, CA: William Carey Library, 1973.
Hiebert, Susan. *Growing Sugar in Manitoba, 1940–1990*. Rosenfeld, MB: The Manitoba Sugar Beet Producers Association, 1990.
Hildebrand, Dianne. *Upholding the Old, Embracing the New: The Life of P.J.B. Reimer – Teacher, Minister, and Mennonite Historian*. Steinbach, MB: Rosetta Projects, 2014.
Hillary, G.A. "Definitions of Community: Areas of Agreement." *Rural Sociology* 20, no. 1 (1955): 111–23.
Hillmer, Norman, Kordan Bohdan, and Lubomyr Luciak, eds. *On Guard for Thee: War, Ethnicity, and the Canadian State, 1939–1945*. Ottawa: Canadian Committee for the History of the Second World War, 1988.
Hinther, Rhonda L. *Perogies and Politics: Canada's Ukrainian Left, 1891–1991*. Toronto: University of Toronto Press, 2018.
Hobsbawm, Eric. *Uncommon People: Resistance, Rebellion and Jazz*. London: Weidenfeld & Nicolson, 1998.
Holm, Gerald F. "Name Authorities Save an Historic Community Name – LaRivière." *Canoma* 25, no. 1 (1999): 4–7.
Howell, Richard W., and Jack Klassen. "Contrasting du/Sie Patterns in a Mennonite Community." *Anthropological Linguistics* 13, no. 2 (February 1971): 68–74.
Igartua, José E. *The Other Quiet Revolution: National Identities in English Canada, 1945–71*. Vancouver: UBC Press, 2006.
Jantzen, Mark, and John D. Thiesen, eds. *European Mennonites and the Holocaust*. Toronto: University of Toronto Press, 2020
Janzen, Jacob H. "Plautdietsch." Translated by Elmer F. Suderman. *ML* 22 (July 1967): 116.

Janzen, William. *Limits on Liberty: The Experience of Mennonite, Hutterite and Doukhobor Communities in Canada.* Toronto: University of Toronto Press, 1990.

Johnson, Gregory A. "The Last Gasp of Empire: The 1964 Flag Debate Revisited." In *Canada and the End of Empire,* edited by Phillip Buckner, 232–50. Vancouver: UBC Press, 2005.

Jolys, J.-M., and J.-H. Côté. *Pages de souvenirs et d'histoire : La paroisse de Saint-Pierre-Jolys au Manitoba.* Saint-Pierre-Jolys, MB: La Paroisse de Saint-Pierre-Jolys, 1974.

Jubilate: 60 years First Mennonite Church, 1926–1986. Winnipeg: First Mennonite Church, 1991.

Juhnke, James C. *A People of Two Kingdoms: The Political Acculturation of the Kansas Mennonites.* Newton, KS: Faith and Life, 1975.

Kappeler, Andreas. *The Russian Empire: A Multiethnic History.* Translated by Alfred Clayton. Edinburgh: Pearson Education, 2001.

Karpiak, Victoria, comp. *Senator Paul Yuzyk, 1913–1986: Father of Multiculturalism.* Ottawa, 2017. https://yuzyk.com/wp-content/uploads/2020/09/paul-yuzyk-book_final.pdf.

Kelley, Ninette, and Michael J. Trebilcock. *The Making of the Mosaic: A History of Canadian Immigration Policy.* 2nd ed. Toronto: University of Toronto Press, 2010.

Kellogg, Michael. *The Russian Roots of Nazism: White Émigrés and the Making of National Socialism, 1917–1945.* Cambridge: Cambridge University Press, 2008.

Kennedy, W.P.M., ed. *Social and Economic Conditions in the Dominion of Canada.* Philadelphia: American Academy of Political and Social Science, 1923.

Keshen, Jeffrey A. *Saints, Sinners, and Soldiers: Canada's Second World War.* Vancouver: University of British Columbia Press, 2004.

Killick, C.H.P. *Manitoba Dairying: A Century of Progress.* N.p.: Manitoba Dairy Association, 1979.

Kirkconnell, Watson. "New-Canadian Letters." *University of Toronto Quarterly* 19, no. 4 (July 1950): 394–433. https://doi.org/10.3138/utq.19.4.278.

Klaassen, Walter. *"The Days of Our Years": A History of the Eigenheim Mennonite Church Community, 1892–1992.* Rosthern, SK: Eigenheim Mennonite Church, 1992.

Klassen, Bertha Elizabeth. *Da Capo: "Start Once from the Front." A History of the Mennonite Community Orchestra.* Winnipeg: Centre for Mennonite Brethren Studies, 1993.

Klassen, Doreen Helen. *Singing Mennonite: Low German Songs among the Mennonites.* Winnipeg: University of Manitoba Press, 1989.

Klassen, Herbert, and Maureen Klassen. *Ambassador to His People: C.F. Klassen and the Russian Mennonite Refugees.* Winnipeg: Kindred, 1990.

Klassen, Jenna. "'She Brought It to Canada in 1926': Intergenerational Preservation and the (Re)invention of Russländer Identity." *JMS* 37 (2019): 305–23.

Klassen, Judith. "Music, Mimesis, and Modulation among Mennonites in Rural Manitoba." In *Contemporary Musical Expressions in Canada*, edited by Anna Hoefnagels, Judith Klassen, and Sherry Johnson, 417–52. Montreal: McGill-Queen's University Press, 2019.

Klassen, Peter P. *Die Deutsch-völkische Zeit: In der Kolonie Fernheim, Chaco, Paraguay, 1933–1945*. Weierhof: Mennonitischer Geschichtsverein, 1990.

– *The Mennonites in Paraguay: Volume 1, Kingdom of God and Kingdom of This World*. 2nd ed. Hillsboro, KS: printed by the , 2004.

Kleinpenning, J.M.G. *The Mennonite Colonies in Paraguay: Origin and Development*. Berlin: Ibero-Amerikanisches Institut, Preussischer Kulturbesitz, 2009.

Klets, Viktor K. "Caught between Two Poles: Ukrainian Mennonites and the Trauma of the Second World War." In Friesen, *Minority Report*, 287–317.

Klippenstein, Frieda Esau. "'Doing What We Could': Mennonite Domestic Servants in Winnipeg, 1920s to 1950s." *JMS* 7 (1989): 145–66.

Klippenstein, Lawrence. "Manitoba Métis and Mennonite Immigration: First Contacts." *MQR* 48, no. 4 (October 1974): 476–88.

– *Peace and War: Mennonite Conscientious Objectors in Tsarist Russia and the Soviet Union before World War II, and Other COs in Eastern Europe*. Winnipeg: Mennonite Heritage Centre, 2016.

Kobelt-Groch, Marion, and Astrid von Schlachta, eds. *Mennoniten in der NS-Zeit: Stimmen, Lebenssituationen, Erfahrungen*. Bolanden-Weierhof: Mennonitischer Geschichtsverein, 2017.

Kroeger, Arthur. *Hard Passage: A Mennonite Family's Long Journey from Russia to Canada*. Edmonton: University of Alberta Press, 2007.

Kroeker, N.J. *First Mennonite Villages in Russia, 1789–1943: Khortitsa, Rosental*. Vancouver: N.J. Kroeker, 1981.

Kuffert, Len. *Canada before Television: Radio, Taste, and the Struggle for Cultural Democracy*. Montreal: McGill-Queen's University Press, 2016.

Kulischer, Eugene M. *Europe on the Move: War and Population Changes, 1917–47*. New York: Columbia University Press, 1948.

Kuzina, Rosemary. "Mennonites and Aboriginals: The East Reserve and Roseau River Beginnings, 1870–1890." *MH* 16, no. 3 (September 1990): 1–2, 6.

Lehr, John C. *Community and Frontier: A Ukrainian Settlement in the Canadian Parkland*. Winnipeg: University of Manitoba Press, 2011.

Loewen, Harry. "Gerhard Loewen (1863–1946): Early Mennonite Poet and Teacher in Russia and Canada." *JMS* 9 (1991): 91–103.

- "Mennonites, National Socialism and Jews 1933–1945: A Historical Reflection." In *A Sharing of Diversities: Proceedings of the Jewish Mennonite Ukrainian Conference, "Building Bridges,"* edited by Fred Stambrook and Bert Friesen, 231–44. Regina: Canadian Plains Research Center, 1999.
Loewen, Harry, and James Urry. "A Tale of Two Newspapers: *Die Mennonitische Rundschau* (1880–2007) and *Der Bote* (1924–2008)." *MQR* 86, no. 2 (October 2012): 175–204.
Loewen, Royden K. "American Nationalism and the Rural Immigrant: A Case Study of Two Midwestern Communities, 1900–1925." In Dueck, *Canadian Mennonites and the Challenge of Nationalism*, 165–90.
- "Beyond the Monolith of Modernity: New Trends in Immigrant and Ethnic Rural History." *Agricultural History* 81, no. 2 (Spring 2007): 204–27. https://doi.org/10.1215/00021482-81.2.204.
- *Blumenort: A Mennonite Community in Transition, 1874–1982*. Steinbach, MB: Blumenort Mennonite Historical Society, 1983.
- *Diaspora in the Countryside: Two Mennonite Communities and Mid-twentieth-century Rural Disjuncture*. Toronto: University of Toronto Press, 2006).
- *Family, Church, and Market: A Mennonite Community in the Old and the New Worlds, 1850–1930*. Toronto: University of Toronto Press, 1993.
- "Mennonite 'Repertoires of Contention': Church Life in Steinbach, Manitoba and Quellenkolonie, Chihuahua, 1945–1975." *MQR* 72, no. 2 (April 1998): 301–19.
- "On the Margin or In the Lead: Canadian Prairie Historiography." *Agricultural History* 73, no. 1 (Winter 1999): 27–45
- *Village among Nations: "Canadian" Mennonites in a Transnational World, 1916–2006*. Toronto: University of Toronto Press, 2013.
Loewen, Royden K., and Steven M. Nolt. *Seeking Places of Peace*. Kitchener, ON: Pandora, 2012.
Lohrenz, Gerhard. *Heritage Remembered: A Pictorial Survey of Mennonites in Prussia and Russia*, rev. ed. Winnipeg: CMBC Publications, 1977.
- *Zagradovka: History of a Mennonite Settlement in Southern Russia*. Translated by Victor G. Doerksen. Winnipeg: CMBC Publications, 2000.
MacPherson, Ian. "'Better Tractors for Less Money': The Establishment of Canadian Cooperative Implements Limited." *Manitoba History* 13 (Spring 1987): 2–11.
- "Manitoba's Blueprint for Power." *Rural Electrification News* 8, no. 8 (April 1943): 6–8.
Marchildon, Gregory P., ed. *Drought and Depression: History of the Prairie West*. Regina: University of Regina Press, 2018.
Marrus, Michael R. *The Unwanted: European Refugees in the Twentieth Century*. New York: Oxford University Press, 1985.

Marshall, Alison R. *Cultivating Connections: The Making of Chinese Prairie Canada*. Vancouver: UBC Press, 2014.
Martens, Hildegard M. "Accommodation and Withdrawal: The Response of Mennonites in Canada to World War II." *Sociale Historie/Social History* 7, no. 14 (November 1974): 306–27.
Martin, Terry. "The Russian Mennonite Encounter with the Soviet State, 1917–1955." *Conrad Grebel Review* 20, no. 1 (Winter 2002): 5–59.
– "The Terekers' Dilemma: A Prelude to the *Selbstschutz*." *MH* 17, no. 4 (December 1991): 1–2.
Millman, Brock. *Polarity, Patriotism, and Dissent in Great War Canada, 1914–1919*. Toronto: University of Toronto Press, 2016.
Mommsen, Hans. "Hitler's Reichstag Speech of 30 January 1939." *History and Memory* 9, nos. 1–2 (Fall 1997): 147–61.
Morton, W.L. *Manitoba: A History*. 2nd ed. Toronto: University of Toronto Press, 1967.
Neufeld, Dietrich (Dederich Navall). *A Russian Dance of Death: Revolution and Civil War in the Ukraine*. Edited and translated by Al Reimer. Winnipeg: Hyperion, 1977.
Neufeld, Jacob A. *Path of Thorns: Soviet Mennonite life under Communist and Nazi Rule*. Edited by Harvey L. Dyck. Toronto: University of Toronto Press, 2014.
Neufeld, Mary. *Prairie Pioneers: Schönthal Revisited*. Winnipeg: Manitoba Historical Society, 2016.
Neufeld, Peter Lorenz. *Mennonites at War: A Double-edged Sword: Canadian Mennonites in World War Two*. Deloraine, MB: DTS Publishing, 1997.
Neufeldt, Colin P. "The Flight to Moscow, 1929: An Act of Mennonite Civil Disobedience?" *Preservings*, no. 19 (December 2001): 35–47.
– "'Through the Fires of Hell': The Dekulakization and Collectivization of the Soviet Mennonite Community, 1928–1933." *JMS* 16 (1998): 9–32.
Neufeldt, Reina C. "Tolerant Exclusion: Expanding Constricted Narratives of Wartime Ethnic and Civic Nationalism." *Nations and Nationalism* 15, no. 2 (April 2009): 206–26. https://doi.org/10.1111/j.1469-8129.2009.00371.x.
– "'We Are Aware of Our Contradictions': Russlaender Mennonite Narratives of Loss and the Reconstruction of Peoplehood, 1914–1923." *JMS* 27 (2009): 129–54.
Neufeldt-Fast, Arnold. "Benjamin Unruh, Nazism, and MCC." *MQR* 96, no. 2 (April 2022): 157–205.
Nolt, Steven M. "Activist Impulses across Time: North American Evangelicalism and Anabaptism as Conversation Partners." In *The Activist Impulse: Essays on the Intersection of Evangelicalism and Anabaptism*, edited by Jared S. Burkholder and David C. Cramer, 11–44. Eugene, OR: Pickwick Papers, 2012.

Osborne, Ken. "Teaching History in Schools: A Canadian Debate." *Journal of Curriculum Studies* 35, no. 5 (September 2003): 585–626. https://doi.org/10.1080/0022027032000063544.
Osokina, Elena A. *Stalin's Quest for Gold: The Torgsin Hard-Currency Shops and Soviet Industrialization*. Ithaca, NY: Cornell University Press, 2021.
Paetkau, Henry. "Jacob H. Janzen: 'A Minister of Rare Magnitude.'" *Mennogespräch: Mennonite Historical Society of Ontario* 6, no. 1 (March 1988): 1–4.
– "Russian Mennonite Immigrants of the 1920s: A Reappraisal." *JMS* 2 (1984): 72–85.
Patterson, Bruce. "The Red Ensign and the Maple Leaf: Canada's Two Flag Traditions." *Raven: A Journal of Vexillology* 23 (2016): 1–17. https://doi.org/10.5840/raven2016233.
Patterson, Sean. *Makhno and Memory: Anarchist and Mennonite Narratives of Ukraine's Civil War, 1917–1921*. Winnipeg: University of Manitoba Press, 2020.
Pauls, Peter. *Bethesda: The First Fifty Years (1937–1987)*. Steinbach, MB: printed by the , 1996.
Peacock, Kenneth. *Twenty Ethnic Songs from Western Canada*. Ottawa: R. Duhamel, 1966.
Penner, Glenn H. "Mennonites and Middle Names." *MH* 43, no. 3 (September 2017): 3.
Penner, Lydia. *Hanover: One Hundred Years*. Steinbach, MB: RM of Hanover, 1982.
Penner, Maria. "Die neue Maedchenschule." In *Gluckliche, sonnige Schulzeit; ein Buch fuer Jung und Alt. Erinnerungen und Erlebnisse der ehmaligen Schulerinnen der Chortitzer Maedchensschule*, edited by Helena Toews, 35–9. Virgil, ON: Niagara, c. 1948.
Perrun, Jody. *The Patriotic Consensus: Unity, Morale, and the Second World War in Winnipeg*. Winnipeg: University of Manitoba Press, 2014.
Peters, Jacob E. "The Forgotten Immigrants: The Coming of the 'Late Kanadier,' 1881–1914." *JMS* 18 (2000): 129–45.
Peters, Jake. *Mennonite Private Schools in Manitoba and Saskatchewan 1874–1925*. Steinbach, MB: Mennonite Village Museum, 1985.
Peters, Victor. "The Immigrant: Part 7. Locked Door, Dust, and Poor Attendance Mark First Teaching Days." *MM* 6, no. 10 (Summer 1977): 7–8.
– *Nestor Makhno: The Life of an Anarchist*. Winnipeg: Echo Books, 1970.
Peters, Victor, and Jack Thiessen. *Mennonitische Namen/Mennonite Names*. Marburg: N.G. Elwert, 1987.
Petkau, Peter. "Low German Drama: A Research Report." *ML* 33 (December 1978): 27–8.
Plett, Delbert F. *Saints and Sinners: The Kleine Gemeinde in Imperial Russia 1812 to 1875*. Steinbach, MB: Crossway Publications, 1999.

Plett, Lynette Sarah. "Refashioning Kleine Gemeinde Women's Dress in Kansas and Manitoba: A Textual Crazy Quilt." *JMS* 26 (2008): 111–31.
Prymak, Thomas M. "The Royal Commission and Rudnyckyj's Mission: The Forging of Official Multiculturalism in Canada, 1963–71." *University of Toronto Quarterly* 88, no. 1 (2019): 43–63. https://doi.org/10.3138/utq.88.1.03.
Quiring, Walter. "The Canadian Mennonite Immigration to the Paraguayan Chaco, 1926–27." *MQR* 8 (January 1934): 32–42.
Quiring, Walter, and Helen Bartel. *Als ihre Zeit erfüllt war: 150 Jahre Bewährung in Russland*. Saskatoon: Modern Press, 1963.
– *In the Fullness of Time: 150 Years of Mennonite Sojourn in Russia*. Kitchener, ON: Aaron Klassen, 1974.
Rasmussen, Kathleen Britt. "Canada and Bretton Woods." In *Global Perspectives on the Bretton Woods Conference and the Post-War World Order*, edited by Giles Scott-Smith and J. Simon Rofe, 167–86. Basingstoke, UK: Palgrave Macmillan, 2017.
Reddig, K.W. "Judge Adamson versus the Mennonites of Manitoba During World War II." *JMS* 7 (1989): 51–70.
Redekop, Calvin. *Mennonite Society*. Baltimore: Johns Hopkins University Press, 1989.
Redekop, Magdalene. *Making Believe: Questions about Mennonites and Art*. Winnipeg: University of Manitoba Press, 2020.
Redekop, Paul. "The Mennonite Family in Tradition and Transition." *JMS* 4 (1986): 77–93.
Regehr, Ted D. "Lost Sons: The Canadian Mennonite Soldiers of World War II." *MQR* 66, no. 4 (October 1992): 461–80.
– "Mennonite Change: The Rise and Decline of Mennonite Community Organizations at Coaldale, Alberta." *ML* 32, no. 4 (December 1977): 13–22.
– *Mennonites in Canada, 1939–1970: A People Transformed*. Toronto: University of Toronto Press, 1996.
– *Peace, Order & Good Government: Mennonites & Politics in Canada*. Winnipeg: CMBC Publications, 2000.
– "Walter Quiring (1893–1983)." In *Shepherds, Servants and Prophets: Leadership among the Russian Mennonites (ca. 1880–1960)*, edited by Harry Loewen, 315–35. Kitchener, ON: Pandora, 2003.
Reimer, Al. "'Derche bloom Räde': Arnold Dyck and the Comic Irony of the Forstei." *JMS* 2 (1984): 60–71.
– "The Print Culture of the Russian Mennonites 1870–1930." In Friesen, *Mennonites in Russia, 1788–1988*, 221–37.
– "*Sanitätsdienst* and *Selbstschutz*: Russian-Mennonite Nonresistance in World War I and its Aftermath." *JMS* 11 (1993): 135–48.
– "The War Brings Its Own Conflict to Steinbach." *MM* 3, no. 8 (June 1974): 15–16.

Reimer, Margaret Loewen. *One Quilt, Many Pieces: A Guide to Mennonite Groups in Canada*. Waterloo, ON: Herald, 2008.
Rempel, David G. "The Expropriation of the German Colonists in South Russia During the Great War." *Journal of Modern History* 4, no. 1 (March 1932): 49–67.
– "The Mennonite Commonwealth in Russia: A Sketch of its Founding and Endurance, 1789–1919." *MQR* 47, no. 4 (October 1973): 259–308; 48, no. 1 (January 1974): 5–54.
Rempel, David G., and Cornelia Rempel Carlson. *A Mennonite Family in Tsarist Russia and the Soviet Union, 1789–1923*. Toronto: University of Toronto Press, 2002.
Rempel, D.D. "The Wonderful Ways of God." *MM* 3, no. 7 (1974): 9–10.
Rempel, Gerhard. "Cornelius Franz Klassen: Rescuer of the Mennonite Remnant, 1894–1954." In *Shepherds, Servants and Prophets: Leadership among the Russian Mennonites (ca. 1880–1960)*, edited by Harry Loewen, 193–212. Kitchener, ON: Pandora, 2003.
– "Heinrich Hajo Schroeder: The Allure of Race and Space in Hitler's Empire." *JMS* 29 (2011): 227–54.
– "Mennonites and the Holocaust: From Collaboration to Perpetuation." *MQR* 84, no. 4 (October 2010): 507–49.
Rempel, Hermann. *Kjenn jie noch Plautditsch? A Mennonite Low German Dictionary*. 2nd ed. Revised by Al Reimer. Winnipeg: Mennonite Literary Society, 1984.
Robinson, Ira. *A History of Antisemitism in Canada*. Waterloo: Wilfrid Laurier University Press, 2015.
Rose, William A., Stanley Z. Pech, S.D. Bosnitch, Bohdan R. Bociurkiw, G.W. Simpson, Leonid Ignatieff, and H. Gordon Skilling. "Discussion of Senator Yuzyk's Paper." *Canadian Slavonic Papers/Revue canadienne des slavistes* 7, no. 1 (1965): 32–50. https://doi.org/10.1080/00085006.1965.11417889.
Ross, Arthur. *Communal Solidarity: Immigration, Settlement, and Social Welfare in Winnipeg's Jewish Community, 1882–1930*. Winnipeg: University of Manitoba Press, 2019.
Ryder, N.B. "The Interpretation of Origin Statistics." *Canadian Journal of Economics and Political Science* 21, no. 4 (November 1955): 466–79. https://doi.org/10.2307/138125.
Safarian, A.E. *The Canadian Economy in the Great Depression*. Toronto: McClelland & Stewart, 1970.
Savin, Andrey I. "The 1929 Emigration of Mennonites from the USSR: An Examination of Documents from the Archive of Foreign Policy of the Russian Federation." *JMS* 30 (2012): 45–55.
Sawatsky, Rodney James. *History and Ideology: American Mennonite Identity Definition through History*. Kitchener, ON: Pandora, 2005.

Schellenberg, John K. *Schools – Our Heritage: From 46 School Districts to Hanover Unitary School Division, 1878–1968*. Steinbach, MB: Derksen Printers for the Board of the Hanover School Division No.15, 1985.

Schmaltz, Eric. "What's in a Name? Russian Germans, German Russians, or Germans from Russia, and the Challenges of Hybrid Identities." In *Jenseits der "Volksgruppe": Neue Perspektiven auf die Russlanddeutschen zwischen Russland, Deutschland und Amerika*, edited by Victor Dönninghaus, Jannis Panagiotidis, and Hans-Christian Petersen, 41–72. Berlin: De Gruyter, 2018.

Shepard, R. Bruce. "Tractors and Combines in the Second Stage of Agricultural Mechanization on the Canadian Plains." *Prairie Forum* 11, no. 2 (Fall 1986): 253–72.

Smith, Douglas. *Former People: The Last Days of the Russian Aristocracy*. London: Macmillan, 2012.

S[mith], W[illard]. H. "Corporación Paraguaya." In *ME*, vol. 1, 718–19. Hillsboro, KS: Mennonite Brethren, 1953.

Smucker, David Rempel. "Faith Versus Culture? The Mennonite Pavilion at Folklorama in Winnipeg, Manitoba, 1980–1982." *JMS* 33 (2015): 235–50.

Sneath, Robyn. "Whose Children Are They? A Transnational Minority Religious Sect and Schools as Sites of Conflict in Canada, 1890–1922." *Paedagogica historica* 53, nos. 1–2 (March 2017): 93–106. https://doi.org/10.1080/00309230.2016.1229347.

Stead, Robert J.C. "Canada's Immigration Policy." In Kennedy, *Social and Economic Conditions*, 56–62.

Steiner, Sam J. *In Search of Promised Lands: A History of Mennonites in Ontario*. Kitchener, ON: Herald, 2015.

Stevenson, J.C., and P.M. Everson. "The Cultural Context of Fertility Transition in Immigrant Mennonites." In *Fertility and Resources*, edited by John Landers and Vernon Reynolds, 47–61. Cambridge: Cambridge University Press, 1990.

Stevenson, Michael D. *Canada's Greatest Wartime Muddle: National Selective Service and the Mobilization of Human Resources during World War II*. Montreal: McGill-Queen's University Press, 2001.

Stoesz, Conrad. "Abraham J. Thiessen (1910–2002)." *MH* 35, no. 3 (September 2009): 5.

– "'Are You Prepared to Work in a Mental Hospital?' Canadian Conscientious Objectors' Service during the Second World War." *JMS* 29 (2011): 61–74.

Stoesz, Dennis. *A History of the Chortitzer Mennonite Church of Manitoba, 1874–1914*. Winnipeg: Manitoba Mennonite Historical Society, 2011.

Sudermann, David. "*Allianz* in Ukraine: More Pieces of the Puzzle." *MH* 23, no. 1 (March 1997): 1–2; 23, no. 2 (June 1997): 6–7.

Sudermann, Leonard. "My First Journey as Deputy in South Russia." In *Family Almanac for the Year of Our Lord, 1896*. Elkhart, IN: Mennonite Publishing House, c. 1895.

Swyripa, Frances. *StoriedLandscapes: Ethno-religious Identity and the Canadian Prairies*. Winnipeg: University of Manitoba Press, 2010.

Sylvester, K.M. *The Limits of Rural Capitalism: Family, Culture, and Markets in Montcalm, Manitoba, 1870–1940*. Toronto: University of Toronto Press, 2001.

Thiesen, John D. *Mennonite and Nazi? Attitudes among Mennonites in Latin America, 1933–1945*. Kitchener, ON: Pandora, 1999.

Thiessen, Jack [John]. "The Plot of Despair." In *Neighbours: Stories in Mennonite Low German and English/Nohbasch Jeschichte opp Plautdietsch enn Enjlisch*, 45–73. Cathair na Mart, Ireland: Evertype, 2014.

– *Predicht fier haite*. Hamburg: Helmut Buske, 1984.

– *Studien zum Wortschatz der kanadischen Mennoniten*. Marburg: N.G. Elwert, 1963.

Thiessen, Janis. *Necessary Idealism: A History of Westgate Mennonite Collegiate*. Winnipeg: CMU Press, 2018.

– *Not Talking Union: An Oral History of North American Mennonites and Labour*. Montreal: McGill-Queen's University Press, 2016.

Thompson, John H. *The Harvests of War: The Prairie West, 1914–1918*. Toronto: McClelland & Stewart, 1978.

Tiessen, Barbara J. *The Schoenfelder Russlaender: A Mennonite Family's History*. Windsor, ON: printed by the , 2015.

Toews, C.P. *The Terek Settlement: Mennonite Colony in the Caucasus, Origion* [sic]*, Growth and Abandonment, 1901–1918, 1925 – Memoirs*. Yarrow, BC: Columbia Press, 1972.

Toews, J.A. *Alternative Service in Canada during World War II*. Winnipeg: Conference of the Mennonite Brethren Church, 1959.

– *A History of the Mennonite Brethren Church: Pilgrims and Pioneers*. Fresno, CA: General Conference of the Mennonite Brethren Church, 1975.

Toews, John B. "The Calm before the Storm: Mennonite Brethren in Russia (1900–1914)." *Direction* 31, no. 1 (Spring 2002): 74–95.

– *Czars, Soviets and Mennonites*. Newton, KS: Faith and Life, 1982.

– "The Origins and Activities of the Mennonite *Selbstschutz* in the Ukraine (1918–1919)." *MQR* 46 (January 1972): 5–40.

– "Russian Mennonites and *Allianz*." *JMS* 14 (1996): 45–64.

Tönnies, Ferdinand. *Community and Civil Society*. Edited and translated by José Harris, translated by Margaret Hollis. Cambridge: Cambridge University Press, 2001.

Unruh, Abraham H. *Die Mennonitische Bibelschule zu Tschongraw, Krim, in Russland*. Winkler, MB: Winkler Printery, 1928.

Urry, James. "After the Rooster Crowed: Some Issues Concerning the Interpretation of Mennonite/Bolshevik Relations During the Early Soviet Period." *JMS* 13 (1995): 26–50.
- "The Cost of Community: The Funding and Economic Management of the Russian Mennonite Commonwealth before 1914." *JMS* 10 (1992): 22–55.
- "David H. Epp: Intellectual, Spiritual, Cultural Leader 1861–1934." In *Shepherds, Servants and Prophets: Leadership among the Russian Mennonites (ca. 1880–1960)*, edited by Harry Loewen, 85–102. Kitchener, ON: Pandora, 2003.
- "Dietrich Heinrich Epp: First Editor of *Der Bote* 1875–1955." In *Shepherds, Servants and Prophets: Leadership among the Russian Mennonites (ca. 1880–1960)*, edited by Harry Loewen, 103–15. Kitchener, ON: Pandora, 2003.
- "A Forgotten Encounter: The C.N.R.'s Community Progress Competitions." *Preservings*, no. 39 (2019): 3–12.
- "Gender, Generation and Social Identity in Russian Mennonite Society." *JMS* 17 (1999): 95–106.
- "Growing up with Cities: The Mennonite Experience in Imperial Russia and the Early Soviet Union." *JMS* 20 (2002): 123–54.
- "The Mennonite Commonwealth in Imperial Russia Revisited." *MQR* 84, no. 2 (April 2010): 227–47.
- "Mennonites in Ukraine during World War II: Thoughts and Questions." *MQR* 93, no. 1 (2019): 81–111.
- *Mennonites, Politics, and Peoplehood: Europe – Russia – Canada, 1525–1980.* Winnipeg, University of Manitoba Press, 2006.
- "A Mennostaat for the Mennovolk? Mennonite Immigrant Fantasies in Canada in the 1930s." *JMS* 14 (1996): 65–80.
- *None but Saints: The Transformation of Mennonite Life in Russia, 1789–1889.* Winnipeg: Hyperion, 1989.
- "Of Borders and Boundaries: Reflections on Mennonite Unity and Separation in the Modern World." *MQR* 73, no. 3 (July 1999): 503–24.
- "Prolegomena to the Study of Mennonite Society in Russia 1880–1914." *JMS* 8 (1990): 52–75.
- "The Reading Worlds of Russlaender and Kanadier Mennonites: Print, Libraries, and Readers in the Origins of Mennonite Creative Writing." *JMS* 27 (2010): 129–49.
- "'The Snares of Reason': Changing Mennonite Attitudes to 'Knowledge' in Nineteenth-Century Russia." *Comparative Studies in Society and History* 25, no. 2 (April 1983): 306–22. https://doi.org/10.1017/S0010417500010446.
- "Time and Memory: Secular and Sacred Aspects of the World of the Russian Mennonites and Their Descendants – Lecture One: Time: The Transcendent and the Worldly; Lecture Two: Memory: Monuments and the Marking of Pasts." *Conrad Grebel Review*, The 2006 Bechtel Lectures, 25, no. 1 (Winter 2007): 4–62.

Urry, James and Helmut-Harry Loewen, "Protecting Mammon: Some Dilemmas of Mennonite Non-resistance in Late Imperial Russia and the Origins of the *Selbstschutz*." *JMS* 9 (1991): 34–53.
Vogt, Erich. *The Steinbach Saga: The Story of the Vogt-Block Family and the Reimer-Wiebe Family*. Altona, MB: D.W. Friesen, 2013.
Voisey, Paul. "Rural Local History and the Prairie West." *Prairie Forum* 10, no. 2 (1985): 327–38.
– *Vulcan: The Making of a Prairie Community*. Toronto: University of Toronto Press, 1988.
Wagner, Johnathan F. *Brothers Beyond the Sea: National Socialism in Canada*. Waterloo, ON: Wilfred Laurier University Press, 1981.
Warkentin, Abe, ed. *Reflections on Our Heritage: A History of Steinbach and the R.M. of Hanover from 1874*. Steinbach, MB: Derksen Printers, 1971.
Warkentin, Erwin. "The Mennonites before Moscow: The Notes of Dr. Otto Auhagen." *JMS* 26 (2008): 201–20.
Warkentin, John H. "Mennonite Agricultural Settlements of Southern Manitoba." *Geographical Review* 49, no. 3 (July 1959): 342–68. https://doi.org/10.2307/211911.
– *The Mennonite Settlements of Southern Manitoba*. Steinbach, MB: Hanover Steinbach Historical Society, 2000.
Warkentin, Margaret. *Descendants of Jacob Heinrich Thiessen, 1781–1994*. Steinbach, MB: Martins Printing, 1994.
Weaver-Zercher, David. *Martyrs Mirror: A Social History*. Baltimore: Johns Hopkins University Press, 2016.
Werner, Hans. *Living between Worlds: A History of Winkler*. Winkler, MB: D.W. Friesen, 2006.
– "More than Just Business: An Historical Overview of Jewish-Mennonite Relations in Winkler." In *Jewish Life and Times: A Collection of Essays*, vol. 9, edited by Daniel Stone and Annalee Greenberg, 19–35. Winnipeg: Jewish Historical Society of Western Canada, 2009.
– "Sacred, Secular and Material: The Thought of J.J. Siemens." *JMS* 17 (1999): 194–210.
Whitaker, Reg. "Official Repression of Communism during World War II." *Labour/Le Travial* 17 (Spring 1986): 135–66.
Wiebe, Jeremy. "Performing Ethnicity in a Pluralistic Society: The 1974 Manitoba Mennonite Centennial." *JMS* 37 (2019): 285–303.
Wiebe, Joseph R. "On the Mennonite-Métis Borderland: Environment, Colonialism, and Settlement in Manitoba." *JMS* 35 (2017): 111–26.
Wiebe, Rudy. *Of This Earth: A Mennonite Boyhood in the Boreal Forest*. Toronto: Vintage, 2006.
– "Tombstone Community." In *A Voice in the Land: Essays by and about Rudy Wiebe*, edited by W.J. Keith, 16–24. Edmonton: NeWest, 1981.

Williams, Austin M.H. "Placing 'Rights and Liberties in Pawn until the Defeat of Hitlerism': Canadian Intelligence Gathering in the Second World War." *The Great Lakes Journal of Undergraduate History* 3, no. 1 (Fall 2015): 70–93.

Wiseman, Nelson. "The Pattern of Prairie Politics." In *Party Politics in Canada*, 8th ed., edited by Hugh G. Thorburn and Alan Whitehorn, 351–68. Toronto: Prentice-Hall, 2001.

Yuzyk, Paul. "Canada: A Multicultural Nation." *Canadian Slavonic Papers/Revue canadienne des slavistes* 7, no. 1 (1965): 23–31.

– "Reply, Rather than Retort." *Canadian Slavonic Papers/Revue canadienne des slavistes* 7, no. 1 (1965): 51–7.

Zacharias, Peter D. *Footprints of a Pilgrim People: Story of the Blumenort Mennonite Church*. Gretna, MB: Blumenort Mennonite Church, 1985.

– *Reinland: An Experience in Community*. Altona, MB: Reinland Centennial Committee, 1976.

Index

Note: The letter *f* following a page number denotes a figure; the letter *m*, a map; and the letter *t*, a table.

Abundant Life Fellowship, Grunthal, 218, 266
Adamson, John E. (judge), and conscription into Second World War, 164
agriculture: egg grading, 187, 194; egg production, 52, 120–1, 172–3, 187, 229; hog production, 49, 172, 173, 183, 187, 256; mechanization, 175; tractors, 24, 175–6, 193. *See also* dairy industry
Alberta: Russländer in, 7, 51, 56, 82, 111, 150, 161, 163, 199; Coaldale, 56
alcohol, 68, 75, 155, 183, 256
Allianz, Mennonite religious grouping, 150
Alt Bergfeld. *See* Bergfeld
alternative service, Mennonite: in Canada, 161–2, 163–4, 165; in Russia, 15, 31, 124, 130, 140, 141, 161
Altona, 128, 160, 174, 249
Anabaptist, 129, 267–8; census category, 267–8; vision, 255
Anishinaabeg (Ojibwa), 5, 6
Arnaud, 16, 188, 206

Baar, Ellen, 8
Banmann, Jake (car dealer), 190
Baratov Shlachtin, 57, 100, 116; reunion (1937), 157
Barkman, J.R. (Steinbach businessman), 247
Beaubien, Arthur Lucien (federal MP), 137
beet. *See* sugar beet industry
Bender, Harold S. (historian), 255
Bergfeld, Alt and Neu, 40, 45, 46, 58, 67, 79, 81, 83, 84, 115, 122, 128, 234
Bergthaler, 165, 184; congregation, 9, 33, 70–1, 128, 216, 222, 224, 234, 264–5; Spencer, 9, 216, 222, 224, 234; West Reserve, 33, 71, 128
Bestvater family, 58; A.J., 113*t*
bilingualism policies: Canadian, 249–50, 253–4; Manitoba school, 21, 74, 76. *See also* Royal Commission on Bilingualism and Biculturalism
Birdsell, Sandra, 3, 4
Bjarnason, John Helgi, 75

Block (Ukrainian family): Ken, 203–4; Steve (garage owner), 126, 191, 204, 261
Block (Russländer family), 113*t*, 132, 155, 157, 164, 206, 233, 242–3, 260; Jacob H., 85, 87–9, 90, 100; Peter J., 155, 164, 169–70
Bolsheviks. *See* Soviet Union
Braun, Johann F. (Kanadier entrepreneur), 74, 104, 121, 124, 134, 173, 243
Braun, Peter (teacher in Russia), 142–3
Braun, Peter A. ("Red Beard"), 45, 49–50, 51, 81, 95, 119, 125
Braun, Peter J. (army volunteer, Second World War), 164
Brazil, Russländer in, 50, 143, 149, 255
Brecht, Georg de (pseudonym). *See* Töws, Gerhard
British Columbia, 232, 238, 255
Bruderthaler. *See* Evangelical Mennonite Brethren
Brunk, George R., II (evangelist), 257–8
Bückert, Johann P. (Elder, Blumenort), 83

Campbell, N.S. (English lawyer), 135
Canadian Centennial (1967), 242–3, 244–5, 245*f*, 260
Canadian Colonization Association. *See* Mennonite Land Settlement Board (MLSB)
Canadian Mennonite Association, 249
Canadian Mennonite Board of Colonization (CMBC), 7–8, 28, 33–6, 44–4, 54*t*, 130–7, 146, 163; debts and, 48, 53, 112–16, 118–19
Canadian Mennonite Conference. *See* Conference of Mennonites in Canada

Canadian National Railway, Community Progress competitions, 91
Canadian Pacific Railroad (CPR), 28, 75, 79; lands, 35–7, 44, 49; loans, 28, 33, 112, 114
Carey, 16, 22, 50, 75, 119
Carillon, provincial constituency, 136, 137, 138, 210–11, 212
Central Mennonite Immigration Committee (ZMIK), 52–3, 131–2, 146
choirs and choir festivals. *See* music
Chornoboy, Ted, 126, 175, 176, 176*f*, 190–1, 200, 247; Luba, 200
Chortitza Colony (Russia). *See* Khortitsa Colony
Chortitzer: Bergthaler and, 128, 184; in Canada, 9, 22, 42, 136, 154–5, 184; congregation, 9, 70–1, 78, 81, 95, 96, 128, 216–17, 222, 266, 313n5; Paraguay, 126–7; rejection of politics, 133–4, 136, 164–5; Russländer relations with, 70–1, 81; schools, 95–6
Christian Life Fellowship Tabernacle, Grunthal, 218
Christian Mennonite Church of Grunthal (CMC), 266
Churchill, Winston (British politician), 136, 165
citizenship, 136–7, 142, 165–6, 251; Canadian, 149, 199, 245–6; Citizenship Act (1946), 248. *See also* Russländer: citizenship
Commission for Church Affairs/Kommission für Kirchenangelegenheiten (*KfK*), in Russia, 141
community: concept of, 7, 10–11; Mennonite sense of, 11–13, 264; Tönnies and, 10

Conference of Mennonite Brethren in North America, 151, 236
Conference of Mennonites in Canada, 33, 53–4, 59, 79, 101, 236, 237, 253, 256. *See also* Manitoba Mennonite Conference
Conference of Mennonites in North America, 79, 81
Conference of Mennonites of Central Canada, 33, 37, 79, 81
conscientious objection, 59, 142–3, 162–3, 164–5
cooperative(s), 183; Dairy Ltd., 173, 181–2; Grunthal store, 122–3, 124, 126, 173, 193–4, 207; movement, 122, 181, 191
Cottonwood Corner Game Farm, 235. *See also* Janz family: Nicholas (Nick)
credit unions, 177; Grunthal, 174–5, 195–6, 234–5; St. Malo, 173, 174

dairy industry, 50–2, 74–6, 126, 183–7, 194, 235; cheese and butter, 119–20, 121–2, 171–2, 171–3, 183–4, 189–90; children's clubs, 200; City Dairy, 50, 75, 122, 126, 172–3; Farmers' Cooperative Dairy, 173, 181–2; Kraft, 183; Medo-land, 183, 202
Dawson, C.A. (sociologist), 262
debts, 39, 50; C.F. Klassen and, 114–16; CMBC, 47, 48, 53, 112–6, 118–9; to Intercontinental and National Companies, 53–4, 112; municipal taxes, 117–19; travel, 101, 112–13, 177
DePape, Gus (dairy farmer), 184
depression, economic. *See* Great Depression
De Salaberry, Rural Municipality, 67, 75
Dominion City, 59, 188

Doukhobors, 37, 40
drama, Low German, 206–7
Dufrost, 16, 43
Dugard, George (music conductor), 206
Dutch, 11, 26; Russländer claims of descent, 20, 143, 147, 148, 163, 267
Driedger family, 57; Abram A., 113*t*; Abram J., 82, 83, 84, 85, 240*t*; Johann A., 38, 89; John A. (teacher), 90, 209
Dyck, Arnold (Abram), (author and publisher), 106, 147, 149, 154; Echo-Verlag series, 177; Low German and, 45, 50–1, 154, 205, 206–7, 226, 289n36
Dyck, Heinrich (publisher), 237–8

East Reserve, 5, 16; cordwood, 46, 67, 120–1, 128, 211; French settlement and speakers, 16, 50, 75, 120, 121, 124, 125, 126, 174, 184, 191, 194, 212, 243, 256; original Mennonite villages, 17*m*, 78–9; religious affiliation, 16, 70–1; saskatoon berries, 40, 72; seneca roots, 71, 120; Ukrainians, 10, 73–5, 125–6
Ebenezer Mädchenheim, 59, 60
education, 16–17, 222–3; districts/divisions, 212, 214*t*, 215, 216*t*, 224; higher, 15–17, 33, 94, 108–9, 207, 214, 223–5, 240, 264; Kanadier attitudes, 21, 33, 66, 94–6, 107, 108–9; Manitoba Royal Commission on, 211–15, 224; in Russia, 16–17, 94–6; Russländer attitudes, 31–2, 61, 65, 70, 96–7, 207–8; reforms, 211–15, 224–6, 249; Second World War, 160, 165–7. *See also* Goodwill School
elections: congregational, 82, 84–6, 136, 235; federal, 18, 137–9,

elections (*continued*)
246; local council, 133–5, 247; provincial, 137–9, 189–90, 246–7. *See also* voting

electrification: dairying and, 181, 183–5; installation, 181; Manitoba Power Commission, 179, 180, 181; planning, 179, 181; women's work and, 179–80, 192, 222

Elim congregation, 91–2, 222, 244; election of ministers/deacons, 83–5, 232–4; Elim Ladies Auxiliary, 223; foundation of, xi–xii, 82–7; Maria Martha Verein, 223; meeting house, 85, 86, 86*f*, 98*f*, 125, 131–2, 125, 205, 217*f*, 234; membership, 165, 264–5; Tabea Verein, 91, 223; youth groups, 87–8, 89, 223. *See also* music

Emerson, 136, 188, 256; federal electorate, 136

emigration, Mennonite: from Canada to Mexico and Paraguay (1920s–30s), 21–2, 22*f*, 154; from Russia to Canada before 1914, 15–16; from Soviet Union to Canada after 1923, 26–9, 29*f*. *See also* Russländer

English language, 18, 59, 63, 64, 65, 75, 90, 178, 220; in schooling, 32, 74, 91, 94–7, 100–1, 105–7, 109, 151–2, 208, 235; transition to, 236–41, 243, 247–50, 257

English people, 155, 170; Russländer views of, 75–8, 120, 133–4, 136, 138–9, 143–4, 152–4, 229, 247–9, 253

Enns family, 57; Anna (Rempel), 232; David J., 57; H.J., 82; Johann J. (Elder), 38, 57, 80–2, 83–4, 85–7, 108, 164, 211, 232*f*, 233–4, 240*t*, 285n12

Enns, David D., 91, 240*t*; Margarethe, 91

Enns, Eva, 91
Enns, Franz F. (Elder, Whitewater), 80, 83, 85
Enns, J.J. (dramatist, Ontario), 206–7
Enns, P.H. (Elder, St. Elizabeth), 84, 86–7, 148
Epp, Frank H., 7–8
Esau, Abram N., 240*t*
ethnic activities, 251–2; grants, 252–3; populations, 6–7, 250. *See also* multiculturalism
Evangelical Mennonite Brethren (Bruderthaler), 71, 216–7, 266
Ewert, H.H., 18

farm machinery dealerships, 121, 125–6, 175–6. *See also* tractors
Fast, David (minister), 84–6
federal constituencies: Emerson, 136; La Vérendrye, 136; Provencher, 136, 138, 169
food, 65, 192; ethnic, 183, 251, 258; women and, 69, 219
friendship, 12, 55, 64, 69, 88, 219
First World War, 144; in Canada, 20–3, 95, 121–2, 161–2, 167; in Russia, 22–3, 24–5, 47–8, 79, 100, 124, 130, 142
Francis, E.K. (sociologist), 9, 36, 64–5, 170–1, 193, 194–5, 196–7, 250
French settlement and speakers, 16, 75, 94, 120, 123, 125, 128, 137–8, 174, 184, 193, 196; language, 236, 248–50, 254; Manitoba Catholic Schools, 94, 95. *See also* Métis
Friesen, A.A. (emigration delegate from Soviet Union), 143
Friesen, Abraham J. (author, professor), 226–8
Friesen, Gerald (historian), 202
Friesen, H.T. (lumber merchant), 191
Friesen, J.J. (baker), 113*t*, 192, 222, 240*t*

Friesen, Peter P., 125
Frisian, Nazi racial classification, 146–7, 163; Heinrich H. Schröder, promotor of, 146–7
Froese, Abraham F. (minister), 84, 234
Froese, A.H., 237
funerals, 68–9, 89, 90, 219–20, 223, 257

garages, 193, 194; dealerships, 126, 176f, 190–1. *See also* Jake Banmann; Steve Block; Ted Chornoboy; John D. Warkentin
Gardiner, J.G. (politician/federal minister), 163
German language. *See* High German; Low German
Gerstein, Baruch (Benjamin), Jewish shopkeeper, 72–3, 124, 149
Glenlea, 39, 56, 58, 123, 125, 157
Gnadenfeld, East Reserve, 38, 47, 53, 57, 60–1, 67, 79, 82–3, 95, 99, 115, 121, 198, 227
Goodwill School, 96, 100–1, 122, 166, 207; board, 207–8, 209–10, 214, 224; collegiate, 224–5; district, 99, 213–14; *Green and Gold* (yearbook), 211, 224–5, 243
Goossen, J.D. (secretary, Hanover RM), 118–19
Graceway Church (Grunthal), 266
Great Depression, 54, 58, 66–7, 121, 103, 116–17, 119–28, 132, 143, 145–6, 155, 170, 173–4, 188, 190, 206–7; prairie provinces, 111–13, 132, 190
green, use of term (for Grün as in Grunthal), 4, 181, 200, 201, 211, 260, 261
Greenway, J.J. (school trustee), 99
Gretna. *See* Mennonite Collegiate Institute
Grigorievka, 58; reunion (1938), 157

Grunthal, 4, 79; auditorium, 204, 205, 205f, 206, 244; board of trade, 194–5; building improvements, 191–2; chamber of commerce, 194–5, 225; co-op, 122–3, 124, 126, 173, 193–4, 207; credit union, 173–4, 195–6, 234–5; fair, 49, 200–1, 253; farming in, 45–6, 50–2, 175–6, 183, 186–7; "Green" adopted as name, 4, 181, 200, 201, 211, 260, 261; Green Valley Riders, 200; Herd Improvement Association, 186; horticultural society, 200; library, 145–6; New 121, 126, 231m; old people's home (Menno Home), 222; population, 193, 222, 263–4, 266–8; property transfer, 229–30; Russländer settlement in, 46–9, 62m, 79, 127m, 182m; school board, 207–8, 209–10, 224; social structure, 66–8, 228; Sports Association, 195; streets, 193, 230–1; volunteer fire brigade, 195. *See also* Bergthaler; Chortitzer; Elim congregation
Grunthal Christian Fellowship, 266
Grunthal Evangelical Mennonite Brethren, 266
Guenther family and store, 58, 113, 192–4, 198, 202, 230; Anna (Penner), 122; Art (Arthur), 154, 164, 230; Eric, 164, 230, 259; Eddie (Edward), 229–30, 259, 304n78; Franz (Frank), 58, 113, 122–3, 124, 158, 161, 176, 202, 230, 259

Hamm, Bruno, 72, 149
Hanover, Rural Municipality, 9, 67, 75, 243, 262–3, 266, 268; council, 132–4; economic issues, 111–12, 118–19, 172, 181, 188–90, 195; education and, 91, 99, 101, 208–10,

Hanover, Rural Municipality (*continued*) 213, 215, 224; highways, 118; reeve, 134; population, 262–3; school division, 213, 224; taxes, 117–18, 118*t*, 126, 208; Ukrainians and, 134–5, 247; voting, 133, 212–13, 215, 246–7; water supply, 195

Hanover Trustees' Association, 209

Heese family, 60, 67; Dietrich, 58–9, 74–5, 113*t*, 163, 211, 234, 237, 244; Elizabeth (Janzen), 59; Heinrich, 58; Margarethe, 59; Nikolai (Nick), 59, 161

Heidebrecht, David (teacher), 100–9, 121, 202, 207, 208, 254; Anna (Fast), 101; German instruction, 105–7, 106*f*, 239

Heidebrecht, Jakob J. (estate owner, Schönfeld), 100

Heinrichs, David (schoolchild), 166

Heinrichs, David (teacher), 97

Heinrichs, William (Bergthaler minister), 128

Herriot, Archibald A. (school inspector), 101, 103–4, 166, 167

Hespeler, Municipality, 133. *See also* Hanover

Hiebert, David F. (restaurant owner), 125

Hiebert, Jacob H. ("Store"), 121–2, 124

High German, 11–12, 20, 63; Low German, suppression of, 63–4, 104–7, 151, 153–5, 161, 167, 238, 254; Mennonite Society for the Fostering of the Mennonite Mother Tongue/*Mennonitische Verein zur Pflege der deutschen Muttersprache in Canada*, 238–40; religion and, 11, 88, 40, 225, 235, 237, 238, 239; Russländer identity and, 76, 152–6, 237–8, 247–8, 256–7; in schooling, 64, 95, 100–1, 105–8, 152, 167, 210, 221; social status and, 65, 66–7, 72, 234, 239–41; transition to English, 236–41, 243, 247–8, 257; writing in, 151, 226, 237–8

highways, 118, 183, 188–9, 189*m*, 197; Piney Highway, 183, 188–9

Hildebrand, J.J., 64, 144, 159, 238

Holdemans, 71, 81

hospitals, 202; Bethesda, 119; Concordia, 119

Hübert, P.P., 82

Hutterites, 27, 193, 267

hydro. *See* electrification

identity, 20, 23, 205, 266–7; Canadian, 248–52, 254–6; census returns, 267–8; "Dutch," 20, 143, 147, 148, 163, 267; "English," 247–8; "German," 143–6, 148–56, 163, 167; Kanadier, 64, 76, 148, 150, 151–2; language and, 76, 152–6, 237–8, 247–8, 256–7; Nazi, 146–9, 221; religious, 140–1; Russländer, 32, 64, 76, 105, 140–3, 144, 148–9, 151–6, 160; Second World War and, 163–4, 167. *See also* nationalism

immigration, Mennonite: to Canada and the United States from Russia before 1914, 15–16, 244; to Canada, Brazil, and Paraguay, post–Second World War, 30, 255; to Mexico and Paraguay, 1920–30, 21–2, 22*f*, 154; Umsiedler/Aussiedler immigrants, 255

Indigenous peoples, 5–6, 7, 72, 123, 230, 243

Intercontinental Company Limited, 42–5, 49, 76, 85, 99, 112, 119; collapse, 53–4. *See also* National Trust

Isaak, Frank (teacher), 97

Janz family, 58; A.P., 113*t*; John, 58; Nicholas (Nick), 58, 234–5; Sara (Peters), 58; Tobias, 45, 58
Janz, B.B. (Elder, Manitoba), 148, 162–3
Janzen family: Heinrich H., 59; Peter H., 59, 113*t*, 132, 187, 212, 240*t*
Janzen, Jacob H. (Elder and author, Ontario), 141, 153, 206
Jewish people: Russländer attitudes towards, 73, 145, 146, 149, 158, 160–1, 167; shopkeepers in Grunthal, 72–3, 121, 149; in Winnipeg, 59
Jones, Cynthia, 8
Jutras, René (federal MP), 137

Kanadier: definition of, 3; immigration and settlement of in 1870s, 4–6; views of Russländer, 65–6
Kasdorf family, 57; A.J., 83
Kauenhoven family, 124
Khortitsa Colony, 23, 70, 84–5, 287n2, 287n13; Civil War, 25, 26; education in, 94, 100, 108, 154; emigration from, 28; Low German and, 63–4, 87, 106; Molochna immigrants and, 56–8, 61; settlers in Canada, 35, 57, 58, 60–1, 79, 83, 84, 227
kinship, 12–13, 15, 33, 35, 55–7, 60, 67, 102, 124, 138, 140, 173, 218–9, 255–6. *See also* marriage
Kirkconnell, Watson (professor, on Low German literature), 226
Klassen, Cornelius F., 114–16, 115*f*, 238
Klassen, Jenna, 8
Klassen, Johann P. (Elder, Winnipeg), 79, 80, 82, 83, 143, 233
Klassen, Julius, 57, 125; feed mill, 170, 184

Klassen, Peter D., 57, 113*t*, 149, 176
Kleefeld, 98, 119, 190
Kleine Gemeinde, 9, 71–2, 133, 135, 154, 257; education and, 96, 210
Kommission für Kirchenangelegenheiten (*KfK*). *See* Commission for Church Affairs
Krahn family, 57; Abraham B., 85, 240*t*
Krahn, Johann F., 104, 121, 134, 135, 173, 243
Kroeger, Arthur (writer), 9
Kroeger, Jacob (Nazi supporter), 160–1

LaFrance, Joseph (agricultural advisor), 76, 185–6, 185*f*, 200
language. *See* English language; French settlement and speakers; High German; identity; Low German; Russian language; Ukrainian language
Latin America, Mennonites in. *See* Brazil; Mexico; Paraguay
Lehr, John, 10
Loewen, Royden (historian), 253, 276n39
Lohrenz, Gerhard (Elder and author), 242
Low German, 11–13, 20, 63, 68, 93; humour, 66, 76, 87, 228; Russländer suppression of, 63–4, 104–7, 151, 153–5, 167, 238, 254; speech and, 6, 35, 63–5, 133–4, 235–7, 253–4, 267; written works in, 205, 206–7, 227–8

mail services, 69, 124, 165, 194
Mackenzie King, William Lyon (politician and prime minister), 137, 179, 301n6
Mackintosh, W.A. (economist), 262

Makhno, Nestor, 25, 26, 136
Manitoba Centennial, 260; royal visit (1970), 243–4
Manitoba Farmers Union (MFU), 199
Manitoba Intercultural Council Act (1984/1992), 250–1
Manitoba Labour Relations Act (1948), 209
Manitoba Mennonite Conference, 223
Manitoba Mennonite Educational Committee, 212
Manitoba Mennonite Trustee Association and Manitoba Mennonite Educational Committee, 249
Manitoba Teachers' Society, 208–9
marriage, 12, 27, 66; debts, 112; mixed, 4, 69–70, 72, 75, 218–9, 265; social relations of, 35, 56–8, 60, 67, 84, 87–8, 125. *See also* weddings
Martens family: Abraham P., 57–8, 240*t*; Jacob, 240*t*
Martens, John S., 240*t*
Mary Martha Home, 59, 60
McCreary, Mennonite settlement, 57, 83–4
medical costs, 72, 101, 112, 119. *See also* hospitals
Memrik Colony, 26, 84
Mennonite Brethren: Canada, 56, 59, 63, 70, 75, 79, 85, 86, 141, 148, 236, 249, 306n23; Grunthal, 58, 101, 150–1, 208, 218, 227, 235; North America, 33, 35, 80, 151; Russia, 33, 63, 141; Steinbach, 81, 92, 208–9
Mennonite Church Canada, 256
Mennonite Church USA, 256
Mennonite Collegiate Institute (Gretna), 16–17, 100, 108, 109, 156, 212, 316
Mennonite Commonwealth, Russian, 18, 24, 222, 264

Mennonite German Language Society, 249
Mennonite Heritage Village (Steinbach), 252
Mennonite Land Settlement Board (MLSB), 37–8, 44, 48, 52; Canadian Colonization Association, 37, 44
Mennonite Literary Society, 253
Mennonite Mirror, 253
Mennonite Society for the Promotion of the German Language in Canada, 249–50
Mennonitische Lehrerzeitung (later *Mennonitische Welt*), 237–8
Mennonitisches Bildungsinstitut (Winnipeg), 249. *See also* Westgate Mennonite Collegiate
Mennonitische Volkswarte (Steinbach), 147. *See also* Arnold Dyck
Menzies, John H. (school inspector), 243
Métis, 4, 6, 49, 79, 243. *See also* French settlement and speakers: Manitoba Catholic Schools
Mexico, Mennonite emigration to, 22, 40, 255
mills/milling, 124, 170; feed, 50, 72, 184, 194; Kanadier, 121–2, 124; in Russia, 18, 23, 24, 50, 59
Mirau, David D. (candidate for minister), 82, 87
Molochna Colony, 24; Schönfelder and, 56–7; Khortitsa immigrants and, 56–8, 61
Müller, Adolf F. (reeve), 134, 135; Elisabeth (Schellenberg), 134
multiculturalism, policy of, 248–53, 258; Manitoba Intercultural Council Act (1984/1992), 250–1. *See also* Royal Commission on Bilingualism and Biculturalism

music, 235; choirs, 52, 87–90, 98, 204–6, 210, 235–6, 244; congregational lead singer, 82, 223–4, 235–6; festivals, 88–9, 89f, 206, 144, 204–5, 218–19; jazz, 144; Kenneth Peacock recordings, 251–2; notational system, 88–90

mutual fire insurance schemes, 90, 132

names, place, 4–5, 61, 67; changing, 198, 201, 260–1; congregations, 79, 82; Kanadier village, 16, 46, 78–9; schools, 95–6, 224; streets (Grunthal), 193

naming, personal, changing, 145 258–60; English, 75–6, 258; French, 260; German, 4, 258–9; Russian/Ukrainian, 59, 258, 260. *See also* nicknames

nationalism, 20, 140–1; Canadian, 244–6, 251, 254–5; German, 72; Russian, 142, 247. *See also* identity

National Trust, 42–3, 49, 53–4, 76, 86, 112, 117, 177

Nazi movement: in Canada, 145–6, 159–60, 167; Deutsche Bund, 146, 169; ideology, 73, 144, 145–7; Kanadier response, 149, 150; literature, 146, 147–8, 147f, 158, 160, 168; Mennonite support for, 145, 146–54, 156–7, 159, 161, 165, 169, 238; name changing, 145

Neufeld, C.F. (builder), 191

Neufeld (Navall), Dietrich (author), 159

Neufeld, George M. (teacher), 96

Neufeld, Hermann H. (editor *Rundschau*), 146

Neufeld, Jacob, 113t

Neustaedter, Paul (teacher), 210

New Bothwell, 215, 230

newspapers, 11, 141, 256–7; *Der Bote (Der Immigranten Bote)*, 90, 234, 239, 240, 257; *Der Botschafter*, 33; *Canadian Mennonite*, 253, 257; *Carillon*, 240, 256–7; *Courier*, 139; *Deutsche Zeitung Kanada*, 146, 160; *Die Friedensstimme*, 33–4; *Manitoba Free Press*, 53; *Mennonitische Post*, 257; *Mennonitische Rundschau*, 101, 146, 149, 160, 163; *Nordwesten*, 139; *Steinbach Post (Die Post)*, 71, 138, 173, 206, 256; *Winnipeg Free Press*, 159, 240; *Winnipeg Tribune*, 159, 165, 240

nicknames, 45, 47, 124, 149–1, 150–1, 187, 291n39

Niverville, 43, 125, 173, 190, 230, 263

non-resistance, Mennonite, 15, 25, 74, 165–6; Canadian recognition of, 15; Russian recognition of, 15. *See also* alternative service, Mennonite

North Dakota, 188, 256

Ojibwa. *See* Anishinaabeg

Old Colony, Russia. *See* Khortitsa Colony

Olfert, Heinrich (minister), 57, 83–4

Ontario, 51, 170; Russländer in, 7, 38, 39, 48, 56, 83, 85, 100, 125, 141, 153, 176, 232; "Swiss" Mennonites in, 7, 8, 20, 151, 162, 171, 243

Orenburg, Russia, 58, 61, 122

Orphans Office, 78, 90

Otterburne, 16, 188

Paetkau, David H. (teacher), 240–1

Paetkau, Henry, 8

Pansy, 125, 230

Paraguay, Kanadier in, 21–2, 42, 66, 67, 75, 121, 126–7, 134, 154–5, 196; Nazi influence in, 149; post–Second World War, 30, 255; Russländer in, 30, 143, 255

356   Index

Pearson, Lester B. (Prime Minister), 248
Penner, Harvey Van, 208
Penner, Isaak (minister), 84
Penner, Jacob J., 83
Peters family, 57, 109, 240; G.A., 132; Johann G. (manager of cooperative), 123, 129, 132, 207, 223, 240*t*; Jessie (teacher), 223; Margaret (Hildebrand), (teacher), 109–10, 223; Margarethe (Warkentin), 123; Mary (teacher), 223; Sara, 58, 223
Peters, Abraham A. (minister), 82, 83–4, 87, 99
Peters, "Dr.," 121, 124
Peters, Gerhard A. (minister), 81, 82, 156
Peters, Gerhard H. (Mennonite Collegiate Institute, Gretna), 156, 238
Peters, Jakob (Oberschulze/reeve), 133
Peters, Jacob H., 135
Peters, J.W. (councillor), 222
Peters, Victor (teacher, writer), 108, 237–8
Peters, Wilhelm J. (minister), 84–5, 233
politics: Anabaptist/Mennonite attitudes to, 129–30; Canadian, 32–3, 138–9, 150, 246; German, 144, 148–9, 160; Russian, 18, 130, 136. *See also* elections; voting
Prefontaine: hockey cup, 203; members of Manitoba Legislature: Albert, 137, 138; Edmond, 137, 138, 188, 210–11, 212
Prussian Mennonites, 13, 66, 88, 93, 94, 100, 129, 154; in Canada, 18, 27, 33, 108
Prymak, Thomas M. (linguist), 250

Quiring, Walter (Jacob), (Nazi sympathiser and editor), 145, 156, 238–9

radio, 76–7, 116; broadcasts, 158, 160–1, 219, 257; CYK, 260–1
Red River: highway, 188, 230; Resistance, 5; sugar beet cultivation, 173
Reesor (Mennonite settlement), 100, 101
Regier, Peter (Elder, Rosenort), 33
Reimer family: Al (professor/ writer), 101, 254; Peter J.B. (teacher), 210, 239
Reimer, Jacob J. (evangelist), 86
Reimer, J.J. (businessman), 135
Reimer, Susanna Nettie (teacher), 102, 103
Reinlander Church, 9, 40, 95
Rempel family, 57; Dietrich J., 82, 85, 113*t*, 124; George, 208, 259; Peter J., 208. *See also* Jacob J. Rempel
Rempel, Jacob J., 48*f*, 80, 82, 91, 108, 113*t*, 121, 124, 126, 131–2, 132*f*, 176–7, 208, 233, 259; agricultural improvement, 52–3, 55, 117; councillor RM Hanover, 134–5; Intercontinental Company agent, 85, 115, 118–19, 121, 135; land settlement and, 38, 47–9; wives: Lena (Woelke), 91; Maria (Thiessen), 57
Rempel, Johann G., 154
Rempel, Peter, 37
Rempel, Peter J. (teacher), 103
reunions, pre–Second World War. *See* Baratov Shlachtin; Grigorievka; Schönfelders; Terek Colony
Reuter, Fritz (Low German writer), 87, 207

Rhineland, Rural Municipality, 190
Robertson, Andrew (agricultural advisor), 49, 117
Robertson, James (landowner in Grunthal area), 42
Roseau River Reserve, 5, 6, 7, 72, 123, 230
Rosthern, 18, 33, 34, 152, 240; German Academy, 108, 240
Royal Commission on Bilingualism and Biculturalism (1963), 248–9, 253
Royal Commission on Education (Manitoba) (1957–9), 211–5, 224
Rural Municipality (RM). *See* De Salaberry; Hanover; Hespeler; Rhineland
Russia: Civil War (1917–21), 22, 25–6, 34, 36, 73, 100, 110, 139; Great Reforms (1860–80), 31, 94, 129–30, 133; pre-revolutionary (before 1917), 18–20, 19*m*, 22, 23, 34, 48–9, 63, 72, 74, 76, 88, 94, 123, 150, 153, 177; Revolution (1905), 25, 94, 130, 136, 141; Revolution (1917), 6, 18, 22, 36, 37, 73, 110, 139, 140, 142, 145, 156, 157
Russian language, 11, 20, 31, 40, 59, 63–4, 74–5, 76, 88, 90, 93–4, 133, 152–3, 156, 247
Russländer: citizenship, 100, 136–7, 142, 149, 161–2, 199, 245–6, 248, 251; definition of, 3; immigration and settlement of, 6–7; internal contrasts among, 56–8; mobility of, 219–20, 226, 232, 255, 264; support for Nazis, 146–57; views of Kanadier, 65–6

St. Malo, 125, 126; cooperative in, 173, 174, 181
St. Pierre-Jolys, 16, 50, 75, 120, 121, 124, 125, 126, 191, 194, 212, 243, 256; chamber of commerce, 195; cooperative, 174; highway, 118, 188–9; hockey team, 200
Sarto, 73, 125, 230, 243, 247, 256; highway, 188–9
Saskatchewan, 38, 51, 95, 199; Depression in, 111; Kanadier in, 5, 7, 18, 21, 31, 33, 34, 37, 40, 64, 79, 83, 108, 151, 252; Rosthern, 18, 33, 34, 108, 240; Royal Commission on Immigration and Settlement (1930), 29; Russländer in, 18, 34, 38, 40, 42, 59, 64, 67, 143, 152, 240; Saskatoon, 33, 164
Sawatzky family: Gerhard W., 37–8, 48, 52–3; Maria (Klassen), 57; Wilhelm W., 38, 52, 57, 67, 113, 227
Schapansky family, 58; Jacob, 233
Schellenberg, B.J. ("archivist"), 107
Schellenberg, Jacob J., 240*t*
Schönfeld settlement in Russia, 23–6, 60–1, 97, 123
Schönfelders: in Canada, 28, 38–9; in Grunthal, 47, 56–7, 60, 70, 82, 100, 116, 123, 134, 227; reunion (1938), 157–8
Schönwiese, congregation in Winnipeg, 79, 81, 82, 90, 143, 164, 233
schools: English named, 96; Gravel Ridge, 109; Kornelsen, 109; Lister, 108; public, 21, 95–6; Spencer, 96, 101, 117, 166, 213, 216. *See also* French settlement and speakers: Manitoba Catholic Schools; Goodwill School
schooling. *See* education
Schmeling, Max (German boxer), match with Joe Louis (1938), 158
Schröder, Heinrich H. (author and Nazi sympathizer), 146–7, 147*f*, 148

Schulz, David (Elder), 128
Second World War: alternative service, 161; Communist Party (Labour-Progressive Party), 168–9; conscription, 161–2, 163–4, 169; economy during, 170–3, 178–9; internment, 160, 164; language use during, 167; Mennonite identity and, 163–4; National Resources Mobilization Act (1940), 161–3; schools and, 165–6
Siberian Mennonites, 26, 29–30, 70, 142; in Grunthal, 58, 235
Siemens, J.J. (cooperative promoter), 122
social relations. *See* friendship; kinship; marriage
Sommerfelder Church, 40, 71
Soviet Union, 6, 142; collectivization, 29, 116, 143; Great Terror, 117, 167; New Economic Policy (NEP), 26, 28, 29; *Torgsin* agency, 116, 117; Umsiedler/Aussiedler immigrants, 255
Spencer, 9, 58, 67, 115, 125, 128, 173; Bergthaler congregation, 9, 216, 222, 224, 234. *See under* schools: Spencer
sport, 258; baseball, 202, 204, 258; ice hockey, 202–4, 203f, 254, 258; youth, 195, 202–4, 207, 224, 225, 258
Stalin, Josef, 116, 117; Nazi Pact, 156, 161, 168; Terror, 167
Steinbach, 218, 252, 256; Arnold Dyck (publisher) in, 149, 154, 205f; city, 263, 266–7, 268; economic centre, 9, 135, 174, 190, 191, 195, 197–9, 230, 256–7; education, 96, 102, 109, 207, 210, 212, 213–15, 224, 226; electricity in, 181; Grunthal and, 49–50, 71–2, 123, 126, 188–90, 198–9, 201, 232; Hanover municipal office, 134, 135, 178; highways, 188, 190, 196–7; hockey in, 203–4; hospital, 118, 119, 202; Kleine Gemeinde, 9, 71; Mennonite Brethren congregation, 81, 92, 208–9; population increase, 187, 263; Russländer, 64, 71–2, 119, 157
Steingart, Franz (Frank), 48, 134
Stroeter, E.F. (evangelist), 238
Stuartburn, 230
Sudermann, Dora (teacher), 103
sugar beet industry, 172, 173, 187

television, 192, 258
Terek Colony, 25, 38, 80, 82; reunion (1938), 157
Thiessen family, 58; Jack (Johann), 4, 151, 155, 218–19, 227–8, 308n27; Peter D, 187, 227
Thiessen, Abraham J. (businessman), 249
Thiessen, Cornelius Van (school principal), 208
Thiessen, Nikolai, 56
Toews, Cornelius L. (teacher), 97
Toews, David (Elder, Rosenort), 33, 54, 83, 159; chairman CMBC, 115, 163
Toews, David F. (blacksmith), 125, 175
Toews, Nick (teacher, Steinbach), 213
Toews, Peter K. (Gnadenfeld), 67
Tolstoi, Manitoba, 230
Tomlinson, Albert A. (school trustee), 99, 289n33
Töws, Gerhard (author Nazi sympathizer), 156; Schönfelder reunion book, 157

tractors, 24, 175–6, 193, 287n24
transport: cars, 116, 149, 188, 190–1; transfer services, 120, 125, 126, 149, 184, 194; trucks, 190, 193. *See also* garages: dealerships
Trudeau, Pierre (Prime Minister), 248, 256

Ukraine. *See* Russia
Ukrainian language, 12, 20, 31, 63, 152, 156; in Canada, 40, 65, 74–5, 133, 253
Ukrainians: businesses in Grunthal, 125–6; East Reserve, 10, 73–5; Mennonites and, 74–5, 128. *See also* Ted Chornoboy; Steve Block
Unger, H.H., 240*t*
unions, trade, Mennonite opposition to, 199, 208–9
Unruh, Benjamin H., 144, 148–9, 209
Unruh, Cornelius (Neil) G. (teacher), 208–11, 224, 225, 239
USSR. *See* Soviet Union

Vogt family (Steinbach): Abram A., 119; Marie 119; Peter, 123
Voisey, Paul, 9–10
voting: congregational, 84, 90–1, 223–4, 233–4; federal, 136–9, 138*t*, 246–7; home defence (1942), 169; local government, 133–5, 208, 212–13, 215, 246–7, 260–1; provincial, 136–9, 246–7; school reform, 212–16. *See also* elections

Ward, John W. (cooperatives registrar), 173
Warkentin family, 57; Dietrich, 57, 240*t*; Franz, 57; Irene, 166; John D. ("Garage"), 125, 176, 191–2, 206, 208, 240

Warkentin, Benjamin (school inspector), 97, 99
Warkentin, Heinrich A. (minister), 234
Warkentin, Irene (schoolchild), 166
Warkentin, Jacob B. (teacher), 97, 99, 103
Warkentin, John D. (garage owner), 125, 175, 240*t*; Margarethe (Voth), 125
Warkentin, John F. ("Post"), 124, 240*t*
Warkentin, John H. (geographer), 9, 197
weddings, 67–8, 219, 252, 284n24. *See also* marriage
Westbourne, Russländer settlement, 38–9, 81
Westgate Mennonite Collegiate, 249. *See also* Mennonitisches Bildungsinstitut (Winnipeg)
West Reserve, 65, 71, 72, 190; Kanadier on, 5–6, 9, 16, 22, 33, 67, 95–6, 133; Russländer on, 40, 49–50, 70, 137, 148, 160, 168; schooling, 96, 213. *See also* Altona; Bergthaler; Mennonite Collegiate Institute (Gretna); Rhineland; Sommerfelder Church; Reinlander Church
Whitewater, Russländer community and congregation, West Reserve, 80, 116
Wiebe, Jacob T. (councillor RM Hanover), 134
Wiebe, Rudy, 9
Wiens family, 57
Wiens, Heinrich J., 80–1
Wiens, Johann, 120
Winkler, Mennonites in, 74, 146, 162, 222, 249
Winkler, Howard (MP), 91, 168

Winnipeg, 34, 76, 120, 230; Folkorama, 251; market, 50, 120, 126, 184; newspapers (*see* newspapers, *Winnipeg Free Press*; *Winnipeg Tribune*); Russländer young women as maids in, 59, 60, 60*f*, 69, 76. *See under* Schönwiese. *See also* Mennonitisches Bildungsinstitut

Woelke family: bachelor brothers, 57; Jacob G., 99, 113*t*, 125; Lena (Rempel), 57, 91

women: congregational roles, 90–1, 136, 219, 222–4; education, 36, 69, 94, 104, 224–5, 265; electrification and, 179, 181, 192, 220; employment, 207, 223; maids in Winnipeg, 59, 60, 60*f*, 69, 76; marriage, 68, 70, 72, 207; organizations, 201, 223; restrictions, 79, 136, 252, 253; status, 90–1, 192; teachers, 107, 109–10; work, 39, 51–2, 69, 91, 172, 191, 192–3, 201

youth, 155–6, 161, 214, 240–1; 4-H Club, 200, 201, 258; concerns about, 225–6, 240–1; higher education, 207, 235, 266; Kiwanis, 199–200; language and, 237–8, 241; organizations, 87–8, 89, 159, 200–2, 205, 224–5; sports and, 195, 202–4, 207, 224, 225, 258

Yuzyk, Paul (senator, scholar), 250

Zentrale Mennonitische Immigrantenkomitee (ZMIK). *See* Central Mennonite Immigration Committee

TRANSNATIONAL MENNONITE STUDIES

General Editor: Aileen Friesen

This interdisciplinary series presents the history and culture of Mennonites within a transnational context. It explores Mennonites as a global people, considering the worlds of both acculturated and traditional Mennonites across the Americas, in Europe, and around the world. Books in the series will address a diverse range of topics from religious practice, migration/mobility, environmental interaction, agriculture, gender, and development/relief work to issues of race, settler colonialism, and non-violence.

1 Mark Jantzen and John D. Thiesen, eds., *European Mennonites and the Holocaust*
2 James Urry, *On Stony Ground: Russländer Mennonites and the Rebuilding of Community in Grunthal*

www.ingramcontent.com/pod-product-compliance
Lightning Source LLC
Chambersburg PA
CBHW030301080526
44584CB00012B/390